THE
BEACH

THE
BEACH

THE

HISTORY

OF

PARADISE

ON

EARTH

LENA

LENČEK

AND

GIDEON

BOSKER

VIKING

VIKING
Published by the Penguin Group
Penguin Putnam Inc., 375 Hudson Street,
New York, New York 10014, U.S.A.
Penguin Books Ltd, 27 Wrights Lane, London W8 5TZ, England
Penguin Books Australia Ltd, Ringwood, Victoria, Australia
Penguin Books Canada Ltd, 10 Alcorn Avenue,
Toronto, Ontario, Canada M4V 3B2
Penguin Books (N.Z.) Ltd, 182–190 Wairau Road,
Auckland 10, New Zealand

Penguin Books Ltd, Registered Offices:
Harmondsworth, Middlesex, England

First published in 1998 by Viking Penguin,
a member of Penguin Putnam Inc.

1 3 5 7 9 10 8 6 4 2

CIP available

ISBN 0-670-88095-7

This book is printed on acid-free paper. ∞

Printed in the United States of America
Set in New Baskerville
Designed by Alexander Knowlton and Betty Lew

To our parents,
who gave birth to us by the sea,
and to our daughter, Bianca,
who makes sure we will always make it
the center of our lives

. . . Do I dare to eat a peach?
I shall wear white flannel trousers, and walk upon the beach.

T. S. Eliot
"The Love Song of J. Alfred Prufrock"

CONTENTS

ACKNOWLEDGMENTS

The closest pleasure to *being* on the beach—especially in soggy, landlocked Portland, Oregon—was researching and writing the story of the making of paradise on earth. In this labor of love, we gratefully acknowledge the help, advice, and encouragement of all whose interest, conversation, and criticism were of such help to us, and especially:

Wendy M. Wolf, who managed this project with intelligence, humor, and grace through all its critical stages. A collaborator—and beach enthusiast—with a wickedly intelligent sense of how to pace a story, Wendy rolled up her sleeves and provided exceptional guidance through all phases of the project, from manuscript development to picture selection. Always offering specific and insightful suggestions, Wendy inspires a writer to keep polishing the stone until the sparkle is just right.

Nelly Bly, for her timely reminders and professional help, and Terry Zaroff-Evans, our copy editor, who deserves marked recognition for her thoroughness and humbling skill and finesse in wielding a red pencil.

Richard Pine, of Arthur Pine Associates, a world-class diving aficionado and beach maven, for providing lighthouselike guidance, and for his rare and deep personal interest in the subject matter he represents.

Arthur Pine, who, with carefully chosen words and aphorisms, inspired us on numerous occasions to keep taking the project to a higher level.

Bill LeBlond, friend and mentor, for launching our first work on the beach.

Mary Homi, for introducing us to some of the finest "paradises by the sea," and Mademoiselle Andrée Brunet, Château du Domaine Saint-Martin; Monsieur Gerald Hardy, Château de la Messardière; Signore Maurizio Saccani, Albergo Splendido; Madame Marie Aastrup, La Residencia; Monsieur Jean-Claude Irondelle, Hôtel du Cap Eden-Roc—for their erudite hospitality by the sea.

Ben Sutcliffe, Melissa Brooks, Alexander "Seth" Young, and Michael Kunichika, meticulous research assistants, and Mark Kuestner and Stephanie Sleeper, of the Inter Library Loan Office, Reed College Library, for their tireless help.

Christian F. Hubert, Chuck Isenberg, Peter Parshall, Michael Foote,

Justin Weir, and Hugh Van Duzen for research tips and pearls of wisdom.

Bibi Lenček, Jimmy Onstott, Catherine Glass, Jack Watson, Mark Christensen, Karen Brooks, Denis Dudouet, and Marc Vantouroux for moral support and spirited comments.

Kim Harker, whose reminiscences about beach experiences provided helpful insights into how this story might be told.

Our parents—Rado and Nina Lenček and Dorka Bosker—for their patience and perspective.

Bianca Lenček Bosker, for putting up with the madness and for being our beach baby.

My love affair with the beach began during the buoyant and serene Eisenhower years. Almost every day of summer during my childhood in sunsplashed Trieste, we made a pilgrimage from our urban apartment to the beach. Among the handful of cheap diversions available during those lean years, seaside bathing was by far the most affordable. And, of course, the most pleasurable. My mother packed us a *marenda,* or snack, of mortadella-filled *panini,* slipped rubber flotation rings like bandoliers across our chests, tucked the latest issue of *Annabella* into her basket, and off we would go for another adventure by the sea.

The best bathing beaches were in Barcole, on the northernmost reaches of Trieste's long, thin crescent, inserted into the narrow lip between stark limestone hills and the sapphirine Adriatic.

For the price of a few hundred lire, we could ride the tram out to the end of the line, then walk a half-mile or so along the shore in the coruscating sunshine—our feet getting hotter and hotter with each step—before arriving at a sparsely populated beach. The umbrella pines and palms that had been planted with Hapsburgian precision along the waterfront a hundred years earlier offered an efficient rhythm of cooling shade.

We usually ended up at the Topolino, so named because the concrete footprint of its changing rooms—men on the left, women on the right—resembled Mickey Mouse's ears. There, we were guaranteed private

Lena and Bibi Lenček at the beach in Trieste, Italy. (Rado L. Lenček, *Children at the Beach,* authors' collection)

changing stalls, the chalky feel of weathered concrete beneath bare feet, and, best of all, the inexhaustibly diverting spectacle of lush *signorine* in bikinis and cork-soled mules studiously ignoring the sexual incantations of Latin males. On Mondays, Wednesdays, and Fridays, the beach was reserved for women, and we could swim without worrying about being teased

Topolino Beach in Trieste, Italy, with Nina Lenček standing at the lower left. (Rado L. Lenček, *Topolino*, authors' collection)

by obnoxious boys. Onc summer my mother made a sensation in a Jantzen "Wonder Girl" swimsuit the color of ripe raspberries.

Virtually every phase of those end- less days—especially, the shifting tem- perament of the beach, the tides, and the moods of the sea, sequentially un- folding from dawn to nightfall— remains indelibly fixed in my mind. The beginning of each day was the time to enjoy the morning's cool, limpid sea and its underwater secrets— pebbles, sea anemones, undulating sea- weed, and the blue-green flashes of iridescent fish—clearly visible in the raking light. And then, with the mount- ing heat, the sea would grow opaque and mysterious, its surface specular in the stillness of noon. When the interminable torment of the siesta's sixty digestive minutes had elapsed, my sister and I would bolt into water that the interval had transformed into liquid sapphire. The waves closed in around us with the density and snugness of a thermal blanket. Our parents slept while we floated on our backs and played at being shipwrecked. Tir- ing of that, we lured fish into pools dug out of the grainy sand. Then,

sneaking up behind my father, we popped the air bladders of seaweed, letting the water drip on his reddening back until he jumped up in mock fury and chased us into the waves. By then, Mother would have joined him, and we'd watch the two of them swim away, far beyond where we dared to follow, where our feet no longer met the reas- suring solidity of sand.

Nothing I had experienced on the shores of the Adriatic would prepare me for the beaches of America. We ar- rived in New York Harbor in 1956. On board the U.S.S. *Constitution*, we had sloshed in the pocket-sized swimming pool and waved madly at our liner's sis- ter ship, the U.S.S. *Independence*, when

The "new" castle at Duino, Italy, overlooking the Adriatic Sea. (Rado L. Lenček, *Duino*, authors' collection)

she passed us in a blaze of fireworks on the Fourth of July. The coincidence seemed portentous. New York City was a blur, and so was the long train ride to Chicago with its hilarious first impressions: beer in a can! convertible seats! monster cars! Then came the Windy City, where my father had come to study at the University of Chicago. It was July 10 when we arrived, and the heat and humidity were infernal. It took us only two weeks to find our way to the beach.

Chicago's North Shore, Navy Pier, and even swank Oak Street Beach at the edge of downtown's Gold Coast stood in stark contrast to what I had known in Europe. The water of Lake Michigan was not salty, buoyant, or, for that matter, refreshing. And there were alewives by the million, wriggly little fish that propagated like locusts and washed onto the shores, making them impassable and mal-odorous. The sand felt like dust. It also heated up, so that walking barefoot was impossible. The long stretches of shore attracted vast hordes, who came equipped with all the conveniences of home, as though in this age of conspicuous con-sumption they dared not venture into nature without the appurtenances of comfort to which they had become accustomed. There were ice chests of colossal proportions, folding tables and chairs, recliners and umbrellas, badminton nets and rubber mattresses, baby cribs and geriatric walkers, record players and radios, and, of course, portable barbecues. Combined with the heat, the unremitting swish of traffic on Lake Shore Drive, the sticky smell of searing meat, the cacophonous cocktail of rock and roll, polka, blues, shrieking children, and shouting adults, the atmosphere was nightmarish.

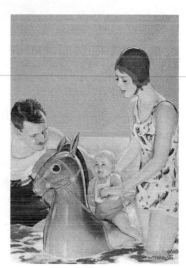

Sun, water, and the parental embrace imprint the template for pleasure that we associate with the beach. (authors' collection)

One magical summer, we managed a month-long stay on Lake Michigan in Wisconsin's Door County. Joining forces with another family, the Van Dongens, we rented a white cottage with a screened porch overlooking the pristine, sandy shore. It was beach living at its landlocked, Midwestern best: barbecues, boating, water-skiing, and, best of all, swimming at every hour of the day and night. The days were hot and humid and the water tempera-ture settled at a very comfortable seventy-four degrees. We swam together as a family almost every day, ate on the patio, and walked along the beach at sunset. Except for the Brobdingnagian mosquitoes, life was pretty much irritation-free. We lived in our swimsuits, even at night, when the tempera-ture and humidity would still hover at the ninety/ninety level. We gathered

Washed by the cold Pacific Ocean, the beaches of the Pacific Northwest invite strolling, riding, and scavenging, but discourage all save the hardiest swimmers. (Givler, *Figures on the Beach*, collection of James Onstott)

around the grainy transmissions of a Zenith TV to watch *Dobie Gillis* and *77 Sunset Strip*. Like so many other nuclear families, we embraced the emotional stability offered by the Ozzie and Harriet decade.

I not only loathed the American swimsuits of my youth—they were a far cry from the elegant swimwear I saw on the shores of Italy—I was *traumatized* by them. In my view, no single item of fashion so thoroughly diminished the physical status of the American male. Though my father remained loyal to the skimpy European brief, all the other males of our acquaintance sported huge, boxer-short-style trunks that weighed in at twenty-five pounds when wet. Mr. Van Dongen himself owned three pairs, not because he was a man who indulged himself, but because it took about three days for a pair of industrial-strength trunks to dry, even under the hot sun. From a fashion standpoint, these suits did nothing for the human torso. Wet, they clung to the thighs, as if they had been glued on or, even worse, vacuum-sealed.

Many years later, I would find my own moods by the shore reflected in the writing of Anne Morrow Lindbergh. At the beach, Lindbergh writes in *Gift from the Sea,* "one is forced against one's mind,

The sight of breakers rolling shoreward delivers a potent jolt of adrenaline. (Frank Clark, *Bathers on the Beach*, 1929, authors' collection)

against all tidy resolutions, back into the primeval rhythms of the sea-shore." In the final analysis, this was why I returned to the seashore with loved ones—and, eventually, my child—year after year. "Rollers on the beach, wind in the pines, the slow flapping of herons across sand dunes, drown out the hectic rhythms of city and suburb, time tables and sched-ules," wrote Lindbergh. "One falls under their spell, relaxes, stretches out prone. One becomes, in fact, like the element on which one lies, flattened by the sea; bare, open, empty as the beach, erased by today's tides of all yes-terday's scribbling."

The magnificent, unpredictable drive to the Neahkahnic beach has al-ways been part of what drew me to the wild Oregon coast. On countless oc-casions, as I headed south on U.S. Highway 101, I would stop the car at a bend high above a swath of sand dotted with craggy monoliths and strain to hear the ragged roar of sea lions through the dull rumble of waves far below. Offshore, twice a year, whales blow clouds of steam, and the odd bald eagle circles warily, ever on the lookout for prey.

The beaches of the Oregon coast flash as many faces as a masked ball. In fact, so eclectic are the topography and climate of the seashore that individual beaches could be grafted onto the wildly varied coastlines of twenty different countries across the world. In early spring, as the fog rolls in from the ocean, you may find yourself driving south from Cannon Beach through Arch Cape, Rockaway, and Netarts, groping your way from one tiny hamlet to another. At least once each winter, in almost every coastal outpost, ominous thunderheads coalesce in the sky. Surreptitiously, as if they had a mind of their own, clouds nestle against the Coast Range and drop torrential showers that produce rock slides and wash away roads. But in the bloom of summer, the coastal complexion changes dramatically. The blazing sun clarifies the atmosphere, and beaches from Seaside to Cape Blanco are kissed by briny offshore breezes. Whether hunting for gemstone treasures or glass floats at Agate Beach, digging for clams near Rockaway, or casting for shad or salmon near Coos Bay, one cannot help being intrigued by the face-off between land and

The grand hotels and opulent resorts of the French Riviera epitomized the civilized beach as Eden. (Hotel brochure: Nice: Negresco, authors' collection)

Slipping beneath the surface of the water, one enters a world where habit dissolves and one's sense of wonder is renewed. (Bibi Lenček, *The Diver*, 1982, authors' collection)

water on the Oregon coast. Here, two titanic forces—one stationary and one in motion—engage in eternal dispute.

After many visits to remote, unpopulated beaches on the coast of Baja California, I have come to the conclusion that this is where the sun comes to refuel, where the wind purifies itself, where the waters draw their sparkle. I have spent countless days narcotized by the natural rhythms of this desert by the sea, and countless days watching the sun sink below the horizon and leave behind a thin fleece of clouds whose edges glow a brilliant orange. And, after many such sunsets, I finally began to understand the siren call of danger that is part of Baja's charm. Here, the beach is peppered with stone upon stone, some larger than Mayan pyramids, and more mysterious than Stonehenge. They have been sculpted and spanked by the wind and water into shapes resembling dolphins, praying Zen monks, and lovers in embrace. Worn to bulbous smoothness by eons of geological torture, these accidental skyscrapers of nature are spot-welded to the beach in perpetuity, constant reminders that the sea is the greatest sculptor of all.

—Lena Lenček

On his deathbed, overlooking a blue slash of the Adriatic, my great-uncle Arturo Manzoni was reputed to have said: "There are three phases of life: birth, *beach,* and death." And with those words, he was said to have expired. True or apocryphal, Zio Arturo's aphorism could have served as the family motto, for, no matter where my peregrinations have taken me over the past forty years, the beach has remained enshrined and unchallenged as a site of spiritual renewal, regeneration, and the stockpiling of sun-warmed memories that would sustain me and my family through hard times and winters of the soul.

From Brighton to Montevideo, the bathing routine of the nineteenth and early twentieth centuries was played out against the standardized props of grand hotel, pier, bandstand, boardwalk, and bathing machine. (Bettmann Archive)

More directly than the written word or painted image, the sensations of the seashore travel with impunity to the heart and mind of the beast, collapsing past and present into a matrix of water, sand, space, and light. Few environments have been more inspirational in our leisure life. Nature's most potent antidepressant, the beach moves us with the power of a drug, the rhythm of its tides and shifting margins reorienting our sense of space and time, its aphrodisiacal cocktail of sun and water firing our slumber-

At the beach, the body becomes a spectacle, put on display according to elaborate unwritten codes of dress and undress, gesture, and custom. (Elliott Erwitt, *Rio de Janeiro, Brazil, 1984,* Magnum Photos)

Seen, since deepest antiquity, as a site of transformations, the beach releases us from the strait-jackets of routine and repression. (UPI/Corbis-Bettmann)

ing hedonism. With its retina-searing vistas and erotic spectacles, it lies at the creamy center of American and European leisure destinations.

There are many threads to this story, but the complete fabric must chronicle, grain by grain, the transformation of the beach from an alien, inaccessible, and hostile wilderness devoted to conquest, commerce, exploration, and the primal customs of tribal cultures, into a thriving, civilized, pleasure- and recreation-oriented outpost of Western life where so many sybaritic impulses of culture have been indelibly concentrated.

The beach as we know it is, historically speaking, a recent phenomenon. In fact, it took hundreds of years for the seashore to be colonized as the pre-eminent site for human recreation. Although the coast was the birthplace of history, before it could be transformed into a theater of pleasure, it had to be discovered, claimed, and invented as a place apart from the messy business of survival. A proscenium for history, the beach has become a conspicuous signpost against which Western culture has registered its economic, aesthetic, sexual, religious, and even technological milestones.

Long before it became a narcotic for holiday masses, the beach was a sacred site, a testing ground of humanity's fitness for survival and capacity for spirituality. After all, it was on the borders of continents and islands that the first living creatures crawled out from the sea to begin their inexorable march toward conquest of *terra firma*. Since deepest antiquity, many of humanity's most fateful battles have been staged on the beach. Agamemnon sent his ships against Troy and spilled the blood of his daughter Iphigenia on the bleached, rocky shores of the Aegean to bribe the gods. From biblical times, the voice of God has sounded loudest and clearest at the seashore, where the tumultuous meeting of elements bore witness to the divine judgment of the Great Deluge or the profound wisdom of creation. The New Testament tells that Jesus began his ministry "by the seaside and great multitudes were gathered unto him." Since the Middle Ages, holy men and women seeking solitude and inspiration have retreated to remote sites by the sea in order to escape the distractions of the world and draw closer to the voices of angels and the whisper of God. Writing in *Mr Bligh's Bad Language,* historian Greg Dening argues that history was likely born "on beaches, marginal spaces between land and sea . . . where everything is relativised a little, turned around, where tradition is as much invented and handed down, where otherness is both a new discovery and a reflection of something old."

Though typically perceived, in contemporary times, as a repository of sweetness and light, the seashore did not always present a smiling face to humanity. Like Alain Corbin, author for *The Lure of the Sea,* I am among those who believe that the story of the beach is also the history of power and conquest. Beaches were portals of entry for death, in the guise of virulent plagues and hostile invaders that equally consumed the fabric of civi-

lizations. They were anxiety-ridden strips of no-man's-land where, according to the journals of Columbus, Cortés, Cook, and Bougainville, Europeans first set eyes on others who, though like them, were yet utterly alien. Here, duels to the death were waged between races and cultures. In modern times, the bloodstained sands of Normandy saw the tide turn definitively against the forces of fascism, and on the innocent shore of Bikini Atoll the first postwar atomic bomb was exploded. On the sandy, shingle, or rocky beaches of the world, humanity has played out the entire gamut of its proclivities.

Whether an isolated stretch of sand staked out by a solitary towel, or a populous strand colonized with

The architecture of leisure turns coastlines into successions of geometric and utopian fantasies. (UPI/Bettmann)

carnivals and casinos, the beach is at once escape valve and inspiration, symbol and playground. At its finest, it invites watchers to unearth not only the dominant, culturally elite themes of a period, but its popular sensibilities: a blank piece of real estate on which each wave of colonizers puts up its own idea of paradise. The site of regeneration, relaxation, and recreation, the beach of modern times is circumscribed by history and rooted in desire, which is why it moves us with the passion it does. From the South Pa-

Once the exclusive province of the affluent, the beach has developed into the premier site for numerical tourism. (Bruce Davidson, *Blackpool, England, 1965,* Magnum Photos)

cific to Miami Beach, these sandy stretches impinge upon us with more directness and force than virtually any other natural environment.

The mileposts along its journey include everything from medical opinions on the value of bathing to fluctuations in the history of taste; from attitudes toward the body and healing to ideas about the spiritual meaning of the shore. Reframing the beach from environmental foe to friend required myriad incremental changes in attitude and literally hundreds of minute— as well as major—technological advances. For example, voyages of global exploration coaxed reluctant Europeans to experiment with the playful variant of the beach found in tropical cultures. Scientific debates and medical breakthroughs broke down resistance to immersing the body in water and paved the way for the therapeutic colonization of the seashore. Writers and artists swept up in the heady spell of early romanticism weaned Europeans from their habit of shunning the shore, and taught them to seek it out as the pre-eminent source for the aesthetic experience of the "sublime." On the pragmatic side, the Industrial Revolution spawned accelerated population growth and urban crowding, both of which fostered the development of seaside colonies as spectacle-based outposts for new mass culture. A series of mechanical contrivances—the bathing "machine," the steam engine, the gas combustion engine—tamed the unpredictable environment of the seashore and brought its benefits within reach of millions.

As a kaleidoscope of culture, the beach is as central to the myths of antiquity as it is to the storehouse of legendary Americana, its associations running the gamut from the gritty and banal to the magical and rarefied. Spanked by a tepid, moist breeze riffling the sands near Tulum on Mexico's Yucatán coast, we can stand among the ruins and experience the vacant stillness of ancient temples, with their worn, mottled façades of dismembered stones and sun-bleached columns slicing into Caribbean skies black as obsidian. Here, on a stretch of shore now crawling with tourists from Cincinnati and Shanghai, stand ruins robed in the silence of advancing moss, unexhumed for centuries, left to decompose in a once forgotten, but now reclaimed, cove of Mayan space.

Other beaches broadcast an entirely different constellation of cultural signals and sensibilities. The carefully curated re-

Shorelines of mild-mannered waves and gently sloping, fine-grained sands invite swimming and basking. (Leonard Freed, *View of the Beach at Nice*, 1981, Magnum Photos)

sorts of the French and Italian Riviera parcel out the beach with the precision of a Mondrian painting. In tiny plots staked out by private clubs and hotels, paying guests recline on color-coded chairs laid out with graph-paper rectilinearity in front of brilliantly painted cabañas. The beach fairly sizzles with the erotic voltage of bare-breasted, bare-buttocked beauties and virile stalwarts, but strict decorum keeps the sensual stew at a steady, socially acceptable simmer. In the Edenic parks of Portofino, Ibiza, Mallorca, and all those exquisite seaside villages and towns discovered by the nineteenth-century British traveler, the refined sensibility of the Victorians is still in evidence. Here, the visitor's approach to the beach is as carefully orchestrated as the destination, with trails leading to small patches of rocky shore laid out through ancient olive groves and lush, fragrant gardens.

And though the beach is universal in its appeal to an increasingly urbanized humanity, it is also a pluralistic outpost of pleasure, taking as many forms as the protean human mind can invent. From the Victorian formalism of Brighton and the fanciful elegance of Biarritz to the topsy-turvy inventiveness of Coney Island or the suave theatricality of southern California,

Humming and flashing with pleasure-and-thrill machines, carnival beaches—such as those at Coney Island or Blackpool—concentrate the sybaritic impulses of civilization. (UPI/Corbis-Bettmann)

We come to the beach seeking rejuvenation, revitalization, and recreation. (authors' collection)

from the earnest utopianism of the Pacific Northwest to the geriatric escapism of Miami Beach, it has spawned a motley swarm of rituals and recreational obsessions.

To explain how this came about—how and why Europeans and Americans came to be enchanted with the liminal landscape of the beach—it is necessary to track the multiple tiny shifts, as well as the macro-movements, that prompted the West to reassess prevailing perceptions of the beach. In this intriguing sense, the story of the beach replays many of the grand themes of human conquest—those heart-of-darkness turnarounds—in which the domesticating and refining propensities of culture eventually triumph over the savage and unknown.

The sensations of the beach are as primary as life itself. "Inhabited by legions of beckoning mermaids and sirens, and by a silently signaling Tadzio on the Lido, awakened by a night sound and shimmer," writes Richard Martin in *Splash,* "the water of the sea is everlastingly reflective, its pools ever fresh and translucent, its promise of youth, its refreshment, an unceasing recreation, a re-creation of womb-life before external life, a re-creation of amphibian ancestors, and even the ultimate recreation that is the joy of bathing." As time goes on, we are drawn to the beach to return to our conscious mind the sensation of the body—not in the private, compartmentalized world of bath or boudoir that contextualizes us by reference to the hygienic or the erotic—but at the infinitely creative junction of elements where habit and convention dissipate and imagination once again takes over. It is to the beach, in other words, that we go to reinvent ourselves.

—Lena Lenček
—Gideon Bosker

THE BEACH

NO MAN AND THE SEA

It all began about four billion years ago, when there were no men, no women, no bikinis, and no sea, an inauspicious start for a journey that would culminate in paradise on earth. From a distant cove of intergalactic space, a fiery mass accelerated as it plummeted through the earth's atmosphere, then dug into the barren surface of a remote plain, raising a thick cloud of debris. Giant, jagged boulders shuddered from the impact of stone on stone and exploded into a shower of shards. Severed by the enormous impact, the thin, hot crust bled lava and ash, as winds swirled and eddied, driving rock against rock, smoothing rough edges, and grinding angular facets into granules of sand. And so it remained for hundreds of millions of years. Vagrant drifts swept across the monotonous flats, abrading the ragged edges of craters dug by comets that, over eons of geological torture, constantly punctured the rocky membrane of the young planet.

Finally, gases trapped in the earth's inner core burst outward, releasing waters that since the very beginning of time had been locked in the depths. Rivulets dripped from crevices of granite and basalt, swelled into streams, and gathered into rivers that gouged out canyons on the way to budding seas. Rains began to pour, carrying sands to the sterile margins of infant oceans. Fingers of sand reached into the waters and sandbars took shape, dissolved, and then re-formed. The shore sands had no loyalty to the ocean, or to the earth. Whatever wind blew, whatever current streamed, the sands followed. Primeval storms assaulted emerging landmasses and blasted away at them until they lay in heaps of shingle and gravel at the feet of wave-washed cliffs. Ribbons of beach began to rim the shores.

Another billion years ground by. The moon, still close to the earth, waxed and waned, gathering the ocean waters into mighty, bulging tides that sucked in and spat out gray tongues of sand, an unending project of sculpting the profile of distant shores. The continents began to drift apart from their primordial oneness. The sands and muds that the rivers pumped into the oceans sedimented into long, sloping shelves. In their

The adventitious roots of coconut palms dig deep into the obsidian sand on the beach at Kaimu, Hawaii. (Rex R. Elliott)

sun-warmed shallows, organic life began to incubate, until, about two billion years ago, bacteria and algae and fungi emerged. Photosynthetic bacteria set about making food out of the anoxygenic atmosphere of carbon dioxide, and in the process spewed enough oxygen to mantle the earth and percolate into the salinity of the oceans. Here, in the planet's uterine depths, multicellular animals with tissues and organs and byzantine anatomies emerged as trilobites and corals, mollusks and shelled creatures, whose intricate skeletons were eventually worn down into soft sands that, one day, would become the floor of paradise.

With the infrastructure in place, the remaining 570 million years of beach-polishing could begin. Flowering plants sprouted in sheltered, fertile pockets of the earth. Other flora clung to the precipitous slopes of monticules and the rocky high ground, sending roots into microscopic cracks and fissures, and, with the gentlest pressure relentlessly applied, pried the hard stone apart. Rain and melting snow sought out the crevices, slipped into them, and dug away at the crystalline bonds of rock. Like a cunning trio of jewel thieves, wind, water, and plant picked away at the basalt, granite, pumice, and quartz masses, which had been impregnable to the assault of wind alone. The weathering of rock accelerated. Sands crumbled down the wrinkled faces of cliffs, and began their laborious journey to the waters draining from mountains.

Bound by the new chaos of roots, riverbanks that had meandered promiscuously, finally began to hold fast, and trapped rocky debris that had been pushed along riverbeds. Obeying the strict calculus of gravity, sediment dropped out, the heaviest particles first, and, as the velocity of the torrent gradually diminished, the lightest of muds at the very end of the stream's journey as it debouched into the seas. Along the continental margins, a profusion of shelled organisms left behind calcareous shales and sandstones, and in the siliceous muds on the bottoms of deep seas, the skeletal remains of infinitesimal basket-shaped radiolarians piled up in layers of ooze. Multicellular sponges effloresced, died, and, battered by the infinite circling of wave waters, were pulverized into grains of pure silica.

Dinosaurs came and went. Sea mammals appeared in their appointed time, but their movements left undisturbed the harmonious *ménage à trois* into which water, wind, and earth had settled. Like a worldly couple with a discreet paramour in the wings, water and earth played out their domestic power struggles, each first yielding ground, then taking back what it had surrendered, alternately provoked and soothed by the wind. Of course, there were conflicts, nasty ones. The margins of the oceans and seas bore marks of tender encounters and tumultuous collisions in gently sloping beaches; in pebbled shelves overstrewn with rubble; and in the bouldery ruins of vertiginous cliffs pounded and lashed by the fury of wind and water.

And then, at last, humans arrived, and the beach party could begin in earnest. Dazzled, terrified, and stymied by the great power of the three elements, man warily hung back from the shores, which expanded and receded without regard for his feeble structures and territorial markings. If he came to the beach at all, it was because hunger, lust for power, or greed lured him there, for only the most urgent drives could counter the terror with which primal man was surely filled at the sight of the sea rising up in murderous waves. All the destructive powers of the universe seemed to be bound up in that treacherous liquid medium, which left the earth battered, bruised, and littered with the stinking corpses of sea monsters and the stench of rotting kelp.

Humans migrated from the warm tropics to all points of the globe; discovered fire, tools, iron; built shelters; contrived boats; and ventured across the seas. Some even domesticated the gentler shores of mild, inland seas and the docile sands of tropical isles, and took a measure of delight in bathing in the surf and basking in the sun. Finally, in 1736, all the microscopic developments of what we call culture and modern civilization came together in an Englishman's whim to open a bathing establishment in the little town of Scarborough, northeast of York. There, a rough, gray smear of shale traced the far reach of high tide. For centuries, the Picts, the Celts, and then the Saxons limped across the shingle to draw in their fishing

After traversing vast stretches of open water, Pacific Ocean swells move into the shallows of the continental shelf and collapse upon themselves in a turbulence of froth. (*Surf Meeting a Beach*, Brett Weston Archive/Corbis)

boats, or dragged skiffs out into the angry sea to make a crossing to the Continent. Now sounds of laughter and merriment reverberated against the white sandstone cliffs as the beach was suddenly transformed into a gateway of health and relaxation. The full, if still-rough, tally of distant lands and shores had just been made by an intrepid fraternity of explorers, and the charts of the seas hastily sketched out. But the beach that was each seawashed country's hostile and barely functional backyard would gradually be claimed as habitable new terrain—the setting for a new garden of earthly delights.

The ocean would become a source of inspiration. The Romantics would consider the beach a place for threshold experiences, where they could study the very soul of Nature and learn from her the riddle of their own. On remote peninsulas where the fury of two oceans erupted in the ceaseless combat of colliding swells, the Romantics would see eddies, tides, and clandestine currents moving into and out of each other like lovers at passion's high tide.

Now, on countless surf-washed August days, nestled into the warm sand, protected from the sun by chemical screens, garbed in fibers that shed water more efficiently than sealskin, men and women ponder the tides, smell breezes at the ocean's edge, and absorb melanizing radiation from their private star millions of miles away. At night, they gaze at the silvery point flares of meteors and comets streaking across the sky, and speculate about that distant time, four billion years ago, when the earth was still young and turbulent, and battered by vagrant asteroids, long before the Sea of Eden was born.

■■■■■■

The beach is not so much a distinct place as it is a set of relations among four elements: earth, water, wind, and sun. Partnered in an endless dance, these elements produce a staggering range of beaches, each subject to constant change, sometimes rhythmical and cyclical, sometimes linear and catastrophic. If there is a single invariant played out on the boundary of land and sea, it is contained in the paradox of ceaseless metamorphoses, in the idea of immutable mutability. Minute by minute, hour by hour, each of the four constituents submits to the action of the others, and each, in turn, bends the others to its influence.

Charles Darwin, who may have seen more species of terrestrial animals than any other human of his day, still marveled when he looked into the depths of the sea. "Our meadows and the forests of the earth we dwell upon," he said, "appear desert and void as compared to those of the sea." Even more remarkable, this prodigious productivity is accompanied by playfulness, by a seemingly aesthetic mimicry that cannot be reduced to mere utility in the service of survival and adaptation.

Ocean plants take on animal forms, and animals have the appearance of stony vegetation or marine flowers. The alcyonium, the Proteus of the sea, is at one moment an animal, at another a fruit. The fertile sea bottom reveals itself to us as an exquisite parallel universe. Looking down upon the reefs of the Pacific, one sees a green carpet of tubiporas, astreas, and brightly colored meandrinae and cariophyllae, swiftly vibrating their rich golden stamina. Majestic gorgonians and the less lofty isis undulate over them like the willows and aspens and climbing plants of our own forests. The plumaria sends out its spirals from one submarine tree to another. And there is still another, more deeply hidden world within this one. Mollusks drag their shells of pearly luster along the submarine labyrinths. Crabs run here and there. Strange fish of golden, turquoise, and yellow hues rove tranquilly about. Purple- and violet-colored annelids alternately roll up and stretch forth their delicate and fragile arms to the descending sunbeams.

SANDS OF TIME

"Sand," Rachel Carson tells us, "is a substance that is beautiful, mysterious, and infinitely variable, each grain on a beach is the result of processes that go back into the shadowy beginnings of life, or the earth itself." There is nothing particularly striking about a grain of sand, unless, of course, you have the misfortune of having one blow into your eye. Then the speck that seems so benign and innocuous reveals its true character as a descendant of the great rocks of the world. But to sedimentologists, geologists, and paleogeographers, the size, shape, roundness, surface texture, and composition of a single grain of sand tell the story of forces that pried it from its matrix and brought it to the shore. If one sifts through a handful of sand, and looks closely at the grains, it is possible to detect many individual shapes, sizes, and colors; these variations are even more dramatic if samples come from different beaches. Some grains are almost perfectly round and smooth, others jagged, rough, and irregular in texture and shape. Light-colored, nearly spherical sand is composed almost entirely of quartz, a common mineral from which the earth's crust is compounded. In contrast, dark sands are made up of volcanic particles and complex silicates that were spewed up from deep within the earth's core.

Nearly indestructible, a single grain of sand can be millions of years old. These fragments can be seen as the original "silicon chip," acid-etched with the story of the rise and fall of mountains, rivers, deserts, and creatures. Lilliputian messengers from the depths of geologic time, grains of sand are the bridge between past and present—the last, hardy survivors of distant islands, deltas, cliffs, mountains, and long-lost landforms. Buffeted by wind, leached by rain, bleached bone-dry by the sun, sands are also made up of the carbonate skeletons of creatures from the tepid tropical seas, and in this respect are geological *cartes de visite* from obscure worlds beneath the waves.

Generally ranging in size from one sixteenth of a millimeter to two millimeters—and sometimes even five millimeters—in diameter, sand is smaller than gravel but larger than silt or clay. The rich tonal variations and range of shapes emerge fully only under a microscope, where sands reveal themselves as pointed and bulbous rays exploding from pillow-shaped centers; creamy lozenges; shiny ball bearings; jagged, striated, and pitted flakes; glossy disks and striped cigars; spheres as bumpy as Trix cereal; shriveled red chiles of volcanic lavas; and crystalline green jelly beans bursting with glauconite from the ocean floor.

Studded with spicules, the calcium carbonate "star" sands are formed in the shallow, agitated waters at the edge of marine banks off Fiji. (Rex R. Elliott)

The mechanics of sand formation are simple. Rocks, reefs, and coral break down through either mechanical or chemical weathering, becoming smaller and smaller as they are pounded by the hydraulic or pneumatic pressure of waves. They are pried apart by ice exerting thousands of pounds of pressure per square inch, or split by the insistent probing and prying of plant roots. Heated by lightning or fire, rocks expand until they break off in chips and flakes. Or, through involved chemical processes, minerals and chemicals within the rocks gradually decompose, and the rock literally decays as if it were an organic substance. The size of each resulting grain is determined by the kinetic intensity of the medium that transported and deposited it. A strong current or a powerful wind, for instance, tends to carry larger particles greater distances. The smoothness or the jaggedness depends on the degree of abrasion during transport. The rounder the sand, the longer it has been weathered by wind or water. By contrast, ragged grains have either not traveled far or been cushioned in their journey by an envelope of mud.

The weathering process that turns rocks into sand, however, is only half the story. The other half involves the consolidation of sands into rock during the vast intervals of geological time. The rock of ages, as it turns out, is impervious to time only in our minds. Sand that once was rock becomes rock once again as it slowly sediments and compresses into layers of sandstone, which, in turn, transmute into sand. Standing on a cliff overlooking a raging sea, we watch waves hurl themselves against the shore, scooping up cobbles at the base of the cliff and lofting them into the crown of seething foam. Then the wave retreats, hauling its load of stone along the sea bottom, until the next swell rushes in to repeat, relentlessly, the work of breaking, grinding, polishing.

In warm waters, abundant sea life provides a steady source of bone and shell fragments, from conches, clams, mussels, scallops, shellfish, corals, fish, and even microscopic plankton. Most of the fabled white beaches of the world are in fact the burial mounds of such sea life. Radiocarbon dating shows that the sand of Miami Beach, for example, is on average thirteen thousand years old, with some material over thirty thousand years old. So, as we dig our toes into the soft shell sands, we quite literally burrow deep into antiquity.

Because sand is derived from a spectrum of substances, it comes in many colors—tan, yellow, white, pink, purple, red, blue, green, gray, and black. The precise shade of each grain depends on the rock or organism from which it came. To a great degree, color alone can identify the origin of a beach with reasonable accuracy. Armed with a strong hand-lens, an experienced geologist can readily distinguish between translucent, light-colored grains of quartz and brown, dullish feldspar, and then link these properties to the geological history of a specific beach type.

Delivered to their site long ago by slowly moving glaciers, the whitish beach sands of the Northeastern United States are mainly mineral in origin. As one moves farther south—to North Carolina, let's say—the sand begins to take on the pinkish and pale-yellow hues of crushed seashells. Florida's eastern flank is rimmed with coarse grains of quartz, but the tip

and the western shore are covered with sand the color and feel of un-
cooked semolina. Along the Gulf Coast, the fine-textured beaches blend
the rosaceous tint of pulverized shrimp and conch with the white, yellow,
and orange colors of minerals—copper, calcium, and quartz—carried
there by rivers from the Appalachian highlands and the Great Plains.

As one moves farther south and west, beach sands begin to broadcast a
flashy, south-of-the-border exuberance characterized by the paintbox tints
of tropical seas. The brilliant white of Bahamian beaches is derived from
the precipitated oolites or calcium-carbonate coating on bits of coral and
whelk. Bermuda's pink sands blush with the calcite of limestone, coral,
and shell. The gray sands of St. Lucia's southwestern rim, on St. Kitts, Saba,
and Domenica—all in the Caribbean—bespeak a volcanic origin. In fact,
the mixture of vanilla-colored shell and coral beaches and dusky volcanic
sands is a formula repeated throughout the tropics. This pangeological
recipe is evident in the golden coral beaches of the Seychelles in the Indian
Ocean, the mauve-and-purple sands of Fiji's Taveuni Island, and in Queensland's kaleidoscopic blends of ground-up shells from the Coral Sea. The
striking hues of Hawaii's shores—the olivine green of Papa-kolea Beach,
the cinder-cone red at Hoku-'ula, and the jet black of Polulu Beach—also
derive from volcanic eruptions, rather than decomposing sea life.

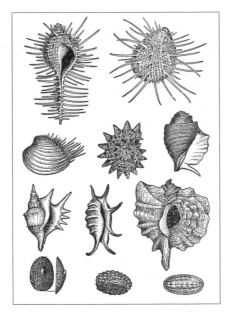

Tropical sands are often repositories of multiple seashell species. Among the various remnants, traces of long-vanished species may be
found. (authors' collection)

As one travels north into the temperate zone, the color palette of
beach sand fades in vibrancy. On
the eastern coast of England, the
pockets of sand deposited among
the shingle are, like the rock from
which they have eroded, light gray.
By contrast, the northern coast
takes on an almost honeyed hue.
Along the northeastern coast of
Wales, the golden beaches have a
faintly rosy cast. All along the Baltic,
the dunes and berms are a soft tan.
Mediterranean beaches—the Costas
del Sol, Calida, Blanca, Dorada and
Brava, as well as the strands on
deltas of the rivers Rhone, Arno,
Po, and Brenta—range from puce
to whitish gray, reflecting the tints
of clay, mud, and river sand transported from deep inland. Up and
down the Côte d'Azur, along Italy's

southern coast, and on the shores of Alexandria, the pale sand flashes an occasional grain of marble, glass, or alabaster that centuries ago was part of some ancient Roman villa. By and large, the meager sands of Mallorca, Sicily, Sardinia, Corsica, and Cyprus—and of other islands in the Adriatic and the Aegean—are coarse, lacking the sustained buffeting of rough winds and waters.

Along the Sea of Cortés and on the Pacific coast of Baja California, the beaches still sparkle with coarse-grained sand colored the buff of desert rock, the white of marlin bones, and the burnt sienna of weathered coral. But along the beaches of the Pacific Northwest, tan and gray predominate. Descended from basalt cliffs that were extruded as sea-floor lavas several million years ago, these sands glisten like oil slicks when wet. The brownish specks scattered among them come from the quartz and feldspar of granites that were spot-welded to the Rocky Mountains of the North American continent, and then spilled down the tributaries of the Columbia River, before draining into the Pacific. Other mighty rivers—the Orinoco, the Amazon, and Argentina's Colorado—enrich ocean sands with grains of gold, platinum, and uranium, to which is added the glint of garnets and emeralds.

In certain beaches, sand exhibits another remarkable property, neither useful nor threatening, but aesthetic. These sands "sing" and "bark," as though they were endowed with vocal cords, although in this instance the musical sounds are produced by the gentle friction of grain against grain. In Kauai, Hawaii, a golden knot of windblown dunes in the shadow of the opal-tinted cliffs of Polihale produce cries in various cadences. In the wind, they rustle like silk; when someone slides down them, they bark like dogs .

Still intriguing scientists, singing sands have been threading through the literature of explorers and travelers for over a thousand years, posing the riddle of their vocalization. Some say the sound is produced by the friction of sand against sand that has been coated with dried salt, much as the violin's melody is produced by the action of resin on the bow. Others speculate that the thin layers of gas which are released between the grains act as percussive cushions capable of considerable vibration and tone production.

Balefully sibilant "singing sands" have been discovered in England and Wales. On the Isle of Eigg, in the Hebrides, the snowy sand at the base of sandstone cliffs gives off an eerie whining. The sands of Oregon's Florence Beach squeak with the high-pitched bark of distant chihuahas. But perhaps the most fabled of these are commemorated in the *Arabian Nights,* which lauds the weird beauty of the sands skirting the Mountain of the Bell, the Jebel Nagous of the Isthmus of Suez. When whipped up by storm winds, these sands chant and groan like deep organ notes; on calm days, they tinkle like bells.

VARIATIONS ON A THEME

For those of us who have grown up on the Eastern Seaboard or in southern California, "sand" and "beach" are interchangeable. But the sandy beach hardly exhausts the range of physiographic forms that take shape on the boundary between land and sea. In Great Britain, for example, much of the coast is covered with "shingle," or flat stones. The fabled French beach at Cannes is mostly pebbles; the beaches of the Adriatic and Tyrrhenian seas are piles of rock. The north shore of Long Island and the coast of Maine are sculpted of high bluffs, stony beaches, and intimate coves and harbors lined with miserly bands of sand and pebbles.

Whatever its composition, the beach is made up of three zones: the "back-shore," set above the swash of normal waves at high spring tides; the "fore-shore," located between the high- and low-water marks; and the "offshore," which extends seaward from the low-water mark to a depth where appreciable movement of material ceases. Geologists tell us a beach can take one of three general forms: a narrow strip of sand separating the rocky cliffs of land from the sea; a spit or a bay-mouth bar; or a barrier island.

The first type of beach, also called a "pocket beach"—narrow, shallow, and seasonally unstable—is geologically young, and results from the under-mining of cliffs and the grinding of rocks associated with wave action. Slung between rocky headlands, a pocket beach usually backs into sheer cliffs. Sandy in the summer, it is often stripped down to cobble and rock in the winter. Many of the beaches along the Cornish coast of England, and the coasts of Norway, Sweden, Scotland, the Hebrides, California, and Oregon, are of this sort.

Steep cliffs meet a rocky beach on the north coast of France. (Martine Franck, *Seascape of the North Coast*, Magnum Photos)

The rate at which pocket beaches form depends on the character of both the rocks and the wave patterns. Porous and soft rocks erode quickly, whereas hard rock is more impervious to wave action. In both instances, however, the mechanical processes at work are the same. As the rock is struck by a wave, air is forced into the cracks and pries them farther and farther apart. When the air is released, it bursts outward with explosive force, sending spray, rocky fragments, and pebbles high into the air. This happens relatively quickly in such porous-rock coastlines as those of East Anglia or the Aegean island of Chios. Where cliffs are made of hard rock, however, pocket beaches take much longer to form. Small, wild, and inaccessible, these hard-rock beaches are littered with logs and tangles of kelp, and perfumed with the briny scent of plankton.

Bay-mouth bars and spits are straight, continuous deposits of sand that run parallel to the shore. Whether the formation is a bar or a spit depends on its point of attachment to the coast. The bay-mouth bar extends across a good portion of a bay, somewhat like a bit inserted into a horse's mouth. Eventually, it may build up to the point where it completely seals the gap between contiguous headlands, enclosing the bay waters to form a lagoon, pond, or marsh. The spit, as the name suggests, looks on maps like a string of saliva dangling from the corner of a lip. Embankment-shaped, it is anchored to the land only at one point, and the outermost end is always surrounded by water.

Both of these sand formations result from the tendency of bodies to minimize the impact of force by presenting the least resistance to it. In the case of beaches, ocean waves strike protrusions from land with more force than they do a flat plane. As waves of equal energy approach the shore, the underwater topography of headlands attracts and focuses their force through refraction. In other words, the projecting formations actually augment the ferocity of the waves as they strike the shore. Over long periods of time, this persistent battering gradually wears away at the land's jagged edges. As the rocky coast is straightened, underwater currents hitting the shore obliquely can transport rocky fragments downcurrent into relatively quiet water at the head of a bay.

A bay-head beach begins to form in the hollow. With time, as the bay is filled in, the jutting headlands are "filed" down, as has happened in the smoothly profiled beaches of Devon, Cornwall, and South Wales. The coastal currents that hit the shore slide past, carrying the accumulated sand to the mouths of bays lying downshore, where fingers of bay-mouth beaches begin to build up. This has been happening, for example, at the mouth of Katama Bay on Martha's Vineyard, where submarine sandbars have formed at the break point of waves. What are now the Norfolk marshes began as this silting in of a bay, and the process continues at the

The berm—the visible, nearly horizontal terrace above the water—is low and wide in the summer, and high and narrow in the winter, when storm waves move most of the sand underwater. The elevation of protruding rocks and "haystacks" also shows fluctual variation. (James Onstott, *Crescent Beach, Oregon,* authors' collection)

rate of half an inch a year, not nearly as quickly as along the coast of Holland or the chalk cliffs at Étretat, in Normandy.

When the process has furnished enough sand, a continuous line of bay-mouth beaches straightens out the shore, so that the currents are able to transport sand much greater distances, to points far away from the shore. Only at land's end, where the water deepens and the currents lose velocity, does the sand drop to the bottom and gradually accumulate until it rises above the surface as a spit, as it does at Sandy Hook and Rockaway at the entrance to New York Harbor, or at the mouth of the Columbia River. The spit need not be straight but, like the one at Spurn Head, across the mouth of England's Humber River, can curl and curve like a hook.

Barrier islands or barrier beaches also run roughly parallel to the shore, and are sometimes erroneously called "offshore bars." In fact, they are quite distinct from the latter, both in appearance and formation. Of much more ancient provenance, they tend to be wider, broader, and heaped up with dunes, and either sit directly on the mainland—in which case they are barrier beaches—or are separated from land by shallow bays many miles wide.

Barrier islands began many thousands of years ago as natural dikes that formed along the edge of the continental shelf where it drops off to the oceanic abyss. As the glaciers began to melt, the sea, which was some four hundred feet lower than it is today, rose over the edge of the continental slope and spilled onto the coastal plain. It rose quickly, working its way into coastal forests. Like gigantic earthmoving machines, the waves pushed masses of soil, mud, rocks, trees, and sand, heaping them up along the shoreline wherever the waves ran out of energy. The wind shaped these pliant mounds into ridges and nudged them into parallel lines along the newly defined shore.

Eventually, as the water level kept rising, the sea broke through the ridges and flooded the predominantly flat land behind them. The ridges, which were anywhere from a few yards to a mile wide—and sometimes dozens of miles long—were now surrounded by water and became the first barrier islands. Most of the East Coast and Gulf Coast of the United States, and of the coasts of Holland and Poland, is made up of these sandy deposits. Although the sea was rising at the same rate on the Pacific, barrier islands did not form here, because this side of the continent lacked the nearly flat slopes characteristic of the Eastern coastal plain.

Geologists estimate that, when the barrier islands off the Southeastern United States were formed, about fifteen thousand years ago, they were located some fifty miles seaward of their present location. Since then, they have been constantly on the move. As sea levels continued to rise, waves drove the islands higher and higher up the continental shelf, sometimes as quickly as one hundred feet a year. As they moved, so did the shoreline of the mainland behind them. When the shoreline retreated more slowly than the ridges—as happened where the coastal plain sloped upward—the barrier island merged with the mainland.

At other times, islands from various eras fused for a geological moment, creating thick, relatively stable formations, such as the islands off the coast of Georgia. But, given the absence of new supplies of sand and the fluctuating sea level, even these islands are not safe. As the ocean level rises, they will get progressively narrower, until only the highest part protrudes above the water, and after several more hundred years, they will begin to move again. By contrast, the barrier islands of recent formation, such as those in the delta area of the Gulf of Mexico, are in perpetual motion, for only by moving—by retreating through overwash, dune movement, and inlet formation and migration—can they survive intact as islands.

SHIFTING SANDS

Powerful ocean waves pulverize rocks, dismantle cliffs, swallow islands. The anatomy of a wave attack mounted against some solid object—a cliff, say, or a breakwater—is an awesome thing. A breaking wave only four feet high strikes an object with 65,600 foot-pounds of energy, or thirty-three foot-tons. The land accommodates itself to this perpetual onslaught by breaking off and crumbling into detritus that re-establishes a foothold elsewhere, farther down the coast, or out at sea. Or it rearranges itself to blunt the force of the attack. The beaches of Aegean and Adriatic islands tend to be rough and coarse-grained because the tides there are gentle and the storms relatively mild. By contrast, the northwestern coast of France, scoured by Atlantic gales, is blanketed with fine sand. The violent clash between land and sea most dramatically demonstrates the pliancy and ephemerality of the shoreline and, conversely, the force of water in motion.

If violence is the modus operandi of water, accommodation is the way of the land. Elastic, the coastline shrinks and expands over the course of the year to take the force of storms, tides, and sea-level fluctuations. For instance, at Finis Terra, the beach at the cusp of Baja California, the seasonal variations are striking. In November, after the heavy surfs and storms of the rainy season, the berm is low at the feet of granite boulders and obelisks that thrust twelve feet into the air. Two months later, these same rocks are a mere foot high, buried under eight to ten feet of sand. The sea takes. The sea gives back. Paradises come, paradises go.

Many of the shores of antiquity are gone. We know that Achilles' Troy used to overlook a large arm of the sea, though it now stands far from the shore. Less than a thousand years ago, the city of Pisa, Italy, now over two miles from the sea, was a port. In the ancient city of Ephesus, on the coast of Turkey, archeologists have uncovered a collonaded marble road from a harbor that is now more than a mile from the sea. For the last two hundred years, archeologists have been uncovering traces of sunken cities and settlements throughout the Mediterranean, from the Minoan-Egyptian port of Pharos and the Phoenician port of Tyre, to the Carthaginian ports of North Africa, and the advanced Roman constructions along Italy's Amalfi coast and in the Bay of Naples.

Fragments of quays, breakwaters, bollards, concrete piers, walls, steps, and grottoes all around the Sorrento Peninsula and Capri attest to once thriving marine resorts. The erosion lines on rocks and buildings, as well as the positions of the buildings themselves, all indicate that in Roman times the shoreline was about sixteen feet lower than it is today. By the twelfth century, the land had fallen some sixteen to thirty feet below the present level and re-

The force of breakers advancing against the shore is so substantial that it can rip apart breakwaters, move blocks of stone many tons in weight, burrow tunnels in rock, and hurl trees like toothpicks. (Chris Rainer, *Natural Tunnel Through Headland at Wedded Rocks Emerging from Sea*, Chris Rainer/Corbis)

mained that low for at least three hundred years. Then, by the sixteenth century, it began to rise again, until it reached its present level. Archeological evidence on Capri, provided by grottoes, the partly submerged Baths of Tiberius, and the structures of the Roman harbor on Annacapri, suggests that the entire island pivoted, rising about twenty-two feet in the east but only twelve or so in the west.

Over the course of a thousand years, the island of Helgoland, in the North Sea, has been reduced from a considerable landmass to a mere rock by rising water and erosion of

In the "Hurricane Belt," powerful winds pile up high seas and push them shoreward, causing flooding and reshaping the coastal profile. (UPI/Corbis-Bettmann)

the land. Mont-St.-Michel, in France, in medieval times an island at high tide, is now continuously connected to the mainland by a bridge of sand brought in by the strong tides. The shape of the United States has changed many times in a much shorter time frame—within the last two hundred years, a mere moment in big-time geology. The older shorelines recorded in maps and deeds do not coincide with the current orientation. In some cases, the newer shore advances seaward across an estuary or merges with the line of a bar.

The general trend in the dialectic between earth and water, however, is toward the expansion of the ocean at the expense of the land. Since the beginning of the nineteenth century, the ocean has encroached by an average of two feet along the Atlantic and the Gulf coasts from Cape Cod, Massachusetts, to Cape Hatteras, North Carolina, and from Mobile Bay to the mouth of the Mississippi. Along the Gulf Coast, the system of elongated peninsulas and islands called "keys" that border the landmass stand at a distance ranging from a fraction of a mile to five miles from the Florida coast, but west of the mouth of the Mississippi, at Mobile Bay, they have retreated five, ten, and even fifteen miles from the mainland.

Although the trajectory and power of the ocean's erosive force are in perpetual flux, so is the movement of the tectonic plates that make up the earth's crust. Entire beaches can appear and disappear at the promptings of shifts in tectonic plates. The sidestepping of these massive pieces of planetary crust causes the land to rise or fall relative to sea level. One can track these seesawing movements in such places as England's southern and eastern coasts, which are sinking even as the northern part rises, giving the entire island a gradual tilt as land lost from one side is returned on the other. Reflecting these tectonic ups and downs, the "drowned topography" of Puget Sound and the Northeastern shore betrays itself in narrow, often rocky beaches of irregular length that were once hills and valleys. The dramatic seaside cliffs of northern California signal erosion at work on a sinking landmass. Interestingly, the long, broad, and straight beaches of the East Coast from New Jersey to Florida indicate a temporary truce in the battle between land and sea. Yet, whether rising or sinking, the beaches are perpetually in motion.

In the encounter between water and land, land is by no means the passive partner. It mounts a series of defensive maneuvers such as "rolling over" and re-forming when its weakest points are breached. In a device of ostensible surrender, the land yields its least defensible zones so as to fortify itself in more protected areas. The land also guides the approach of the swells—gently in some places, abruptly and crudely in others. Sometimes, it thrusts a rough fist of headlands into the sea. Then the swells bend and wrap long arms around the land and expend their energy in one titanic burst, the foam exploding and seething and flying in strips of creamy spray. Sometimes the land extends a sloping shore face under the waves that acts like a wedge in the water. Made of sand, gravel, and rock, the shore face drags at the feet of incoming waves, slowing them down and causing them to increase in height. In Waikiki, for instance, the shallow offshore coral reef—its form constant from year to year—slows down waves so that their breaking lasts several minutes and spans a distance of almost a mile.

The continental shelf itself influences the potency of ocean swells. Retaining the topography of the submerged continent, its mountains and valleys, ridges and abysses weaken or intensify wave energy. Deep submarine canyons cutting into the continental shelf close to shore, for instance, debilitate waves and take from them their load of sand and gravel, so that eventually shoals build up. These new deposits in turn influence and attenuate the power of the waves. With each fluctuation of the water, some minute change is introduced into the underlying landmass that will leave its imprint on the subsequent wave.

TIME AND TIDE

Think of water on the earth's surface as a loose skin draped on the more tightly stretched crust of land. This mobile skin is exquisitely responsive to the gravitational pull of celestial bodies. The closer the bodies, the stronger the attraction, which is why stars in the outermost corners of the universe exert almost no pull, and why the sun, vastly more massive than the moon but some ninety-two million miles more distant, has to play a mere supporting role.

Each day the moon rises some fifty minutes later, and each day the time of high tide is correspondingly set back. A constant twenty-four hours and twenty-five minutes intervene between crest—or high tide—and trough—or low tide—regardless of the moon's phase. But as the moon cycles about the earth, it affects the height of the tides. Twice each month, when the moon is full and again when it is at its thinnest, the sun, moon, and earth are neatly lined up so that the gravitational pull of both bodies is combined. These are the springs, when high tides are at their highest. Twice each month, when the moon is in its first and third quarters—and sun and moon oppose their gravitational forces—low tide is at its lowest, the neap tide. The moon's elliptical orbit contributes yet another set of variables. At its perigee, or the nearest point of its orbit, the moon is fifteen thousand miles closer to the earth, and from this position raises the tide about 20 percent higher than normal. And at its apogee, or the farthest point of its orbit, it produces tides that are correspondingly lower. When, at least twice a year, the perigee coincides with a full moon or a new moon, the highest tides of the year occur.

All the earth's waters dance to the waxing and the waning of the moon, but the actual impact of tides on a given beach will vary. Factors such as the shape of the land over which the water passes, and the rate of oscillation specific to each body of water, determine the way tides manifest themselves. Think of tides as water sloshing around in a basin. The basin's shape and depth, as well as the slope of its sides, determine how the water within will move. This movement will be most pronounced at the periphery, and least observable in the center. Broadly speaking, tides behave as though the ocean were divided into a system of basins, with natural periods of oscillation lasting about twelve to twenty-four hours. The length and depth of each basin determine the period of oscillation, and the stimulus for these movements is provided by the gravitational pull of the moon and sun.

A rule of thumb states that, whereas the tides in the deep oceans ebb and flow in accordance with the changing positions of the celestial bodies, the tides in coastal seas, such as the English Channel or the Red Sea, are secondary effects, meaning that their oscillation depends on the oceanic tides. If these coastal seas are entirely cut off from the oceans—as is the Mediterranean—their tides are almost imperceptible. Islands in the middle of oceans tend to have similarly nondescript tides. In Tahiti and other oceanic islands, the range is only about a foot.

The highest tides occur in the Bay of Fundy, in Nova Scotia, where a spring tide will raise the water some fifty feet. Puerto Gallegos, in Argentina; Cook Inlet, in Alaska; Frobisher Bay, in Davis Strait; the Koksoak River, at Hudston Strait; and the gulf of St.-Malo, on the Rance River estuary in France, also have dramatic, thirty-foot tides. One of the great curiosities of tidal variation is the fact that two places in proximity may have wildly divergent ranges. The eastern end of the Panama Canal has a tidal range of not more than one or two feet. But only forty miles away on the Pacific side, the range is twelve to sixteen feet. In some parts of the Sea of Okhotsk, which has a dominant range of two feet, the tide rises ten feet, and in one part—the Gulf of Penjinsk—the range from zenith to nadir peaks at thirty-seven. The variation is even more dramatic when we compare the foot-high tides of Nantucket Island with the towering forty- or fifty-foot tides of the Bay of Fundy, only a few hundred miles away.

Tidal scientists explain such wide fluctuations by invoking the theory of tidal oscillation. The immense discrepancy between Nantucket and the Bay of Fundy is due to their respective positions in the oscillating basin: Nantucket in its center, the Bay of Fundy at its terminus. Within this basin, the natural period of oscillation is approximately twelve hours, which means that it neatly coincides with the period of the ocean tide. The influx of oceanic high tide greatly augments the oscillation-driven rise, and both are even more exaggerated by the extreme narrowing and shallowing of the bay's upper reaches, which funnel the rising water through an increasingly narrow aperture.

Finally, just as tidal ranges vary from place to place, so do tidal rhythms. Both shores of the Atlantic Ocean have a rhythm of two high tides and two low tides each day. Twice each day, the high tides and the low tides reach roughly the same levels. These are semidiurnal rhythms. In the Gulf of Mexico, the Atlantic Ocean's inland sea, however, the tides are diurnal, with only one high water and one low water each lunar day of twenty-four hours and fifty minutes. This diurnal rhythm predominates in a scattering of places around the globe, such as St. Michael, Alaska, and Do Son in French Indochina. Most of the coasts around the world—including the Pacific coasts of North America, the European coasts, the shores of the Indian Ocean—have mixed tides, a combination of diurnal and semidiurnal: they have two highs and two lows a day, but usually of markedly unequal heights.

Scientists are hard put to explain this rhythmical variation, although they invoke such factors as local geographic features, the changing relative positions of the sun, moon, and earth, and the shape and depth of the specific basin. One of the most interesting examples of tidal rhythms is the island of Tahiti, whose semidiurnal tides occur like clockwork, with high tide at noon and midnight, and low tide at six o'clock in the morning and the evening. The tidal rhythm here is completely independent of the schedule of the moon, which elsewhere advances each successive tide by some fifty minutes. Instead of obeying the gravitational pull of the moon, Tahiti's waters seem to respond to that of the sun. Why they do this is still a matter of speculation.

In coastal waters, strong tidal currents can stage awesome spectacles as they rush through narrow passages at speeds of as much as two or three knots. The tidal waters passing through the straits between the Shetland Islands and the Orkneys in the North Sea are, at certain points, maelstroms of eddies, domes, and sinkholes, similar to the one described by Edgar Allan Poe in "A Descent into the Maelström":

> Here the vast bed of the waters, seamed and scarred into a thousand conflicting channels, burst suddenly into phrensied convulsion—heaving, boiling, hissing—gyrating in gigantic and innumerable vortices, and all whirling and plunging on to the eastward with a rapidity which water never elsewhere assumes except in precipitous descents.

Between two of the islands of the Lofoten group off the western coast of Norway, which presumably inspired Poe's text, lie gigantic whirlpools caused by tidal currents, with cavities in the shape of inverted bells, eddying and funneling with a wild circular motion. Poe describes such a vortex as a "terrific funnel, whose interior, as far as the eye could fathom it, was a smooth, shining, and jet-black wall of water, inclined to the horizon at an angle of some forty-five degrees, speeding dizzily round and round with a swaying and sweltering motion, and sending forth to the winds an appaling voice, half shriek, half roar, such as not even the mighty cataract of Niagara ever lifts up in its agony to Heaven."

MAKING WAVES

The tidal ebb and flow makes up the basso continuo of the ocean's orchestral ensemble, a kind of oceanic metronome—regular, reliable, predictable. At the opposite extreme are the tsunamis—impulsively generated waves—and the terrifying rogue waves that suddenly tower in the high seas. In the ocean, an earthquake, a volcanic eruption, a landslide, or a nuclear explosion can set off waves that are only one or two feet deep, but as much as 150 miles long. Moving at high speeds, these waves carry tremendous amounts of energy, but are not noticeable to ships at sea: in deep water, their slope is negligible. Only when a tsunami touches the bottom of a coastline does it discharge its energy with devestating force. There it literally trips over itself, rearing up as much as one hundred feet, as it advances deep into the shore.

Charles Darwin described one such titanic inundation, which he witnessed on February 20, 1835, while visiting the coast of Chile. He reported that, in the early hours of the morning, huge formations of seabirds were spotted flying landward, and dogs ran from the coastal settlements. Later that morning, shock waves were felt throughout central Chile. The first were little more than tremors, but in a matter of minutes they gathered terrifying momentum. The ground heaved, buckled, and split open. The stench of sulfur swept from the fissures that zigzagged through fields and villages. The sea drained out of the harbor and then, with a hideous roar, rushed back in as looming walls of water. Ships were hurled about like pieces of driftwood. Houses were picked up and carried far inland, only to be sucked back out to sea with the next wave. In six seconds, the entire town of Concepción was demolished, and its population virtually disappeared.

If tsunamis become lethal only when they hit land, rogue waves pack their destructive force exclusively on the high seas. Solitary and anomalous, the rogue wave surprises mariners by the extraordinary height of its crest, towering anywhere from fifty to one hundred feet above its fellows, or by the precipitous depth of its trough. A ship that is assaulted by such a freak wave has a good chance of swamping or breaking. In fact, most of the ships that have disappeared tracelessly on the high seas have succumbed to these monster waves. Although they can occur anywhere, these supercrests and supertroughs—or "holes in the sea"—are more prevalent in some areas than others. The Bermuda Triangle and the "wild coast" of South Africa, between Durban and East London, are notorious for such killer waves. The closest we on land can come to experiencing the might of these rogues of the deep is the "sneaker" wave, an extra-powerful breaker that occasionally darts out of the line of surf to race far up the beach, where it can cause considerable mischief.

Regardless of their size, all waves share basic physical features that permit oceanographers to describe them in terms of their height, the distance from trough to crest or between crests of contiguous waves; and period, or the length of time it takes succeeding crests to pass a fixed point. As a wave forms, travels, and breaks, these dimensions are constantly changing, although they all bear a specific relation to the wind, the depth of the water, the character of the sea bottom, the force and direction of any colliding waves. At the beach, one usually thinks of waves as inseparable from the moving water, yet this is not so. For the most part, the water that demarcates a wave does not move with the wave across the sea. Rather, each drop of water is set into motion as the wave energy passes through it and travels in a limited circular or elliptical orbit to return nearly to its original position. Watch what happens to an apple thrown a reasonable distance from shore. It will not be borne back to us, but will stay more or less in one spot, gently moving forward and backward as the waves succeed each other. Only very close to shore does wave energy actually influence the backward and forward movement of water. Here, the movement of the water beneath the wave crest is responsible for carrying sand, pebbles, and gravellike material toward the coast and high onto a beach.

Most waves are born far out at sea, engendered by the slap of the wind passing over water. The minute particles that make up air collide with the molecules of water. The friction of the air current breaks the surface tension of the water, which now becomes furrowed with alternating grooves and ridges. A gentle breeze breathing across calm water raises tiny ripples or capillary waves one or two millimeters high and a few centimeters from crest to crest. These tiny ripples, in turn, snag more of the wind's energy and ripen into wind chop, which, if augmented by fresh agitation, assumes a confused, irregular pattern called a "sea." How high the waves will eventually develop depends on the "fetch" or distance the waves can run without meeting an obstacle as they are driven by a wind blowing in a constant direction. The stronger the wind and the longer the fetch, the bigger the waves, which is why really big waves cannot be produced in the confines of a protected bay.

The complexity of waves only increases as they draw near to the beach, where the concealed topography of the submerged shore comes into play. Snagging on the peaks of submarine mountains, waves move closer and closer to the continental shelf, which rises abruptly from the oceanic depths about fifty miles from shore. As the wave progresses across this gently sloping plateau, between fifty and a hundred fathoms below, it slows down perceptibly until it enters shallow water.

From this point on, a series of rapid changes takes place. The wave shrinks in length and, dragging on the bottom, slows down. The crests of following waves crowd in toward it. Thus compressed, the wave now radically alters its profile from the horizontal to the vertical. The crest rises abruptly into a high ridge of water and continues to steepen. When it reaches a height about four-fifths of the depth below it, the wave no longer has enough water ahead of its advance to maintain a stable symmetrical shape. The smooth crest begins to cascade over the trough in front of it, and the wave begins to break. Swelling, the tip balloons, reaches wildly upward, and then bites into the shore, sucking up shale, fish bones, and the exoskeletons of mollusks and crustaceans before it swirls and churns them in its oxygenated foam and then spits them out again with a long hissing sigh.

The British poet Gerard Manley Hopkins captures the nuances of the approaching surf in his journal entry of August 10, 1872:

> I was looking at high waves. The breakers . . . are rolled out by the shallowing shore just as a piece of putty between the palms whatever its shape runs into a long roll. The slant ruck or crease one sees in them shows the way of the wind. The regularity of the barrels surprised and charmed the eye; the edge behind the comb or crest was as smooth and bright as glass. It may be noticed to be green behind and silver white in front: the silver marks where the air begins, the pure white is foam, the green—solid water. Then looked at to the right or left they are scrolled over like mouldboards or feathers or jibsails seen by the edge. It is pretty to see the hollow of the barrel disappearing as the white comb on each side runs along the wave gaining ground till the two meet at a pitch and crush and overlap each other.

BEACH, WIND, AND FIRE

Radiation from the sun warms the earth's atmosphere and its surface—which is 29 percent land and 71 percent ocean—but heats them unevenly. At the equator and in the tropics, the earth lies closer to the sun, and so the air here receives more direct rays than the air at higher latitudes. The warmed air rises and into its place moves cooler air from the north or the south, which, in its turn, is heated, ascends, and leaves room for a fresh supply of cool air. These movements, driven by the sun and orchestrated by the earth's rotation, produce the major winds. Near the equator, in the region of the doldrums, there is barely any wind at all, but in the lower latitudes to the north and south, the trade winds begin to blow, always steadily to the west. Then, when we reach the higher latitudes of 40° to 50°, the winds suddenly change direction and blow from the west to the east, becoming the "westerlies" or "roaring forties."

Winds over the sea surface raise waves by transferring part of their energy to the water as a current. The trade winds provide the initial impetus for the equatorial currents, which stream close to the surface of the water in a westerly direction until they collide with a landmass that deflects them from the equator. Then the currents head north or south, and eventually swing back up, forming huge loops which turn clockwise in the Northern Hemisphere and counterclockwise in the Southern. The prevailing winds themselves take on this shape as they describe vast eddies corresponding to the oceanic currents. These movements are determined by the spinning earth, which exerts a steady, deflecting force that turns all moving objects to the right in the Northern Hemisphere and to the left in the Southern.

Each ocean has its major currents—the Gulf Stream and the Benguela Current in the Atlantic, and the Kuroshio and the Humboldt in the Pacific. Because the ocean is the great regulator of the earth's climate, affecting the temperature and humidity of the atmosphere, the currents that sweep past the continents play a great role in shaping their weather. Together with the winds and coastal topography, they determine whether a given area will feel the moderating effect of the sea or will know only the harsh extremes of the continental climate. The North American Eastern Seabord, for instance, gains little from its proximity to the ocean, because the prevailing winds blow in an easterly direction. By contrast, Europe, wide open to the sea, profits from "Atlantic weather" for hundreds of miles inland. Similarly, the Pacific Northwest lies in the path of westerly winds that have traversed vast stretches of warm ocean and, laden with water vapor, encourage lush vegetation in a mild climate.

Sometimes, proximity to the ocean produces an arid climate, as in the Atacama Desert on the Chilean coast. The decisive factors here are the combination of a western coast in the lee of the prevailing winds and the cold Humboldt Current. As air that is heated by the hot land rises, it draws the cold sea breezes inland, forcing them up over the mountains, where they remain cool for long periods—and distances—before the warm land can heat them. Never given a chance to condense at the shoreline, the water vapor that is contained in the sea air rarely returns to the coast as precipitation. This scenario is replayed wherever marine deserts occur, as in Africa's Kalahari or Mexico's Baja California.

By and large, the major currents follow the wind system and have a well-defined and predictable trajectory. But there are exceptions. Weaker currents often vary their direction under the influence of local weather, but even the stronger currents, moving at speeds as high as four or five knots, may shift with the seasons or respond to wind fluctuations caused by solar storms. The monsoons of the Indian Ocean, for example, cause the currents to shift seasonally. Fluctuations over a longer time span can have a dramatic impact on the climate. Every few years, at irregular intervals, the Humboldt Current is deflected from the coast of South America by a warm current of tropical water that comes down from the north. El Niño, as the current is called, brings torrential rains to the land and raises the temperature of the sea so that the marine flora and fauna, accustomed to cold, die in large numbers, and the birds that feed on them perish or migrate.

Wind and current fluctuations leave perceptible traces even when they produce less dramatic phenomena. We have all experienced sudden warm currents which render usually frigid water bearable, and which deposit un-

expected marine specimens on the beach. In much subtler ways, the harmony and counterpoint of wind and water generate fogs of various densi-
ties, some hanging as massive gray banks on the horizon, others shrouding
the beach for a depth of twenty to thirty feet, and others still eerily hovering above the surface of the sand, exposing only the legs of beachcombers
as they move spectrally along a line of surf.

THE BEACH OF ANTIQUITY

Baiae, 15 B.C. The sun climbs slowly in the transparent, brilliant sky. The Mediterranean, heavy, still, and dark, flashes an occasional whitecap and, at its edge, reflects the covered galleries, porticoes, and alabaster walls of a luxurious villa rising from a verdant grove of cypress and umbrella pines.

The perfume of jasmine and lime blossoms sweetens the air, adding an aromatic high note to the briny pungency of the sea. A small party of Roman noblemen descends a gently sloping path to a platform built out into the bay. Their laughter and animated chatter resonate across the still water and alert the group of slaves waiting in the wings of a spacious pavilion.

Gliding across the floor of tiny ceramic tiles laid in a pattern of waves, the attendants solicitously escort the guests into the pavilion. There, under the gaze of marble Nereids set

At the seashore, affluent Romans spared no effort to provide the proper environment in which a sound mind might dwell in a sound body, in keeping with Juvenal's maxim mens sana in corpore sano. (*Coastal Landscape*, first century A.D. mural, Museo Nazionale, Naples)

into niches and sea serpents cavorting in bas-relief across the walls, the visitors are helped out of their cream-colored colobia, or tunics, and wrapped in capes of soft wool. There is still a hint of cold in the air, but the angle of the sun is already giving promise of the incandescent heat that will soon drive them back into the shady gardens and cool chambers of the marine villa. With an imperious gesture, the portly host urges his guests to follow him down a short flight of steps into a spacious, artificial bay.

Massive stones, capped with blocks of marble, compose the two arms of a breakwater that encloses the swimming basin, whose waters the gentle Mediterranean tide had replenished some hours earlier. With shouts of glee, the men throw off their wraps and dive into the warm water. Like young boys, they splash each other, squiggle under the surface, and race each other to an artificial grotto built into the sides of the breakwater. Slaves in gaily painted boats follow their progress, prepared to row the swimmers back to the pavilion. There, oiled, perfumed, and garlanded with roses, they pick at dainties, sip wine, and laugh at what the poet Horace had said of rich men like themselves, who "on the verge of death contract for blocks of marble to be hewn, and unmindful of the grave, are rearing mansions and are all eagerness to thrust back the shores of the sea that roars against Baiae."

■■■■■■

Societies inhabiting the mild shores of the Mediterranean spent many centuries relishing the beach, whereas their distant neighbors on the seas of the north shrank from recreational bathing. The raw winds, the invisible currents snaking beneath the surface of the water, the mysterious creatures lurking just offshore, and the slippery, jagged shingle underfoot assaulted the body in unpleasant and sometimes deadly ways. Even the sun was treacherous, its potency amplified to turn pale, bare skin into a flaming carapace of pain. Not surprisingly, the approach to the boundary of land and sea was made cautiously, haltingly, each step nudged along by a conceptual breakthrough, attitudinal shift, or technological advance.

Regardless of climate, the domestication and exploitation of the beach as a source of pleasure came only as an offshoot of civilization. For centuries, of course, the beach had been the liminal space of encounters between Manichean forces of good and evil: between earth and water, man and nature, the civil and the savage, life and death. It was the fragile staging area for expeditions of survival, colonization, and military conquest. But except among the classical Greeks and Romans—for whom the sea was as much playground as workplace—it was not a place of diversion, of things sweet and light. First we had to grow radically *alienated* from nature, by, paradoxically, gaining systematic and wide-scale mastery over it. As demonstrated by the Romans, who were devout worshippers of the beach, it was first necessary to gather into cities, secure a measure of independence from the earth, barter and trade, build ships and roads, and organize the business of survival into spells of labor and of leisure. Free time, that most radical and most elusive of human commodities, had to be invented.

THE SEA OF MYTH

Long before Steven Spielberg, there was myth. The beach was anything but paradisiacal, as confirmed by a mythopoetic tradition that spewed forth visions of the sea as a flesh-flagellating aqua-pit, completely inhospitable to domesticating, civilizing impulses. In fact, *Jaws*-like deterrents to safe sea-bathing drew their inspiration from ancient lore which painted the turbulent depths as miasmic stews of bellicose, limb-chomping creatures that guarded their domain with jealous ferocity. Judging by the diversity and richness of the sea-monster lore transmitted through the ages, the primordial mental blocks to sea bathing must have been prodigious.

The first voluntary step into the sea required people to shed the shackles of mythology, which rendered the beach as both a life force and, for centuries, an unpredictable geological zone that bred fear and loathing among the natives. After all, antiquity viewed the ocean as the mother of all mysteries, the sign of all that was impenetrable, unknown, and immense. She was a divider of peoples; her limitless horizon concealed singular sights, unintelligible customs, and barbarous tongues. The shore was the limit of the known and familiar world, the ragged selvage of human experience. In fact, etymologists tell us that the English word "shore"—derived from the Old English *scieran*, meaning "to cut, to shear"—was literally construed as something that was "shorn off." At any moment, the sea could rise up against coastal inhabitants, dash their frail sailing ships into smithereens, sever the fragile threads of life, and still have enough fury left over to wreak havoc on land.

Utilitarian motives brought early civilizations to the shores of rivers, lakes, seas, and oceans: Babylonia on the Tigris and the Euphrates rivers, Egypt in the Nile Valley, Jericho on the River Jordan, Phoenicia—then Crete and Troy, Athens and Rome—along the shores of the Mediterranean. Water was their lifeline to survival, commerce, conquest. From the sea, these peoples harvested fish and salt. They drew on the waters of lakes and rivers to irrigate their crops. As mariners and warriors, they plied aquatic routes to foreign markets and territories. And so the cosmologies, or origin tales, of all these littoral civilizations pay tribute to the crucial role water played in their genesis and survival. Their myths speak of that distant past when earth and sky and water came into being through a cosmic mating ritual. Hesiod, in the *Theogony*, recounts how the earth "lay with Sky and gave birth to Ocean with its deep current," which became the wellspring of creatures good and evil.

For the Sumerians, the earth emerged directly from the *mar* the moment the storm god Huracan touched her. The ancient Akkadians weave a sea-based love legend in which the primordial chaos of ocean lying beneath the earth mates with the goddess Tiamat to trigger the pulse of life. For the Japanese, too, the sea was the crucible of earth; it was the home of a giant carp that, upon awakening from a deep slumber, thrashed with a violence so savage that it churned up an enormous tsunami, on whose crest rode the shards of land that became Japan. The landlocked tribes of North American Indians theorized that some demiurgical intermediary delivered earth from the bottom of the sea to create landmasses that became the bedrock of human civilizations. Against the background of such powerful myths, the beach was charged with a very special meaning. It was revered as a meeting place for mighty deities, where daily was staged the drama of the earth's origin in the intimate—and sometimes violent—mixing of elements along its unstable boundaries.

Homer's "deep-flowing Oceanus," that immense river that encircled the earth, was the gateway to Hades, the realm of the dead, shrouded in mist and cloud. The Bible makes frequent reference to Leviathan, a mysterious marine monster, who is the embodiment of an evil so enormous that only the vastness of the ocean can contain it. Other maritime people also told of many-headed serpents, dwellers of the deep, who threaten destruction unless mollified by unthinkable offerings. Among the ancient Greeks, this wandering tale was fleshed out in the characters of Andromeda, the beautiful daughter of Cepheus, king of Joppa, and Perseus, the stalwart slayer of Medusa. Learning of the impending sacrifice of Andromeda, Perseus rushes to the side of the horror-struck maiden, who, bound to a rock, vainly struggles to escape the abominable serpent approaching through the waves. In the ensuing struggle, Perseus pierces the dragon with his sword, in one fateful stroke ridding Joppa of its sea scourge and gaining Andromeda's hand in marriage.

Memory of such ancient terrors underlay later, Christian, legends of marine monsters, most notably in the story of St. George and the Dragon and, still later, in the tale of an aquatic serpent that was rent asunder by the archangel St. Michael on the site of Mont-St.-Michel, on the coast of France. In their peregrinations, Irish monks such as St. Brendan were called to do battle with godforsaken filthy beasts that crawled out of the watery depths. The northern sea, in fact, was teeming with gnarly creatures, the Kraken of Norway and the man-eating Grendel immortalized in *Beowulf*. The ancient Scandinavians populated their shores with uncouth and hellish creatures and stocked the depths of the seas with noisome serpents, the most terrifying of whom was the Jormungandur, that "loathy worm" who, from time to time, ventured to the shore to challenge the very gods in foul combat. Among the people of Iceland, Nikr, or Neck, was said to infest the waters in guises that ranged from a beautiful nixie enticing sailors to their doom, to a bearded, capricious old man casting spells on hapless beach scavengers. Given such frightening perceptions, one could hardly expect coastal dwellers to imagine that swimming in such a witches' brew could offer anything remotely resembling pleasure. Indeed, it filled them with horror.

THE CLASSICAL ROMANCE OF THE BEACH

Ancient Greek and Roman myths depicted the sea and the beach as equivocal environments, at once threatening and caressing, terrifying and soothing. The poets of antiquity—Homer, Hesiod, Pindar, Aeschylus, Sophocles, Herodotus, and Aristophanes in Greece, and Ovid, Apuleius, and Virgil in Rome—told stories of nature animated by the same passions that rule the lives of mortals. The seas and seashores teemed with deities whose temperaments were as inconstant as the weather, and whose moods were pegged to the volatile forces that rule human lives.

The Aegean, Ionian, Black, Adriatic, and Mediterranean seas were ruled by an entire pantheon of deities: Proteus, Poseidon, and Ocean, the Titan who comanded the great river that girdled the earth. The deity Pontus lorded over the mysterious deep; Nereus, the gentle "Old Man of the Sea," presided over the placid Mediterranean, "thinking just and kindly thoughts," as the Greek poet Hesiod tells in the *Theogony*. With the prolixity of all beings oceanic, this Nereus and "fair-haired Doris, daughter of the pure Oceanstream," spawned fifty lovely Nereids, sea maidens so captivating that they "inspired many hearts with love." Among them was Amphitrite, who was a calm ing influence on the waves of the dark sea and the blasts of its stormy winds. In the Atlantic, on the outer fringes of the known world, Oceanus brewed destructive gales and currents, and the foul-tempered Hesperian nymphs Sthenno, Euryale, and Medusa plotted the destruction of mortals. The duplicitous songs of the Sirens, the treachery of the rock-fiend Scylla, and the fierce upheaval of Poseidon brought many Greek sailors to a watery grave and killed Odysseus' compan-

Mythical monsters swarmed in the depths of the seas, preying on sailors and unwary swimmers. (authors' collection)

ions in that greatest of all sea yarns, the *Odyssey.* Likewise, in Virgil's *Aeneid,* the sea struck fear in the hearts of sailors.

Aphrodite, cunning goddess of love and beauty, who beguiled mortals and gods alike, was born of the sea. Risen from the foam, she emerged out of the waves near the island of Cythera, growing out of the sexual organs of divine Sky, which his own son Cronus had sheared off and cast into the waves. As inconstant as the sea, Aphrodite presided over "the whispers and smiles and tricks which girls employ, and the sweet delight and tenderness of love." Wherever she passed, Homeric hymns tell us, beauty followed in her footsteps. The wind and the sea waves were calmed, the clouds dispersed, flowers sprang from the ground. But she could also be deceitful, maliciously turning on mortals and wielding over them a deadly, destructive power.

In classical myth, the shoreline is typically a place where identity itself is imperiled and the self becomes unrecognizable—sometimes diminished, sometimes augmented, according to the whimsy of the gods. On the margins of water and land, divinities assume the form of men and wild beasts, and from the amorous embraces of mortals and immortals are engendered hybrid creatures with extraordinary powers. The Greek tragedian Aeschylus and the Roman poet Ovid recount charming tales of young maidens playing on beaches who were carried off by gods. Persephone was abducted into Hades by Pluto, who seized her on the shores of Sicily while she was gathering roses, hyacinths, and narcissi.

Europa was also gathering flowers by the beach with her friends when Zeus, smitten by her charms, transformed himself into a dazzling white bull, lured her onto his back, and bore her off across the wide water. The Greek pastoral poet Moschus relates that, as Zeus cut the waves, a whole procession of beings from the deep rose up to accompany him: sea gods, delectable Nereids astride dophins, handsome Tritons sounding their horns, and even Poseidon himself, the mighty master of the sea. Ensconcing his new bride on the island of Crete, Zeus sired her famous sons and rendered her the tribute of giving her name to an entire continent. Europa's grandmother, Io, had been courted, abducted, and metamorphosed into a cow by the philandering Zeus. Recognizing her odious rival in the heifer, Hera, Zeus' wrathful wife, sent a gadfly to torment the girl and drive her, frenzied, from sea to sea—the Ionian, named after her, and the Bosporus, or "Ford of the Cow"—until at least she reached the shores of the Nile, where Zeus restored her human form.

In the *Metamorphoses* (A.D. 1–8), Ovid celebrated this transformative power of water as the simultaneous and identical source of the prodigious creativity of nature and the magical gift of the poet. In the Allen Mandelbaum translation, this paean reads as follows:

I found some water, moving without a ripple,
Without a sound, clear to the very bottom,
You would not think the water was even moving,
You could count the pebbles, and the silver willows
And poplars shaded the sloping banks. I stood there
Paused, dipped my toes in, waded to my knees,
And this was not enough. I took my clothes off
And hung them on a willow, bending over,
And plunged in naked, and while I beat the waters
With one stroke and another, and turned and glided,
I thought I heard a curious kind of murmur
From deep down under. . . . wherever I moved,
There seemed to be a pool, and even quicker
Than I can tell the story I was changed
To a stream of water.

LOOKING AT THE SEA

To the Greeks, and later the Romans, who had a keen appreciation for the beauties of the natural world, the sea was the noblest and loveliest sight. Describing the marvels of creation, the Roman orator Cicero exclaimed, "How mighty is the beauty of the sea, the view of its hugeness, the manifold isles, and delightful coasts." The pleasures of the sea were infinitely renewable and varied. The short-lived third-century Emperor Marcus Aurelius Marius so loved the shimmer of morning light on the water that he had a passage cleared between his house and the coast to open up a view. In the fourth century, the Greek philosopher Plutarch thought a sail along the coast or a stroll along the shore a supreme pleasure. Next came the first zoning law for the beach. Coastal vistas were so cherished, and the competition for them was so keen, that by the sixth century the Emperor Justinian the Great was compelled to pass an ordinance barring construction within one hundred feet of the shore to protect sea views.

Interestingly, the architecture of the ancient Greeks and Romans contains even more evidence of their irrepressible love for the beach than their literature does. The history of this passion is eloquently told in the ruins and remnants of elaborate villas, palaces, baths, and piers they constructed along the coasts of Greece, Italy, Sicily, and Egypt. In a description of his villa at Laurentum, the Roman statesman and writer Pliny the Younger explains that the dining room was built far out into the water so that it could capture a magisterial spectrum of marine moods. When the wind blew from the southwest, dinner guests could enjoy the sight of spray splashing against the windows. In calm weather, they could look out at the broad, still sea through folding doors and floor-to-ceiling windows. In various alcoves and upper stories, the fenestration was designed to afford a variety of views, and even the warm sea-bath was constructed in a way that allowed bathers to glimpse the reflections of trees and palaces that flickered on the sea's placid surface.

Wild, savage, unbounded nature—the expanse of the ocean or the heights of mountain peaks—inspired fear or, at the very least, distaste. The natural world, in a sense, was completely satisfying only if it was reassuring, and it could only be so by clearly incorporating recognizable elements of human industry. Valleys, hills, coastlines that curved into coves, or bays gracefully defining the horizon possessed great appeal. In the first century A.D., the Roman rhetorician Quintilian, for example, thought a beautiful natural site had to be "level, charming, and marine," meaning that mountainous, rough terrain and arid stretches of land were unaesthetic and consequently inappropriate for human habitation. During antiquity, as today, aesthetic conventions determined which seaside outposts were aggressively colonized, and which were bypassed in favor of "location, location, location."

ATHLETES ON THE BEACH

There was a saying among the aristocrats of ancient Sparta and Athens that an imbecile was a person "who could neither read nor swim." The Greeks understood that both literacy and physical prowess were required to navigate through life. Accordingly, the Greek passion for exercise was broadcast from virtually every artifact their hands fashioned: statuary, friezes, vases, pots, and amphorae. The *Iliad* and the *Odyssey* provide elaborate descriptions of the funeral games celebrated by Achilles in honor of Patroclus, athletic competitions held outside Alcinous' palace, and the bow-stringing trials in Ithaca. The French historian Robert Flacelière emphasizes that almost all Greek cities harbored two buildings that, between them, embody the intellectual and athletic cornerstones of their civilization: the theater and the sports stadium. Beginning at the age of eight, every Athenian lad could expect to spend the next ten years working out in a beautifully appointed palaestra or gymnasium, an open-air sportsground flanked by covered lobbies with changing rooms, resting rooms, baths, and shops ornamented with fine statuary. Here, young boys performed their exercises, always stark naked, to the rhythmic melodies of the flute.

In Athens, by the fifth century B.C., swimming had grown so popular that the palaestrae and gymnasia were frequently equipped with swimming pools. In Delphi, the gymnasium featured a circular bath ten yards in diameter and nearly six feet deep, into which the athletes plunged for a communal swim after their workouts. Swimming was not represented among the sports of the Panathenaic Festival, which was introduced in the sixth century B.C. Presumably, aquatic activities were reserved for pure pleasure and refreshment. However, we know that children learned to swim in the sea—or the nearest river—and that Spartan children and men took a daily dip, winter and summer. Women did not bathe in public, except during certain religious festivals—the Posidonia or the Eleusinian Mysteries—when they immersed themselves in the seawater for ritualistic purposes.

ROMAN HOLIDAY

In Rome, seaside pursuits were the lifeblood of civilized pleasures. If, as the available evidence suggests, swimming in ancient Greece was a hygienic necessity or a physical regimen, among the ancient Romans water and aquatic rituals became a way of life. Baths were the cornerstone of Roman hygiene and sociability, and each city of the empire, no matter how small or insignificant, had *thermae* that catered to the needs of the body as well as the spirit. Likewise, the seashore was a site of rest, meditation, collective pleasure, and boundless hedonism. Rome's finest thinkers and writers—among them Cicero, Pliny the Younger, Statius, Seneca—have left behind chronicles of their pleasurable sojourns by the sea. Here, intelligently curated sur-

The ancient Romans prized the waters of the Adriatic for their buoyancy, their alleged restorative powers, and their luscious harvests of sardines, squid, sole, and mackerel. (*Seascape*, mural, c. 520 B.C., Tomba della Caccia e Pesca, Tarquinia, Italy)

roundings, refined architecture, and a variegated schedule of contemplation and physical activity supported a concept of cultivated leisure that the Romans called *otium*.

A sort of "working weekend" by the sea, *otium* involved rest without laziness or boredom, a carefully calculated program of self-development that provided respite from the taxing affairs of state and a preparation period for future serious endeavors. Cicero writes of *otium cum dignitate* or relaxation with dignity, as befitting the best citizens of the state, a special time set aside as a momentary break from the pursuit of honor and glory. In a serene beachside villa filled with charm—or *amoenitas,* as the Romans called it—*otium* was a way of living by the seashore. The Roman elite were fanatical about the aural and visual effects of the sea. They loved to hear the sound of water: splashing in fountains, gurgling in streams, and rhythmically breaking on the shore. In their coastal retreats, they were free to organize their time as they wished: reading, corresponding, sorting their collections of amulets or coins, engaging in philosophical conversation, strolling on the sand. They delighted in the company of friends as they swam in warm water or gathered pebbles on the shore. Early in the morning and in the heat of the day, Roman ladies donned a simplified togalike garment that had been customary water dress since Praxiteles' Greece, around 350 B.C. Younger women wore an abbreviated two-piece garment, depicted on the mosaic wall of a fourth-century-A.D. Sicilian villa, which did double duty as a gymnastics costume and, many costume historians agree, anticipated the modern bikini.

From the end of the republic until the middle of the second century of the empire, resorts thrived along the shores of Latium and Campania, and an unbroken string of villas extended along the coasts near Ostia, between Terracina and Naples. A fine system of roads connected these sites with the capital, and fleets of boats comfortably ferried travelers to islands and remote seaside destinations. The Romans of the early empire were, as Pliny put it, fundamentally "migratory and curious," addicted to collecting new impressions, information, experiences. As Seneca the Younger observed, many of his contemporaries "make sea-voyages, endure long journeys alone, for some remote sight." Perhaps this explains the remarkable flightiness of wealthy Romans, who seemed always to be in transit from one seaside resort to another. The affluent, born to a life of ease and leisure, only lightly encumbered by the demands of civic life or toil, undertook these rambles by sea in search of a change of scene, to allay weariness and boredom.

Climate and urban crowding drove both the masses and the upper crust in seasonal migrations from sultry and vapor-ridden Rome. The ingredients for beach holidays were already in place. Population density, teamed with a relatively high standard of living, a well-established economic and social elite, and a superb infrastructure of roads, provided the material conditions for annual excursions to the seashore—and with it the precursor to the summer traffic jam. As spring blazed into summer, the Via Appia—the most famous thoroughfare of the classical world—choked with travelers heading over the Alban Hills to Campania, and then on to Puteoli and Brundusium, the two main harbors that served Rome.

The Via Appia in fact offered a moving spectacle of Roman society indulging in a preview of the festive antics of the coast. Here, a wealthy merchant rushed at a furious clip, frantic to reach his Alban villa for a refreshing interlude from his pressing urban affairs. Behind him, proceeding at a more stately pace, came a fine lady's carriage surrounded by a swarm of elegantly attired men, some young, some old; like most sophisticated Roman matrons, the lady drove her own horses. Much laughter and banter passed among the members of the merry company, which certainly included a poet to extemporize verses in praise of the lady or to satirize a rival following at a discreet distance in his silk-curtained carriage. As in modern times, the nouveaux riches—in this case, upstart freedmen—hustled through the crowd in flashy vehicles drawn by expensive horses. The throngs streaming to the glittering beaches of Campania or the Gulf of Naples hummed with an air of excitement, impatience, exhilaration. A select few were headed for quiet, private villas on the sea, but most streamed to the Lotus-Eaters' land of Baiae, seeking health, recreation, and dissipation in the first of antiquity's pleasure cities.

The immaculate and cultivated setting, the beauty of the palaces, the luxury, the clear air and bright sky all combined to make Baiae delightful. Festivals followed each other endlessly against the daily rhythm of rest, fine food, and physical exercise. By day, boating parties were organized. On board the barques and galleys there was music, laughter, and drinking—constant drinking—and the tipsy guests tossed their rose wreaths onto the gentle sea. Songs and other music echoed from dawn to dusk. As the cool evening descended, the glimmer of countless torches reflected in the black silky waters, and the strains of serenades carried across the waves, broken only by the rough shouts of rivals pitched in heated quarrels.

For five hundred years—a record the modern era has yet to break—Baiae reigned as the greatest fashionable beach resort of the ancient world. In Baiae Rome's gilded youth paraded their pomaded hair and tunics of the finest wools, and dissipated bons vivants squandered borrowed money on women, wine, and oysters. This gay outpost by the sea was legendary for its dissoluteness, and Romans found its erotic spell irresistible. Seneca the Younger, the first-century philosopher, called Baiae a vortex of luxury and a harbor of vice. When he visited the city for a protracted stay, he had the bad fortune of taking up residence directly above the great bath, and was greatly annoyed by the incessant noise—the din of splashing bathers, groaning weight lifters, shouting ballplayers, singing drunks, and barking vendors.

According to myth, the water of Baiae had once been cold—too cold, in fact, to allow for the pleasures of bathing. One day, Venus made Cupid swim in it, and a spark from his torch fell into the bay, which then burst into flame. From that time on, everyone who bathed here fell in love. Licentiousness and ribaldry were always in the air: maidens were common property, old men turned into young bucks, youths experimented with homosexuality, no man escaped without a broken heart, and few women left with their virtue intact.

Roman "beach culture" matured into a full-fledged obsession in Baiae, whose cocktail of pleasures set the tone for the general experience of the beach, and established the standard of luxury to which the affluent aspired. The elite of the republic had lovely summer residences—the more, the better—on the Latian and Campanian coasts. Cicero kept villas at Arpinum, Tusculum, Pompeii, Puteoli, Cumae, Astura, Formiae, Antium— one, it would seem, for each mood and each season. The emperor-philosopher Marcus Aurelius, as Caesar, enjoyed as many residences as a modern CEO's luxury oceanside hotels. Every climate and every season had its own villa. "In Naples," he wrote in A.D. 143, "the weather is good but changeable. The nights are mild, as at Laurentum; at cockcrow, it is as cool as Lanuvium; at sunrise as cold as on the Algidus; the forenoon as sunny as at Tusculum; the midday as hot as at Puteoli; the afternoon and evening temperate, as at Tibur."

Imperial villas proliferated along the entire coast, from the seashore close to Rome to the white cliffs of Terracina and the islands. Today, however, only ruins and some scattered literary fragments attest to the grandeur and charm of these sybaritic retreats. Pliny the Younger described the Emperor Trajan's estate at Centum Cellae, today's Civitavecchia, as a magnificent villa set in brilliant-green fields only a stone's throw from the coast. There, a grandiose engineering project was under way in 107–6 B.C. to create a sheltered bathing-and-boating retreat. Slaves from all corners of the empire excavated a harbor and were bludgeoned into hauling massive stones to create an artificial island to dampen the force of the breakers. At Alsium, near Palo, Pompey the Great and, after him, Verginius Rufus, the consul, built charming resorts to which they planned to retire in old age. The ruins now extend along the seacoast a distance of 950 feet, swinging back inland another six hundred feet, enclosing mosaic floors, marble walls, antefixes, lead water-pipes, and isinglass panels.

In Ostia, a bustling destination at the mouth of the Tiber, which is now far inland, second-century philosophers engaged in fevered discourse on the use of virtue to confer happiness as they strolled along the winding shore. Christians and pagans debated the merits of the new morality over the old while sitting on the edge of the breakwater and idly watching boys splash in the sheltered water. The entire stretch of Italian coastline from Ostia to Lavinium, now called Prattica, was dotted with a series of little towns and country houses devoted to pleasure and relaxation. But the jewel among Italy's sea cities in republican times, and even more during the empire, was Antium. Situated on a long, rocky promontory, this bastion of exquisite temples and ornate palaces was a favorite resort of emperors such as Caligula and Nero, who were born there. Some of our most cherished Roman masterpieces—the *Apollo Belvedere* and the Borghese gladiator—were created to adorn Antium palaces. Today, only ruins remain to suggest the refinement and luxury with which the Romans surrounded themselves on their sea holidays. The adventurous modern-day swimmer can look down through the crystalline water that has since invaded the land and see scattered remnants of terraces, galleries, and precious marbles that long ago graced glittering white palaces by the sea.

If Antium was the Palm Beach of classical times, Naples was Coney Island and Blackpool rolled into one. Even under the late republic, visitors came here for the full round of seaside pleasures civilization could deliver. When not swimming or rowing, they visited the Sibyl's grotto at Cumae, then strolled through the vineyards of Bacchus, and hiked the slopes of dormant Vesuvius. Some came to gaze at the magnificent villas dotting the harbor of

While excavating a luxurious fourth-century Roman villa, the Italian archaeologist Gino V. Gentili discovered a mosaic that depicts female gymnasts sporting an early version of the bikini. (A. Ascani, *Villa Romana del Casale*, authors' collection)

Posilipo. The most notorious—whose impressive ruins now bear the name
Casa degli Spiriti—belonged to Vedius Pollio, friend of Augustus Caesar,
who was in the habit of feeding his fattest and most disobedient slaves to
the pet lampreys with which he stocked his pools. Revels, carnivals, and festivities went on in covered and uncovered assemblies, columned palaces,
and open-air theaters, in full sight of Mount Vesuvius, whose eruption in
A.D. 79 brought this glorious chapter in the history of hedonism to a fiery
close.

THE DARK AGES OF THE ANCIENT BEACH

The Edenic pleasures of the Roman beach were not to last. In A.D. 476, the
Western Roman Empire collapsed and the beach, as a site of sybaritic indulgence, went down with it. For the next millennium, the body, the beach, and
even pleasure would be shrouded with a mantle of dread and prohibition.
Greco-Roman culture disintegrated, as did its rich storehouse of legends
that depicted the beach as a valuable source of psychological and physical
restoration. The Judeo-Christian tradition, filled with equivocal representations of the phenomenal universe, emerged as civilization's powerful new
matrix. As the new cultural "master text," the Bible would shape approaches
to life, from religion and politics to science and recreation. But its influence
would interact with and overlie another potent cultural tradition—the
pagan belief system of the Northern and Eastern European tribes.

Just as potent in molding attitudes toward the beach as religion were the
entirely material conditions of life. If ancient civilization had centered on
the Mediterranean, in the Middle Ages the centers of population moved
north and westward, to regions either landlocked or washed by inhospitable, cold seas. Plato had written that "the earth is very large and that we
who dwell between the pillars of Hercules and the river Phasis live in a
small part of it about the sea, like ants or frogs about a pond." These waters
of the Mediterranean had remained for centuries the center of the Roman
world, even after the imperial conquests had dramatically expanded that
world. Roman imperialism had disseminated a uniform way of life along
with its Pax Romana. A senator from Aquitania could pursue his career in
the Bosporus, own vast estates in Macedonia, and holiday in Baiae—and he
would always be in a single universe. But when the Roman Empire disintegrated, the equilibrium was destroyed.

One after another, the territories of the empire succumbed to the invasions of the "Barbarians": Italy to the Ostrogoths and the Lombards, Britain
to the Angles, Saxons, and Jutes; Gaul to the Franks; Spain to the Visigoths.
Differing in language and social organization, these peoples brought with
them habits and patterns of thought that had little in common with the

mentality and customs of the subjugated. As they swept south across the Rhine and the Danube, they left deep scars. By A.D. 500, all vestiges of the Western Roman Empire had virtually disappeared, along with all knowledge of Greek learning and social institutions. Roman cities, so essential to the spawning of leisure and the love of the beach, deteriorated. Many never recovered from pillage or evacuation. Some disappeared entirely. Others sank to the status of mere hamlets.

Cultivated land diminished sharply, and, in consequence of constant strife and starvation, the population plummeted. Europe's most important towns had no more than a few thousand inhabitants each. Vast expanses of wilderness—forests, scrub, dunes, wasteland—surrounded them and separated them from the nearest settlements. The system of roads feeding the coastal communities fell into disrepair. Bridges were no longer maintained, and as they disintegrated, nothing took their place at river crossings. The aqueducts that delivered water to the towns and supplied the *thermae* were destroyed. Gradually, the magnificent villas and natatoria of the Romans crumbled, and because their function had evaporated, no one thought to maintain or restore them. Instead, the rare marbles and statuary were dismantled and pressed into service for constructing the rude dwellings of a brutalized population.

Finally, nature itself mounted an assault on the seashores. Over the course of centuries, the water level gradually rose in the Mediterranean, submerging cities, ports, and harborworks along its entire serrated and jagged coastline. Because the mountains of the Alpine system—which includes the Atlas, Pyrenees, Alps, Carpathians, Caucasus, Himalaya, and the island chains of the East Indies—are of recent formation, having been uplifted in the Tertiary period, the entire region surrounding the Mediterranean has been and still is adjusting to the residual stresses of this upheaval. Earthquakes, tremors, faults, and volcanic outbreaks have been a continual reminder of the region's geologic youth. Bordered by the mountains of this system, the entire Mediterranean coast—and especially the coastal cities of its ancient civilizations—were susceptible to the devastating forces of tectonic unrest.

Although in the Eastern Roman Empire—centered in Constantinople, now Istanbul—the life of luxe continued unabated, in the Western territories a new set of conceptions about the beach and the sea prevailed. As might be expected, invading Barbarian tribes had no use for the Romans' refined tastes and rituals, in and out of the sea. With the spread of Christianity, classical notions of hedonism and hygiene were gradually supplanted by a more disquieting perspective of the sea—one promulgated by the biblical "abyss"—that made a full circle back to the horrific Homeric sea-theories of antiquity.

Bathing, eroticism, and female wantonness were linked into a single associative chain long past the waning of the Middle Ages. (Lucas Cranach the Elder, *Donne al bagno*, Collezione Conte Segre-Sartorio, Bettmann Archive)

From the Christian point of view, the aquatic extravagances of the ancient world were a vanity among vanities. Oriented to the otherworldly, medieval spirituality denigrated the value of the body and looked askance at institutions and practices that catered to the pleasures of the flesh. Except during strictly limited periods of permissiveness—the carnival and a few scattered holidays—the body's needs were largely denied. For the Middle Ages, the model of the new paradise was the monastery and the nunnery— ideal ascetic communities whose members starved, froze, and lashed their bodies into religious ecstasy. Bathing did not rank high among the duties of a good Christian. In fact, dirt was often the earmark of sanctity: not for nothing did people speak of the "odor" of sanctity. Though bathhouses did not entirely disappear, they developed an increasingly maligned reputation as little more than dens of ill repute, where strumpets cavorted with wastrels, and the devil himself lurked in the red coals of brick ovens.

Water's moral and hygienic prestige plummeted beginning with the fourteenth century, when plagues began to rampage across Europe, issuing from ships and port towns and passing from body to body in crowded cities, in cramped bedchambers, chilly churches, smoky taverns, and in the damp heat of steambaths and bathhouses. Measures were taken to suppress practices believed to open up the body to infected air. Violent exercise or hard labor and, above all, exposure to water were seen as prime culprits. The pressure and warmth of water, the French scholar Georges Vigarello explained, was thought to open the pores and penetrate the skin. Steambaths and water baths were feared precisely because they most efficiently and mechanically opened up the body to pestilential influences. Though in certain cases the mechanisms of hydrotheraphy were prescribed—for dissolving kidney stones, or restoring substance to systems that were "too dry," or correcting sour or vicious temperaments—baths were thought to upset the organism's equilibrium. Ordinances were passed that shut down baths and medicinal pools. The permeable human body was thought to be so ill-equipped to defend itself from pernicious fluids and emanations that merely being naked was perilous. The shape of clothing and the nature of the material were important. The safest attire consisted of layers of smooth, dense fabrics, wrapped to cling tightly to the body, so that infected air could slide over them without being able to gain entry.

As late as the sixteenth century, bathing as a hygienic protocol was quite unthinkable. Cleanliness was manifested in clothing, not the body. And the bath, on the rare occasions when it was undertaken, was circumscribed by bedrest, protective clothing, lack of drafts. Quite contrary to the classical paradigm, water was thought to enfeeble. It is difficult to plot precisely the twists and turns in the evolution of attitudes. But an aversion to baths gradually came to encompass aversion to immersion in any kind of water and thence erupted into a generalized horror of the beach.

The biblical text, selectively understood, could also be made to furnish ample motivation for what might be called beach phobia. The medieval imagination gravitated to those depictions of the ocean and its shores that were most terrifying and forbidding. While the classical age had fashioned these elements into the stuff of Utopia, the Middle Ages transformed them into its antithesis. The ocean—inhospitable to terrestrial life—is a damned world in whose darkness grotesque creatures cannibalistically devour each other and where the powers of hell rage unrestrained.

From earliest childhood, the medieval Christian was introduced to a horrid host of diabolical sea creatures in depictions of the Last Judgment and hell on the walls of churches. To late-medieval sailors, the agitation of the stormy ocean seemed to be caused by the devil himself and by the circling of souls condemned to eternal damnation. In fact, so firmly linked with hell was the spectacle of the raging ocean that Dante, in his *Divine Comedy,* weaves these strands into a magnificent tapestry depicting the Inferno as a region where "All light is mute, with a bellowing like the ocean / Turbulent in a storm of warring winds, / The hurricane of Hell in perpetual motion. " As he descends deeper into the circles of hell, Dante retraces the symbolic topography of the ocean as a vast pit, a veritable maelstrom or spiral that sucks everything into its insatiable center.

In Genesis, the sea is introduced as a "great abyss," a site of great mysteries, an uncharted and undifferentiated liquid chaos that is as unknowable

For centuries, Europeans clung to images of distant shores as populated with cannibals, freaks of nature, and monsters as terrifying as those inhabiting the depths of the sea. (Anonymous, *New World Scene*, c. 1505, New York Public Library, Spenser Collection)

as the Spirit of God. "In the beginning of creation . . . the earth was without form and void, with darkness over the face of the abyss, and a mighty wind that swept over the surface of the waters." This formless primal expanse, filled with "great sea monsters and all living creatures that move and swarm in the waters," was forbidding in and of itself. Tellingly, there is no sea in the Garden of Eden. The landscape of paradise is enclosed, reassuringly bounded, and within it everything has its knowable, fixed place. This in part is what gives the Edenic world such a compelling hold on the psyche. In subsequent Christian theology, the "Garden of Eden" paradigm had profoundly shaped attitudes toward the sea. In the biblical paradise, there was no vista of limitless horizon beyond an expanse of water, because such an image lures the imagination, disquiets the nerves, and spurs sacrilegious inquiry. Moreover, to penetrate into the secrets of the ocean was almost blasphemous, since it suggested a satanic discontent with the limits enshrined by the Creator. The Psalmist, after all, had equated divine wisdom with the image of the ocean when he said, "Thy judgements are a great deep," and God himself reproached querulous Job with the words, "Hast thou entered into the springs of the sea? or hast thou walked in the search of the depth?" In this sense, the beach is a line drawn in the sand beyond which the human mind should not venture; like all sacred thresholds, it could only be approached with the greatest trepidation.

It is hard to overestimate the impact of the Deluge on the Western perception of the ocean and the beach. Anyone growing up in the Judeo-

Christian culture was bombarded with images of the Flood from infancy to death. The biblical account of the invasion of the waters was broadcast in homilies, poetry, in the paintings on church walls and ceilings—the Sistine Chapel among them—and even found its way into protoscientific cosmogonies. As late as the seventeenth and eighteenth centuries, scholars were obsessed with the Great Flood as the climactic event that scarred and defaced an originally perfect creation. Influential theorists such as Gottfried Wilhelm von Leibniz and Thomas Burnet probed the causes for the catastrophe, interpreting and reinterpreting Genesis, and sifting the evidence of the "book of the world" for clues to the physical, moral, and aesthetic impact of this event.

Before the Deluge, Burnet argued in his *Theory of the Earth,* "The face of the Earth . . . was smooth, regular and uniform, without mountains, and without a Sea. . . . It had the beauty of Youth and blooming Nature, fresh and fruitful, and not a wrinkle, scar or fracture in all its body; no rocks or mountains, no hollow Caves, nor gaping Channels. . . . The Air was calm and serene." According to his account, the earth's beautiful youthful body was then ravaged by divine retribution. The great abyss of the waters was once again opened up, and chaos spread across the surface of the earth, so that geological anarchy replaced antediluvian harmony and moderation. The coastline—deformed, confused, monstrous—became a tumble of ruins with no order, no pattern, and no trace of the exquisite beauty that had been the aesthetic imprint of the original divine creation. Indeed, the sand, cliffs, boulders, and chasms of the shore—the heaped-up debris of a fallen universe—also summoned the spectator to reflect on a scenario of future devastation.

The New Testament reinforced this vision of the sea as God's weapon. Although the Book of Revelation predicted

It was at the seashore that Christ recruited his disciples, thereby offering a spiritually positive alternative to the horrifying vision of the beach brokered by the Old Testament account of the Deluge. (Pellegrino di Mariano, *Christ Calling St. Peter,* 1471, Bernard H. Breslauer Collection)

that the world would perish in a final conflagration, the impending apocalypse was to be presaged by the rising up of the waters. And because scholars tended to conflate the history of the world with the history of mankind, seeing the two as simultaneous, they read in the ruined and sterile landscape of the seashore the tangible evidence of man's spiritual degeneracy and the deterioration of human civilization. When pious Christians, imbued with these views, came to the shore, it was to stand on the line of contact between the elements, a front along which good waged its allegorical battle against evil. Here, in the burning sands and the sucking mudflats of the beach, they reflected on the terrifying desolation of the sea bottom exposed by the retreating tide. Holy men and women in search of the living theater of Divine Justice staked out solitary habitations on desolate, brutally inaccessible pockets of seashore—from fabled Mount Athos to anonymous outcroppings in the North Sea—where they communed fearfully with their Creator. The naked spectacle of the shore was to them a foreglimpse of Gehenna as much as it was a recollection of the biblical Flood. Only the masochist, only the sinner in search of terrible vistas with which to flog a recalcitrant conscience into repentance, sought out oceanic sites that had been scarred by the force of divine wrath.

POISED FOR THE PLUNGE

Scarborough, on the northeastern coast of England, May 1627. A small party of ladies and gentlemen cautiously descends along a precipitous cliff of pure limestone. A sharp wind tugs at their dark wool capes and tears at the feathers ornamenting their wide-brimmed hats. Carefully balancing on high-heeled shoes, the ladies, very pale and frail, raise their layered skirts to avoid snagging them on the rough rock. Bringing up the rear in an obviously goutish limp is a stout stalwart leaning heavily on a finely carved cane. Overhead, birds of myriad species circle and dip, darting into the crevices and caverns in the lofty crags. At the base of the cliff, on a projecting ledge, stands a ramshackle wooden building. Here the visitors stop and, within, find the goal of their excursion: a spout gushing continuously with a potent quaff of iron, soluble salts, and carbonic acid.

Some of the ladies recoil from the stench issuing from the russet-colored spring and are reluctant to follow the example of their stout companion, who, however, shows uncommon energy in downing three tumblers-full of the potion. The gentlemen follow suit, and remind the timid in their party that anything that smells so bad could only do one good. The fainthearted are persuaded, at last, to sip the waters. Their therapy accomplished, the visitors turn their attention seaward.

Beyond the ledge, a wide beach encircles the margin of the North Sea. Stepping carefully to avoid the seaweed and tide pools, the invalids take a measured turn along the strand before making the ascent back to their lodgings. Few if any of them reflect that they might be pioneering what would become a landmark seaside experience. Probably none reflects that in just forty years cure-takers will be instructed to drink seawater for their health. Or that they will be directed to plunge into the icy sea in order to restore vigor and vitality to their failing protoplasm.

■■■■■■

The approach to the beach was made gingerly, slowly. Not knowing whether they would find pleasure or pain, Europeans at the beginning of the seventeenth century set out on a journey of discovery that, in its own modest way, would change their experience of everyday life nearly as much as the voyages of global exploration that had been under way for two hundred years.

The path that finally brought them to the beach twisted and turned through some rather remarkable cultural terrain. Part of the route lay through thickets of intellectual constructs: myths, prejudices, and explanatory schemes that envisioned the shore as a dangerous frontier. Another portion of the way was entangled with purely physical impediments: the inclemency of nature, the seashore's inhospitality to terrestrial routines, and the body's unsuitability for aquatic habitation. Still another part of the way disappeared into the uncharted domain of habits and rituals of sociability: How was one to be social in this most asocial of all sites? What sort of activities could take place here? How could they be organized? What would they mean? And what would be their value: positive or negative, socially redemptive or degenerate, politically correct or subversive?

EXOTIC SEASHORES

Travel to exotic outposts by the sea helped Europeans to reshape their thinking about the beach in general. The great period of global exploration—the age of Ferdinand Magellan and James Cook in the Pacific, James Bruce and Mungo Park in Africa, Louis-Antoine de Bougainville in Tahiti—catalyzed the gradual reorientation of attitudes that would excite the imagination of Enlightenment Europe and coax it, among other things, to reassess the value of the seashore. Travelers' accounts and letters streaming back to England and the Continent offered enticing sketches of untouched paradises inhabited by indigenous peoples as pure and innocent in their hedonism as the noble savage eventually portrayed by the revolutionary Jean-Jacques Rousseau.

Expeditions to the Western Hemisphere had set out in search of new lands. In the sixteenth, seventeenth, and eighteenth centuries, adventurers, driven by a lust for riches, power, and knowledge of what should not be known, risked their lives in uncharted seas. When Europeans finally caught sight of the islands of the Pacific—the beaches of Hawaii and Fiji, Tonga and Tahiti—they looked upon them as the earthly paradise about which sailors had always fantasized: ports-of-call of sunshine and mild breezes, food, water, and an inexhaustible supply of lovely, amorous women.

The shores of tropical islands were magical in the full sense of the word. The European seamen—starving, filthy, riddled with scurvy and sores,

For Northern Europeans accustomed to the spectacle of the rough Atlantic, global exploration opened up new perspectives on the seashore as a picturesque site. (John Clevely the Younger, *HMS Resolution and Discovery at Moréa*, Picture Library, National Maritime Museum, London)

Records from global voyages depicted exotic islanders through the lens of Jean-Jacques Rousseau's notion of the noble savage as naturally good, sociable, and innocent. (Gustave Alaux, *Arrivée de Bougainville dans la baie de Matavai à Tahiti*, Musée de la Marine, Paris)

their senses dulled by the desperate monotony of survival at sea—saw rosy beaches ringed with turquoise and emerald waters. Verdant hills rose steeply from groves of feathery palms. Waterfalls sparkled in the distance, and everywhere there were flowers in brilliant shades of red, violet, yellow, and orange.

The tropical paradise shocked the straitlaced Dutch explorers who visited the Friendly Islands in 1643. They found the inhabitants to be "a good and peaceful people, but excessively lascivious and wanton." No sooner had the ships dropped anchor in the bay than they were surrounded by a flotilla of canoes. Bronzed, half-naked islanders nimbly piled on board, and to the amazement of the seamen, Abel Janzoon Tasman recorded in his diary, "some women took off their clothes and bartered them for nails. Others felt the sailors shamelessly in the trouser-front, and indicated that they wished to have intercourse, while the men of the island incited our ships' company to such transgressions."

Interestingly, sex and the beach were natural bedfellows long before the age of Club Med. As it turned out, sexual favors were customarily offered as a ritual form of greeting newcomers throughout the South Pacific. When the French visited Tahiti in 1767, they received the same sort of welcome. In typical Gallic fashion, however, they were most anxious to reciprocate. "The canoes were full of females, who for agreeable features are not inferior to European women," wrote Bougainville, the leader of the expedition, "and who in beauty of body often surpass them." He continued:

> Many of these fair females were naked, and the men pressed us to choose a woman and come ashore with her; and their gestures, which were nothing less than equivocal, denoted in what manner we should form an acquaintance with her. It was difficult, in these circumstances, to keep at their work 400 young French seamen who had seen no women for six months. In spite of all our precautions, a young girl managed to climb aboard and placed herself upon the quarterdeck, near one of the hatchways which was open, to give air to those heaving at the capstan below. The girl carelessly dropped the cloth which covered her, and appeared to the eyes of all beholders as Venus showed herself to the Phrygian shepherd, having indeed the celestial form of that goddess. Never was capstan wound in with more alacrity.

Steeped in the Judeo-Christian sense of sin, the Europeans associated this guiltless sexuality with the only prototypes with which they were familiar: Eden before the Fall, or pagan antiquity. Indeed, Bougainville named

Tahiti La Nouvelle Cythère, after the island off the coast of the Peloponnese where the ancient Greeks believed the goddess Venus had risen from the sea. For the time being, at least, Europeans were ready to assume that innate goodness was synonymous with a state of nature, and waited eagerly to have their newfound optimism confirmed by fresh reports.

One of the most influential publications shaping attitudes toward the beach was Bougainville's journal. Published in 1771, his long-awaited *Circumnavigating the World on the Royal Frigate "La Boudeuse" and the Armed Transport "L'Etoile"* caused a great stir in Parisian salons and philosophical circles. His glowing descriptions of native islanders were instantly seized upon by intellectuals seeking support for the myth of the "noble savage"— the idea so popular in the eighteenth century that man in his natural state is both good and happy, and that all his vices and miseries stem from the greed and sophistry of civilization. Both Bougainville and his readers were all too glad to think of the Polynesians as incarnations of an ideal. On the beaches of Tahiti, they imagined idyllic islanders whom they endowed not with actual virtues, but with virtues they thought, as noble savages, they *ought* to have. A philosophical fantasy, in short, determined what they saw.

And so, in their elegant salons and drawing rooms, the legislators of fashion, both sartorial and intellectual, argued that Bougainville had actually found people living in that idyllic state that Jean-Jacques Rousseau had hy-

Missionaries and moral ameliorationists tended to take a dim view of native beach culture, seeing in its hedonism evidence of degeneracy and backwardness. (George Baxter, *The Rev. J. Waterhouse Superintending the Landing of the Missionaries, Rev. Charles and Mrs. Creed, at Taranaki, New Zealand,* Rex Nan Kivell Collection, National Library of Australia)

pothesized in 1755 in his *Discourse on the Origin of Inequality*. Here were human beings who practiced family love in small benign communities, who were free from sin and untouched by the greed, envy, and territoriality that had derailed Western civilization and set it on a road to decline. Accounts like Bougainville's came as a refreshing anodyne to the pessimistic reflections on man in a state of civilization. The genuinely happy islanders inspired confidence in man's innate goodness, and suggested a recipe for recouping it in the lap of nature. After all, the explorers had proved unequivocally that the noble savage was not a myth. And if he did exist on the distant shores of Polynesia, what was to keep him from materializing on the near shores of the Atlantic? Perhaps the proximity of the beach would help coax to the surface the hidden but innate good in the citizens of civilized Europe?

SEEING THE SEA

It was all very tantalizing, but before Europeans could be persuaded to go down to the beach and luxuriate in its physical and spiritual bounty, they had to learn to see it. The eye that had been trained by Scripture, harsh nature, and tradition to view the beach with fear or disgust had to be taught to gaze upon it with approval. For those Europeans who had much traffic with the sea—captains, sailors, merchants, fishermen—the ocean was something to be negotiated safely and expeditiously, and the seashore was worthy of attention only to the degree that it facilitated or impeded these necessities of commerce and conquest.

Even to the Britons, the most maritime of people, the sea without any human traces was a "waste." When, for example, William Shakespeare wrote about the sea in such plays as *The Tempest, Pericles, Hamlet,* or *Richard III*, he did so only if it had some immediate connection to human affairs. The bottom of the sea, where one would not expect to encounter any such traces, appears in his *Richard III* as the site of carnage and drownings:

> *Methought I saw a thousand fearful wrecks,*
> *Ten thousand men that fishes gnawed upon,*
> *Wedges of gold, great anchors, heaps of pearl,*
> *Inestimable stones, unvalued jewels,*
> *All scattered in the bottom of the sea.*
> *Some lay in dead men's skulls, and in those holes*
> *Where eyes did once inhabit there were crept,*
> *As 'twere in scorn of eyes, reflecting gems,*
> *Which wooed the slimy bottom of the deep*
> *And mocked the dead bones that lay scattered by.*

THE BEACH GOES RESPECTABLE

Two developments helped to correct this sea-and-shore blindness: tourism and souvenirs. The first was the practice of the Grand Tour, without which the education of any self-respecting gentleman of the sixteenth through eighteenth centuries was deemed seriously deficient. "A man who has not been to Italy," wrote Dr. Samuel Johnson, the eighteenth-century British man of letters, "is always conscious of an inferiority, from his not having seen what it is expected a man should see." The beaches of Italy, as it turned out, were mandatory stopping points on the road to enlightenment and self-perfection.

This practice was especially instilled among the British aristocracy, though by the end of the eighteenth century it had also gained popularity among the Germans, Scandinavians, and Russians. Eventually, even the middle-aged and the middle class came to embrace the practice. In its early years, however, none but the wealthiest could afford the Tour, the most expensive form of education yet devised, but essential for the young peer who wished to learn manners, war, and diplomacy—the latter two being the only trades open to aristocrats. The journey usually lasted four or five years, during which the young man was accompanied by two tutors: one for academic subjects, the other for the arts of riding, fencing, and war. The tutors were often illustrious intellects, such as the economist Adam Smith, the philosopher Thomas Hobbes, the historian William Coxe, and the essayist Joseph Addison. Typically, one personal servant came along, and others were hired as necessary along the way. The wealthiest brought their own carriages; others rented coaches and put up with the inconvenience.

It was *de rigueur* for young gentlemen to travel to the Continent, a rite of passage that qualified them for inclusion in the esteemed society of cultivated men. In most instances, the peregrination took the amateur scholars to designated ruins, fortifications, and harbors in an itinerary that was strictly prescribed. One unexpected destination was of particular importance to the revival of the beach's reputation: the seashore of Holland. The Grand Tourist perceived Holland as a monument to the Dutch genius for taming the ocean. Everywhere he looked, his eye encountered markers of civilization's harmonious colonization of the sea. The seaports and the horizon—both in actuality and rendered in innumerable landscape paintings—were filled with Dutch merchant ships, loaded with riches from distant ports-of-call, and were teeming with fishing boats full of herring. Coastal villages and towns were sites of prodigious activity, the strands echoing with the hammering and sawing of boatwrights building ships, the shouting of fishermen hauling in their nets and of fishwives hawking their wares. Thanks to the elaborate system of dikes and canals, fertile fields and verdant meadows thrived where once the ocean had raged. In short, here was a unique spectacle of humanity harmoniously completing—rather than retreating from—the work of divine creation.

The new genre of seascape painting developed by seventeenth-century artists such as Jan van Goyen and Salomon van Ruysdael shaped what the eye took in. Perceptions of the beach were softening. With a scrupulous attention to detail, these artists showed the beach as a pragmatic and integral part of life, not as a pernicious, allegorical remnant of the biblical Deluge or a stern admonition to repent. By depicting what was actually taking place in front of their eyes, the seascape painters paved the way for a new appreciation of the utility of the beach. And, to reinforce the pedagogical and exemplary dimension of their art, they always inserted somewhere in their tableaux the image of a leisured observer who served as a role model for the actual observer of the painting. "Behold the beach," they seemed to be saying. "Behold its readiness to serve our human needs." Taking their

A grounded whale prompts an excursion to the seashore. The litter of casks, baskets, and timber bears witness to the beach's purely utilitarian function as late as the eighteenth century. (authors' collection)

cue from paintings and engravings of seascapes, foreigners looked upon the Dutch beaches as marvelous sites of production, imbued with ethical as well as aesthetic values.

Although early realists eschewed the enjoyable aspects of life by the sea, the next generation of Dutch artists—Simon de Vlieger, Jacob van Ruisdael, and Adriaen van de Velde—expanded the range of characters on the beach to include the elegant bourgeois, conversing strollers, and dashing horsemen who began to frequent the seashore. Their inclusion of these newcomers helped legitimize and popularize the novel image of the beach as a pleasurable destination for urban excursions.

Primed by such representations, tourists gravitated toward coastal sites where they might contemplate the productive interaction of the human and natural spheres. Scheveningen, on the North Sea, was the destination of choice. Situated on a beautiful expanse of seashore, this simple fishing village could be reached by one of the most agreeable land routes in the world, according to accounts of such eminent visitors as Samuel Ireland, Denis Diderot, and Ann Radcliffe. About half a mile long, the road cut across the dunes and was bordered by trees and shrubs. Benches dotted the way, and the ensemble—the road, the framing verdure of the trees, and the contemplative resting spots—paved the way for an appreciation of the picturesque character of the sea.

At Scheveningen itself, Grand Tourists watched the bustle on the beach, hired fishermen to take them on excursions, feasted on fish freshly caught, and made sketches. They wandered in the dunes or clustered around a beached whale—as they had seen strollers doing in many paintings and engravings. In the process, they laid down the template for a new beach experience: the inspirational pilgrimage to the boundary of land and sea.

Farther south, Campania, famed from Roman times for sybaritic celebrations of the seashore, was the grand finale of every Englishman's and continental tourist's journey to Italy. Reared on Latin classics—Virgil and Horace accompanying them from childhood to deathbed as conduct guide, taste manual, and civic handbook—the travelers "read" the Italian coast through the scrim of classical literature and mythology. Stops at the great excavations at Herculaneum (begun in 1737) and in Pompeii (begun in 1748) were obligatory. The vistas of the sea inspired paeans of rapture from the likes of Johann Wolfgang von Goethe, who in the *Italian Journey* waxed poetic about feasting and taking in "the most magnificent sights. They can say, tell, and paint whatever they want, there is more here than all of that. The shores, bays, and gulfs of the sea, Vesuvius, the suburbs, the citadels, the pleasure grounds! I forgave all those who lose their minds over Naples." The ruins—classical arches, obelisks, columns and temples, villas and porticoes—spoke of the mythical origins of civilization and legitimized hedonism with the stamp of tradition.

The impact of the Grand Tour on the history of taste—and leisure at the beach—was nothing less than revolutionary. Neoclassicism as an aesthetic movement was the direct offspring of Grand Tourists who experimented with classical motifs in architecture and decoration and modeled their own literary works on classical prototypes. Equally impressive was the influence of the Grand Tourists on travel. Their needs and habits established the institutions and practices along which European travel to seashore destina-

Fraught with dangers, the sea inspired awe and terror, emotions that contributed to the aesthetic of the sublime. (John Singleton Copley, *Watson and the Shark*, National Gallery of Art, Washington, D.C.)

tions was to develop. "Hotels, couriers, foreign exchange facilities, specialized transport to beauty spots," writes historian J. H. Plumb, "the whole paraphernalia by which the aristocrats were housed, fed and informed came into being in eighteenth-century Europe." These early travelers scouted out the destinations that would soon become the playgrounds of Europe—the Swiss Alps and, most notably, the French and Italian Rivieras. The educational motive that drew the Grand Tourists to these Mediterranean sites gradually gave way to more frivolous objectives as the Grand Tour, democratized and commodified, eventually degenerated into recreational tourism. But to this day, an integral part of every seaside holiday—whether on an exotic South Sea island or in a nearby gateway—involves shopping for curios and exploring the cultural, artistic, or ecological merits of local sites.

SIMPLY SUBLIME

When the French philosopher Denis Diderot visited Holland in 1772, he looked out across the flat sands at the looming expanse of the sea and was seized with fear. He could not imagine how people, knowing that at any moment it could overflow its bounds and rush across the lowlands, could live equanimously within sight of such a mass of water. He himself could only "wonder and shudder" at the ominous spectacle. His mixed reaction, interestingly, was of more than personal significance. For in characterizing his response as a combination of awe and fear, Diderot placed himself squarely within a fledgling subculture of marine aficionados for whom the seashore was the newest gateway to profound sensations. The discovery of terror—and of certain terror triggers—as desirable was of tremendous importance in the history of feelings and in the cultural evolution of the beach. And a brand-new aesthetic category—the sublime—was taking shape to valorize a gamut of traumatic sensations.

The ocean breaking on the shore was one of the foremost stimuli for the sublime, and writers and artists approached this psychogeographical site guided by aesthetic treatises on the subject by Immanuel Kant, Anthony Cooper Shaftesbury, Joseph Addison, and Edmund Burke. "Of all objects that I have ever seen, there is none which affects my imagination so much as the sea or ocean," wrote Addison in his essay on the sea, published in the *Spectator* in 1712. "I cannot see the heaving of this prodigious bulk of waters, even in a calm, without a very pleasing astonishment; but when it is worked up in a tempest, so that the Horizon on every side is nothing but foaming billows and floating mountains, it is impossible to describe the agreeable horrour that rises from such a prospect."

Edmund Burke, Addison's intellectual protégé, thought the human spirit derived far more benefit from the sea than from dry land. "A level plain of a vast extent on land," he wrote in his 1757 treatise *On the Sublime and Beautiful*, ". . . [can never] fill the mind with anything so great as the ocean itself." But the sea's expansiveness and ungovernable turbulence not only mirrors the scope and the mysterious movements of the soul; it also produces "a sort of delightful horror, a sort of tranquillity tinged with terror." Burke grasped the principle that terror inspired by danger, darkness, solitude, and the prospect of the infinite, when experienced in *safety*, can give a most enlightening and satisfying conjunction of pleasure and pain.

Burke's theory of the sublime gave a potent impetus to representations of the seashore as a site of spiritually productive encounters. Whereas earlier seascapes had narrowly focused on scenes of human labor and industry, in the late eighteenth and early nineteenth centuries, artists depicted the beach as the setting for meditation. In the wake of the new aesthetic of the sublime, Europeans began to overcome a blind spot about the shore, especially of the north. A rage for windswept Nordic landscapes followed hard on the heels of Burke's *Philosophical Inquiry* and picked up energy only with the publication of James Macpherson's spurious *Fragments of Ancient Poetry Collected in the Highlands of Scotland and Translated from the Gaelic or Erse Language in 1760*. Filled with stirring scenes of heroism set in a majestic landscape, the work encouraged readers to extend their notions of beauty to include seaside caverns, cliffs, and rocky coastlines. From "Ossian," as the alleged bard of these fragments was named, the fad for all things wild, desolate, and northern came to be called Ossianism. Book in hand, an entire generation began to prowl Scotland's Caledonian coast on the North Sea, the Hebrides, and Scandinavia. If their forebears—had they bothered to look at all—had seen the seashore as an arid waste, the Ossianic adepts now strove to find in the sea and the shore the traces of hidden meanings and the portal to the sublime.

THE BATH AS GATEWAY TO THE SEA

To contemplate the sea from the beach was one thing. Actually to bathe in it was quite another. Indeed, had it not been for the practice of mineral-spring bathing, sea bathing might never have emerged as the complex social ritual it became in the latter half of the eighteenth century. Through the ages, the public mineral bath had served motives of cleanliness, health, pleasure, and congregation. More important, it had nourished a set of practices, rituals of comportment and of sociability, that would gradually find their way to the beach. In this very important sense, the inland spa was the direct progenitor of the coastal holiday, generating protocols that survive to the present day.

Although little is known about the mineral baths of the Middle Ages, they appear to have been modest and crude structures, cobbled together from the remains of Roman facilities, if available, or thrown up as rude wooden huts. By the twelfth century, however, descriptions of more sophisticated facilities began to appear, largely in connection with legislation aimed at curbing the licentious behavior within. In 1161, the records of Pisa show that a captain was appointed to the neighboring baths of San Giuliano to keep away the pimps and courtesans who made the baths their base of operations. In 1176, the administrator of a bath in Teruel, Spain, was so provoked by the unruly behavior of his clients that he appointed separate bathing days for men and women and appended a prohibition against the theft of women's clothing by men. But nothing short of closing down the baths—which one of the Alfonsos did in the early fourteenth century—availed against the erotic spell of the Spanish baths.

French records from the period offer an equally salacious image. In the thirteenth-century *Roman de la rose,* we find a description of the feasting and love play staged in the communal baths. A portal of the Gothic cathedral at Auxerre, France, depicts the sinful life of the Prodigal Son through the single image of the young wastrel in a steambath being massaged, scrubbed, and tended by several women. The lesson was evidently lost on lay members of the Church, and even men and women of the cloth found it difficult to keep away. In 1441, the Synod of Avignon tried to put baths off limits to the clergy, with little success. At certain establishments, abbots, monks, brothers, and priests outnumbered laymen. Heads crowned with wreaths, the servants of the Church frolicked with loose women in a common pursuit of hilarity and hedonism. In 1415, an abbess of Zurich so craved the diversion of the baths that she sold certain lands to cover the expense of her visit to Baden. And in Italy in 1494, one Matteo Franco, canon of Florence and author of a book of ribald sonnets, presided over the baths of Pisa for fifteen delicious years.

By the fifteenth century, swept up in the Renaissance revival of the teachings and art of classical antiquity, Europeans began self-consciously to model bathing establishments on ancient Roman prototypes. At Baden in Argau, two public and twenty-eight private baths were constructed and linked to a hotel. Visitors spent the better part of the day in the water. They invited friends to join them, played at cards, and had their meals served on floating tables. Jokes flew from tub to tub. Musicians plucked at zithers and shook tambourines. Raucous singing voices resonated against the stone walls. Wine flowed, supposedly to counteract the soporific effect of the hot water, and the longer visitors soaked, the more they drank.

At Plombières, in Lorraine, a large oval building was flanked by several bathing rooms, beneath which ran a system of pipes with hot water from the springs. Broad stone steps descended to the pools as in a Greek amphitheater, and the baths themselves were divided into small zones by poles or partitions. Most establishments supplied chairs and small tables on which bathers could read or write or gamble while immersed. Dressing rooms for ladies were richly appointed, with polished floors, painted wainscoting and ceilings, and windows set with colored glass.

Though the facilities took a marked turn for the better, the mores displayed therein were still abysmal. Men and women shared the same tubs, touching, caressing, and even copulating. It was customary at these aquatic orgies to elect and crown a king of the feast in parodic imitation of the world beyond the spa. In effect, this microcosm deliberately inverted the protocols and virtues of the outside world, establishing a

Bathing establishments often doubled as assignation sites and bordellos. (authors' collection)

"free zone" in which the rules that held society together could be over-turned without any danger to the status quo.

During the fourteenth century, however, an interesting change had begun to appear in attitudes toward mixed bathing. Tolerance for the min-gling of sexes and age groups in the nude was being replaced by an insis-tence on physical distance. Separation of the sexes—either within the same facility or in separate locales—was increasingly insisted upon, though, in practice, it never became universal. By scant degrees, perceptions of de-cency and modesty changed.

Respectable folk adhered to the rules of gender segregation. Bons vi-vants sought to subvert it, and measures taken to deal with them were dras-tic, though not consistently enforced throughout Europe. The British seem to have been the most severe. In 1450, for instance, Bishop Beckyngton of Bath threatened to excommunicate anyone found bathing nude in the spa. Presumably, segregated bathing had become so deeply ingrained as a norm that when, a century later, Michel de Montaigne, the great French essayist, came upon men and women bathing together at Plombières, he was amazed to find that "the greatest decorum is observed; the men, however, bathe quite naked, with the exception of a slight pair of drawers, and the women with the exception of a shift."

At about this time, an interesting bifurcation in domesticated aquatic culture occurred: the regular bathhouses took over the respectable func-tions of hygiene and health, while the steambaths were differentiated into sites of sin and urban disorder. In no uncertain terms, the steambath be-longed entirely to the world of lust, lawlessness, and license. In many Euro-pean towns, the steambath was nothing more than a bordello, and the expression "going for a steambath" carried the very precise connotation of steamy sex. An air of anarchy, unrest, and dissipation hovered about the lo-cale. In Dijon, France, a certain Jehannotte Saignant, proprietess of steam-baths, was brought to trial and sentenced to death for the evildoings on her premises. "So much shouting, bawling and jumping about was heard," at-tested the court record, "that it was amazing that the neighbors put up with it, the law ignored it, and the ground supported it."

The delinquent sociability of steambaths was increasingly ill-tolerated. At the beginning of the fifteenth century, Henry V banned them from the city of London and its suburbs, referring to the "grievances, abominations, damages, disturbances, murders, homicides, larcenies, and other common nuisances" perpetrated by the "men and women of bad and evil life." The last steambath in Dijon was shut down in 1556, in an ordinance citing the "clamours, complaints, and protests about wicked and scandalous doings there, and the fact that many serving women were debauched and drawn into wrongdoing." When the Estates General of Orléans outlawed all brothels in the realm in 1566, the death knell sounded for the steambath as an institution of lawlessness in France and, soon, in all parts of Europe.

THE SEA SPA TAKES SHAPE

But the closing of steambaths did not mark the end of the association between water and pleasure. The steambath had catered to a sociability that explicitly subverted order. In contrast, respectable bathing establishments and mineral springs thrived in part *because* they encouraged order and enforced norms of behavior. Integrating aquatic activities with other licit pleasures—eating, conversing, resting, dancing—the water baths legitimized the sensuous propriety of water. Eventually, the ornate and decorous seaside resorts of the eighteenth and nineteenth centuries would perpetuate this high road of development. The steambaths' low road of lawlessness and libido, on the other hand, would eventually debouch in the carnivalized beach—the Blackpools and Coney Islands of the nineteenth and twentieth centuries, where orgiastic, transgressive pleasure would find its expression in theme parks, wild rides, and congregating masses.

By the sixteenth century, a distinct bath *season* had emerged. In Baden, Lucca, and the Bagnères-de-Bigorre, visitors began to arrive in June and depart in September, leaving the baths quite deserted by October. At Aix, the baths were used only in the spring and autumn, because in the heat of the summer months they were uncomfortable and insalubrious. The public for these facilities came from two main segments of the population, both affluent: those suffering from maladies, whether actual or imaginary, and

Callot's fanciful idyll depicts the primitive innocence of frolicking villagers whose nudity and eroticism seem entirely unproblematic. Enclosed and domesticated, the southern seashore would have to wait until the late seventeenth century to be discovered as a fashionable destination. (Jacques Callot, *Medici Landscapes: Bathers*, National Gallery of Art, Washington, D.C.)

those suffering from boredom. The former had to make their way through a thicket of discordant medical theories about the benefits of mineral waters. The latter, by contrast, had nothing to fear but exhaustion from an excess of diversions.

Armed with prayers, incantations, and sacred songs, patients sought out hydrotherapy in medicinal pools in confident expectation of amelioration. In sixteenth-century Germany, pilgrims undertook "spiritual" journeys to the baths, combining therapy of the soul with the healing of the body. Around this practice appeared an entire genre of devotional songs that had their roots in ancient pagan and, eventually, early Christian medical incantations. As late as the seventeenth century, aquatic therapy was being promoted as a vehicle for spiritual regeneration. Sir John Floyer, the patron saint of modern bathing, wrote in 1697 that the secularization of bathing was the chief factor in the decline of the therapeutic efficacy of baths. In *On the Use and Abuse of Baths,* Floyer noted, "As the virtues of the waters formerly supported the reputation of the Saints, so now the want of a proper religious office to be used by the devout at the time of bathing and drinking waters, leaves all to a general debauchery of manners in such public places."

In the seventeenth century, when the medicinal spa entered into its own as a fashionable institution, poisonous-tasting, foul-smelling, villanously tinted water was prescribed for a broad spectrum of disorders. Patients suffering from gout, the pox, dropsy and melancholy, ulcers, the "dry itch," and a host of other maladies congregated at medicinal wells to sip the waters and discuss their physical condition. Most establishments offered the option of bloodletting in a "phlebotorium," a room especially set aside to accommodate this procedure. Gossip about various digestive and excretory phenomena flowed freely, unchecked by contemporary norms of propriety. Madame de Sévigné wrote from Vichy, which she visited in 1676 and 1677, "People converse confidentially about the operation of the waters. Nothing is talked of but that till noon." This unabashed preoccupation with corporeal functions would eventually travel to the seashore resort as a practice of scrupulous introspection and scrutiny, directed at the body and to the soul as part of the invalid's active responsibility in advancing the medical cure.

Medicinal-bath fever surfaced wherever mineral springs were found. The baths of Pyrmont, in the north of Germany, drew far more visitors than could be accommodated in the neighboring villages and farmhouses. Invalids pitched tents in the woods, and spontaneous camp communities formed. Still more kept coming—ten thousand in one four-week period alone. Finally, a local entrepreneur had the inspired idea of putting the mineral water into casks and distributing them in the environs, so that those who were turned away could benefit from the healing liquid.

With time, Pyrmont joined Schwalbach as one of Europe's fashionable bathing spots, so popular that young women stipulated in their marriage contracts that they be allowed to travel there annually. Health was often one of several motives for their visits. Fertility was another. Since antiquity, medicinal springs had been thought beneficial for correcting various reproductive ailments. Certain baths, such as the one at Bormio in Italy, acquired renown as "the paradise of ladies," because, it was said, as medievalist Marc Bloch noted, "so many sterile ladies as bathe in this spring suddenly become prolific, whence it happens that one sees come thither every year duchesses, matrons, and most noble ladies, without any other malady except the hope of offspring, and never yet has one been seen defrauded of her hopes!"

Were the waters truly responsible for the spontaneous reversal of infertility? Or did the presence of men in the baths have something to do with it? Some medical authorities of the period insisted that bathing in mixed company could lead to pregnancy without intercourse. An aquatic immaculate conception could result when sperm floated in the tepid water and entered an unsuspecting woman's body. Georges Vigarello, historian of attitudes toward hygiene, reports that seventeenth-century medicine believed a woman could conceive merely by using baths in which men had bathed.

Which brings us to yet another reason for the popularity of baths among women: they provided a legitimate, medically authorized escape from domesticity and monogamy. According to a renowned physician of the seventeenth century, there were precisely 479,001,600 sorts of mineral waters. The number of bathing establishments across Europe and the British Isles fell far below that figure, but there were more than enough sites to keep a lady traveling, if she was so disposed, throughout her reproductive years.

Across the Atlantic, the American colonists were also quite devoted to spas. Medicinal bathing acquired a certain prestige among the more progressive members of colonial society. Specialized mineral springs were established at points along the East Coast, and elegant ladies, among them Martha Washington, frequented establishments such as the one at Berkeley Springs, West Virginia. The contrast between the elaborate facilities at Bath, England, and those in the colonies could not have been more dramatic. Whereas Bath was regal, with inspiring architecture and refined design, Berkeley Springs featured picturesque pine groves and lush stands of fern. A collection of simple log huts and canvas tents was thrown up around a bathing pool, which consisted of a large hollow scooped in the sand. The bathing pool was used alternately by ladies and gentlemen, and the time set aside for each sex was announced by the blast of a long tin horn. A screen of pine brush provided privacy.

Given the copious evidence that mineral baths came to enjoy ever greater popularity, it is easy to overlook the persistent strain of skepticism directed at the salubrity of water, both as a medicinal quaff and as a hygienic medium. Practices of cleanliness and hygiene were viewed with caution far beyond the Middle Ages, and recurrent deadly illnesses did little to increase their regard. Not surprisingly, the devastating pandemics of plague and syphilis in the fourteenth, sixteenth, and seventeenth centuries had an immediate and dramatic impact on bathing culture. At each occurrence, the cause of bathing—public or private—was critically set back, and the practices of collective immersion virtually disappeared, at least for a spell.

The story of Europe's bouts with the great contagions can be plotted in three acts, each with a subplot signifying a successive breaking point in the culture of bathing. The Black Death of 1347–50 was the first such rupture. Syphilis, introduced at the end of the fifteenth century and reaching its apogee in the sixteenth, was another. The plague pandemic that ravaged Europe in 1665–66 and produced the so-called Great Plague of London was the final break. At each of these three points in the history of European diseases, contemporary medical theorists believed that the disease was transmitted by the penetration of the skin by noxious elements, or by the malfunctioning of internal organs triggered by exposure to water. Medical literature was rife with speculations about the potentially injurious effect of any sort of water—hot or cold, mineral or plain—upon the body. Any encounter between these two required the utmost vigilance.

Even after the epidemics disappeared from Europe, medicinal baths were still regarded with wariness in some circles. As late as the end of the seventeenth and the beginning of the eighteenth centuries, when water therapies began to be introduced into medical protocol, isolated voices still questioned the practice on various fronts. Daniel Defoe objected to the baths on what were most clearly aesthetic grounds: "The smoke and the slime of the waters, the promiscuous multitude of the people in the bath, with nothing but their heads above water, with the height of the walls that environ the bath, gave me a lively idea of the several pictures I had seen of Fra Angelico's in Italy of Purgatory, with heads and hands uplifted in the midst of smoke, just as they are here." With his characteristic vitriol, the writer Tobias Smollett articulated the more substantive fear of contagion by the various diseases and ailments that came in contact with bath waters. From his own experience at the spa in Bath, England, which he visited as both patient and physician, Smollett drew some rather disquieting conclusions:

Two days ago I went into the King's Bath by the advice of our friend Charleton, in order to clear the strainer of the skin, for the benefit of a free perspiration; and the first object that saluted my eyes was a child, full of scrofulous ulcers, carried in the arms of one of the guides, under the very noses of the bathers. I was so shocked at the sight that I retired immediately with indignation and disgust. Suppose the matter of these ulcers, floating in the water, comes in contact with my skin, when the pores are all open, I would ask you what must be the consequence? Good heavens! the very thought makes my blood run cold! We know not what sores may be running into the waters while we are bathing, and what sort of matter we may thus imbibe; the King's evil, the scurvy, and the cancer, and, no doubt, the heat will render the virus the more volatile and penetrating.

This fear of dermal infection extended as well to drinking the thermal waters. Smollett speculated that the bathwater might be regurgitated into the pump room so that the patients would imbibe "the scourings of the bathers, medicated with the sweat, dirt and dandruff and the abominable discharges of various kinds, from twenty different diseased bodies, parboiling in the kettle below."

Although repelled by the unhygienic properties of communal mineral baths, Smollett remained persuaded of the merits of hydrotherapy. In 1752, he published "An Essay on the External Use of Water, in a Letter to Dr. ———, with Particular Remarks upon the Present Method of Using the Mineral Waters at Bath, in Somersetshire, and a Plan for Rendering Them More Safe, Agreeable, and Efficacious," a revolutionary tract in the annals of therapeutic bathing, in which he argued for the superiority of pure cold water over warm mineral water. By the middle of the eighteenth century, Europeans were ready to explore a pharmacological alternative to mineral springs. Though this was never universal, physicians were sufficiently concerned about the safety of spa waters to prescribe aquatic cures *elsewhere* than in public baths. On the medical front, the world was ready to plunge into the hitherto untried apothecary of the sea, to test saltwater as an internal and external agent of fortification.

THE WATERS OF CONVIVIALITY

By the seventeenth century, the wealthy hypochondriacs and upper-class invalids who made their way to medicinal springs were not only reviving the ancient Roman ritual of the cure, but also rediscovering its social potential. In the bracing culture of the Enlightenment, the heady politics of England's Glorious Revolution, and the pomp of Louis XIV's reign, bathing had taken on a complex social function. Dignified by an elegant architectural setting, the bath came to be seen as a place where the rich could publicly indulge their taste for extravagance. Medical therapy, though still ostensibly the primary reason, was in practice only one of a varied number of activities staged around the waters. By the eighteenth century, when colonial entrepreneurship and the industrial and political revolutions in England, France, and America had reconfigured the social matrix, the baths had turned into marriage mills, stairways to status, and fields of social competition. The crowds that gathered here were wonderfully heterogeneous: ladies young and old, gentlemen, sprightly priests, worn-out monks, "*petit-maître*" abbés, nuns, grisettes, and bourgeoises came to rendezvous for the pleasure and profit of each other's company.

The watering hole evolved a menu of diversions that, despite minor local variations, have remained quite fixed since the sixteenth century. The morning hours were given over to bathing; men and women, dressed in togalike garments or in brown linen, immersed themselves in the healing springs. Following this, visitors could mingle freely with other guests from various countries or pass the time over a friendly game of bowls. A promenade or an excursion to notable sights came next. The midday repast was taken at the table of some hospitable noble or at private lodgings, after which the company broke for a brief interval of digestive solitude. Once the heat of the day had passed, gentlemen gathered at the bowling green or joined the ladies for a stroll in the gardens and fields. The evening program began with a sumptuous meal, and then proceeded to dancing, gambling, and the theater, each diversion emphasizing self-presentation and parade, the more lavish the better.

A great deal of interest centered on diet: expeditions were made to open-air markets to inspect produce, the merits of diverse eating establishments were debated, and new culinary concoctions were sampled. The watering hole, in fact, was often the crucible of new cuisine. Increasingly cosmopolitan in its clientele, it launched such culinary imports as coffee and "twist," a popular beverage consisting of a mixture of tea and coffee.

BATH, ENGLAND:
THE FIRST FOUR-STAR WATER RESORT

The medicinal baths and spas had produced a cultural template that would find full expression in seaside resorts, predominantly in England. More than a thousand years after the Romans had colonized England, Bath had been rediscovered, and Buxton and Harrogate were flourishing. All who had claims—or merely aspirations—to gentility headed for the mild-tasting waters of Buxton or the sulfurous springs, impenetrable snobbery, and horticultural splendor of Harrogate. But the most illustrious and venerable among the inland resorts was indisputably Bath. Here, more than at any other European watering spot, can the contemporary prototype for beach resorts be found. The beach was discovered by the British, and it was shaped by them to replicate the practices and rituals already familiar to them from Bath.

In Bath, with its many remarkable houses, its lovely streets, its Roman ruins, its Crescent and its Circus, a representative section of English society gathered, as nowhere else in England: noblemen, squires, rich merchants, affluent professional men, politicians, authors, gamblers, and ladies of kaleidoscopic virtue. Its life as a fashionable resort spanned roughly 150 years, from the middle of the seventeenth century to the end of the eighteenth, coinciding with the era of the spa. As a watering place, Bath was no more or less remarkable than a dozen other locales. But, as permanently caught in the pages of such novelists and dramatists as Henry Fielding, Tobias Smollett, Jane Austen, Samuel Foote, and Richard Sheridan, it remains a symbol of a unique way of life. If it had not been a resort for those seeking a cure, Bath would not have drawn to itself such a heterogeneous assemblage of strangers as those who formed the nucleus of the new cosmopolitan society of leisure. Around the genuine and sham invalids who came to imbibe its waters also gathered a group that considered Bath to be the only place in England that could provide social intercourse unhampered by differences in rank, and a change of air and scenery.

At Bath one could find pleasure, easy companionship, all the amusements of London without its discomforts, and, most important, a freedom from troublesome social duties. From June to September, members of the aristocracy and the gentry stayed in Bath rather than in the country because they could thereby save themselves the great expense of maintaining a manor house. In Bath they also had the advantage of a space more circumscribed than London in which to affirm status and contract favorable marriages, as Jane Austen shows in *Persuasion.* The limited circuit of bookstores, boutiques, theaters, meeting rooms, and promenades gave carefully premeditated meetings the appearance of accident and augmented the chances of felicitous encounters. Young people enjoyed greater freedom here from the surveillance of parents and clergymen.

The mixing of classes that went on at Bath was quite unprecedented in the history of England. Christopher Anstey, author of *New Bath Guide,* noted: "Every upstart of fortune, harnessed in the trappings of the mode, presents himself at Bath, as in the very focus of observation. Clerks and factors from the East Indies, loaded with the spoil of plundered provinces; planters, negro-drivers, and hucksters, from our American plantations, enriched they know not how; agents, commissaries, and contractors, who have fattened, in two successive wars, on the blood of the nation; usurers, brokers, and jobbers of every kind; men of low birth, and no breeding, have found themselves suddenly translated into a state of affluence, unknown to former ages; and no wonder that their brains should be intoxicated with pride, vanity, and presumption. Knowing no other criterion of greatness, but the ostentation of wealth, they hurry to Bath, because here, without any further qualification, they can mingle with the princes and nobles of the land." Ironically, the gaffes of the parvenues simply confirmed the fact that the aristocracy and the gentry still set the tone and defined the horizon of social expectations. As long as they were aped—however clumsily—they still reigned.

The city and the baths themselves were recast in the pleasing forms of classical architecture under social arbiter Richard "Beau" Nash's inspiration and the design genius of architect Joseph Wood. Everyone understood that, by his rule, Nash earnestly wished to make Bath's amusements and facilities pleasant and accessible to all, and people tamely agreed to follow his decisions and live by his rules. This legislator of style set in place the principle according to which subsequent seaside resorts would be organized: the primacy of aesthetics and pleasure over politics, finance, and, eventually, therapy. An orchestra was established to make the baths agreeable as well as healthy. Writers and artists assembled, drawn as much by the availability of generous patrons as by the prospect of observing and recording the manners of a new social ecosystem. Thomas Gainsborough and Sir Thomas Lawrence, the fathers of British portraiture and landscape painting, recorded, idealized, and disseminated the distinct features of Bath for the new middle-class art lover, who would also soon patronize the seabathing resort at Brighton. Men and women of letters spent week after week at Bath, meeting for conversation or readings and engaging in the practice of copious letter-writing.

THE SEASHORE AS SCHOOL

One does not immediately associate scholars and scientists with beach holidays. And yet the discovery of the beach was very much indebted to the interest they focused on this strip of land. The global peregrinations of merchants, explorers, administrators, and Grand Tourists—as well as the intellectual ferment of the Enlightenment—all left their mark on prevailing attitudes toward nature. As knowledge of the world beyond their horizon broadened, people seemed more ready to admit their ignorance about what lay at their doorstep. To the typical European of the late seventeenth century, the local beach was as much a *terra incognita* as Tahiti, Formosa, or Alaska. Not much was known about the flora and fauna inhabiting the ocean's depths. The inventory of known marine species was limited to the creatures that fishermen hauled up or storms left on the sand. Engravings and paintings of the period often depicted a cross section of humanity drawn together on the shore around a beached whale, swarming like Lilliputians around Gulliver, poking and tentatively prodding the hulk, as if desiring to penetrate the mysteries of the deep through the intermediary of the beached whale.

But the same *libido sciendi* that had lured explorers such as Cook and Bougainville across the Pacific coaxed the isolated eccentric onto the sands of his own country. In the first decade of the eighteenth century, the British "scholarly travelling gentleman" was born. This was typically an aristocrat schooled in the classics and polished by the Grand Tour, who based his travels on some intellectual interest, and who had come to regard with some skepticism an assertion made by the archbishop of Usher in 1650, that the world was created at precisely nine o'clock in the morning on October 23 in the year 4004 B.C. Instead, this scholarly gentleman preferred the theories and findings of more contemporary philosophers and scientists whose empirical observations suggested that the creation was not an event but an ongoing process that could easily be read in the shifting margins of landmasses.

Throughout the ensuing decades, gentlemen scholars avidly studied theologians, natural scientists, and philosophers who were re-evaluating the beach from a number of vantage points. Enlightenment scientists had begun to resent the scriptural reading of the seashore as the outcome of the Deluge, the result of direct divine intervention that intentionally scrambled the order of creation and rendered the universe unintelligible. These rationalists were attached to the idea that the only possible world God could have created would be one that was thoroughly understandable. Otherwise, they argued, why would God have given us reason and curiosity?

Fascinating new interpretations of the Book of Genesis appeared. Some scholars accepted its account of the Great Flood, but others tried to establish a correlation between the archeological ruins they were discovering and the biblical text. Still others—Benoît de Maillet, Voltaire, Holbach among them—simply dismissed the Flood as myth. New theories were put forth that ascribed to the sea a fundamental role in the *formation* of the earth, rather than its destruction. The tides, currents, and fluctuating levels of the sea, argued such scholars as Benoît de Maillet, are "entirely responsible for all the physiographical, lithological, and structural characteristics of the earth's crust." The discovery of marine fossils and marine strata far inland also led scientists to hypothesize that what was now dry land had been submerged a long time ago. By implication, notions of time altered, as discrepancies began to appear between the physical record and the biblical chronology, which had always tended to equate the history of the planet with the history of humanity.

The marine landscape itself began to suggest new ways of viewing natural history. The waves, continuously building up and breaking, yielded an analogy for the uninterrupted changes that make up the world's development. Measurements of the shoreline established its instability and subverted its image as a stable boundary. Many fascinating implications followed: that the seas were slowly drying up; that the rocky underpinning of the ocean was not fixed but mobile; that continents did not abruptly end at ocean's edge, but continued far beneath its surface; that the ocean bottom and dry land shared identical topographical features.

As a result of such minute paradigm shifts, Europeans began to appreciate the shore as integrally linked and relevant to dry land, which was a reassessment of monumental importance. If the beach was no longer a firm line of demarcation where dangerous, aberrant, or exceptional events took place, it now became a transitional zone. And whatever lay here had a direct bearing on the entirety of the continent.

THE HEALING SEA

Among staunch advocates of the beach were those who practiced the healing arts. In 1667, Dr. Robert Wittie, a physician practicing in Hull, made an outing to Scarborough, on the northeastern coast of England. Perhaps he was lured there by the geological oddity of the sandstone cliffs, or by the diverse species of seabirds nesting in the crags and crevices. Then again, he might have been looking for a way to expand his practice and wanted to see whether the mineral springs that gushed from the sea cliffs, which had been attracting a meager following of invalids since 1627, might warrant his moving there. Perhaps, too, one of his patients at Hull had come back from Scarborough with a leather bottle full of the spring waters and in good health.

Whatever his reasons, Dr. Wittie sampled the mineral waters and promptly proclaimed them sound. The springs were well situated, and with a little judicious advertising Dr. Wittie was convinced he could successfully resettle on the coast. He issued a pamphlet extolling Scarborough's springs as helping in cases of apoplexy, epilepsy, catalepsy, vertigo, and nervous disorders. Not inclined to understatement, he then went on to specify that the water "cleanses the stomach, opens the lungs, cures Asthma and Scurvy, purifies the blood, cures Jaunders both yellow and black, and the Lep-

rosie, . . . and is a most sovereign Remedy against Hypochondriack Melan-
cholly and Windiness."

But even with such an impressive catalogue of benefits, Scarborough's
mineral water did not really offer anything that dozens of inland spas had
not been supplying for decades. Dr. Wittie, still driven by a respectable desire for financial gain, unleashed his stroke of brilliance. Why not offer at
Scarborough what no inland spa could give: an inexhaustible source of
water impregnated with the most benign and vitalizing minerals in existence? Why not offer the *sea*?

4

REVOLUTION ON THE BEACH

Scarborough, 1748. Under the pale morning sky, a broad band of sealskin-colored sand curls around the tidy blue bay. Headland after ragged headland stretches into the distance. Across the generous expanse of sand, an elegant party of ladies and gentlemen canters their horses past a file of twenty or thirty bathing machines waiting by the rocks. The contraptions are really only wooden changing rooms mounted on a carriage base with a door on each end and a tiny window on each side. A young woman walks hesitantly past them until she finds one to her liking, an attractive wooden cabin set on broad wheels and hitched to a horse. She gives the matron at the door a shilling and sixpence and mounts the three steps.

Inside, she slips out of her promenade dress and into a severe flannel smock that hangs heavily to her ankles. Then she settles herself on the velvet-cushioned bench for the short, bumpy ride to the surf. She can hear the driver coax the horse forward. The crisp crunching of sand against wheels quickly gives way to a soft lapping against the underside of the floorboards. The machine stops. The driver unhitches the horse, fixes it to the other end, and then comes back around again to lower a kind of awning over the door and hook a ladder to the tiny platform. The young lady steps out. Water is sloshing over the top step. It feels cold on her bare ankles. She hesitates, waiting for the matron, or "dipper," to approach.

Seeing that she is reluctant to descend, the matron, who is waist-high in the surf, lifts her gently and lowers her into the water. Still maintaining her hold on the girl's waist, she waits for a wave to form, and just as it is breaking, she plunges the bather headfirst into the swirling foam. The young woman struggles in the dipper's grip, as the shock of the icy water takes her breath away. She feels a surge of water rushing up her nose and pressing against her eyelids. Beneath her feet, the sea bottom swirls and eddies, knocking lead disks in the hem of her smock against her legs. She opens her mouth to breathe, but takes in water instead. She fights to raise her head, but the dipper holds her fast. With a sense of overwhelming panic, she feels herself suffocating.

Just as she is about to lose consciousness, she is hoisted up and deposited on the bottom step of the ladder. The attendant rubs her wrists and back vigorously to revive her. Blue-lipped and trembling from cold, but wide-eyed from the rush of adrenaline, the girl cries, shouts, and weeps, begging to be taken back to shore. There are other bathers in the surf and spectators on the shore, but no one takes any particular note of her struggles, even when the dipper submerges her again. Not until this ordeal of immersion and revival has been repeated five or six times is the shaken patient finally allowed to return to the haven of the bathing machine.

Once inside, she quickly strips, and steps on the foot warmers, vigorously toweling her extremities to restore circulation. As the machine lurches to shore, she slips into dry clothing and tidies up. Now she will return to her hotel for a cup of hot tea or a bracing bouillon, rest for an hour, and then, after lunch, join her friends for a stroll about the promenade. She will try not to think about the sea and the terrifying experience she has just survived. Because tomorrow morning—and every morning for the next five weeks—she will once again be subjected to this therapeutic immersion in the cold currents.

■ ■ ■ ■ ■

Similar life-and-death, illness-and-health scenes were played out at seaside locations throughout the British Isles—in Eastbourne, Newquay, Bournemouth, Falmouth, Yarmouth, Weymouth, Brighton, and Torquay—as a growing number of British gentlefolk willingly endured various degrees of trauma in order to reap the novel, health-restoring benefits of seawater. Paradoxically, they sought out the sea precisely because it aroused terror. The shock it administered to the nervous system was thought to revitalize the organism, soothe anxieties, help restore harmony between body and soul, and revive vital energy. The lure of the beach, in short, stemmed from the combination of two powerful but diametrically opposed emotions: fear and hope.

Sea bathing as a form of therapy and penance was invented by the British, the same nation that gave the world, nearly simultaneously, the cold bath, the steam engine, and the Industrial Revolution. Indeed, without the latter two developments, the likelihood that sea bathing would have become anything but an anecdote in the history of leisure is rather slim. Without efficient means for transporting large numbers of people across relatively long distances, the beach would have remained largely beyond

Until bathing machines became standard equipment at British beaches, bathers were rowed out to boats or barges moored a short way from shore. (Corbis/Bettmann)

reach for those who stood most to benefit from it. And without the rise of factories, there would not have been the wholesale migrations from the countryside that produced overcrowded and unsanitary cities, from which the public for the beach would be drawn. Eventually, sea bathing would shed its penitential character, though it would never quite lose its association with medicinal cures and moral improvement, two objectives that had been promulgated by British high-class culture.

Sea-bathing spas displaced inland spas as gathering places for the aristocracy and the upper bourgeoisie when Bath and Harrogate, Tunbridge Wells and Matlock began to attract large numbers of upstart traders and monied social climbers, and "cheapened." The lust for exclusivity was then, as now, a powerful motive for keeping status-conscious elites on the move. Rather than adapting to the "coarse" newcomers, the nobility and high bourgeoisie did what social snobs do today: they went elsewhere.

A few pioneers took up the seawater therapy offered at Scarborough. Soon the British royals gave their imprimatur to several new seaside spas: George III at Weymouth, his son at Brighton, his daughter at Southend. As in the case of the spas, where royalty led, the aristocracy followed. For a time, seaside resorts were the exclusive preserves of the affluent, who frequented expensive hotels and elegant rooming houses. Then the inevitable trickle of nouveaux riches swelled to a flood, and the snobs were once again on the move. Queen Victoria gave the signal when she discovered Brighton overrun by what she considered "flashy vulgarians" and fled to the Isle of Wight, taking with her the most conservative elements in her court. More adventurous aristocrats, however, took steamers across the Channel to the coast of France, where an elite beach culture was slowly taking root on the Atlantic coast.

By 1850, the British upper classes were in full retreat from well-established oceanside spots such as Weymouth, Brighton, and Blackpool, leaving the English coast clear for settlement by the middle class and, later, the laboring masses of London and Manchester.

After the 1830s, the British beach would be the creature of the steamer and the railway, obeying the laws of the marketplace rather than the taste of the court. But during the hundred-odd years of its heyday, the British seaside resort would set the standard

Virgil in hand, eighteenth-century tourists in Italy retraced the steps of Aeneas, concentrating most on the shores of the island of Capri, beloved getaway of Roman emperors. (A. Bierstadt, *Capri Beach*, Bettmann Archive)

on both sides of the Atlantic for sea bathing. Such was the international prestige of British culture, aristocracy, and medicine that the British anhedonic model of sea bathing became the norm. As the eighteenth century drew to a close, British bathing rituals appeared on the North American coast and in resorts on the Continent, from Dieppe and Boulogne in France, to Bad Doberan and Norderney on the Baltic and the North seas.

SEA THERAPY: NO PAIN, NO GAIN

The British invented the ordeal of immersion-cum-drowning—a healing ritual prescribed and carefully monitored by reputable physicians—as part of their most advanced medical arsenal. In fact, only in the early nineteenth century would the British "discover" the warm Mediterranean coast and become ready to take lessons in aquatic hedonism from the French, Italians, and Greeks. At that point, the experience of the sea would shift away from aquatherapy to a new center of gravity: physical *pleasure.*

Put another way, the human body on which the eighteenth century rode into the waves was not healthy but diseased. This distinction is fundamental, because it determined which bodies came to the seashore and what they did once they got there. The pioneering dip in the North Sea that defined nearly a century of fashionable practices was constructed as a therapeutic response to a set of medical conditions that ranged from vague psychological ailments to grave physical maladies. Fortunately, the therapy met with compliant patients. Members of the elite worried about their fevers and diseases, not only for themselves, but also for their class as a whole. Debility, feeble-mindedness, reproductive difficulties, digestive abnormalities, and all sorts of nervous tics and tremors appeared to be running riot among the aristocracy. If things continued on this course, they feared, there would be no one left to inherit the title, properties, and privileges. For this state of affairs they blamed the court, with its stresses and "unnatural" pressures; the city, with its contagions and noxious fumes; and the "softening" effects of civilization, which natural philosophers, theologians, and physiologists had been telling them was linked with geography and climate.

As an antidote to the pathologies plaguing the ruling class, the evolution in attitudes toward seawater passed through two stages.

First, the discovery that cold water is good for the body led to the finding that cold *salt* water is even better. Sometime in the late sixteenth century, physicians began to tout the miraculous healing properties of cold water: dying bodies convulsed back to life after the application of ice water, and travelers on the verge of expiring from heat stroke were restored in glacial streams. The shock effect of cold water appeared to offer a promising remedy for a range of complaints that were viewed as especially worrisome at the time, melancholy being chief among them. The disorder had been attested in antiquity, but became especially marked in sixteenth- and seventeenth-century Europe, when large numbers of people were found to be depressed, dejected, gloomy, and irascible. Paintings and engravings of the era depicted melancholics slumped against messy heaps of ruins or vegetation, heads drooping, eyes unfocused. Body language conveys mental torpor, disengagement, despair, and profound lassitude.

For a while, melancholy enjoyed a vogue among the aristocracy, for it carried the connotation of spiritual depth and emotional refinement—as it would again two hundred years later, when the Sentimentalists cultivated melancholy as the mark of the superior soul. The French were the first to abandon it. In the France of Louis XIV, melancholy went out of style, because the demanding pace of court life left no time for depression. In Britain, however, it took such firm hold that it came to be known on the Continent by its English name—"spleen." British gentlemen in particular cultivated the splenetic manner far into the nineteenth century, and young Anglophiles on the Continent adopted the pose of the melancholic as one more fashionable British mannerism.

The diagnostic popularity of melancholy was partially the fault of an influential treatise published in 1621 by the English clergyman Robert Burton. Entitled *The Anatomy of Melancholy, What It Is, with All the Kinds, Causes, Symptoms, Prognostickes & Severall Cures of It,* the thirteen-hundred-page tome detailed the numerous varieties, gradations, and causes of melancholy, its physical and mental manifestations, its origin in a multitude of often contradictory conditions ranging from "rumbling in the guts or fumes arising from the stomach" to "immoderate heat of the sun" and "idleness or overmuch study." Burton's catalogue for this psychopathology was so far-ranging that hardly a complaint, mental or physical, could be found that would not in some way qualify for inclusion. Schizophrenia and lovesickness, excessive piety and social snobbery were all accommodated in the often witty and always satirical dissection of melancholy.

Physiologists of the late seventeenth and early eighteenth centuries described other illnesses that were thought susceptible to hydrotherapy. At this time, the diaphragm, working in tandem with the brain, came to be considered as the master regulator of sensitivity and was thought to be linked to various disorders of the nerves, such as vapors, hysteria, nymphomania, menstrual irregularities, and the diffuse listlessness of the aristocracy. Sudden immersion in cold water appeared to energize the diaphragm, thereby igniting seaside bodies into engines of activity. It was further postulated that cold contracted the body in its very deepest zones,

To augment the prestige of swimming, early proponents of the sport appealed to its antecedents in antiquity, and took pains to depict it as a practice rooted in classical values. (Corbis/Bettmann)

and in so doing stimulated circulation of humors, the evacuation of viscera, and the shrinking of tumors. Cold water caused masses to retract, organs to quicken. Louis de Préville, a French physiologue, envisioned water-based cold therapy in terms of a conflict between relaxation and contraction, softening and hardening. In his view, there was nothing superior to cold water when it came to "dissolving blood or evacuating glutinous matters attached to the linings of the vessels," or inducing "abundant filtration of animal spirits or make them run more rapidly in the nerves."

SEA BATHING AND THE BODY

When Dr. Robert Wittie in 1667 pioneered the therapeutic sea bath at Scarborough, he described seawater in his brochure both as a quaff and a medium of immersion. This was a brilliant tactic. By inventing the medicinal equivalent of a better tool for the job of curing gout, worms, and other ailments for which mineral waters had been indicated, Dr. Wittie created a need where no need had existed before. He had hit on a new, improved formula for the elixir of health.

To us, of course, the idea of drinking seawater seems outlandish and even revolting. Most seventeenth-century Britons, however, did not share these qualms. In fact, the objection to drinking seawater on the grounds of taste was easily circumvented by the simple expedient of "cutting" the salt water with some fresh milk. The more substantive question of therapeutic efficacy was soon laid to rest by a growing chorus of support from medical authorities with impeccable credentials.

One of the most influential in this respect was the Englishman Sir John Floyer, who in his authoritative *History of Cold Bathing,* written in 1701–2, advocated the therapy on purely scientific grounds. He appealed to such irreproachable experts from antiquity as Hippocrates, Celsus, Caelius Aurelianus, and Galen, as well as to modern-day physiologists and English intellectual authorities. Floyer prescribed cold baths to urbanites, shut-ins, frail children, adolescent girls, and young people as a corrective for bodily and spiritual infirmities.

> Cold baths cause a sense of chilness, and that, as well as the Terror and Surprize, very much contracts the Nervous membrane and tubes, in which the aerial spirits are contained, and they being kept tense and compressed, do most easily communicate, all external expressions to the Sensitive soul. Not only the external senses are more lively in cold water, but all our animal actions and reasonings are then more vigourous by the external compressure of cold air.

Floyer recommended immersion in water colder than ten degrees Celsius and insisted that it be followed by some form of vigorous exercise, such as riding or walking in the cold air. The conscientious Floyer tested this therapy on himself and was delighted with the results. "To bathe in the sea," he claimed, "is to have not only a cold bathe, but a medicinal cold bathe."

Floyer's regimen was subjected to much professional scrutiny, some no doubt spurred by patients clamoring for the new cure, and some by erudite invalids who, fed on a diet of Greek and Roman authors, were rediscovering forgotten medical therapies such as Dioscorides' seawater diluted with honey. Now medical science deigned to take note of these antique nostrums and folk remedies. It was recalled that the common people in England took seawater to counter worms, and in Spain to cure them of yellow fever. In 1748, a physician by the name of Richard Frewin tested these claims on an enfeebled aristocratic youth. From November through January, the young man was made to bathe daily in the sea and drink nearly a quart of salt water. Three months later, his health was completely restored. Both antiquity and folk medicine had been vindicated.

The results of aquatherapy by the sea impressed another physician, Dr. Richard Russell, who was at work on a scholarly treatise entitled *A Dissertation on the Use of Seawater in the Diseases of the Glands, Particularly, the Scurvy, Jaundice, King's Evil, Leprosy and the Glandular Consumption*. Published in 1750, Russell's work was to the beach cure what *Listening to Prozac* would be to antidepressants: a permission slip to experiment with a new elixir of health. Persuaded by his piety and science, an entire generation of physicians was converted. Russell believed that salt water was nature's own best medicine, provided by Divine Providence as a defense against decay and putrefaction. Chemical analysis of the seas surrounding the British Isles revealed a composition comparable to mineral waters. He praised seawater for its heavy traces of iodine, bromine, chloride of sodium, muriate of magnesia—a salt considered particularly beneficial to humans—chloride of potassium, Epsom salts, sulfate of lime, and carbonate of lime. Beyond these elements, the organisms that live and die in the sea were thought to add a unique stimulating power that produced an oceanic bouillabaisse equivalent to the modern-day multivitamin.

With the sea as his "magic [and aquatic] bullet," Dr. Russell felt secure in claiming, "Nature cures many diseases by her own Power," and for this reason she is justifiably called the "Healer of Diseases." In his view, the physician's best strategy was to imitate the ways of nature. By regulating glandular secretions, seawater cleansed the system, controlled the rate of internal putrefaction, and invigorated the entire organism. A combination of daily bathing and consumption of a half-pint of seawater in the morning, and still another *after* the bath, was his prescription for healing. In some instances, this could be supplemented with seaweed massage and hot sea-water showers.

A heavy-jowled and heavy-lidded man, Dr. Russell sent his patients, virtually all of them rich, idle, and constipated, to drink seawater at Southampton or at Brighthelmstone, the latter location being much preferred for its proximity to London. According to his prescription, a pint of seawater was "commonly sufficient, in grown Persons," to unlock the most recalcitrant of bowels, although a story—apocryphal, one hopes—was told about a patient who drank twenty-five gallons in an uninterrupted "course of Purging" before he obtained the desired relief. Russell took up residence in Brighthelmstone, patients came and went, and the town came to be known throughout England by its native pronunciation as "Brighton." His clients were splenetic gentlemen, gout-ridden bons vivants, and patients in the grip of dementia and what we would now call neurosis. Among the latter were patients suffering from hydrophobia. If hydrotheraphy did not always cure them, at least it gave them a fair sense of why they so feared and detested water. Most numerous among the invalids were pubescent girls who were being prepared for the physical ordeals of womanhood. The icy water, the constraining embrace of the bath attendant, the sudden suffocation followed by equally sudden release were ostensibly contrived to toughen girls up for menstruation and the arduousness of childbearing.

The medical establishment climbed aboard the sea-therapy bandwagon with uncharacteristic enthusiasm. In the late eighteenth century, hospitals were erected at many of the seaside watering places, including Margate, where they regularly prescribed salt water to their patients. At Scarborough, Brighthelmstone, and Margate, bathers awaiting their turn in the dippers' arms were given flasks of seawater to down. At simpler resorts, such as Lyme Regis, bathers simply walked down to the surf and scooped up a pint pot of water. Inland invalids who could not make it to the shore could purchase bottled seawater. Newspapers carried advertisements announcing that "seawater from Brighthelmstone, in Sussex, took off the main Ocean by T. Swaine," could be purchased at various inns. The habit became widespread, then gradually tapered off. By about 1850, it had all but disappeared, replaced by the continental mode of drinking bottled mineral water, which is still going strong.

The quality of the ocean air was no less important. Physicians undertook detailed investigations of various coastal resorts and compiled comparative data that recommended one set of conditions above another for patients suffering from a particular constellation of complaints. After 1783, the theories of the French chemist Antoine Lavoisier underlining the crucial role of oxygen in maintaining the organism and the nearly simultaneous increase in pulmonary consumption focused anxiety on respiration. Benjamin Franklin spoke of the air bath with great enthusiasm. Rising early each morning, he threw open the windows and moved around the house naked for "an hour or a half-hour, according to the season."

Scientific investigations of the period demonstrated sea air to be purest and most saturated with oxygen, superior even to mountain air. The faith in the restorative combination of marine air and water brought patients flocking to the shore. For, as Jane Austen wrote in *Sanditon,* her satirical novel of the seaside:

> No persons could be really well . . . [or] in a state of secure and permanent health without spending at least six weeks by the sea every year. The sea air and sea bathing together were nearly infallible, one or the other of them being a match for every disorder of the stomach, the lungs or the blood. They were anti-spasmodic, anti-pulmonary, anti-septic, anti-billious and anti-rheumatic. Nobody could catch cold by the sea; nobody wanted appetite by the sea; nobody wanted spirits; nobody wanted strength. Sea air was healing, softening, relaxing—fortifying and bracing—seemingly just as was wanted—sometimes one, sometimes the other. If the sea breeze failed, the seabath was the certain corrective; and where bathing disagreed, the sea air alone was evidently designed by nature for the cure.

COLD SEA BATHING AND MORAL CHARACTER

Parallel to these physiological studies and testimonials, eighteenth-century scholars and philosophers were busy extending the benefits of the cold bath far beyond the body, speculating on its contributions to the moral character of the individual, the nation, and even the species. Physiologists speculated that the internal organs of humans behaved very much like those of other organisms. If cold water could stiffen and invigorate plant stalks, then, by analogy, it could contract and make turgid the interior of the human body. Furthermore, the action of water on the human body was not seen as an isolated phenomenon, but as part of a larger system that incorporated a broader vision of the cosmos.

Many educated Europeans had read that the North Sea was of great benefit to humanity in a curious work entitled *The Telliamed or The Dialogue of an Indian Philosopher with a French Missionary,* published in Amsterdam in 1748. Widely read and discussed, the treatise was the work of the scholar Benoît de Maillet, who, upon observing that land and sea creatures were related, hypothesized that all life originated in the sea. The theory was not uniquely his, of course, but his formulation had the virtue of summarizing a growing scientific and philosophical consensus that the sea was the cradle of life. Marine creatures, Maillet argued, were gradually "terrestrialized" in deep watery caves in the northern seas along such fogbound coasts as Greenland and Hudson Bay. Sea-dwelling humans gradually learned to breathe air, moved inland, then headed south, in the process losing bits of vigor and discipline. Thus, Maillet reasoned, water—especially the cold water of the north—is the natural element of *Homo sapiens.*

Comte Georges-Louis Leclerc de Buffon, the pre-eminent French natural philosopher, took these insights a step further. He observed that the size and quantity of marine life decreased as one moved into the warmer latitudes. Southern waters had nothing to rival the teeming schools of herring and the mammoth whales of the polar seas. He concluded from this that fertility and robustness decrease proportionally with distance from the poles. In a strange eugenic twist, Buffon proposed that the sturdy barbarian of the north had weakened into the physically and—the step was instantly taken—morally debilitated citizen of the south. Supposed physical superiority was quickly given a spiritual and ethical twist. Suddenly, the symbolic value of cold seawater skyrocketed: not only was it the source of all life forms, it was also the font and origin of moral vigor. On the Continent, T. Tronchin, physician to the Encyclopedists, recalled, "As long as the Romans, on leaving the Champ de Mars, went and plunged into the Tiber, they ruled the world. But the hot baths of Agrippa and Nero reduced them gradually to slaves." In Tronchin's ethical paradigm, softness was opposed to virtue, physical weakness to moral force, and *cold* water was the pivot on which the oppositions turned.

The philosopher Jean-Jacques Rousseau also proclaimed himself a defender of the cold-water bath in the sea. He pointed to the example of the noble savages and ancient heroes who immersed themselves in cold water so that they might be rendered invincible. In *Émile,* his novel of education, Rousseau observes, "Multitudes of people wash newborn children in rivers or the sea as a matter of course. But ours, softened before even being born by the softness of their fathers and mothers, bring into the world a temperament already spoiled." His protagonist, Émile, is made to emulate the teachings on education through cold of the British philosopher John Locke and to study the example of classical heroes who had followed this practice. He is washed in ever colder water until he grows accustomed to bathing in icy streams, and develops into a paragon of manly virtue and reason.

The moral hardening that was a consequence of such bathing was put to use in training soldiers. In 1776, for example, the royal military school in

France introduced not only cold-water bathing but also an entire regimen based on cooling down the body by means of lighter clothing and bedcovers and more extensive ventilation. There were even proposals afoot to introduce river baths for "important employees of the State" so that these pillars of autocracy might benefit in health, vigor, and valor. Even after the revolution, the utopian impulse of shaping robust and virtuous servants of the state included water. In 1801, the revolutionary J.-A. Millot came up with a scheme for establishing a pedagogical public bath. He described his idea for a circular bath on the Seine in his *Art d'améliorer et de perfectionner les hommes (The Art of Improving and Perfecting Man):*

> Whenever the government wishes, it can change the feeble constitution of our Parisians, and make them as robust as our German neighbors: all that is needed is the construction of a bath at the edge of the Seine, near the Invalides; this bath would consist of an ellipse cut into the waste land on the bank which would be dug out to four feet only, and constructed like an amphitheater, in stages each raised only four or five inches above the next, to seat children of all ages after teething.

Had it been implemented, Millot hoped that his project would change the course of French history, but since nothing was done, we will never know.

THE PRACTICE OF BATHING

From a beach-marketing perspective, the near-frigid temperature of seawater during the winter season was one of its greatest assets. In fact, because many of the therapeutic effects associated with ocean immersion depended on the temperature of the water and the air being cold, sea bathing was nearly exclusively limited to the late fall and winter months. Frances—known as Fanny—Burney, author of a fascinating late-eighteenth-century diary, bathed in the English Channel in winter. So did the Dukes of Gloucester, York, and Cumberland, brothers to the King, who started coming to Weymouth in 1756. The Prince of Wales attempted to cure his goiter in the winter sea of Brighton for forty-four consecutive years. The Princesses Amelia and Charlotte of Wales were dipped at Worthing and Southend in the late fall of 1789 and 1807. King George III braved the cold waters of Sidmouth in 1791, and Charles X sought to soothe his nerves in the cold waves at Cowes.

With its two thousand miles of sea frontage if all the windings are measured, Great Britain offered elaborate and varied opportunities for ocean bathing. Still, the earliest developers concentrated on locales that were within easy reach—by coach and horse—of London, and which met a precise set of medical specifications. Topography, climate, hydrology, and even architecture all had to be right to optimize therapeutic effectiveness of beach-pegged cures. The site had to offer fine, hard sand with deep water close to shore—ten yards or so was ideal, for this allowed sufficient maneuvering space for the cumbersome bathing machine. The beach had to be broad, several miles long, not seriously compromised by high tide, and free from the ooze left by the ebb tide. Visitors did not like excessively loose sand, which made walking difficult. Indeed, soft sand was of no use to them. Unlike today's beachgoers, they did not come to lie down in the sand and expose their bodies to the sun. Instead, they looked for a firm, smooth surface for walking and horseback riding. The ideal beach had to lie far from marshes, brackish water, or large deposits of putrefying seaweed. Pebbles were undesirable, as were weeds, slimy rocks, and mudflats. The air had to be fine, pure, and soft, without a taint of putrefaction—neither too damp nor too arid.

A reliable source of good fresh water was indispensable, as was the proximity of fertile farmland and good pasturage, so visitors had access to crisp vegetables and fresh milk. A stretch of land suitable for a park or a promenade would allow visitors to view the sea at a comfortable distance and breathe the healthy breezes. A cliff or two or some sort of natural elevation would afford picturesque panoramas, and, in the environs, a ruin or a deserted abbey would provide a pretext for excursions.

Toward the close of the eighteenth century, a saltatory change took place in the orientation of buildings by the seashore. New residences were built *facing* the sea and providing unimpeded glimpses of nature. By contrast, traditional coastal dwellers who had made their livelihood by the sea had avoided looking at it when not working. From the typical seaside village, as Jane Austen notes, "the sea is not only invisible—even its sound and smell shut off in all but the worst of weathers. Sea views are only for urban folk, who never experience its menace. The true sailor prefers to be landlocked rather than face the ocean."

The southern coasts of England, especially those of Sussex, were most promising. When it became clear, by the end of the eighteenth century, that sea bathing was commercially lucrative, a great deal of rivalry appeared among neighboring seaside towns. Competing municipalities solicited experts to analyze and endorse the allegedly superior alchemy of each beach locale, and competing claims drove the market for a new genre of guidebooks, dedicated to helping the customer maneuver the bewildering terrain of therapeutic bathing.

FASHIONS OF THE THERAPEUTIC BEACH

Among the British, the very earliest sea-bathing costume was skin. For a long time—in fact, for about a hundred years after that first dip in Scarborough—ladies and gentlemen in England bathed in the nude at the same time and in the same place without apparently suffering any affront to modesty. That they did this in the depths of winter merely impresses us with their superior tolerance for discomfort. A 1735 engraving of Scarborough Bay shows an assortment of bathers of both sexes—some standing on the shore, some swimming—and all are stark naked. No one appears to care. To our sexual sensibility, this state of affairs appears both odd and paradoxical: we know that the seventeenth century had very strict views on the chaperoning of young women, and on land the period demanded concealing costume for both sexes.

True, some women bathers donned calico or flannel gowns, and customs varied from beach to beach. At Margate, Blackpool, and Scarborough, total nudity was the norm at least until the last decades of the eighteenth century. Then, if the evidence of period is to be trusted, prurience reared its head, and nudity fell from its state of grace. Some lady bathers still did without dress, but they did so at the risk of being ogled by gentlemen-in-name-only. At the turn of the century, Peeping Tom–ism was at its height. Seaside gawkers came equipped with telescopes to spy on female bathers, and apparently ladies showed a marked interest in returning the compliment. Scattered resorts took various steps to discourage the practice, not severely

Nude bathing was the norm in British resorts throughout the eighteenth century and well into the nineteenth. Only the elderly, frail, and timid opted for shapeless gowns. (William Tegg, *The Beach at Margate*, 1819, Margate Public Library)

enough to dissuade visitors, but sufficiently to reassure the timid and prud-ish. In some resorts, a token penalty was imposed for telescopic voyeurism: a bottle of wine as an offering of appeasement, a reprimand from the local magistrate, plus a small fine.

Male nudity continued to be the norm far into the nineteenth century. King George III took his ceremonial plunge at Scarborough unclothed. At British resorts in the eighteenth century gentlemen were rowed out a short distance from the shore, where they stripped and then jumped into the water. Across the Channel—at Scheveningen, Dieppe, Biarritz, and Ostend—gentlemen disrobed at the waterline and handed their clothing to local young women—daughters of fishermen—who also rubbed them down and helped them dress. Apparently the class differences were so pro-nounced—and the fishy smell clinging to the girls so nauseating—that no sexual improprieties occurred between swimmer and attendant.

THE BATHING MACHINE

Although bathing costumes were in an embryonic state of development, bathing itself was surrounded by rather involved appurtenances and proto-col. The wooden bathing machine was the most cumbersome of these. His-tory is sadly reticent on the subject of who first conceived the idea of putting a cabin on wheels and towing it into the water to provide a shelter and staging area for the bather. But by the 1750s and 1760s, the con-trivance is ubiquitous in drawings of various British seaside resorts, and by the end of the century it had nearly displaced the stationary cabin with which it had originally shared the beach.

In describing these contraptions, Tobias Smollett says nothing about the rank smell that clung to their walls, or about the dampness, or the sand that stuck between the floorboards, or the tiny flyblown mirrors and ratty win-dow curtains that were standard furnishings. He does mention the projec-tions or "tilts" with which some of the machines at Scarborough were equipped, extending outward from the seaward door. Fashioned of canvas and attached to the doorframe of the cabin, the hood was an aquatic "jet-way" of sorts that resembled a curved caterpillar when its edges were ex-tended to touch the water. It provided a shelter roughly eight feet by thirteen feet where the bather could float in a manner consistent with the most refined delicacy.

This so-called Modesty Hood was the invention of a Quaker, Benjamin Beale, who introduced it at the Margate beach in the 1750s. Beale's con-trivance was greatly appreciated by ladies loath to bare their nakedness or *déshabillé* to the pitiless scrutiny of strangers, as the following verses, al-legedly found inside a bathing machine in the late 1790s, attest:

> *Though oft I have been*
> *In a Bathing Machine*
>   *I never discover'd till now*
> *The wonderful art*
> *Of this little go-cart,*
>   *'Tis vastly convenient, I vow*
> *A peg for your clothes,*
> *A glass for your nose*
>   *And shutting the little trap-door,*
> *You are safe from the ken*
> *Of those impudent men*
>   *Who wander about on the Shore.*

The Modesty Hood was adopted at Scarborough and Weymouth, but it never quite caught on with the bathing-machine operators at Brighton. Perhaps the ladies who frequented the former tended to be genuinely ill and consequently in no mood to expose their wasted, crippled, and fevered bodies to public scrutiny. Some were no doubt shy and so preferred to patronize facilities that spared their sensibilities. Though it does not necessarily follow from this that Brighton's bathers were neither ill nor modest, it is a fact that the resort tended to attract an exuberant clientele. Along with rakes, parvenus, and philanderers, bustling Brighton was filled with young women of easy virtue, euphemistically called "little French milliners" and the "Cyprian corps." According to the *Morning Herald* of August 9, 1784, "Brighthelmstone is the centre of the system of pleasure. . . . The women, the pretty women, all hasten to see the Paris of the day."

THE BIG DIPPERS:
BEACH ATTENDANTS STAKE THEIR SAND

Therapeutic bathing was altogether too serious an affair to be left to the devices of an inexperienced, and often frail, bather, and the cold sea was too dangerous to be ventured into without a guide. Besides, the leisured people who came to bathe in the sea in the eighteenth century were accustomed to doing nothing without a servant at their elbow. Throughout the eighteenth century—and a good part of the nineteenth—a professional attendant, called "bather" for men and "dipper" for women—was engaged to supervise the therapeutic descent into the water and to monitor the extent and duration of the immersion. Male swimmers sometimes dispensed with the attendants' services.

By 1770, protocol dictated that attendant and client be of the same sex. The typical dipper was a brawny woman in a large sunbonnet wearing a black bodice and skirt. Often, she was married to the man who drove the horses which drew the machine in and out of the water. At Margate, eleven dipper-attended machines were at the disposal of visitors during the 1760s. Twenty years later, the number had tripled, and the crude huts in which invalids waited their turn at the machines had been replaced by elegant bathing rooms where one could read the newspaper and drink tea or, of course, seawater, while waiting to be called.

Bathers began to assemble at these stations at six o'clock in the morning and gave their names to a receptionist who chalked them on a large slate. Competition developed for a turn with the most famous dippers, whose names were passed around by fashionable ladies much like the names of hairdressers or physicians. At Southend, a Mrs. Glascock and Mrs. Myall dipped the most stellar members of society. At Ramsgate, Mrs. Nash did the honors. At Brighton, Mrs. Martha Gunn and a redoubtable bather named "Old Smoker" were in great demand.

THE HEALING SPACE OF THE BEACH

The eighteenth-century resort was an idealized and sanitized microcosm of the world of leisured aristocracy. Here, Eden was parceled out among the hours of the day with the pragmatic precision of a railroad timetable. What made the beach resort unique among other kinds of spas and retreats was its results-oriented pursuit of health—physical, intellectual, cultural, and social. Within the generous allotment of six weeks to six months, the visitor could easily register progress on all these fronts. Resort life revolved around several points of attraction, each of which had a particular therapeutic role. Bathing invigorated the body. Vigorous exercise, such as horseback riding, promoted deep breathing and the discharge of diseased air. Strolling, riding in a beach chair, or sailing in a boat manned by hired hands soothed the nervous system.

Morning was the accepted time for bathing, which was synchronized, as much as possible, with high tide. Sometimes, this meant that bathers had to rise before sunrise and trudge down to the bathing machine in the dark, or if too feeble to make the trek, hire a bath-chair man to transport them in a straw contrivance resembling a rickshaw. It was desirable to get one's bathing out of the way early so as to avoid the sun's rays, which were thought to cause congestion, dry out the body, and give skin the hue of the working classes. The precise duration and type of immersion were individualized to each client's medical needs, and were usually carried out in the privacy afforded by the bathing machine. Care was taken to maintain distance among bathers, who, unlike the present-day beachgoer, did not come for the mass spectacle of unclothed bodies but for deeply personal health reasons.

After the morning bath, time was devoted to reading, music, and drawing, in the case of the ladies; yachting, cricket, and riding, for the gentlemen. Subscription libraries, where visitors paid a small seasonal fee for the privilege of perusing newspapers and borrowing books, provided intellectual stimulation, and opportunities to make new acquaintances. In the better resorts, booksellers posted lists of the visitors to enable newcomers and habitués to take stock of each other.

The afternoons were for social calls, shopping, charity work—one was not exempt from this duty even on therapeutic holiday—the marine promenade, and intellectual stimulation. Botanical, geological, and archeological excursions satisfied the need for self-improvement. "Scientific" parties were organized for amateur naturalists to study and sketch the varieties of marine life, birds, and geological formations. Wearying of these natural curiosities, the resort guests explored customs of the lower classes—the peasantry and fisherfolk. Visits to marketplaces, local festivals, and fairs were raised above the level of idle gawking by being conducted in the spirit of intellectual inquiry. Ruined abbeys, picturesque cemeteries, medieval fortresses and towers were sought out as memorials to ancient heroic deeds and tragic love affairs.

For invalids, a good part of the afternoon was devoted to updating a daily therapeutic log. Patients who took their sea-bathing therapy seriously—and most of them did—were encouraged to take an active part in monitoring the state of their health and keeping track of their physiological responses

The therapeutic beach increasingly shared the spotlight with recreational activities. While fishermen could still be seen drawing in their catch, gentlefolk exercised horses, excursionists pondered the waves, and ladies pored over novels. In the sea, a group of naked women cavort in the waves, seemingly without attracting any notice. (Culver Pictures)

to the various sea therapies prescribed for them. Since physicians expected detailed reports about evacuation, sleep, appetite, and circulation, paying attention to oneself was promoted as a legitimate discipline that was critical to maintaining one's health. Instead of examining one's conscience at the end of each day, as had been the practice in more pious times, one now examined one's body and recorded the findings.

The evenings were entirely given over to elaborate dinners, assemblies, and dancing at private residences and hotels. Card parties and gambling were available at the more cosmopolitan resorts of Brighton and Scarborough. The busy social whirl usually excluded actual invalids, who had to husband their energies and usually retired to bed about ten o'clock after a light supper. But, on the whole, a balance developed between the therapeutic demands of the holiday and its social dimensions.

THE EDIFYING SEASHORE

Valetudinarianism made the eighteenth century beach a haven for invalids, real and imaginary, but scholarship made it a laboratory for scientists, scholars, and the intellectually curious. Certainly the most stellar example of the scholarly beach ramble was provided by the German naturalist-poet-philosopher Johann Wolfgang von Goethe, who, on the occasion of his Italian journey, sought out every opportunity to study the flora and fauna—as well as the archeological remains—of the Mediterranean. "I heard a loud hollow murmur—" Goethe reported from the Lido on October 8, 1786, "it was the sea!" Goethe describes some "remarkable detritus" gathered on his beach hunt. Among the predictable particles of limestone, there were also fragments of precious stones and minerals which, Goethe speculated, must have been remnants of old buildings and accordingly gave evidence of "how the waves can play before our eyes with the splendors of the ancient world."

By the middle of the eighteenth century, the ranks of scholars and scientists studying the seashore were swollen by gentlemen and ladies—as well as recruits from the bourgeoisie—who wanted to examine with their own five senses the wondrous world of the beach. Armed with manuals on geology and natural history, a notebook, a sketchbook, a sturdy bag, and a stout walking stick, amateur savants swarmed about the shores of England and ranged farther afield, to the corners of the British Isles and to the Continent. Every ramble along the shore was an opportunity to discover an unfamiliar specimen, perhaps to expand the frontiers of knowledge, to make a contribution—no matter how minor—to science. Specimens were carefully harvested, scrupulously documented, and eventually transported home to be sorted and entered into domestic archives of "curios."

In their quest for knowledge, marine enthusiasts scaled crumbling cliffs, scrambled up slippery rocks, crawled into narrow caves, dodged advancing tides, and braved the mockery of bemused rustics. A certain aura of heroism, of grave dangers surmounted in the sacred work of learning, began to attach to these amateur naturalists, at least in their own accounts. "Without thinking of the danger," writes the Genevan geologist L. A. Necker de Saussure of his 1806 coastal rambles in Scotland, "I wormed my way as best I could by clinging to tufts of dry grass that were growing . . . [on the sand hill] in abundance, and by way of steps, I used the tops of columns that sprung from the earth." He noticed, however, that his native guide, in the meantime, had taken the customary path to the top of the dune, where he awaited Saussure with considerable merriment.

By the 1760s, beachcombing had become a full-fledged mania among people from all walks of life. They came to Margate and Sidmouth and Branscombe, lured by the prospect of vast deposits of seaweed and shellfish. Even the locals, largely indifferent to marine life except for its commercial dimension, took an interest in beach flora and fauna once they realized there was a market in seashells, pebbles, and preserved seaweed. They even developed a thriving cottage industry in framed compositions of dried seaweed laid out in the form of baskets and bouquets of flowers. Beach Kitsch was born.

Visiting young ladies set out at low tide, armed with collecting baskets, drawing paper, pencils, pressing boards, eye shades, and shawls. They poked about the muck left by the receding water with a mixture of disgust and delight, marveling at the revelations of the sea bottom thus exposed. The more artistic among them set up easels and proceeded to record the finds in watercolors. Their gentleman escorts obligingly waded into the water, shoes and all, hoisted the ladies over rocks, and entertained them by reciting snatches of poetry and rhapsodizing about the shore in the modish vocabulary of the sublime.

BUILDING THE BEACH

Brighton was the jewel among British seaside resorts, polished to dazzling perfection through its association with the Prince of Wales. From his very first visit on September 7, 1783, the future regent and king brought a new inflection to the seaside. On the occasion of his first visit, the Prince of Wales found Brighton undistinguished, and the beach—a vacant expanse traversed by a dirty little stream—was shared by fishermen drying their nets and pigs rooting for stinking fish heads in the seaweed. There was no promenade, no wooden pier. Strollers set their own itineraries. By 1830, however, the town had become brilliant and beautiful, as befitted its standing as virtually a second capital during the Regency and the reigns of George IV and William IV—and the members of the aristocracy who rushed there to take lodgings.

In a transformation strategy that would become paradigmatic for the gentrification of fishing villages into elegant resorts from St.-Tropez to Long Island's Southampton, the prince commissioned the fashionable architect Henry Holland to renovate a local farmhouse into a tasteful classical villa. With its circular drawing room, semicircular lounges, and bow-windowed reception rooms, the prince's first residence was tame by comparison with subsequent lodgings he would commission in the same locale. At the turn of the century, he had the residence expanded, adding stables in an "Indian" style which he so fancied that several years later he commissioned a whole new pavilion from landscape designer Humphrey Repton. But financial problems and amorous intrigue interfered with the execution of Repton's Oriental design. The prince fell in love with the wife of architect John Nash—Repton's partner—and when he was again "flush," the prince switched his patronage to Nash. The Royal Pavilion, which took shape in Brighton between 1813 and 1820, was the work of Nash.

One of the decorative wonders of the world, the Royal Pavilion is festooned with minarets, onion domes, lacy trelliswork, and zigzag moldings. The creamy confection rises from a reflecting pool, like the Taj Mahal at Agra, which inspired it. But whereas the Taj Mahal is all about restraint and spatial clarity, the Royal Pavilion is a fantasy straight out of the *Arabian Nights*. It would serve as inspiration for the whimsical Orientalism of British beachfront hotels and American amusement parks well into the nineteenth century.

The Royal Pavilion signaled the start of the "architecturalization" of the beach. For the first time, people viewed the seashore as a place where they could establish fashionable residences, and where they expected to stay in accommodations every bit as refined as the manor houses and spa hotels between which they divided their time. On the Royal Crescent in Brighton, fourteen elegant lodging houses were erected between 1798 and 1807. A formal promenade was installed along the seafront to connect the residential zones that developed on the east and west sides of the town. As the site of the royal residence, Brighton, like all the capitals of Europe, now offered a grand promenade, which, like the Bois de Boulogne, in Paris, was the stage for ceremonial display of dress and rank. Along this strip, benches were set facing out to the sea, and people came to stroll, read, chat, and watch children play. A terrace rising more than two hundred feet above sea level provided a vantage from which to observe fine carriages, impeccably groomed riders, and fashionably attired pedestrians, who passed back and forth continually, taking in the air, the view, and each other's company.

Once started, the beach building boom only gained momentum. After the unstable area of the Steyne, a favorite strolling strip, was reclaimed in 1793, and then landscaped and paved in 1806, construction of residences began in earnest. Between 1823 and 1827, Brighton added sea terraces, a square, the lovely wings of Lewes Crescent—these according to the plans of John Nash—and additional residences of even greater beauty and more impressive dimensions.

Travelers were fascinated by the vitality and splendor of this former fishing village. Not surprisingly, other resorts followed Brighton's pioneering example with their own similar architectural programs. Scarborough offered a promenade gallery in the neo-Gothic style, full of sharp little towers and arched windows opening out to the sea, where visitors congregated in good and bad weather. So-called marine houses—small-scale hotels with attached cold and hot baths—were built here at the high-tide line. By 1841, Blackpool boasted fifteen hundred houses at the foot of its cliff, and a handsome terrace and promenade leading to the vast sandy beach.

Scarborough and Brighton, Weymouth and Margate attracted a diversified clientele of pleasure seekers, husband hunters, dowry hounds, and bons vivants of both sexes, in addition to the usual assortment of invalids. When the two factions were not harmonious, the infirm usually quit the premises and took up abode in a quieter locale. The only prerequisite for admittance was the heft of one's purse, so the spas were gradually overrun by parvenus. Eventually, merchants, farmers, cloth makers, stockbrokers, entrepreneurs, and bankers followed the royalty and aristocracy to Scarborough and Brighton. But the diversions they craved were not to be found in the Assembly Room or in the Library. What the masses wanted was not the soothing, edifying rituals of the therapeutic spa, but spectacle— pleasure, excitement, and nonstop entertainment.

DRIFTING TO THE CONTINENT

The British—geographically advantaged with easy access to the seashore— were the first to put cold water and sea bathing together in the seaside resort. From there, the fashion for sea bathing spread to the Continent, where it became more and more popular with each succeeding year along the coasts from Helgoland to Biarritz and San Sabastián. By the late eighteenth century, Smollett had popularized the seaside holiday in France. He settled in Nice for a long therapeutic visit in 1763 and kept a daily record of its climate, seeking to establish a correlation between the state of his health and the atmospheric conditions. His scrupulous notations circulated widely among his fellow countrymen, persuading them that there was much merit to be found in the winter waters of the Mediterranean.

Resorts based on the British model were being established along the

At Biarritz on the Normandy coast and at Brighton and Weymouth across the Channel, swimmers could rent flotational devices in the form of air bladders which they attached to their waists. (Culver Pictures)

Atlantic coast in France, Belgium, Holland, and the German states. Largely founded by companies of merchants, civil servants, and physicians, these, like the British prototypes, blossomed once they had received the blessing and patronage of royalty and aristocracy. Shortly after the French Empress Hortense visited Dieppe in 1813, aristocratic Parisians followed, to see the sea and eat fish, but more and more frequently to indulge in the newest "Anglomaniacal" fad—bathing in the sea. The first German sea-bath was installed at Doberan in 1794 by Dr. Vogel, with the financial assistance of the Grand Duke of Mecklenburg-Schwerin. The Duchess of Oldenburg bequeathed a bath chair to the new resort on the island of Wangerooge. The King of Prussia urged the construction of a sea-bathing facility in Kolberg and invested in the resort at Swinemünde. By 1827, this resort boasted twelve hundred bathers, mostly aristocrats and members of the upper-middle class, with an unrecorded number of commoners who continued using the sands for casual outings.

The mixing of classes, however, was not to go on for long. Sensitive to social pressures, the authorities carved up the beach into five zones, two for men, two for women, with the fifth zone—some five hundred paces wide—forming a no-man's-land in between. The female and male sectors were each divided along class lines. Those for the well-born and the well-heeled provided changing cabins, bathing chairs, and a boardwalk. Those for the commoners had no amenities. A similar arrangement prevailed at

Scheveningen, which developed into a thriving resort after 1818, and such other northern bathing sites as Ostend and Blankenberge.

THE POPULAR BEACH

The common people had been congregating on the beach for centuries. Along the coasts of the Baltic, the North Sea, the English Channel, and the Atlantic, sea bathing was practiced among working-class families not as a therapeutic activity, but purely as recreation. British fishing and farming families were said to have bathed in the sea since well before 1750. Children, adolescents, and adults splashed together in the waves without regard for decorum or for segregating the sexes. But because they tended to be loud and rowdy, the authorities in the emerging resorts discouraged their presence, fearing that their free manners and boisterous play would offend the finer patrons.

In fact, on their excursions abroad, cultivated Britons encountered models of beach practices that were very different from their own. What they saw were sea bathers driven by spontaneous whim, weather, and desire for pleasure, attitudes that stood in stark contrast to their own medically mandated practices. In France, at Biarritz, the last Sunday in September would find entire villages of Basques leaving their mountain homes for a festive dip in the sea. Seventeenth-century travelers to the region were often surprised by the sight of grown girls and young fishermen mingling in the water and then going to dry off in the caves that were veritable chambers of love. Erotic play was an expected part of the fun of bathing for locals, along with, as on the shores of Boulogne, cooling off from the summer heat.

In the course of their Grand Tour, British tourists came across native bathers in the Mediterranean joyfully splashing in the cool, clear waters, playing for hours in the waves like bands of dolphins. To these northern travelers, sights such as these seemed to re-create legendary sea frolics from classical mythology. There was a decidedly aesthetic vein in their appreciation of bathers—exclusively male—whose strong, tanned, nude bodies recalled the sea gods or dolphins of ancient art. In France and Italy, Grand Tourists, bewitched by the presumed similarity between bathing natives and the descriptions of mythological scenes in their Virgilian and Ovidian texts, imitated the behavior of the Mediterranean youths. They hired boats to take them to picturesque coves and, attended by local boys, went for a swim. They dared not sail too far from settlements, because Mediterranean beaches were then still plagued by pirates, brigands, and robbers.

In July 1787, when Goethe visited the Bay of Naples, he delighted at the sight of a young horseman who, as a swineherd played on a flute and a goatherd on bagpipes, rode his horse into the sea. "It was indeed a fine sight," Goethe wrote, "when the well-built lad came so close to shore that one could see his whole form; and then he went right back into the deep sea, where nothing could be seen but the head of the swimming horse and the boy's head and shoulders." Earlier, at the villa of Sir William Hamilton in Posilipo, Goethe had been treated to a similar performance pre-arranged by the host. "After we had eaten, a dozen boys swam in the sea, which was a fine sight. How variously they grouped themselves and posed as they played! He pays them for it, in order to enjoy this pleasure every after-noon."

SPIRITUALITY AND ROMANCE
COME TO THE BEACH

Dorset, 1826. Bare toes wedged into the granular sand, the young, thick-haired British aristocrat clutches a tattered, leather-bound volume of George Chapman's *Whole Works of Homer* and Lord Byron's *Childe Harold's Pilgrimage*. His thoughts swirl in the mental foreplay to epiphany. He has come to the beach for a reason. Scanning the horizon, he seeks a spiritual anodyne to his life in London, where he finds himself chafing under the tedium and constraint of social privilege. He understands his seaside mission. The English Romantics—Byron, Shelley, and Swinburne—have taught him that the beach is nothing less than an outpost for reflection and self-discovery, a place where nature, in her infinite dynamism and enigma, presents a subtle script through which the human spirit cryptically reveals itself.

The shivering water of the North Atlantic stretches out before him, its tremendous distance shrouded in haze. Seabirds ride the ridges close to shore. The voice of the sea is at once seductive and terrifying, a never-ceasing, whispering, clamoring, murmuring invitation to wander in an abyss of solitude. All along the white beach, up and down, there is no living being in sight. A true Romantic, he cherishes the physicality of the moment, rapturously attending to each of nature's minutest inflections: the moaning wind, the high, watery walls rolling in and tumbling into surf, the polyrhythmic drone of incoming billows, the flying blotches of sea foam. Here, he contemplates a luminous moment of freedom, and slowly slips under the spell of the ocean's fatal attraction. He undresses and pauses, naked, on the sandy threshold. Then, suddenly, as if compelled by an untamable passion emanating from the root of his being, he throws himself into the turbulence, and feels a glorious, epiphanic wave crash against the very interstices of his soul. Bobbing in the buoyant, whirling current that now enfolds his body in a soft, close embrace, the young man feels himself a newborn creature, opening his eyes in a familiar world, but one he had never fully known. The beach as therapist is born.

Once Parisians found their way the beaches of Normandy during the Second Empire, nothing could stop their advance to the sea. (Louis Eugène Boudin, *Fashionable Figures on the Beach*, Museum of Fine Arts, Boston)

■■■■■■

The titled, landed, and wealthy of Britain measured the physical limits of their own bodies against the limitlessness of the water, and, clinging to the margins of the sea, sought spontaneous healing from their real and imaginary maladies. Under the pretext of curing infirmities and easing anxieties, however, they discovered an entirely new range of physical sensations. The melding of pleasure and pain that came from sudden immersion at the beach led to strictly medicinal ends. Unfortunately, too many spiritual and physical agendas were made to ride on the cresting waves to leave any room for the unadulterated pleasures of the senses.

Gradually, however, the beach evolved into a powerful and, as the Romantics demonstrated, even a dangerously seductive force. The view of miles of uninhabited land, submerged and uncovered along the shore every day and subjected to the perpetual motion of the sea, had itself become the lure. By the beginning of the nineteenth century, the beach experience had taken on potent spiritual and aesthetic dimensions. A tenuous, unpredictable zone between land and water, the beach inspired a generation of artistic rebels to experience the thrill of the sublime and to contemplate the depths of their own souls. By 1820, the physician who had supervised and devised activities at the shore would be replaced by the artist as legislator of attitudes about nature in general, and toward the beach in particular.

What happened can best be described as classical case of spin-doctoring. Between 1810 and 1850, the beach was claimed by the Romantics, who would discover in the sea and its environs unexpected psychological and spiritual meanings. In turn, literate travelers began to appropriate the bundle of Romantic sensations as the frame through which they themselves experienced and described their responses to the sea and the beach. Influenced by poets and artists, the public became curious about this shifting margin of land and learned to find it interesting and deserving of inspection, study, and contemplation as a mirror held up to the introspective self. Travel writers did their work of turning the luminous insights into clichés.

ROMANCING THE SEA

The "new" British poets—among them, Wordsworth, Coleridge, Shelley, Keats, and Byron—sensed in the vast organic entity of the sea the same amalgam of spirits that stirred in the depths of the human soul. Viewed through this optic, the seashore became a site for visionary experiences, for epiphanic encounters, and for liberating physical sensations, and this, in turn, would help shape the way subsequent generations of visitors would perceive, inhabit, and enjoy the beach. Confirming the observation that there is nothing new that is pleasurable that is not, in some way, based on something *old* that is pleasurable, Northern Europeans began to cultivate a passion for the seashore that extended well beyond its healing properties. In this important sense, they not only were on the road to resuscitating the oceanic hedonism of ancient Rome, but taking the possibilities that lurked in the sea even deeper.

What the thinkers of the Enlightenment had reduced to mute, organic matter now revealed itself to Romantic observers as vibrantly alive. Herman Melville, in *Moby-Dick,* wrote in 1851, "There is, one knows not what sweet mystery about this sea, whose gently awful stirrings seem to speak of some hidden soul beneath." In a thoroughly Romantic vein, Charles Dickens views a tempest at sea as the temper tantrum of a monster. "As the receding wave swept back with a hoarse roar," he writes in *David Copperfield,* "it seemed to scoop out deep caves in the beach, as if its purpose were to undermine the earth. When some white-headed billows thundered on, and dashed themselvees to pieces before they reached the land, every fragment of the late whole seemed possessed by the full might of its wrath, rushing to be gathered to the composition of another monster."

Guided by the new authority of inspired intuition, writers and philosophers approached nature as a living, breathing, sensing organism, capable not only of acting on the psyche, as the theory of the sublime had proposed, but also as a gateway to self-knowledge. The philosopher Immanuel Kant had taught young Romantics that the sublime feelings inspired by such frightening spectacles as storms at sea would make them conscious of their moral worth, by giving them a measure of their own inner powers. Poets and artists took this to mean that by contemplating the elements uniting on the seashore—air, water, and earth—we came to discover the true self as a perpetual battlefield of irreconcilable elements: intellect, emotion, and instinct. "There is a rapture on the lonely shore," wrote Lord Byron, "There is society where none intrudes, / By the deep Sea, and music in its roar: / I love not man the less, but Nature more, / From these our interviews, in which I steal / From all I may be, or have been before, / To mingle with the Universe, and feel / What I can ne'er express, yet cannot all conceal." On a more prosaic level, Lord Byron also recognized the uplifting powers of the sea. Afflicted with clubfoot, he found the exhilaration of unhampered movement only when swimming. "I delight in the sea," Byron remarked to a friend, "and come out with a buoyancy of spirits I never feel on any other occasion."

When it came to the beach, the Romantics played fast and loose. Far from intending scientifically neutral descriptions of physical nature, the Romantics rendered it as an extension of their own internal states. "You sea!" wrote Walt Whitman in *Song of Myself*. ". . . Sea breathing broad and convulsive breaths, / Sea of the brine of life and of unshovell'd yet always-ready graves, / Howler and scooper of storms, capricious and dainty sea, /

For Romantic artists, the luminous, variable surface of the sea was the looking glass through which they entered into the essence of nature and the depths of the self. (John Constable, *Seascape Study with Rain Clouds*, c. 1827, Royal Academy of Arts, London)

I am integral with you, I too am of one phase and of all phases." The ocean's vastness, the cyclicity of tides, the ephemerality of the shore, all mirrored the fate of humans.

The egoism of the Romantics was as boundless as the sea, and their perversions of intellectual confluency knew no bounds. "I feel, therefore I am," the philosopher Jean-Jacques Rousseau had said, validating sensation as the gateway to truth. His spiritual progeny, artists such as J. M. W. Turner, John Constable, Richard Bonington, Eugène-Louis-Gabriel Isabey, and Caspar David Friedrich, delivered paintings of the seashore that transcribed the agitation of the soul. With their blurred horizons—where sea, sky, and sand mingle in an indiscriminate swirl of elements—these evocative seascapes eloquently proclaimed the Romantics' love of indeterminacy and perpetual agitation. The restlessness of the human psyche found countless expressions in Romantic writings of the period. John Keats, for instance, saw the sea wave—"Down whose green back the short-lived foam, all hoar / Bursts gradual, with wayward indolence"—as a mirror for man's own instability.

The Romantics worshipped dynamism. They loved to travel and were constantly on the move, scaling mountains, trudging across moors, prowling the seashore. If the Grand Tourists of an earlier epoch had orchestrated their itineraries and responses to sights according to the texts of classical authors, the travelers of the first half of the nineteenth century put Lord Byron's *Childe Harold's Pilgrimage* to the same use. The protagonist of Byron's narrative poem lived out his life on the premise "Where rolled the ocean, thereon was his home." Real-life Childe Harolds used the work as a guidebook to beaches and bathing experiences. The descriptions of the physical sensations available at the shore—the chromatic riff of sounds, the chill of wind on sun-warmed skin, the sting of salt on chapped cheek—taught readers what to feel and how to extract maximal value from their beach experiences.

The Channel resorts of the French coast were filled with women and children. On Sundays and holidays, husbands commuted from Paris on what wits dubbed the "cuckold trains." (Edward H. Potthast, *At the Seaside*, Museum of Fine Arts, Boston)

For the Romantics, a walk on the beach was as much a spiritual as an intellectual exercise. Ann Radcliffe, author of Gothic novels, spent many hours taking solitary walks along the southern coast of England. The craze for walking on the beach spread to Germany and France in the 1820s and 1830s. The artist Caspar David Friedrich retired for long periods of time to the island of Rügen, where he wandered along the desolate shore, painting and sketching, oblivious of the weather, and always driven by the desire to experience the "spiritual resonances" of the beach. On the Continent, artists of the French Restoration—Eugène Isabey, Le Poittevin, Paul Huet—logged hundreds of miles of walking trips along the Atlantic shore, which they captured so copiously on canvas that within a few years they were in danger of transforming beach scenes into stale clichés. Heinrich Heine so popularized Norderney Island, where he had retired to re-create an aestheticized Robinson Crusoe, that by 1826 the island was overrun by tourists.

Most Romantics found reassurance in the positive potentiality of the sea, in its teeming life forms, and in its eternal youth. Many linked it with the thought of childhood, the world's and their own. The last British Romantic, Algernon Charles Swinburne, was a rapturous swimmer from his earliest childhood, which he spent on the Isle of Wight. He recalled being held naked in his father's arms there, and "brandished between his hands, then shot like a stone from a sling through the air, shouting and laughing with delight, head foremost into the coming wave." In his imagination, this idyllic childhood re-created the primordial experience of humanity. As he lay on his back for hours, floating like a seal off the Isle of Wight, he imagined himself in the "Aegean of his Hellenic dream-world."

Like hyperactive children, the Romantics bored easily, and incessantly clamored for fresh sensations. Anything that remotely resembled stability smacked of death to them. Not surprisingly, their marriages were by and large tumultuous, their affairs explosive, torturous, and convoluted. They were drawn irresistibly to social turmoil, to every kind of upheaval and revolution. If the Romantic admirers of the sea could not emulate the example of Lord Byron, who had perished fighting for Greek independence at Missolonghi, they dreamed of a spectacular death in nature's turbulent aquatic coliseum.

The merriment of resort life was frequently marred by drowning incidents as inept swimmers succumbed to the currents. (*Scenes and Incidents at Coney Island: Life-savers at Work*, undated illustration, Bettmann Archive)

The prideful Romantic artists so disdained the trivial audience and the company of all but their fellow creators that they thought only the savage sea constituted a worthy adversary. Swinburne nearly drowned off the Normandy coast. Others wrote of mariners and swimmers who met their death in the waves, where treacherous encounters were built around the hypnotic and consuming image of the sea. Even though many of them were poor swimmers, they threw themselves into the waves for the thrill which the very real possibility of drowning offered. The sea best illustrated for these artists what they most cherished in the human psyche: perpetual dissatisfaction and ceaseless striving for an ideal that knit into one soul-affirming whole the disparate elements of love, self, society, and God. The precise identity of the ideal mattered little, as long as it was inaccessible and glimpsed only in rare moments of ecstatic transport: orgasm, inspiration, drug-or-alcohol-induced intoxication, or close encounters with the sea as a near-death experience.

BEACH BIVOUAC

The Romantics wrote knowingly about the sea and the beach, largely because they spent considerable amounts of time there. Between 1800 and 1840, artists and topographers scrupulously recorded the shoreline of the British Isles. Such masters of the seascape as Constable, Turner, and Cotman made extensive journeys along the seashore, painting wild natural scenes, vignettes of simple fisherfolk, and the seaside holiday to satisfy an increasingly clamorous market. Hotel life held no appeal for them, nor did crowds, or the society that went by the name of *le monde*. They wanted no resorts, only a quiet spot by the sea where the scenery was unspoiled by modern contrivances and day trippers.

When they ventured into the waves, they discovered a world where one lived and moved in harmony with heavenly sensations. If the sea was "sacred" it was so because still untouched by modern civilization. Ideally, they looked for sites associated with legend and myth, much as the pilgrims of the Middle Ages had congregated at sacred shrines. In many respects, their excursions to the beach had attributes of religious or spiritual pilgrimages. To this end, they made a virtue out of necessity, profiting from the restrictions on travel to the Continent imposed by England's armed conflict with France between 1792 and 1815 to turn inward, to their own native landscape. They explored the infinitely winding perimeter of the British Isles, whose coves, caves, cliffs, and shale-strewn shores were imbued with poetic pathos and populated by the spectral torments of various literary creations. They visited the cave where the bard Fingal allegedly sang his doleful songs, and scanned the horizon for traces of Coleridge's accursed Mariner. On Dover's chalky cliffs, they pondered King Lear's unsuccessful attempt to hurl himself to his death; on the black rocks of Morven, they read aloud the resounding cadences of Ossian.

Beach cultists *à l'extrême*, the Romantics traveled to the eastern, western, and southwestern coasts of England, to look at land across the broad expanse of estuaries such as those on the shore of Southampton Water, or the pebbled banks of the River Ore where it drained into the sea, or the wooded banks of the Orwell, or the flats by the Wash. They were captivated by the Lincolnshire coast, with its cornfields running down to the verge of sand dunes, or the Isle of Wight, where wheat crowned the lower cliffs and ripe corn toppled over onto the beach. With its rocky cliffs and tight, shingled beaches looking out over "nothingness," this lozenge-shaped island was in great vogue among solitary wanderers until it was discovered by Queen Victoria. Seeking solitude, they then retreated to Suffolk's shores, where the land met the sea in a blaze of bracken and purple heather. There, they took up residence in roomy, moss-grown farmhouses nestled into a rare clump of fir or oak in the heather-clad hills, from which they could glimpse a dim Holland across the sea. The charm of these rustic retreats lay precisely in their sense of timelessness and remoteness.

When peace was restored in 1816, after more than two decades of war and revolution, Britons once again traveled freely on the Continent. The institution of the Grand Tour, the classical bent of education, and the intense archeological exploration of the Mediterranean coastline continued to inspire new generations to visit ancient ruins. Members of the venerable Society of the Dilettanti, young British aristocrats joined by their love of classical literature, ranged over the sun-spanked excavations at Pompeii, studying the frescoes and statuary and retracing the seashore promenades of the early Romans. One of the most prominent members of the beach literati was Lord Byron, who, alone or in the company of friends, mistresses, and admirers, made frequent pilgrimages to the sites of ancient beaches commemorated by Virgil, Cicero, Pliny, and Juvenal. On one occasion, his friend the beautiful Countess of Blessington made her way through an orange grove and came across some ruins at the very edge of the sea. She surmised that they had once been part of the baths attached to Cicero's old villa, and, "tempted by their seclusion and the purity of the water . . . bathed therein" and "felt invigorated by the briny element."

Byron voyaged to Greece, Turkey, Sardinia, and Malta. The poet's prodigious swimming feats earned him the adulation of all Europe and the moniker "The English Fish." At the age of twenty-two, he succeeded in crossing the Hellespont, now known as the Dardanelles, on his second try. "The current," he wrote to a friend, "renders it hazardous, so much so, that I doubt whether Leander's conjugal powers must not have been exhausted in his passage to paradise." He was referring to the legendary swimmer who had crossed that treacherous, narrow strait, through which the waters of the Black Sea pour into the Mediterranean. In antiquity, Helle, for whom the straits are named, drowned here. Since then, swimming the four-mile channel that separates Europe and Asia has been a rite of passage for intrepid youths seeking maturity, and mature men longing for youth.

Another tutor of aquatic pleasures was the Romantic Shelley, who consummated a lifelong, almost pathological love affair with water by drowning, a volume of Sophocles in hand, off Viareggio, in the Ligurian Sea. Shelley had never learned to swim, as much for want of athletic ability as on principle: Some years before his death, the poet, carefully coached by a friend who had mastered a series of aquatic moves learned from South Sea Islanders, plunged into a deep pool in the Arno River. But instead of floating on his back, as he had been instructed to do, he sank to the bottom and lay there, unmoving. Had his friend not intervened promptly, Shelley would have drowned on the spot.

The poet loved to watch the surface of the water for hours at a time, lost in its stillness and entranced by the mathematical precision of ripples agitating its serenity. In the mutable faces of water he read the moods of nature. Caught in the throes of poetic inspiration, he intoned verses to the sea, which was at once his muse and his ideal, mute interlocutor. It was said that, away from water, Shelley languished so acutely that only by plunging his head into a washbasin could he revive his spirits. He was never happier than on the Italian coast. Dividing his time between translating and composing, he recharged his creative batteries by bathing, frequently alone but sometimes accompanied by the voluptuous Claire Claremont, half-sister of his reticent bride, Mary Wollstonecraft Shelley. Boating on the Bay of Baiae, he was entranced by the "hollow caverns clothed with the glaucous sea-moss, and the leaves and branches of those delicate weeds that pave the unequal bottom of the water."

The beach, for Shelley, was the threshold to the lost world of classical antiquity and to that ultima Thule (ultimate reach) of experience, still shrouded in mystery and awaiting human exploration. It was the last frontier, a horizon beyond which lay a road map for transmutation into a better, perfectible self. Beneath the pellucid waves lay the submarine palaces and towers of lost civilizations and startling, bizarre forms of natural life. But, most of all, the poets, schooled on the myths of Narcissus and Hermaphroditus, sought in the depths of the sea to look deep into their own souls, to contemplate their own images, and to emerge transformed. There was, in Shelley's passion for water, also a distinct trace of the death wish. During his final voyage across the Gulf of Spezia, his boat was foundering in the heavy seas when an Italian vessel hove into view with the intention of lending assistance. Shelley refused all help. As the legend is recounted, he physically restrained his companion from lowering the sails, which would have kept him from sinking.

AN OCEAN OF EMOTION

Where these Romantic poets led—and died—others followed. It is hard to overestimate the power of their example and their grip on the imagination of their contemporaries. Byron's and Shelley's mixture of narcissistic self-absorption and flirtation with death would mark the Romantic attitude toward the sea. Their poetry, deeply autobiographical, and their deeds shaped the aesthetic tastes and the life habits of privileged young men and women in England and on the Continent for decades.

Some years after Shelley's drowning, the poet Matthew Arnold found his way to the same "soft blue Spezian bay," where he, too, felt the lure of the deep. Ever since early childhood, Arnold had nurtured the rather peculiar fantasy of being a corpse at the bottom of Lake Windermere. Now, lying on the soft sea floor and looking up at the surging ceiling of water, he realized how difficult it was "ever to bring one's head up out of it." Laden with associations of antiquity, the warm sea was to him, and to other Romantics, the entombing womb, the resting place of everything classical and ideal, a spiritual home, a forbidden realm from which lesser mortals recoiled, but to which the true sons and daughters of Homer went for inspiration and succor. The sea was, to them, another lost universe.

Swimming historian Charles Sprawson, author of *Haunts of the Black Masseur,* argues that it was the Romantics who actually invented swimming in the postclassical era. Until they took it up, this activity served no purpose other than traversing water. Not many people bothered to swim, or even had the occasion to learn. The Romantics, of course, were not particularly interested in the practical applications of swimming; only the moderns would make a virtue out of the therapeutic value of aquatic exercise. Rather, it was the access that swimming afforded to the psychological or, more broadly, the spiritual dimension that drew Romantics to this sport. Aquatic immersion gave them an unprecedented way of experiencing the body. Suspended in water, they imagined themselves released from the tyranny of gravity, hovering high above the earth, carried along by waves and currents.

In fact, most Romantics describe being transformed in some fundamental way by their immersions at the beach. For the British painter Benjamin Haydon, swim-

Because of its stability in the surf, the catamaran was a dependable lifesaving device on better-equipped beaches. (Bettmann Archive)

ming catalyzed a heart-of-darkness metamorphosis, releasing him from the rigid intellectual corset of civilization, and returning him to a redemptive state of innocence. The artist wrote about bathing at Brighton, where he "rolled in the sea, shouted like a savage, laved [his] sides like a bull in a green meadow, dived, swam, floated and came out refreshed." The French Symbolist Paul Valéry described experiencing a forgotten primal and authentic version of himself in the water. "It seems to me," he wrote, "that I discover and recognize myself when I return to this universal element. My body becomes the direct instrument of my mind, the author of its ideas. To plunge into water, to move one's whole body, from head to toe, in its wild and graceful beauty, to twist about in its pure depths, this is for me a delight only comparable to love." All in all, the unique physical sensations associated with swimming offered a psychological release, a sense of being reborn, rejuvenated, and reconnected with nature, that no other medium could provide.

It was during the same period that Swinburne spoke of his swims as forays into a "paradise lost," where "another and better world" awaited the beach enthusiast. Swinburne adored the cold northern seas off Northumberland. In his novel *Lesbia Brandon*, he describes the powerful sensations experienced by his autobiographical protagonist, Herbert, as he confronts this body of water for the first time. On the beach, the face of his hero "trembled and changed, his eyelids tingled, his limbs yearned all over: the colors and savors of the sea seemed to pass in at his eyes and mouth, all his nerves desired the divine touch of it, all his soul saluted it through his senses." For Swinburne, swimming was a religious experience. He wrote about his beach encounters with an unbridled passion. "I ran like a boy, tore off my clothes, and hurled myself into the water," he writes of a November dip off the southern coast of England. "And I was in Heaven! The whole sea was literally golden as well as green—it was liquid and living sunlight in which one lived and moved and had one's being. And to feel that in deep water is to feel—as long as one is swimming out, if only a minute or two—as if one was in another world of life, and one far more glorious than even Dante ever dreamed of in his paradise."

What all this meant to the beach was nothing short of revolutionary. Of the beach and the sea, the Romantic artist and poet made one vast metaphor for emotion. From now on—until the bourgeoisie surged in great numbers to the shore in the 1840s and 1850s—the beach enjoyed the highest spiritual prestige it ever would. The social elites, which in this period comprised the aristocracy of intellect and talent—artists, writers, musicians, philosophers, and their hangers-on—were drawn to the symbolic value of the beach. The ways in which they confronted the seashore—the poses they adopted, the experiences they recorded, the meanings they discovered—became the templates for a new sensibility and a novel set of practices that developed on cusp of land and sea.

EROTICISM ON THE BEACH

The intense physical experiences of the seashore—the scouring of the sand, the stroking of the wind, the slapping of water—were interpreted by Romantics as impersonal analogues to erotic contact. Poets such as Jean-Paul, Chateaubriand, and Shelley spoke of the body's immersion in water as a sexually tinged encounter, and sexualized the beach as a realm of orgasmic sensations. The sea was both mother and mistress, at once a source of vitality and an agent of debilitation. The German Romantic Novalis longed to dive into what was for him the cosmic equivalent of the waters of the maternal womb. Valéry described swimming as "fornication with the wave" and a "delight only comparable to love." Under the increasingly erotic spell of late Romantics, it was no longer sufficient to find a vantage point from which one could contemplate the grandiose vistas of the ocean. Now, tutored by lust-longing poets and artists, visitors came to the seashore to enter into a much more intimate relationship with the shore: to actually sit on the sand, to swim in the water.

STEAMING TO THE SEASHORE

In 1808, at Euston Square in London, a large crowd of gawkers gathered around a wooden palisade, craning their necks and jostling for a look at the sturdy Cornishman who was standing in the center barking orders at a

With its spectacular cliffs, arches, and "needles," the beach at Étretat was frequently recorded by such celebrated artists as Boudin, Courbet, Corot, Le Poittevin, and Monet. (Eugène Le Poittevin, *Bathing at Étretat*, 1865-56, private collection)

handful of workers. A peculiar track had been laid in a large circle, and on it the workers were straining to lower a sort of large iron barrel on wheels, with a stovepipe on one end and an open carriage on the other. When the contraption was in place, the Cornishman adjusted a few levers and, with a low roar, the thing began to move on its flanged wheels, hissing and clanking, gushing smoke and sparks as it picked up speed. Round and round it chugged, eliciting cries of amazement and shrieks of alarm from the bystanders. This noisy chunk of metal was Richard Trevithick's locomotive, *Catch Me Who Can,* and within seventeen years it would graduate from a fairgrounds novelty to a potent force in everyday life, hauling everything from coal and hay to hogs and crowned heads of state, and, of most interest to our subject, bringing people of slim means and limited time to the seaside.

As the Romantic fashion for sojourning at the shore gained ground and converts, it was getting increasingly difficult for the "sacred" adepts to find the requisite isolation and virginality of seaside sites without being trailed, sooner or later, by a "profane" crowd. As long as access to the beach was arduous and expensive, solitude at the seashore was not hard to find outside such established resorts as Weymouth and Brighton. But rapid improvements in travel and the invention of the public holiday would set the stage for the recreational inundation of the seashore.

Throughout the eighteenth century, when travelers coped with only the most rudimentary infrastructure of tourism, travel to the seashore was a complicated and time-consuming proposition. Everything—linens, chamber pots, pillows, tables, wine, food, books—had to be transported by private carriage. The trip from London to Brighton required several days of bone-jarring discomfort along rutted roads, with frequent stops for changes of horses and horseshoes, replacement of broken wheels and axles, long waits for boat transfers, and overnight stops at inns. A mail coach introduced at the turn of the century cut travel time to just under two days. Then, in 1815, a steamboat line opened between London and Gravesend. The service expanded to Margate five years later, and soon ran to resorts up and down the coast. The expense of a trip to the beach was now no longer beyond the means of the middle class.

In one of those fascinating ironies of history, the taste for the natural was begotten by the machine. The first passenger-carrying railway was inaugurated amid great fanfare in Liverpool on September 15, 1830. Brass bands entertained the spectators, and various personages of distinction—including the Duke of Wellington, who some years earlier had dismissed trains as useless—were on hand. Enormous crowds lined the road, shouting and waving hats and handkerchiefs as the cars flew by.

By current standards, there was nothing the least bit enjoyable about these early rail excursions. Passengers were stuffed into open "tubs" with-

For those who did not wish to swim, seaside resorts offered a plethora of diversions: donkey rides, puppet shows, strolling minstrels, fortune-tellers, and exhilarating turns on the toboggan slide. (Culver Pictures)

out seats, showered with soot and hot ash, assaulted by sparks, buffeted by wind, and deafened by the belching, screeching, clanging, and roaring. But for the most part, those early excursionists cared only for the thrilling sensation of speed and the prospect of seemingly limitless mobility.

During the next seven years alone, ninety-three railway acts were passed, with dozens more to follow shortly. To be sure, it was not always smooth going. Large estate holders put up a fuss about tracks destroying fox hunting, and barge and stagecoach companies raised the alarm about unfair competition. Staunch traditionalists feared cheap train travel would distract the laboring classes from their main duty, which was to work, and erode the very foundations of social order. Physicians added to the anxiety by issuing cautionary bulletins about the pulmonary complications of smoke and cold rushing air, and worrying about the effect of noise and rapid movement on "nervous" dispositions. By 1841, however, medical science had more or less conceded that the hazards of train travel were minimal compared with the benefits of quick and inexpensive passage to the healing seaside.

The upshot was that, within three or four decades, railroads succeeded in completely altering time-honored patterns of work, leisure, and play.

The biggest impact was felt in the cities, where, driven by the intensification of the enclosure system, workers had been streaming from the countryside since the mid-eighteenth century. Penned together into claustrophobic, sordid slums, they were mired in an oppressive, unhealthy landscape of slag heaps, factories, smokestacks, and brick walls. The only alternatives to work were boredom and the cheap gin shop. "Moral decay" was also endemic. Between the start of the 1800s and 1870, Britain's population doubled to twenty-six million, the better part of it squeezed into slum housing.

Rail travel offered one way out of hell. Now the word "holiday" became part of the common vocabulary of workers, and, come Sunday, they crowded into trains for boisterous, exciting, thoroughly modern outings. The passage of the Bank Holiday Act of 1871, which set aside a fixed number of leisure days at Christmas, Easter, Whitsun, and the beginning of August, established the public holiday, and seashore "day tripping" became an institution. Entire families moved coastward, laden with collapsible stools, umbrellas, buckets, shovels, and hampers bursting with food and drink.

Every weekend, a trainload of boisterous men, women, and children would spill onto the bucolic serenity of a Blackpool or Brighton. London artisans and their families crowded into hoys, raffish young men boarded fast coaches for the Steyne at Brighton, the wool merchants' daughters took over the Assembly Rooms at Scarborough. They came not for their health, to decipher nature's code, or for spirituality, but for sheer delight. Imagine them swarming at the water's edge, squalling and screaming at the novel sensation of waves, or prowling town streets in search of cheap eats and a pint of ale. As the day wore on, a cloying smell of spirits mingled with the vapors of sweaty bodies and wet wool. The confrontation between the urban hordes and the genteel holidaymakers on the beach was a collision of cultures, and in those resorts within easiest reach of the cities, it was the genteel who first decided to cede.

MID-CENTURY SEA CURES

If melancholy and spleen were the disorders that drew patients to the beach in the eighteenth century, in the nineteenth, tuberculosis was the *maladie du jour* for the Romantic generation. Known as the great white plague, this pulmonary affliction was the dark underbelly of urban industrialization and crowding, spreading from city to city, reaching into every class, and leaving its imprint on virtually every aspect of life. It influenced ideas of feminine beauty as ideally pallid and frail. It shaped notions of feminine behavior, integrating fainting spells and excitability into the expected repertoire of female responses. In fashion, it motivated the adoption of high collars among men to conceal the scrofulous scars left by the disease.

In the preantibiotic era, there were no "magic bullets" for tuberculosis. In desperation, physicians experimented with various palliatives, including the papaya-juice "cure," injections of carbolic-acid solutions, inhalations of menthol oil, and even sulfur-gas enemas. Although these strategies somewhat ameliorated the symptoms, they left the infection untouched. The most hopeful avenue seemed to be one that would provide a global attack on the disease by controlling every possible variable, from diet to environment to exercise. And the beach seemed the perfect solution. Practitioners seized on the armamentarium of coastal nature with high hopes. The wind, the water, even the texture of the land itself, the quality and quantity of picturesque views, the disposition of the promenade, the invalid's residence, diet, and water—all these variables were entered into the pharmacopoeia of the nineteenth-century regimen.

In this respect, Southampton offered an intriguing case study for advanced research into the "science" of medico-topography. Situated on a high, gravelly bank that separates the River Itchen from the bay, Southampton boasted excellent drainage, which meant that dampness—bane of the British climate—did not compromise the salubrious effect of the atmosphere. The stone-shingled beach, though a deterrent to bathers and riders, possessed the unexpected therapeutic effect of warming the feet of walkers, the mechanics of which a contemporary physician cited by A. B. Granville extolled: "With each step, the sole of the foot, pressing upon a plane of loose polyangular or round bits of flint, produces friction and, consequently, heat. This repeated every half-second, as each step is taken during a long walk, ends by exciting considerable warmth in the foot, and the promenader returns to his home with a quickened circulation in the lower extremities." The same practitioner specified precise therapeutic guidelines for all stages of tuberculosis. Seriously consumptive patients were to be lodged close to the sea, overlooking the promenade by the very center of town. The bustling activity and merriment of the promenade would divert their minds from morbid thoughts. They would also be assured a constant supply of vitalizing air, which was wafted in by a generally southerly wind—the only sort recommended for invalids. Sites that caught easterly winds were to be avoided at all costs.

So important a role was environment thought to play in the therapeutic outcome that even the layout of accommodations fell under medical scrutiny. Severely affected consumptives were lodged only on the first floor. In winter, windows facing east and north were to be hung with double sashes, and they were to remain closed at all times. If ventilation was required, it could come only from a southerly or westerly window, opened only at noon on a sunny day. City planners and developers took all these prescriptions to heart and designed the streets in formations of crescents and terraces so as to provide seaside lodgings that conformed as closely as possible to medical specifications. With the sea as its principal design generator, the architecture of leisure, perhaps for the first time in history, was elevated to the pantheon of medical therapeutics.

The annals of seaside resorts were filled with lachrymose accounts of tubercular patients, preferably frail and beautiful young ladies, wasting away on the strand. Interestingly, a sort of literary genre emerged from the hybridization of medical case histories with the morality tale, whereby the beach resort figured as a repository of ambiguous, marginal values. Although the sea is where young women came to be healed of their tuberculosis, often they instead fell prey to some handsome scoundrel, who invariably seduced and abandoned them. Before expiring, the violated maiden died a double death—of both reputation and spirit. In a not-too-subtle manner, these literary accounts linked physical deterioration with moral turpitude, and implicated the beach, with its shifting borders and transitional figures, as the cause for the patient's sudden loss of ethical orientation. Thus, by degrees, the beach acquired in the popular mind the typically doubled and oxymoronic meaning of the *pharmacon*, a drug that can both heal and kill.

Not only was the beach seldom able to heal a patient definitively; it was also terribly expensive, unwieldy, and elitist. Only the wealthy could afford to sequester themselves for up to six months of the year in a resort, with personal servants and physicians. The overwhelming majority of the population had either to hope that their infection would spontaneously resolve, or to look for deliverance in death. Other strategies for treating tuberculosis were eventually found to have better results; by 1860, the virulence of the disease showed a marked decline.

The bathing beauty graced innumerable picture postcards. (authors' collection)

In turn, the specifically therapeutic function of the beach began to atrophy, leaving room there for other activities, which satisfied a different set of social and cultural agendas. Not until the years immediately following World War I would the beach once again enjoy a therapeutic prestige—though this time the lure would be not water or air, but sun.

THE DISCREET CHARMS OF
THE BOURGEOIS BEACH

Regina Palace Hotel, Nice, 1892. A warm, silky breeze sweeps in from the horizon's edge, which, under the gaze of the morning sun, glows the color of a ripe persimmon. The sea is smooth as oil. A respectable collection of British *hivernants,* as the seasonal visitors are dubbed, begins the day with a leisurely breakfast on the hotel's canopied terrace with a commanding view of the sea. Surveying the dazzling beaches of the Mediterranean, the guests swell with a sense of superiority and election. In this hotel, where Queen Victoria had stayed, they discuss Sunday's sermon at the English church and cluck over the carnival, with its storms of confetti and the low behavior of the Niçois. To them, the idea of the British as the most just of the just, the bravest of the brave, the most honorable of the honorable, seems perfectly natural, and there is nothing in the least implausible to them in the idea that if God had to choose a nationality he would not hesitate to be British.

Graciously accommodating, the hefty and ornate grand hotels along the Riviera gear their service to the British standard of good taste. White-gloved waiters in dress suits serve an English breakfast and offer English newspapers. Then follows the constitutional, a stately stroll along the manicured paths of the hotel grounds, richly planted with palms, succulents, bougainvillea, and Australian mimosa, and then out to the Promenade des Anglais, which, since the early days of the English colony in the 1790s, was laid out to accommodate their predilection for strolling by the sea. By midmorning, the sun has overtaken the sky, and it is time for a plunge.

The gravelly beach slopes gently into the still sea. Two rows of changing cabins—ocher, pink, and blue—radiate from the central pavilion. In front of it, a mobile dock is wheeled into position, its enormous front wheels deep in the water, its small ones high up on the beach. The swimmers walk along the length of this wooden structure and dive from its far end. Ladies in promenade dress occupy chairs in front of the cabins, balancing dainty parasols in their hands. Deeply tanned *baigneurs* hand the children into the waves.

After the bathe, a group of friends forms a boating party. Their destination is a nearby fishing village, with an obligatory stop at a fishmonger's shack for fresh shellfish, *socca*—the traditional Niçois crêpe made of chickpea flour, oil, and water—and a glass of fortifying wine. Lunch overlooking a tranquil cove comes next, and segues into a siesta to "kill" the hottest part of the day and sleep off the digestive torpor of too many rich courses.

By mid-afternoon, they are ready for another excursion. With the beach to their backs, elegantly dressed men and women load into carriages for a ride through the fig-filled paradise of Provence, where velveteen hillsides sprawl like sheared sheep loins, and shaggy eucalyptus hover over peach-colored villas. They head for a church celebrated for its medieval frescoes, an art gallery, or an antiquarian curio listed in one of the various guidebooks. Baedeker's, Murray's, and Cook's vade mecums in hand, the tourists peruse the day's attraction, dutifully registering its key points, some sketching in their notebooks. One or two wander off with easel, paper, paints, and brushes, to dabble in the fad of *plein-air* painting, recording picturesque vistas of cerulean seas, verdigris cypresses, and madder bougainvillea.

Upon returning, they file into the palm court for tea. A small orchestra plays Strauss waltzes and muted marches. Fortified by watercress sandwiches and lemon-curd tarts, they retire to dress for dinner and the whirl of entertainments. Gentlemen don formal attire; ladies slip into frothy, décolleté gowns, pin fresh gardenias in their hair, and wriggle their fingers into

The beach resort offered city dwellers opportunities to re-experience nature without sacrificing comfort and familiar urban routines. (Eugène Boudin, *Approaching Storm*, 1864, Art Institute of Chicago, Mr. and Mrs. Lewis Larned Coburn Memorial Collection)

long, tight gloves. Evening is the culmination of the day's excursions into fantasy: a perfectly staged enactment of a society better than anything that could be imagined. Cheeks flushed from sun and the evening's glass of port, the guests gossip in subdued voices and attend distractedly to the music, magic shows, and recitations staged for their benefit. If they think at all of the world outside the walls of their resplendent hotel, they do so only with condescension and pity.

■■■■■■

The beach resorts that erupted along the shores of the Atlantic, the Baltic, the Mediterranean, and the Adriatic were the children of the cities and the great town-planning movements of the nineteenth century. Banks and private individuals invested heavily in new forms of transportation—railways and steamship lines—and created new destinations, utopian seaside recreational towns, dedicated to the proposition that life is to be enjoyed in a place and time entirely removed from the messy business of survival.

For all their local variations, seaside resorts of the nineteenth century invariably crystallized around the nucleus of grand hotel, casino, and bathing establishment. In each of these, the architecture, appointments, service, and behavior heightened and transformed everyday life, giving the visitor a sense of power and mastery. In the grand hotel, an army of deferential workers was disciplined to provide guests an experience of luxurious ease, of control over their time, of access to natural and cultural resources, and, not to be minimized, the secret pleasure of knowing that, at least for the time being, the staff that waited on them had none of these things. With its around-the-clock schedule of excursions, teas, dances, dinners, and games, the grand hotel invited its clients to engage in public rituals of leisure and an organized sociability.

The casino intensified, celebrated, and exposed the power of the money that made resort life possible. With its grandiose architecture—a hybrid of temple, stock exchange, and opera house—the gambling casino was a shrine to the mysterious laws of chance operating in the marketplace of the real world. Long banned in France, Italy, and Germany, the first seaside gambling casino was founded in 1863 as a concession of the Société Anonyme des Bains de Mer et du Cercle des Étrangers à Monaco. Where Monte Carlo led, other resort cities, such as Deauville and Cannes, followed, as the ban on gambling was lifted. In sumptuous chambers, on parquet floors polished to mirror-brilliance, in the glare of crystal chandeliers, the tedious business of making money was transformed into an elegant and diverting game. The roulette wheel and the baccarat table were the casino's analogues to the border experience of the beach: potential sources of plea-

An armada of bathing machines at Margate, England, hauled visitors to and from their dip. The Modesty Hood, a retractable canvas awning suspended over the bathing platform, was featured only at the more conservative resorts. (Bettmann Archive)

sure and of pain, gateways to regeneration or ruin, that stimulated a powerful rush of adrenaline.

The magnet for all these activities—their raison d'être and justification—was the bathing establishment. Within the span of half a century, large tracts of Europe's undifferentiated beachfront were split up, divided by fences, ropes, and walls into postage-stamp-sized plots bristling with awnings, cabins, umbrellas, and furniture, all marshaled together in the service of the human body. Even more than in the eighteenth century, when largely naked bodies were delivered to the waves by lumbering bathing machines, in the nineteenth century, the hoopla surrounding aquatic immersion reached extravagant proportions. Nothing about contact with water was simple in these retreats. The bathing hut on wheels, largely eliminated from Western European resorts, was replaced by an elaborate bathing costume. The body was shod, covered, clad, and bonneted according to entirely urban notions of dress. The medical regimen of abrupt immersion evolved an entirely new physical dimension with the introduction of swimming as therapeutic exercise.

In prerevolutionary France, the life of the mind rather than of the body had lured the first holidaymakers to the seaside. For the British, the taste for the sea had been inculcated by therapy and the search for a new experience of spirituality. Through the psychosensory filter of the sublime, the very concrete experience of the body—its reactions to the shock of immersion in cold, rough water, and to the terror of the ocean's limitless expanse—was found to open the door to a fresh sense of wonder. There, at the beach, the Englishman fused the imperative of his questing scientific mind with the spiritual demands of his soul. Each immersion in the waves was a kind of baptism into renewed vigor, health, mental acuity. Fortified by the briny air, the wan British aristocracy could resume its hereditary work of leading the nation to fresh global conquests. Breasting the waves, the members of the ruling class symbolically re-enacted Britannia's supremacy on the seas. There, at the limit of its home territories, the Briton read all the symbolism of his culture.

In France, too, the invention of the seashore holiday was the work of the aristocracy. But health was less important than it had been in shaping attitudes in England. For the French, fashion—or the art of subjecting the practicalities of life to a ruling intellectual or aesthetic design—moved the aristocracy to the beach. Daniel Roche, the French scholar of the Enlightenment, has told the fascinating story of how the classical model of *otium, cum dignitate,* or leisure, with dignity, gradually penetrated into the intellectual life of the French *ancien régime.*

The ancient texts of Cicero, Propertius, Horace and Ovid, Seneca and Pliny, had told of the special sociability of bathing resorts, where the intimacy of blood and the kinship of the spirit formed the basis of a community dedicated to pleasure. On the French seashore, the constraints and intrigues of court life could hold no sway. Among the rocks and sand, some of the more independent members of *ancien régime* found the opportunity to create private worlds of elective affinities, select circles of family and close friends, exempt from the mandated sociability of the official court. An oasis of leisure, the seacoast was recast in the image of the classical retreat.

In his memoir *Voyage dans le Finistère,* the Frenchman Jacques Cambry described one such nest of gentlefolk on the French coast. The year was 1795, and the revolution had just reshuffled the nation's social order. In the new French Republic, the vogue for all things dating from the Roman republic held every patriot in its spell. The great revolutionary painter David filled the walls of the Académie's salons with his rousing evocations of Roman virtue. Supporters of the revolution donned approximations of Roman costume: delicate sandals and diaphanous, body-revealing frocks for women, and for men clinging trousers and hose that came as close to the nudity of classical statuary as costume had yet dared. The new mythology and iconography of reform tapped into Roman republican imagery.

Cambry arrived at the home of his friend Mauduit, a "noble sage," who self-consciously strove to re-enact the cultivated hospitality of his Roman models. The texts of Tibullus, Juvenal, Martial, and Virgil, and other Augustan writers crowded the shelves of his library, where he retreated with friends to browse in the universe of the mind and to read Tasso, Ariosto, and Petrarch. He had built his house according to the recommendation of the ancients: situated between the two antithetical domains of civility and savagery, where one could be appreciated always by contrast to the other. The windows overlooked the beach and, beyond it, the jagged coast. Landward, the house looked toward the woods, a finely cultivated orchard, and a flower garden bearing the clear imprint of human cultivation. Accompanied by his wife, his daughter Roxane, a young engineer, and a scattering of young ladies, Mauduit strolled the grounds, conversing on Molière, Rabelais, and Bayle. Weather permitting, they descended to the beach and, in a merry, mixed group of gentlemen and ladies, bathed and swam in a cove of rocks they called "Diana's baths."

ADVENTURES IN THE LEISURE TRADE

Until 1816, crossing the Channel was something of an undertaking. In his travelogue, Smollett describes the trip as a combination of high comedy and melodrama. The human constitution, ravaged by seasickness and strained by tedious negotiations with various ill-disposed sea captains, porters, draymen, and customs officials, seldom survived the ordeal with equanimity. In 1816, however, the first steamships crossed the Channel, and within five years, the French had established regular ferry service between Dover and Calais. In 1818, the American Black Ball Line began offering bimonthly transatlantic crossings on sailing vessels that took three weeks to reach Europe, and five to return to the States. By 1838, steamships dominated sea travel, and sailing time was reduced to nine or ten days. Affluent Americans and Europeans from the "leisure class" devoted anywhere from three months to a year to touring each other's countries.

British tourists trooped abroad at a brisk pace. The half-million who left their native land in the early 1790s swelled to nearly a million in a little over a decade. These were a new brand of travelers, no longer adventurers but tourists proper, the founding members of a new human subspecies that had no tolerance for inconvenience, discomfort, or unfamiliarity in the basic arrangements of life. When abroad, they expected a British diet, deferential service, and an English newspaper in the sitting room.

The French were less demanding. They tended to stay closer to home. Also, travel, plain and simple, was to them as much a necessity of life as a baguette and a bottle of Beaujolais. In 1860, the newspaper columnist Benjamin Gastineau wrote that, for Parisians in particular, "Traveling is to live. It is to feel disengaged from all social restraint and prejudice." In his *Fleurs du mal* of 1857, the poet Charles Baudelaire had extolled train travel as a means of escape from the pressures, the ugliness, and the venality of the city and the city-bred self. The venue par excellence for this self-renewal was the beach. Not by chance did the French invent the axiom "Nearness to the sea destroys pettiness."

In the mid-1830s, the first major railway line was inaugurated from Paris; within sixty years, over fifteen thousand miles of track existed, serving all of France. The system of canals was dramatically expanded. Trams as well as fleets of the *omnibus américain*—double-decker horse-drawn buses—provided cheap, efficient service between city and country, railroad depot and center of town. The Parisian bourgeoisie, followed closely by provincials, bought up parcels of land, first on the shores of the Atlantic and then the Mediterranean, and constructed villas with names such as Ma Petite Folie (My Little Folly), Pif Paf, Blondinette, and Mimosette. But the majority of the haute bourgeoisie still preferred the pampering of grand hotels, with their cosmopolitan clientele and impeccable service.

Newly created travel agencies rose to the occasion, both in England and on the Continent. Shrewd in gauging the drift of the travel market, professional travel brokers set about creating a special tourist world, with all the appearances of the real world but actually carefully insulated from it. They encouraged the construction of grand hotels in Cannes, Monte Carlo, Baden-Baden, Carlsbad, and the great capitals of the world. They chartered steamers and trains to transport their clientele in comfort, cleanliness, and familiar surroundings.

When Thomas Cook began organizing weekend excursions to British seaside resorts, he inadvertently paved the way for mass invasions of exclusive resorts by economizing holidays for middle-class families and impecunious day trippers. At the same time, he created a market for travel to foreign destinations that served both the privileged and the upwardly mobile. Under the press of "commoners," the elite were again in full retreat to new sites of uncommon pleasures.

Spearheaded by Cook and abetted by a host of emulators on both sides of the Atlantic, the organized tour took the shape of a small number of strangers banding together under the leadership of an experienced traveler to savor the novelty of modern modes of transportation and alien cultures. In the four decades since his virgin venture—a trip to the sea at Liverpool from Leicester in 1845—Cook and his meticulously groomed staff of tour guides ferried and guided hundreds of thousands of Englishmen, Americans, and Europeans to historical, cultural, and recreational sites in each other's lands. A great many more signed up fo day trips to the seashore, where their sheer numbers and simple ways horrified visitors of distinction and refinement.

Travelers abroad, of course, came from a higher cut of society. Newly monied or aspiring to aristocratic polish, they were keen to imitate the itineraries and reactions of their betters. The Victorian tour abroad was a good way to accomplish some social objectives: giving parvenus cultural depth, a veneer of sophistication, opportunities to meet genuine folk of breeding— all indispensable aids to climbing the next rung in the social ladder. Entire libraries of guidebooks appeared to counsel the neophyte traveler in what to look for abroad, how to behave, and even, upon returning home, how to parlay the experience into social capital. Dr. Abraham Eldon, author of *The Continental Oracle, or Maxims of Foreign Locomotion,* suggested that by "saying little, smiling less and listening not at all you will soon obtain what you claim: a *toto vertice* superiority over the multitude who have had the misfortune of having a home and of never leaving it."

Achieving such social distinctions came at a great expense, not so much to the wallet as to the nerves and digestion. The *terra incognita* that British travelers at the beginning of the Victorian era were entering when they set off for the south of France was a double jeopardy. First, there was the novelty of the natural setting: a sun twice as hot as the watery haze to which they were accustomed on the British shore, and rocky beaches full of unfamiliar flora and fauna. For another thing, the practical arrangements of life abroad were a challenge in themselves and, if the solicitous advice in guidebooks of the period is any indication, fraught with peril. Most travelers of this age were venturing beyond their national borders for the first time and traveling among people whose ideas of cleanliness, appropriate conduct between men and women, table manners, standards of privacy, and even volubility in public were quite different from their own.

From all accounts, it took a certain amount of courage, forbearance, and, perhaps most important, a steamer trunk full of prophylactic implements to prepare for a beach holiday in Normandy, Nice, Portofino, and eventually, in the more exotic reaches of Egypt, Turkey, and the North African coast. The first leg of the journey inevitably involved crossing the English Channel, a nauseating ordeal which dampened the ardor of all but the most wanderlust-bitten. Once on the Continent, the traveler had to cope with a plethora of challenges, for most of which even the most conscientious guidebooks left him unprepared. Thomas Cook's *The Excursionist* published copious advertisements for preparations and gadgets that would mitigate the assault of the alien setting. Among them were Keatings Powders, "the remedy for bugs, and beetles"; Dr. Collis Browne's chlorodyne to cure diarrhea; and Seymours' Patent Magnetic Amnyterion Appliances, which provided protection against seasickness.

For the personal safety of the traveler, there was the portable doorfastener and a Gladstone bag with a rope and pulley that could be attached to the window frame and used as a fire escape. Then, as now in Third World countries, a most irksome anxiety concerned facilities for accommodating the natural needs of the body. It was not uncommon for the respectable traveler to open a dresser drawer and find deposited therein something best flushed down the toilet. Except for the highest category of accommodations—if available at all—hotels and rooming houses had no sanitary facilities. The conjunction of intestinal traumas, inevitable then as now, with repugnant toilets made a nightmare out of a natural necessity. And so it was with considerable relief that travelers regarded a most ingenious offering in the pages of *The Excursionist,* a portable chamber pot recommended as an alternative to the "wretchedness, contamination and defilement of the public toilet." Designed specifically for women, this metal pail was disguised as a hat box and had a removable polished mahogany rim and a metal lid. The elegant "porto-let" spared a lady's "having to encounter, to meet and glide by the mustached foreigner (be he noble or peddler) with his waistcoat unbuttoned, cigar in mouth, and his hands fumbling at his braces, in the corridor . . . nor will they be subject to the insult of coming upon such a personage seated with the door open."

By the 1870s, the situation took a decisive turn for the better, at least for the monied, with the introduction of the first sleeping cars. Veritable grand hotels on wheels, they were the brainchild of George Nagelmackers, a Belgian, whose Wagons Lits Company made them available for commercial use in 1872. Initially, Nagelmackers had some difficulty persuading railway companies to include one of his cars in their trains. Newspapers were full of cartoons depicting satirists' speculations that these beds on wheels would turn into mobile bordellos. One panel of drawings depicted a succession of compartments as seen in cross section. In each, a fully dressed Victorian gentleman dallies with some curvaceous beauty in corset and bloomers. How many of these fantasies actually materialized is not known, but the erotic association they forged with travel remained firm.

By the 1880s, seven guineas could buy a ten-day trip to Menton, Nice, and Cannes, with a sideline to Monte Carlo for a bit of gambling. Foreign excursions to the beach—especially on the Riviera at the end of the century—were not always associated with respectability. Landlocked by public opinion, many Victorians simply would not admit having been there. After all, the self-appointed moral legislators of British society clicked their tongues over the "smart set" that gathered there, deeply convinced, as one correspondent to *The Times* scoffed, that "at Monte Carlo is to be found the very scum of all Europe."

Beach travel also, in an important sense, advanced the emancipation of middle-class women, helping them acquire a global perspective, test themselves, and open their minds. Women had begun traveling to distant beaches on their own in the eighteenth century. Hester Stanhope, Emmeline Stuart Wortley, Ida Pfeiffer, and others were in the vanguard of an army of peripatetic women who found exotic ports of call—including locations to which figures such as Lord Byron had pointed the way—to be a romantic escape from the restrictions and tedium of their lives. Women with more limited appetites or purses for adventure were particularly well served by Thomas Cook and other travel agents like him.

THE INVASION OF NORMANDY

The leisure invasion of Normandy began in July 1824, when Marie-Caroline, the Duchesse de Berry, introduced the French to the British fashion of bathing, by being carried, fully and magnificently dressed, into the water in a gilded sedan chair. Prior to this aqua-spectacle, Parisians had come to the sea only to see it and to eat freshly caught fish. By force of her charisma, passionate devotion to the shore, and superb sense of style, the Duchesse de Berry succeeded in transforming the modest fishing town of Dieppe into an aristocratic residence. Each year, her arrival in town was greeted by light shows, cannonades, recitations of poetry, and speeches of welcome by beribboned and decorated city fathers. The gracious duchess distributed gifts all around, then proceeded to a comedy and a ball staged in her honor.

On the historic occasion of her first visit, Marie-Caroline was driven to the sea costumed as an Amazon: a white blouse tightly gathered at the neck with a large black silk tie, and a hat festooned with a floating veil. As the official patron of the bathing establishment, she proceeded onto the beach, where she was then "exposed to the waves" by the inspector of the baths. The season was formally inaugurated. During the following weeks, as she would for years to come, the duchess bathed early in the morning, always in the company of ladies-in-waiting dressed as naiads, to the great admiration and delight of the local populace. Other members of the fading Restora-

In beaches without private bathing masters, the initiative for rescuing poor swimmers fell either on volunteers or on municipal employees. (Bettmann Archive)

tion aristocracy flocked to emulate her example, and joyously embraced the "Anglomania" of bathing, promenading, sightseeing, sketching, and easing the misery of the poor by bestowing alms and tending graciously to the sick.

After Marie-Caroline's advent, life at Dieppe took on a glorious, gilded edge. Until June, when the aristocracy descended, the town moved to the stately rhythm of invalids and convalescents, most of them British, guided in their therapy of immersion by physicians and dippers. After that date, however, the resort exploded into festivities. The fashionable Parisian crowd surged from beachfront to amateur concerts, whirled at masked balls thrown by the duchess, congregated on the promenade, sailed around the bay, and staged charitable bazaars. Within a few seasons, the bathing beach appeared like a fabled Oriental city, crowded with pavilions, tents, bazaar, vendors' booths, covered galleries, and gardens planted with shrubs and seeded with lawn.

The French Revolution of 1830, which ushered in the "Bourgeois Monarchy," brought a temporary suspension to the gaiety. Hearing of the change of regime, British visitors immediately returned to England, and the French bourgeoisie, anxious to dissociate itself from the discredited nobility, retreated to inland thermal spas. Only a handful of French aristocrats lingered in coastal spots, where they strolled despondently by the sea, the gentlemen on foot, the richly dressed ladies astride donkeys.

But this melancholy state of affairs was short-lived: Parisians soon returned. Most of them, however, were still reluctant to emulate the Duchesse de Berry's aquatic extravaganzas, preferring to promenade along the waterfront while the English colony indulged in what to most Frenchmen of the 1830s still seemed to be the eccentric practice of swimming. Only in the second half of the nineteenth century would the French themselves take up this peculiar activity and begin to frequent the salt water therapy center, a veritable "Versailles of the sea" built in 1856. When completed, the wood, stone, terra-cotta, iron, and bronze edifice would be hailed as a masterpiece of engineering and architecture. But, for the time being, the closest the French came to swimming was to follow the somberly clad British community on Sunday mornings as it trooped down to the beach, there to gather about a Union Jack and sing religious hymns. At other times, the French liked to keep count of the number of Britons out walking along the shore, recognizing those from across the Channel by their walking sticks, without which no self-respecting Englishman or lady ventured abroad.

Later in the century, the resort would once again receive the official stamp of approval by the Emperor Napoleon III and the Empress Eugénie, who, unstinting in their love for seaside diversions, commuted between

Dieppe and Trouville, sparking the erection of the spectacular *planches,* or boardwalks, and magnificent grand hotels and casinos. In 1853, they ordered the construction of an imperial palace, which housed the French royalty during their visits but was otherwise open to the Dieppe public. A cosmopolitan clientele frequented both resorts.

When, in the 1840s, the French bourgeoisie embraced the seaside holiday as a class prerogative, pleasure and leisure replaced the British-dominated penitential practices of the beach. European beach resorts, though continuing to supply therapeutic bathing facilities, gave therapy a position decidedly ancillary to recreation and leisure. In 1848, with the onset of Paris–Dieppe train service from the airy cast-iron-and-glass sheds of the Gare St.-Lazare, the second invasion of Normandy was under way. Rumbling toward the coast, past picturesque towns with Romanesque churches and Norman fortresses, the comfortable carriages transported the Parisians with well-behaved children in sailor suits, nannies in somber wools, ladies' maids, Pomeranians, and mountains of luggage.

In the long summer months, the Channel resorts of the French coast filled with a preponderance of women and children, who stayed for weeks at a time. During the week, when society was dominated by women, informal attire prevailed. Henry James, among others, was to discover a special charm in this loosening of the otherwise strict sartorial code. "You wear old clothes," he wrote, "you walk in canvas shoes, you deck your head with a fisherman's cap. . . . You lie on the pebbly strand most of the day, watching the cliffs, the waves, and the bathers." On Sundays and holidays, husbands commuted from Paris on what wits dubbed the "cuckold trains," and another, more formal rhythm prevailed.

THE AMUSING BEACH

The monopoly of the therapeutic British beach was gradually challenged all along the Atlantic seashore. At Ostend, Dunkirk, Dieppe, and Trouville, villages of brightly striped tents, colorful changing huts, and straw beach chairs gave the resorts the madcap aspect of a carnival. Stately palatial hotels stood far back from the water, fronting on broad boardwalks that were punctuated by ornate cast-iron benches. Flies—light, horse-drawn carriages—sped across the sands.

With its magnificent seawall stretching between town and sea, Ostend offered excellent promenades. Promptly at six o'clock in the evening, Ostend's seawall was transformed into an impromptu theater of strollers and diners, each contemplating the other, engaged in their respective pleasures. It was a custom in Ostend for the great houses and hotels lining the promenade to throw open the windows of their dining rooms so that it appeared as though the fronts of all the houses had been removed to display the whole of Ostend at table.

The bathing at this Belgian beach was largely confined—as it was at the majority of European resorts—to the morning hours. During the season, Ostend bathers took to the water from machines that were rolled into the surf after the bather started to prepare for the dip. Like the British, the Belgian bathing masters followed the ebb and rise of the tide religiously. As a result, it often happened that bathers found that their machines had been shifted many feet from their original positions, and the sodden, chilled swimmers were then compelled to spend many weary minutes hunting for their own particular van. Since the little houses on wheels were nearly identical, the unfortunates were likely to ruffle the tempers of the occupants of other vans by breaking in upon their privacy. Some entrepreneurial bathing masters found ways to individuate their machines by decorating them with advertisements for patent medicines and ladies' corsets.

At Scheveningen—Holland's most fashionable watering place—horse carriages and omnibuses ferried visitors throughout the summer season. From the vast veranda of the hotel, one could scarcely see the sea through the thicket of oddly shaped beach furniture, which visitors rented for the day. As tall as a man and wide enough to fit around a generous crinoline, the Dutch beach—or "wind"—chairs were monumental wickerwork baskets in the shape of large peanut shells hollowed out on one side to enclose the bather as in an upright cradle.

At Scheveningen, Holland, bathing machines, bath chairs, and canvas tents filled the beach from late fall through early spring, when the fashionable clientele took up residence in the luxury hotels. (Culver Pictures)

The resort at St. Malo constructed a remarkable bathing station for transporting swimmers from the beach into deep water. This consisted of an elevated platform on wheels that ran along a track extending from the shore halfway into the bay. At low tide the tracks were evident but at high tide, both the tracks and the scaffolding on which the platform rested were under water. As the contraption moved, it appeared to be gliding through the waves of its own accord. For a small fee, visitors were ferried out into the middle of the bay, and many took the ride for the sheer novelty of the experience.

Étretat and Trouville did not provide bathing machines. Instead, they constructed stationary bathhouses—narrow, wooden changing cabins set in rows parallel to the beach just beyond the high-tide line. Here all who wished to bathe changed out of the street clothing in which they had arrived at the beach. The strict etiquette of these resorts did not permit bathing attire for any activity other than actual swimming. For this reason, bathing dress could be seen only in the brief space between changing cabins and the sea. Elsewhere, as the French writer Guy de Maupassant wrote in his novel *Pierre and Jean,* the beach at Trouville was filled, from the pier as far as the Roches Noires, with "sun-shades of every hue, hats of every shape, dresses of every color, in groups outside the bathing huts, in long rows by the margin of the waves, or scattered here and there . . . [which] looked like immense bouquets on a vast meadow."

To prepare for swimming, bathers availed themselves of the services of bathhouse attendants, who stood ready to rent them a variety of implements and services, each of which could be paid for separately or purchased as a package. A *cabinet de luxe*—a large van near the surf—could be had for two francs. A towel cost ten centimes, a peignoir of white muslin another fifteen, and a bathing costume twenty-five centimes. A bathing box could be provided for thirty-five centimes and, for timid bathers, a *baigneur,* or bathing master, came along for forty centimes. The complicated negotiations that preceded the dip could be considerably reduced by purchasing a ticket for a *bain complet,* which included everything but the *baigneur.*

After shedding their street attire in the rickety canvas tents—which most bathers preferred to the more solid but also mildew-ridden wooden cabins—male and female bathers put on bathing attire and wrapped themselves in the voluminous peignoirs the bathing master held out for them. Thus enveloped from head to toe, they made their way to the water, where they discarded the outer garment for the duration of the swim. Upon emerging, they again donned the loose white gowns and, ghostlike, made their way back to the bathhouse, where the attendant had readied a basin of hot water to revive the numbed extremities.

Of all the British beach customs they adopted, the French were particularly fond of the institution of the bathing master. It was difficult to see a group bathing without remarking the dark blue or black clothes and hat of the *baigneur.* He was logically found at such places as Étretat, where the waves pounded the shore with great ferocity and force, but was also a fixture in the mildest of surfs and the shallowest of waters. Visitors to the beach at Trouville were often amused by the sight of a fastidious Parisian belle, in her ungainly bathing dress, clinging to the *baigneur* in water scarcely a foot deep, while he stood immovable, silent, and solemn. More than coquetry was at stake, for Frenchwomen were by and large less athletic and daring than their English or American sisters, who consequently had much less use for aquatic assistance.

IMPRESSIONISTS' EDEN

If in England it was the Romantics who had pioneered new perceptions of the beach, for the French it was the psychosis-plagued Impressionists who elevated the seaside holiday to its sybaritic status, applying dollops and splashes of paint to create an epiphany of light that gave God's own rainbow a run for its money. Though royalty and aristocracy legitimized bathing resorts and put them on the social map, it was in fact the artists and writers who scouted out most of the shore sites that would develop into vacation destinations. From the 1830s, cultivated Europeans were able to piece together a new "narrative" of the southern beach from the works of artists such as Jean-Baptiste Corot, George Sand, Frédéric Chopin, Johan Jongkind, Jean Courbet, Charles-François Daubigny, and Antoine Chintreuil. Their seashores were animated by the thought that one could become a better and more moral person through contact with the *isolated* beach. Inspired by their example, visitors to the sea expected to come away automatically restored in spirit, purified of vanities and petty worries—and, most important, spiritually reborn.

The next generation of artists—the Impressionists proper—reworked and elaborated this image of the beach into a social place for visitors from the city, civilized and organized, where the body came into carefully monitored contact with the waves, and the rituals of domesticity prevailed over therapy. Their idea of the beach did not involve wandering for hours in search of a desolate vantage from which to chronicle an uninhabited nature. Instead, they planted themselves squarely in the midst of seaside resorts that were easily accessible by train or steamer and already filled with people. In short, theirs was a tourist-based beach, celebrating the ideal marriage of city and nature as consummated in the fashionable resort. Between 1874 and 1886, artists such as Claude Monet, Alfred Sisley, Camille Pissarro, Pierre-August Renoir, and Berthe Morisot visited and painted the strip of coast running along the English Channel from Deauville to Étretat. Their beachscapes were beautiful, simple, and prosperous Edens of sailboats and loose-limbed bathers, fishermen, washerwomen, and urban tourists elegantly decked out or in charming *déshabillé* who came to gape at them.

Impressionist painters were also fixated on transmitting the hedonistic physicality of the seashore. Superb spectators, they moved their contemporaries to view the beach as a source of fresh sensations of the flesh. Their beach was a brilliant light-show of fluid, living, unstable forms bursting with color. At the same time, the activities on which these artists focused were also groundbreaking. The subject matter of their seascapes was the new domesticity that had taken shape on the beach. Their human tableaux depicted family groups doing nothing more exceptional by the sea than what they did in their salons at home, or on the boulevards and in the cafés of Paris. By giving scenes of familial intimacy such aesthetic cachet, the Impressionists did much to reassure the public as to the legitimacy of their new pastimes on the beach.

Impressionists on both sides of the Atlantic Ocean celebrated the sensual pleasures of the beach, integrating them into the rhythm of bourgeois domesticity. (Joseph Milner Kite, *Sun and Shadows*, Bettmann Archive)

What brought Monet here in the mid-nineteenth century was the prospect of painting from a nature that had yet been untouched by industrialization, where at dusk fisherfolk still set off in boats in costumes worn for countless generations, and where a new culture of leisure was quickly taking root. Yet the destinations of escape which the Impressionists so accurately recorded were locations dear to the urbanite, oriented to fashionable Paris, and bearing the unmistakable traces of its civilization. The Impressionist beach was as far a cry from the beach of the Romantics as the "madding crowd" was from the solitary stroller.

The Impressionist painters were only the high end of a great army of draftsmen, printmakers, and popular illustrators who were recording the changing physiognomy of the French seashore. In a way, works by Monet, Renoir, and Degas created the most compelling—and expensive—travel brochures in the history of tourism. Because of paintings they had seen, visitors came to Étretat to view the spectacular geological formations: archways vaulting out over the sea, needles thrusting out of the waves, and limestone cliffs descending to azure waters. Primed by travel books, they knew precisely which paths took them to the views that painters had made famous, what they would see when they got there, and even what feelings they would experience. At the top of the cliff of the Porte d'Aval, they would stop to look over the side into what the Baedeker guide described as the "yawning gulphs . . . out of which the agitated sea sends up tones like the voice of a bard singing the destruction of his race."

By the 1860s, the resorts were fully established. The local fishermen sold their modest homes to entrepreneurs and developers, who erected hotels, casinos, inns, and villas. Some fishermen became bathing attendants; their wives and daughters took up work as cooks, cleaners, and servants. In fact, the age of anthro-tourism was formally inaugurated at the beach. Since the eighteenth century, when travelers began to pay attention to peasants in local costumes, more and more economically strapped villages and hamlets, encouraged by the local chambers of commerce, realized the benefits of turning their citizenry into folkloric sideshows.

What tourists took for authentic rituals of everyday life, in fact often turned out to be carefully curated performances—Disneyland *avant la lettre*. Shrewd businessmen, the locals quickly realized that urban visitors found special charm in the "primitive," and that it made good business sense to stage picturesque, "old-fashioned" customs. Oblivious of the guile, vacationers wandered down to the beach to watch and sketch laundresses in local costume kneeling by the bank of a freshwater stream and washing clothes. On one end of the broad stretch of sand, well away from the bathing cabins and beach chairs, they inspected boats of the herring-fishing fleet, the nets drying in the sand, piles of seaweed entangled with gull feathers and fish bones, hopping with flies. For the benefit of the tourist spectators who marveled at the strength of peasant women, fishwives did the backbreaking labor of launching the fishing boats and of winching them up on the shore. When the boats came in, the women of the village rushed to the beach to crank the windlass by which each smack was hauled up high above the watermark. Men customarily took no part in this arduous undertaking, but looked on impassively. Here the two cultures of the beach collided: the traditional one of labor, and the new one of leisure, each having become a spectacle for the other.

In 1883, Monet took up residence in Étretat, on the second floor of the Hôtel Blanquet, where room and board cost a reasonable eight to ten francs per day, and painted multiple canvases of the famous Porte d'Aval and Porte d'Amont from his window. Visitors promenaded on the shaggy slopes of La Passée, which a British vacationer by the name of Anthony North Peat recommended, in 1868, "to the serious attention of all persons

The beach at Trouville combined the strict fashion of the ballroom with the therapeutic regimen of the sanatorium, the opulent trappings of the opera with unlimited doses of ozone. (Culver Pictures)

engaged in love-making or flirting of any kind. The romantic woods which clothe the hillside is . . . rich in spots particularly appropriate to those têtes-à-têtes wherein brown hats are to be seen in close propinquity to scarlet berres [sic]."

In the summertime, Étretat's shingle beach was transformed into a playground, ringed with changing cabins rising, in two or three tiers, along the far side of the strand. The beach itself, along with its rocky projections and dramatic cliffs, constituted the main attraction for the elegant Parisians who came here. This clientele had little interest in anachronistic local color, but preferred all the modern conveniences of the great metropolis. Local developers and railway companies modernized the town, tearing down historic monuments such as an ancient round tower in order to install the ubiquitous facilities of fashionable resorts: a casino, a studio, inns, hotels, and a Protestant church. The work of redecorating Eden for Parisian visitors even went as far as reshaping the topography of the beach. The municipality realized that, in order to capitalize on the growing popularity of swimming, they must install more shorefront than nature had allotted. They decided to extend the beach toward the east by carving away at the cliff which formed its natural boundary. Steps and railings were installed to give visitors easy access to the exquisite views. At the top of the point, one could always find groupings of sightseers on collapsible bamboo chairs, beneath linen parasols, and attached to the narrow end of binoculars aimed at the distant horizon.

Immortalized by the French Impressionist painters, the *planches,* or boardwalk, at Trouville ran about eighteen hundred feet between the beach and the grand hotels. Describing the celebrated Hôtel des Roches Noires and its grounds, the British travel writer Katherine Macquoid noted that there was "not so much as a beggar to destroy the illusion. Truly Trouville would have seemed a paradise to that Eastern philosopher who wandered about in search of happiness; and the paradise would last—perhaps till he was called on to pay his hotel bill." In the 1880s, at the height of its glory, the beach at Trouville was perceived by observers such as Guy de Maupassant as a veritable Babylon, "a love-market where some sold, others gave themselves—some drove a hard bargain for their kisses while others promised them for love." The warm air, fragrant with seacoast odors—with gorse, clover, and thyme, mingling with the salt smell of the rocks at low tide—seemed especially conducive to affairs of the heart. Marriages were contracted, romances launched and aborted on the boardwalk, in the elegant tearooms and gambling casinos.

In the 1880s, horse racing was added as a diversion. Every August, for a week, some of the greatest races in Europe were held on the beach, attracting all varieties of sports, from millionaire playboys to ambitious jockeys and calculating gamblers, who crowded the bars and club rooms of continental hotels. Toward the end of the century, bicycle races began to be held on the beach. Both men and women—the latter in short, tightly fitting white knickerbockers, sailor hats with heavy white veils, and white kid gloves—took part in these energetic contests.

PLANTING PARADISE: THE MEDITERRANEAN BEACH

British colonialists came to the Mediterranean to cast their net of affluence around the pleasure ports of the French Riviera. The southern coast of France, according to Côte d'Azur historian Mary Blume, was invented as a hedonistic destination by Lord Henry Braugham in 1834, when he was detained in the village of Cannes by a quarantine. The former lord chancellor of England at once fell in love with the mild climate, the clear skies, and the deep blue waters. He commissioned a villa to be built in the Italianate style on a hill overlooking the bay, and settled in for the winter. Friends came to visit and they, too, soon bought up parcels of land and erected residences of their own—Moorish casbahs, Italianate palazzi, Russian izbas, Provençal *mas*—surrounded by gardens filled with native cypress, tropical hibiscus, water-hungry lawns, and desert succulents.

The pellucid water, the transparent sky, and the harmonious setting were a powerful magnet to northerners with a predilection for landscapes enshrined in classical art. Unlike resorts on the Atlantic, the humble villages and towns along the stretch of Mediterranean from Bandol, in the west, to Menton, on the Italian border, had a venerable history of settlement since Greek and Roman times. Nice had once been Nicaea, Antibes had been Antipolis, and Monaco was said to be named for Heracles Monoikos, or Heracles the Solitary Dweller. Something of an antiquarian dignity touched the seasonal life of northern visitors to the south. Until rather late in the century, British, German, Russian, and Scandinavian visitors led quiet, decorous lives of repose by the shore, and took well-tempered exercise in the sea.

The southern coast of France and the Italian Riviera began bit by bit to resemble a British colony. Convinced that one must have the maximum of sea air, sea bathing, and sun to do "oneself good" by restoring one's constitution, affluent Britons set about commissioning residences in the environs of Nice and Cannes. They instructed their architects and builders to design homes as adjuncts to swimming, sun and air bathing, sailing, and inhaling ozone. Just as medical opinion of the eighteenth century had dwelt sadly on the noxious smells arising from the ocean and the ague-bearing east winds blowing in off the sea, nineteenth-century healers swore by the vivifying effects of what they called "ozone." In their view, this "heavy" air, charged with saltwater vapor, was formed by the passage of wind currents over cresting waves, and was produced in greatest quantities offshore during storms—as well as, more to the point for beachgoers, close to shore. They theorized that, to obtain the most benefit from sea air, visitors must stay as level with the water as possible. The higher one went, the less of this healthful benefit was to be obtained.

When first they arrived, lured by rumors of a golden light, of a warm and fragrant air that quickened the senses, and of a caressing, tranquil sea that healed the soul, British visitors were greeted by a pristine but oddly spartan paradise. For eyes accustomed to the shaggy verdure and floral kaleidoscope of English gardens, the scenery of the Midi was barren: rock, distant peaks, and wild scrub. Descending to the shores of the Mediterranean, the English found largely arid hills covered with wild thyme and little country houses of blinding whiteness which the natives called *bastides*. Each had a small garden of olives, almond trees, glossy laurel, and towering clumps of cane. Orchards of citrus alternated with the humble *potagères,* or vegetable patches, of the natives. The tranquil sea stretched to the horizon in an expanse of deepest blue, its surface ruffled into little waves sparkling in the sun.

Waves of cultivated Britons, Americans, Russians, and Parisians flocked to the unspoiled shores and set about reshaping paradise according to their notions of perfection. They bought up parcels of land, dug up the indigenous orchards and stands of olives, transplanted the vineyards, and planted a mind-boggling range of exotic plants that they had gathered from nurseries, botanical gardens, and tropical lands. From Marseilles to Sorrento, they went about creating huge, exquisitely curated gardens, invariably oriented to the sea as to a vast, ever-changeable, shimmering fountain.

Along the rugged coast of Liguria, in a sheltered bay tucked into a fold in mountains covered with heather, umbrella pine, and olive trees, a handsome park gradually took shape in the course of the nineteenth century. At its heart lay the small fishing village of Portofino, colonized by the ancient Romans and named Portus Dolphini, or the Port of the Dolphins. In the tenth century, monks, endowed with an unerring sense for heavenly sites, had claimed an elevation overlooking the bay for their monastery. Richard the Lion-Hearted tarried with them in the twelfth century, on his way to the crusades in Syria. Time and again, Saracen pirates swooped in on the small settlement, until at last, in the sixteenth century, the discouraged Benedictines abandoned their abbey to sheep and retired inland.

Centuries passed, and life for the natives continued in its accustomed groove. In spring and summer, as men fished the sea, women and children picked wild thyme, cultivated vegetable plots and olive groves. In the autumn, all harvested chestnuts, olives, and grapes. Late in the nineteenth century, however, a new band of invaders arrived, this time by land as well as by sea. Their intentions were peaceable enough: they sought not tangible booty but the invisible "spoils" of beautiful vistas, lush verdure, and fresh air. The visitors were largely British, and because they were inveterate lovers of gardens and picturesque architecture, they set about restyling the rugged beauty of the land into a gentle Arcadia of manicured gardens that spilled over the stone and iron walls girdling their villas. Unlike the French Riviera, this stretch of the Mediterranean remained serene and introspective, attracting artists, writers, and composers for protracted sojourns of intense creative labor. No other stretch of beach had summoned forth such rich effusions of the imagination, or inspired such an eclectic array of talent deployed in redecorating the seashore to make it reflect human notions of the picturesque.

The topography of the northern Mediterranean—a generally craggy coastline interrupted by pebbled inlets and episodic deposits of estuary sands—discouraged the expansive rituals of the Channel beaches. There was no room for bathing machines, horses, donkeys, boardwalks, bandstands, or bath chairs. Often, there was only enough space for a tight cluster of bathing cabañas and a rash of recliners.

By 1905, the French and Italian Riviera had become a land of legend where, from all accounts, a bad reputation had done no one any harm. Princes, princesses, marquises and dukes, real and false, bankers and swindlers mixed indiscriminately and joyously while moneyed widows and neglected wives passed their days sightseeing and bathing, and whiled away the nights waltzing with *danseurs mondains* hired by the hour.

DRESSING FOR THE BEACH

For a long time, chaos and improvisation had marked the domain of bathing apparel in England and on the Continent. When nakedness was no

longer deemed appropriate—or the cold was far too intolerable—ladies
had donned heavy woolen dresses with no pretensions to fashion. Gentlemen largely confined themselves to Adamic nudity. Gradually, however,
morality, therapy, and exercise conspired to fashion a more or less standardized and uniform bathing costume that, depending on one's point of
view, either challenged or reinforced standards of decency.

In the matter of bathing costume, no category of bathers was more in-
tractable than British males. Smollett's fictional Jerry Melford—and, we are
safe in assuming, the author himself—had expressed a firm preference for
bathing nude in the 1770s. Nearly one hundred years later, when not a single naked lady was still to be found on the public beaches and a confining
morality was creeping up on the male bather on the Continent, pockets of

resistance were still to be
found among respectable
Britons. At Margate, for
example, male nudity was
still the rule, but other
British resorts had adopted
the continental fashion of
wearing bathing drawers
called *caleçons*. These
string-waisted, knee-length
trousers were introduced
by Dr. Augustus Bozzi
Granville, an Italian who
changed his name and be-
came the period's leading
authority on therapeutic
bathing with his multivol-

Mid-nineteenth-century bathers exhibited wild extremes in attire:
elaborate dress on shore contrasted with the most dégagé bathing
deshabillé in the water. (Bettmann Archive)

ume reviews and guides to the principal spas and sea-bathing places of Europe and England. As late as 1841, Granville was still offended by the
spectacle of men bathing naked from the machines with "their persons
wholly exposed." He decried the practice as "a stain on the gentility" of
Brighton.

Thirty years passed, but male nudity still persisted, even at beaches where
men and women bathed together. At most bathing establishments, costumes could be rented for a small fee. The *caleçons* went a long way toward
maintaining decency, at least as long as the bather did not leave the water.
In rough surf, great dexterity was required to keep the garment from washing away, and many gentlemen suffered the embarrassment of emerging
from the waves in full adamic splendor.

Finally, in the 1880s, the introduction of a new style of male bathing attire took the uncertainty out of bathing. This was the so-called University Costume, so named for the swimming contests at which it had been worn since 1517, when the vice-chancellor of Cambridge University banned nude bathing in the Cam River. The striped, one-piece, short-sleeved garment encased the entire trunk, covering nipples, navel, and pubis, and ended snugly at the knees. Encased in this suit, the bather did not have to fear being stripped by the waves.

Women had been confronting the same liability in their ankle-length flannel smocks since the inception of public sea-bathing but, aside from segregating themselves from male bathers, had done nothing concrete to protect decency. The situation in 1856, as described in *The Observer,* called for decisive measures: "The water [at Margate and Ramsgate] is black with bathers: should the sea be rather rough, the females do not venture beyond the surf, and lay themselves on their backs, waiting for the coming waves, with their bathing dresses in a most dégagé style. The waves come, and, in the majority of instances, not only cover the fair bathers, but literally carry their dresses up to their neck, so that, as far as decency is concerned, they might as well be without any dresses at all. . . . And all this takes place in the presence of thousands of spectators."

The journalist went on to point out that these seaside follies were "looked upon much as a scene at a play would be, as the gentlemen are there with their opera glasses." He wondered how ladies, who in London were reputed for unsullied virtue, could so suddenly be perverted into voyeurs and exhibitionists on the beach. His solution was pragmatic: cover up the ladies and virtue would take care of itself. "Ladies' dresses should at least be so constructed as to prevent a wholesale exposure of their natural perfections or imperfections as now momentarily takes place."

True, as early as the 1840s, some fashionable ladies had begun slipping trousers under their smocks. But not until the 1860s did modesty finally triumph in a formal bathing costume that concealed every part of the anatomy. The Englishwoman Amelia Jenks Bloomer had just introduced the divided skirt, to dress women appropriately for the new sport of bicycling. Voluminous about the waist and gathered tightly about the ankles, these newfangled trousers—or "bloomers," as they came to be known— seemed ideal. Securely anchored to the waist and ankles, they had no chance of riding up. In the space of a season, Amelia Bloomer's knickerbockers made the leap from bicycling to bathing. Usually concealed beneath a knee-length skirt, the trousers supplanted the Modesty Hood, long since vanished from British beaches, in the role of guardian of decency. Some decades thereafter, young women also began to wear one-piece costumes closely resembling the male University Costume, but only if they were young and fit. Sensible matrons from the provinces still opted for

Ladies' bathing dress developed drawers at about the same time that *caleçons*, the male equivalent, became compulsory at British and Eurpean bathing resorts. (Bettmann Archive)

"flannel cases," draw-stringed at neck, waist, and knee, or for shifts worn over ankle-length "harem" pants brought by travelers from colonial outposts.

Elegant ladies were swathed in some eight yards of wool, another eight of cambric lining, and an assortment of metal stays, fasteners, and whalebone notions. Dress-makers made skirts short and very flouncy, so that the very bulk of the fabric would serve to screen the buttocks and the groin. Above the waist, stiff lining was added to blouses and jackets to conceal pro-truding nipples. Arms disappeared into leg-o'-mutton sleeves that bal-looned at the shoulder and tapered to a snug fit at the wrist. Legs were encased in drawers festooned with bands of white serge, rows of braiding, and cascades of frills.

Although petticoats and crinolines were put aside for bathing, the corset continued to be worn well into the 1890s imparting a machine-stamped uniformity to the most diverse female anatomies. Made to stiffen the spine, constrict the waist, and thrust the bosom and buttocks into prominence, the corset was the sartorial device par excellence of an age that fervently believed man not only could, but should, improve upon nature. That this improvement should, in sociologist Thorstein Veblen's words, "lower the subject's vitality and render her permanently and obviously unfit for work," mattered less to Victorians than upholding decency and their peculiar vi-sion of the ideal female form as an explosion of bust and buttocks con-nected by a waspish waist. Representing male opinion on the matter, the naturalist Charles Darwin pronounced the resulting projecting posterior of the hourglass figure "wonderful to behold."

Thrilling as the sight might have been to the male of the species, it was often lethal for the female. Restricting the free intake of air, the practice of tight lacing and corseting led to a host of medical disorders, especially among sedentary, housebound gentlewomen. Ranging from hemorrhoids and poor digestion, to cancer and tuberculosis, corset-linked maladies were responsible for dispatching countless women to cures at sea resorts. There, ironically, the patients were thrust into costumes that only aggravated the medical conditions they had come to treat. Corsets induced life-threatening cramps in the water and, rusting through, broke and stabbed the wearer. Eventually, a patent was obtained for a "seaside corset" that the advertising copy touted to be "rust-proof, as light as a feather and as strong as those worn in winter." No matter. The corset continued to compromise lung capacity. And, combined with the drag of some twenty-two pounds of sodden fabric, the female bathing dress effectively rendered the Victorian female unseaworthy.

When not bathing bareheaded, British women pioneered the use of white waterproof oilcloth bonnets or caps, the fashion for which soon spread to the Continent. For their part, Frenchwomen donned broad-brimmed straw hats inspired by the "cottage bonnets" of peasants. Sometimes, silk face-masks were worn against the sun, as well as various kinds of fabric visors cantilevered from the crowns of bonnets. Other precautionary devices included cotton wool for plugging up the ears, wooden clogs or canvas ankle boots to keep the feet free of sand, and fur-lined coats to receive chilled, wet bodies.

All was well as long as flannel, calico, or wool was used for male and female bathing attire. Although uncomfortable and itchy when wet, these fabrics had the merit of opacity and what seamstresses call "body," or the ability to maintain their own shape under pressure. But once jersey, cotton, and silk were introduced, the game was up. Modesty was again under assault. No doubt tenfold more wearable, these fabrics clung to every curve, cleft, and dimple of the wearer's body. As a result, many a Victorian child received graphic lessons in comparative human anatomy while playing on the beach. The French novelist Gustave Flaubert recalled that his ideal of female beauty was born on the sands at Trouville, where, as an impressionable adolescent, he was enraptured by the "shape of luxuriant bodies in wet bathing dresses." Outside the cabaret and the bordello, the beach was the only place where voyeurs could indulge their secret vice. The British novelist John Cowper Powys described the male's "maniacal quest for provocative feminine forms basking in that blazing sunshine," gloating "like a satyr on hundreds of bodies as they bathed or extended themselves for his delight along the sand, fastening his feverish gaze on any leg, knee or ankle that chanced to be revealed."

Many fashionable resorts segregated the sexes according to locale and time, and barred onlookers of the opposite sex from the scene. Until 1865, ladies at Blackpool were summoned to the water by a bell ringing at flood tide and, according to Anthony Hern, historian of British seaside resorts, "no gentleman was afterwards to be seen on the parade, under the penalty of a bottle of wine." In the spring of 1862, the city of Margate mandated a distance of not less than sixty feet "between the Bathing Machines from which Females are bathing and those from which Males are bathing." Poles colored red for men and white for women demarcated the segregated areas. Boys over the age of ten were considered male. Pleasure boats were to keep at least two hundred yards away from bathing machines. Although similar regulations were passed at other British resorts, demographic pressures made their policing impracticable. The situation was quite different on the beaches of France and Belgium, where laxity regarding the commingling of the sexes was the rule.

By the last decade of the nineteenth century, the gradual betterment in life that had helped erode the distinctions between the aristocracy and the middle class began to have an impact upon the lower strata of society. Karl Marx and Friedrich Engels formulated a political philosophy that placed the blueprints for the future in the laborer's hands. Charles Darwin shook the confidence of the higher classes with his theory of evolution, which saw dynamic change rather than stasis underlying the organic world. Relocated squarely within the natural world, human history, too, could be seen in terms of a savage competition for survival. Doubt and uncertainty began to gnaw at the deep core of faith in Manifest Destiny on both sides of the Atlantic Ocean. Artists and thinkers delved deep into this rift of unease; some, like Fyodor Dostoevsky, found comfort in ardent religiosity; others, like Friedrich Nietzsche, in an elitist doctrine of cultural superiority; still others, like

As railway lines were laid from the urban centers to the seashore, holidaymaking spread to the masses. By 1841 even aristocratic Brighton was linked to London, and shopkeepers, servants, and artisans found their way to the beach. (Bettmann Archive)

Richard Wagner, who hypnotized thousands in his annual Bayreuth Festivals, in multimedia stagings of immutable myths. It was too early for despair, but the time was ripe for full-blown escapism.

7

THE PLEASURE BEACH

Philadelphia, August 1896. The sky stretches over the squat tenement of row houses like a suffocating blanket. There is no wind to stir the bedsheets, underclothes, and faded smocks that hang from lines strung between fire escapes and windows. Dogs lie comatose on the pavement, oblivious of screeching children emptying buckets of water over each other's heads. Men in sweat-sodden shirts trudge past, cigars clenched between their teeth. Women are nowhere to be seen. They are deep inside the boxy three-deckers, moving like somnambulists in kitchens dense with the sticky smell of boiled cabbage and grease. The air is thick with heat and a discouragement that turns into explosive irritation as the evening wears into night.

Sunday dawns gray and even more oppressive. But inside, the cramped bedrooms and dingy kitchens are already buzzing with a festive current of excitement—day-tripper delirium. Towels are stuffed into hampers; bread and sausage and bottled water and beer are tucked into the spare corners. Children are squeezed into outgrown clothes, and grown-ups pull on whatever old things they have on hand.

After a hurried breakfast, a ragtag crowd of men, women, and children, loaded down with rugs tightly rolled and bound with rope, straw hampers, hats, and umbrellas, moves briskly to tram stops that line Philadelphia's Spruce Street. Animated with a single urgent idea—to escape the heat— some of the urban refugees head for the steamboat landing on the Delaware River; others make their way to Penn Station. But they are all moving in a single general direction: to the Jersey shore, to the promised land of the beach, for a brief respite from the urban inferno.

By eight o'clock, several thousand people are crowding into trains made up of as many as thirty-five cars that run at short intervals from Philadelphia to Atlantic City, before continuing to Cape May. And several hundred more are packed into every corner of deck space on the soot-stained steamer that plies the Delaware between Philly and Long Branch. After one and a half hours, the train, having rattled over a bridge built across the Delaware by the Pennsylvania Railroad Company for two million dollars, disgorges sweaty, rowdy passengers at Atlantic City; the remainder descend at Cape May just a short while later. Three and a half hours after its departure from Philadelphia, the yawing steamer pulls up to the dock at Cape May, where by ten o'clock in the morning the pier is already teeming with life, as wave after wave of fresh arrivals from Philadelphia swell the numbers.

A pilgrimage of pleasure is now in full swing. With meager but bulky provisions in hand, hordes of visitors stroll on rickety boardwalks; others make a beeline for the tepid waters crashing on the beach. The day trippers' pale faces and anxious eyes stand out in sharp contrast to the flushed visages and the air of knowledgeable determination that mark the "cottagers" and boarding-house guests. For the former, the beach is a jungle, a *terra incognita* bordering an even more mysterious ocean. They stand squinting their eyes at the glittering expanse of blue water, at the tattered lines of white foam, at the black figures flung about in the surf, at the teeming, bustling, laughing, varicolored multitude of bodies swarming on the white sands.

■■■■■■

At the turn of the century, seaside life at the Jersey shore was a burlesque for the masses. Everyone was welcome, and the price of admission was the cost of a bathing suit—frequently, even that was not necessary. For Americans, much as for Europeans, resort and public beach were very much about status, social climbing, and health. And about vanity and fashion. But, beneath it all, they were also about sex and sensuality. Paintings of the period, in which late-Victorian bathing beauties bared milky limbs and pneumatic bosoms, interpreted the beach as a vast erotic theater. Humorous trade cards in the 1880s depicted day trippers cavorting in the carnival atmosphere of the strand and decorous couples strolling past bathhouses filled with embracing lovers.

Cape May, nestled at the southern tip of New Jersey, where the Atlantic meets Delaware Bay, culminated the string of resorts marching down either side of Barnegat Bay from Sandy Hook, at the north end. In the 1880s, the hundred-mile stretch was punctuated by some fifty-four seaside cities— Long Branch, Asbury Park, Ocean Grove, Beach Haven, Atlantic City, and Ocean City among them—that swelled and shrank with the seasons. The bigger and older communities, such as Cape May, the pioneer of American seaside resorts, and Atlantic City, its younger stepsister, had commissioned the construction of boardwalks several miles long running parallel to the beach. During the summer season, which extended from the beginning of

July to the end of August, more than three million visitors came for fortnight holidays, with day trippers contributing another eight million. Money
flowed into coastal towns at the rate of $150 million each season, or $1.5
million per acre of barren sand.

THE DELICIOUS SEA

By the end of the nineteenth century, beaching it, American-style, meant
abandoning limits. The train ride to the Jersey shore would leave day trippers ravenous, and upon their arrival they would look around for an inexpensive eatery along the boardwalk or just beyond, where they could
hunker down to a hearty meal for a few cents. The food may have been
poorly prepared, but no one came to eat fine meals. People came to cool
off and breathe the fresh sea air and have some fun—all for the small price
of a round-trip excursion ticket and a cheap meal. The ocean itself was
free.

Their bellies full, the day trippers trudged down to the sand. The best
spots—in the shade thrown by the bathhouses arranged in lines a hundred
feet deep and at right angles to the beach—were already occupied by
overnight guests. But no matter: the sand was just a temporary dumping
ground for their modest belongings. Those who could afford the price
went to one of the small frame bathhouses, where they could change into a
bathing costume—if they were lucky enough to own one—or rent one
from the attendant.

Bathing suits were built on a single pattern, designed, apparently, by
some misanthrope and emphasizing every weak point of the human
anatomy. The thin looked thinner in them, the fat more aggressively ro-
tund. One leg of the breeches was invariably shorter than the other, and
buttonholes were too large to exercise the slightest control over the small
buttons. The doleful shade of blue, relieved by braid that had once been
white, invariably brought out the ashen tones of the skin. The straw hats
donned as protection against the sun were tied under the chin with white
tapes that demoralized even the most self-confident.

But all apprehensions were swept away the moment bathers reached the
forgiving shelter of the sea. Nothing in their experience had prepared
them for the unexpected motion of the waves, or the instability of the sand
beneath their feet, or the sting of salt spray in their eyes, or even the sudden weight of clothes filled with water and sand. They stood stunned for a
few minutes, while their senses registered these new impressions. And then
they looked around to see how the other bathers were dealing with the situation. Their apprenticeship in the sea had begun.

The beach at Atlantic City—as at most of the South Jersey seaside

The stylish, form-fitting bathing dress of the 1880s was unforgiving, dramatically dividing the beach into the anatomical haves and have-nots. (Bettmann Archive)

resorts—slopes so gently that one can wade out shoulder-deep and bathe in perfect safety, with no seaweed to tangle the feet, or shells or stones to bruise them. After the initial joyful shock of immersion, bathers would look around for friends and family, and join hands to form a circle where the water was waist-deep. As each "roller" came in, they would jump up and let its great bulk throw them high out of the water. Up and down they leaped and fell, shouting with wild enthusiasm. To one side, other bathers lay prostrate on the water, bobbing up and down, their hands linked, waiting for a giant wave to sweep and catapult them to an upright position. A little farther out, more intrepid bathers stood facing the advancing wall of swells. The moment one came rushing in, they put their backs into the great moving mass of water. As it arched up into a white, seething, boiling foam, they sprang into the curling wave so that it tossed them round in a complete somersault. This tricky maneuver demanded a fine sense of timing. Those who misjudged caught the full force of the white "curl" on the back of the head, neck, or spine, which could lead to a nasty fracture or even drowning.

The sea was a place to improvise and explore. It offered not only new occasions for aimless fun, but also opportunities for transposing land-based activities to water. Surf-dancing was a case in point. The rage for the waltz and the polka at some of the more fashionable resorts instantly spread to the surf, where couples performed intricate maneuvers that allowed for considerable love play. A correspondent for *Harper's Weekly* observed that, knee-deep in the frothing surf of Atlantic City, gentlemen in clinging tights "handed about their pretty partners as if they were dancing water

"WASHINGTON-POST"

Knee-deep in the waves, gentlemen in clinging tights led their partners through elaborate dance steps. The sport, requiring strength, precise timing, and impeccable balance, was especially popular at East Coast resorts. (Culver Pictures)

quadrilles." As this new activity gained in popularity, many of the hotels set aside certain times for surf-dancing, and ran up a red flag to announce that the beach had been reserved exclusively for this use.

In 1902, *Outing* gave a cachet of formality to this graceful sport, laying out detailed protocols and choreographic hints. "And now, if you are indeed a good surfman, both courtesy and inclination may lead you to offer escort to one of the sex . . . that can meet surf almost with the best." But this treatise warned: "Unto such activity go you, in fitting humility of soul. Make no promises. . . . Above all, *never* agree that a woman won't get her hair wet, for of such agreements come disappointment and distrust." Steps for arabesquing in the surf were then spelled out in exacting detail: "Standing . . . in the break, there are two ways of putting a woman through the surf," ran one set of instructions. "One is to place a hand on each side of her waist. . . . [The other involves] both standing sideways to the breakers, you with your right hand holding her belt, and your left, her right elbow; she with her right hand holding your left elbow and her left resting on your shoulder."

This intricate water ballet little resembled its rudimentary surf-bathing forerunner, as practiced at the eastern end of Long Island. "Every Saturday morning or afternoon, as the tide willed, throughout the summer," wrote a correspondent for *Outing* in 1902, "big farm wagons trundled down to the beach and were swung around abreast of the line of breakers. Old fish houses served the purpose of modern bathing pavilions, and the sea costumes were those of last year's village street." A long rope was secured to the wagon wheel, and some sturdy ex-whaler or sailor wrapped one end around his wrist and waded out with it into the surf. In his red flannel shirt and old trousers, he pulled the line as taut as it would go while women and children clung to it, shrieking and wallowing and exulting in the foaming breakers.

S E A S I C K N E S S

The beach was such a novel experience that most were completely unfamiliar with the health hazards—and risks to life and limb—it posed. Half an hour was the physician's absolute limit on a surf bath, but the newcomers lacked knowledge of the rituals that the "better sort" of people had evolved over the past hundred years for dealing with the dangers of the beach. They did not know that medical authorities had established a precise protocol. The first few baths of the season should be short, doctors insisted. At the first sense of cold, fatigue, or discomfort, the bather should exit the sea and take a quick shower of fresh water, then rub down briskly with coarse towels or with a "flesh strap"—a muslin or linen cloth surfaced with bristles. Anyone who went into the water had to be prepared for the consequences of precipitous and prolonged exposure, which included "headache, nausea, and the other symptoms which are generally associated under the term 'biliousness,' " according to bathing guru John H. Packard, M.D., surgeon at the Episcopal Hospital of Philadelphia.

American medical authorities went so far as to promote ocean bathing as a living lesson in the evolution of species. Dr. Woods Hutchinson, a well-known promoter of aquatic sports, painted bathing as "a return to primitive ancestral conditions, the halcyon days of the sea-squirt and the amphioxus, [which] sets the nerves vibrating as almost no other influence can." The same observer discriminated between bathers of superior and inferior constitution, implying that short dips in the surf were a sure admission of evolutionary inferiority. "The strong and rugged and red-blooded find sea-bathing a bracing and exhilarating sport, and may indulge in it freely," the good doctor noted, but he cautioned: "The weak and relaxed and undervitalized and especially all who know themselves to be below par in any respect, heart, lungs, kidneys, or what not, must indulge in it sparingly." The surf, in short, emerged as an arena in which the strong were separated from the weak, where young males played out the drama of natural selection before the eyes of discriminating females.

After a morning in the surf, it was usually hunger that finally drove bathers back to shore. Those who had rented costumes returned to the bathhouses. They surrendered their soggy garb so it could be dried, cleaned of the sand that had insinuated itself into every stitch, and made ready for the next wave of renters. The bathers washed as much of the sand and salt from their bodies as the cramped and mildewy showers allowed, then put on their dry clothing and looked about for a spot to stretch out for a long rest. A cool claret punch and biscuits helped quiet the more noxious hunger pangs until the lunch gong went off, precisely at two o'clock.

Long rows of tables at the eateries filled up quickly. Great trays of food were brought around by the waiters and were passed unceremoniously, from one end of the tables to the other, adults helping children saw through the tough cuts of beef, chattering gaily with neighbors who twenty minutes earlier had been total strangers. A bold spirit of democracy descended on the group, and grew stronger as ale, beer, and "spirituous liquors" began to circulate. Faces already red from the sun grew ruddier still from internal combustion.

The more energetic visitors went off for a few hours of fishing in the bays or inlets, hoping to land a sheepshead (a gamy fish with a shark's bite) or even a bluefish. Wielding a pole rigged with a stout line that had a silver spoon over the long sharp hook at the end, the fishermen waded out chest-deep into the still water. Then they tossed the line out to sea perhaps sixty to eighty feet and hurried back to shore, until the tug on the line drew them back into the surf for the lively struggle with the four-foot fourteen-pounders. Those without the foresight to pack a fishing pole rummaged about the shallow bottom of the bays for crab.

The racy picture postcard burst upon the Victorian bathing scene with a joyous bawdiness. Filled with voluptuous bathing beauties, visual puns, and double entendres, such cards were inspired by raucous music hall acts and burlesque humor. (Bettmann Archive)

It was the hottest part of the day, and the sun beat down ferociously. A few bathers returned for an ill-advised second swim after the lunch. People of the "better sort" did not as a rule bathe in the afternoon. Only servants and those unfortunates who were compelled to come down from town late in the day bathed after one o'clock. Weighed by a heavy meal and overconfident of their ability to negotiate the waves, some came to a bad end. They knew nothing about the dangerous undertows, which varied at different stages of the tide and with different strengths of the surf. No one had warned them that, the stronger the surf, the greater the undertow. If they were fortunate, they found themselves struggling valiantly against a current that dragged them a hundred yards or so beyond their points of entry. But if they were caught in the dangerous swirl of the "sea puss" or the "sea purse," they had little chance of surviving.

This kind of undertow, quite common along the Jersey shore, resulted from a sudden shift of wind that whipped up a current running contrary to the current along the shore, creating a powerful whirlpool that sucked hapless swimmers out to sea. So unfamiliar an environment was the sea that these urbanites were illiterate when it came to reading its signals. They even went out of their way—inadvertently—to add handicaps by wearing bathing costumes that, when wet, added between ten and fifteen pounds to their weight.

Dr. Packard, the Philadelphia bathing authority, speculated that the greatest number of drowning accidents occurred among these day trippers, who "know nothing of the beaches, and venture far more than those who do; often they cannot swim, and are helpless when in danger. One reason for this is, the want of the habit of self-possession, and of thinking for themselves, which is the result of higher mental training." However, even "higher mental training" was of no use when the swimmer was seized by a sudden cramp. A burst of panic, a few quick minutes of struggle, a few scattered bubbles, and another casualty was added to the list of drownings.

At some of the better-organized beaches—and Atlantic City was certainly one of them—the local government made some provisions to safeguard bathing. Volunteers and, eventually, municipally sponsored beach guards attached stout ropes to poles driven deep into the sand. The ropes were then stretched out into the water, where they were held in place on the surface by means of buoys attached at regular intervals. Life preservers on long lifelines were placed at many points along the beach. At the height of the season, surfboats patrolled the water. The "surfmen," as lifeguards were then called, were good swimmers of cool temperament sponsored and trained by the Volunteer Life-Saving Association of New Jersey.

These formal arrangements were augmented by concerned citizens, largely athletic males who assumed that patrolling beaches was another divinely ordained duty reserved for their sex. Some of the stronger men made it a habit to carry attached to their belts reels the size of large spools holding about five yards of stout rope. The spool could be thrown to a drowning person, who would then be reeled in to safety. Even without any equipment, swimmers often assisted inexperienced bathers who got into trouble. If an unusually large and strong wave carried a surfer seaward beyond his or her depth, the frantic thrashing signaled trouble to the bathers closer to shore. Quickly a line of men would form. Joining hands, they would ease out into the deep water until they were close enough to grab the drowning bathers and haul them into shore. Invariably, there were tragedies, more frequent than they are today in advanced countries where learning to swim is a standard childhood ritual. In those days, most bathers were seriously unprepared for the sea. A panicked, inexperienced swimmer would drag the would-be savior under; a wader stranded on a sandbar by the incoming tide drowned while attempting to return; a solitary bather vanished in a deep submerged hole; a body surfer was swept out to sea by a riptide; an exhausted swimmer was battered to death while clinging to the poles of the pier.

As the afternoon wore to a close, the day trippers began to keep a close eye on the clock. Their trains would be starting back to town soon, and they had just enough time for a quick cup of tea—or something more fortifying—and another nasty meal on the pier. Then, dragging with exhaustion, they crowded into the train carriages for a dispiriting ride home. The seats and aisles were full of sunburned, feverish bathers suffering the aching heads and sick stomachs of the beach novice. Nausea bleached quite a few faces, and the nasty smell of vomit hovered in the air.

Urban day trippers returned to the city often bearing painful traces of the beach, the surf, and the sun on their bodies: sunburn, windburn, sand-blasted eyes, faces and hands swollen from contact with jellyfish, water sloshing in their ears. They bore their scars proudly, however, for these were, unlike the farmer's and the fieldworker's ravaged skin, badges of pleasure and leisure. As they dropped off to sleep, they were already thinking of ways to improve the next outing and pondering how to scrape together enough money during the year so that next summer they could afford a week in a cheap boarding house or even a rented cottage.

THE BEACH HOTEL

By 1900, Atlantic City boasted four hundred hotels, some capable of housing as many as one thousand guests; together they accommodated an average of fifty thousand visitors each summer. Full room and board could run as much as nine dollars a day for a room overlooking the sea.

A typical day began with a surf bath in the Atlantic. Hotel guests wrapped themselves in ample dressing gowns and shuffled downstairs in their slippers. At that early hour, a gentleman could swim nude, and so dispense with the orthodox bathing costume that was obligatory at the regular bathing hour. Following breakfast, the visitor stretched out on a wicker chair or lounge in a breezy corner of the spacious veranda for a casual perusal of the morning papers, brought by special train from Philadelphia or New York. A forty-piece orchestra played softly in the background, serenading the late risers at their breakfast. About eleven, the hotel's public rooms

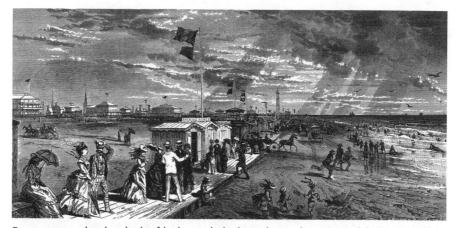

Every summer day, hundreds of bathers splashed together in the waves, while hundreds more watched them from the shore. (Culver Pictures)

emptied briefly, to refill a few minutes later with bathrobed and dressing-gowned guests trailing down to the beach for the swim. They changed into bathing dress in the bathhouses, where they had handsomely tipped the attendant on their first day to assure that the suits they were handed would be dry and free of sand. Then they joined the awkward day trippers, the cottagers, and the rooming-house clients in a democratic tumble in the surf. Unlike British and French bathers, Americans dealt with the waves directly, without the intermediary of a *baigneur* or "dipper" or the encumbrance of a bathing machine.

Thirty to forty minutes later, they were back on the hotel veranda in dry clothing, sipping tea and munching on biscuits for a good two hours of rest before being summoned for a sumptuous lunch. Afterward, those who could muster the energy retired to the hotel's common rooms for a round of chess, cards, or backgammon. More often than not, however, they returned to the veranda for a healthful nap in the oxygen-laden air. In the late afternoon, they could choose between boating parties or swimming in the indoor bathing pool, which was equipped with flotational devices, boards, rings, and ropes.

Before the dinner hour, while the heat of the day still hung heavy over the land, guests strolled out onto the pier to cool themselves in the refreshing breeze and to contemplate the onrushing waves from a new vantage. Several of the watering places of the Jersey shore had built up piers extending many hundred feet into the ocean. These were largely impermanent structures, regularly swept away by the winter storms. And though they had a poor effect on the topography of the beach, deepening the water or encouraging the formation of sandbanks, still they were immensely popular with the public, who relished the cooling breezes they could always find there, and especially the novel views of the shore. At dusk the piers were particularly magical, filled with twinkling electrical lights, whose reflections snaked and twisted in the inky waves.

At seven, after the dinner hour, the proper thing was to drive or ride on the beach. When the tide was out, the hard sand formed a natural boulevard some two hundred feet wide. Across this surface, carriages glided noiselessly and the hoofbeats of horses were muffled. The evening beach presented an altogether different aspect from the merry congestion of the day. The desolation of the dark ocean mirrored the emptiness of the sand. The blue sky paled, turned lilac, and then, with the deepening twilight, closed down around the carriage. The last gulls flew swiftly by. An eerie feeling took hold of the heart. The silence, the solitude, the damp darkness gradually grew oppressive, and visitors looked with longing at the blazing strings of lights of the great hotels, miles away. The carriage was turned around, and soon snatches of band music drifted across the sands, and the horse was urged into a brisk trot, so that in no time at all the sightseers were back in the crush and clatter and chatter of the festive crowd, swept up in the whirl of dancing the "German" until the wee hours of the morning.

THE BLUE-CHIP BEACH

A world of difference separated the beach experience of urban workers from that of the wealthy entrepreneur in whose employ they often labored. The millionaires of Philadelphia, New York, Boston, and the factory towns of New England had two seaside destinations, depending on the length of time money had been in the family. "Old money," or the class that was deemed richer in mind and manners than in mere money, favored the host of small and large seaside resorts on the New England coast—Nahant, Marblehead, Nantucket, Bar Harbor—where strolling and sketching the rocky, picturesque coast claimed as much attention as yachting and picnicking and surf bathing.

The astronomically wealthy and those newly gilded streamed to Newport, Rhode Island, the mecca of the millionaire. If, as wits were fond of saying, all good Americans went to Paris when they died, all *rich* Americans went to Newport. Newport came into being in 1639, when dissenters from the Massachusetts Puritans settled on the plain between the high bluffs and cliffs fronting the Atlantic and the quiet bay. The town was superbly situated to develop into the finest commercial harbor of the New World, which it was until 1767, when its supremacy was challenged by Staten Island, New York. Then it entered into a century of decline as the city on the Hudson grew, prospered, and eventually lost its natural beauty to massive buildings,

tentacular streets, and overcrowding. Although New York surpassed Newport in business, when it came to leisure, New York's merchants carried
their wealth back to Newport—to its strange little crooked streets and grass-
grown squares fronting on the oldest Jewish synagogue in the United
States, and on the house in which the first American newspaper was
printed and published by one of Benjamin Franklin's nephews, and on the
"old mill" which inspired Longfellow's verses. Newport had charm and history. Here, the first Baptist church was opened and introduced a "religious
dip" long before the "social dip" was established. The French who came
with the Americans after the War of Independence fell in love with it and
agitated to have it ceded to France. This was the magnetic Newport.

The great beach resorts of Europe had taught cosmopolitan Americans
that elegance and high living were not antithetical to the seashore. Newport became the first American sea town to legitimize the beach as a theater where the robber barons could flaunt their wealth as they retreated
from steamy summers in the city. To afford even a brief a holiday in Newport in the 1880s, one needed an annual income of at least fifty thousand
dollars, and many spent five times that sum in a season. Hotels were virtually nonexistent; visitors had either to own their own homes or to be well
connected to those who did. Along Newport's avenues the Vanderbilts, As-
tors, Belmonts, Lorillards, Mortons, and Bigelows commissioned the country's finest architects to design magnificent summer houses that were
"cottages" only in name.

In the 1840s and 1850s, Richard Upjohn, the leading architect of his generation, came from New York to design half a dozen handsome "cottages"
and "villas." In the 1860s and 1870s, when Newport was "invaded" by
wealthy New Yorkers, the residential-construction boom was on. The architects of choice were now the Bostonian Henry Hobson Richardson and
New Yorker Richard Morris Hunt, both trained at the École des Beaux-Arts
in Paris. The new wave of summer residents now wanted grander and
grander homes to match their inflated standard of living and obsession
with flamboyantly conspicuous consumption. Leading the way to baronial
magnificence was the brilliant young Eastern architectural firm of McKim,
Mead and White. The partners had been architects to the wealthy at
Elberon, Newport's Jersey rival of the late 1870s. With Newport as a laboratory for castles by the sea, McKim, Mead and White took beach architecture to unprecedented, proportions. Their diverting and derivative fancies,
based on the Queen Anne style and the Loire châteaux, were full of gables,
bays, dormers, elegant porch columns, rough and refined shingles, superbly crafted interiors, and marvelously proportioned volumes. One of
McKim, Mead and White's best creations was "Southside," built for Robert
Goelet in 1892, a fantastical estate of disparate parts assembled under a vast

mountain range of shingled roofs pierced by tall, red brick chimneys. The commission followed on the heels of the firm's design for the Newport Casino, where the *crème de la crème* would meet for billiards, concerts, and plays in the vaulting theater, drinks on the piazza, and lawn bowling in the courtyard.

According to legend, the Casino was commissioned by James Gordon Bennett in a fit of pique, but actually answered a serious need for a social center that would be the heart and soul of the community. So energetically had the summer colony expanded by the late 1870s that hostesses were hard-pressed to keep up with the demands of social obligations—lawn parties, luncheons, tennis matches, dinner dances, and theatricals—much less orchestrate their own. The Newport Casino, the first of those suburban and country clubs that would spring up all over the country in the 1880s, was designed to look more like a country house, though of vast proportions, than a public edifice, and accommodated its social mandate with grace and ease.

No residence exemplified the spirit of Newport with more aplomb than "The Breakers," a stately white marble pile built for Cornelius Vanderbilt between 1892 and 1895 to replace the earlier, more modest Gothic Revival cottage that had burned several years earlier. Conceived on an imperial scale and modeled upon Renaissance merchants' palaces in Genoa, it boasted interiors sumptuous beyond anything then seen in Newport. Filled with blue marbles, golden swags, cartouches, and festoons, the rooms soared to vaulted ceilings crowded with decorative motifs thickly overlaid with gilt. The billiard room, a submarine harmony of blue marbles and tawny alabasters, looked out over the Atlantic. From here, the Vanderbilts studied the spread of ocean in the early-morning light, watching the shadows of the islands on the horizon gradually materialize out of the pearly mist. On moonlit nights, they retired here to enjoy a last cigar and contemplate the silvered sea dissolving into fleecy foam at the base of a cliff.

Until the close of the century, manor houses and châteaux and palaces sprang up along Newport's avenues. Trianons out of glazed terra-cotta that simulated marble stood next to vast *hôtels particuliers* that mimicked the ones the newly rich magnates had built in eighteenth-century France. By the magic of precisely detailed drawings, palaces from the Faubourg St.-Germain were transported to Newport's Bellevue Avenue. Soon there were full-scale replicas of all the more elaborate examples of European residential architecture. From here, the pattern for architectural settings spread to other expensive resorts on the eastern, southern, and western shores of the United States: to Narragansett, Bristol, Providence, and then to Palm Beach and Catalina. Wherever the newly rich could afford fantastic expense, they re-created the architectural model of Newport.

When Henry James revisited Newport in 1907, he was offended by the waste and the ostentation paraded by these behemoths. "What an idea," he wrote, "originally, to have seen this miniature spot of earth, where the sea-nymphs on the curved sands, at the worst, might have chanted back to the shepherds, as a mere breeding ground of white elephants! They look queer and conscious and lumpish—some of them, as with an air of the bran-dished proboscis, really grotesque—while their averted owners roused from a witless dream, wonder what in the world is to be done with them." James sadly concluded that there was absolutely nothing to be done with them.

But the millionaires had no such dilemmas. In these palaces they lived the life of royalty, and prodigious hospitality banished any possibilities for boredom or reflection. Polo, yachting, riding, driving, lawn tennis, and a round of social life filled every minute of the day and night. The "smart set" did not always spend much time in the water, but the beach was a constant magnet, where everyone came to stroll and observe. Bathing costume, nat-urally, assumed great importance, since undressing for the dip actually in-volved dressing for ceremonial display. What the ladies in Newport wore into the sea became the standard for what would be worn at resorts throughout the nation.

In the summer of 1866, beach fashion dictated something called the Zouave Marine swimming costume. This outfit prominently displayed *trousers* beneath a diminished skirt that had shrunk to about three inches above the ankles. By the end of the century, swimwear for women was sim-plified to a voile-and-cotton ensemble covered by a short skirt and com-pleted with black hose, low rubber shoes, and an oiled silk cap. The corset was no longer obligatory.

Disseminated through miniature patterns in such publications as *Godey's Lady's Book, Peterson's Magazine,* and *Demerset's Monthly Magazine* and the full-scale patterns introduced by Butterick's in the 1860s, the lighter, short-sleeved bathing dress took over American beaches. In Newport, Narra-gansett Pier, Cape May, and lesser resorts, lightly clad young women—the so-called summer girls, full of winsome camaraderie, free ways, and bold manners—waded into the surf. European observers were frequently scan-dalized by their casual dress. Light flannels, cottons, linens, and muslins were used much more extensively in the States than they were abroad, where heavy, dark, and ugly bathing apparel was customary. American women, according to a reporter for *Harper's Weekly,* were known for their "suggestive or indecent" costumes: thin white suits that, when wet, became more or less transparent and clung "as if dipped in glue."

The impression made by the gentlemen who accompanied them into the waves was not dissimilar. Their two-piece wool knit suits were even more re-vealing than the skirted female version. On men of an athletic build, the short-sleeved or sleeveless pullover and knee-length trousers were quite handsome-looking. On the thin or the corpulent, however, the effect was hilarious, as one victim confessed in 1891. "Barefoot as a mendicant," a contributor to *Demerset's Monthly Magazine* wrote, "your hair disheveled in the wind, the stripes on your clothes strongly suggestive of Sing-Sing, your appearance a caricature of human kind, you wander up and down the beach a creature that the land is evidently trying to shake off and the sea is unwilling to take."

Newport set the pace for the rest of America. From the 1860s on, summer travel had become an established part of life for wealthy Northeastern city dwellers. Newspapers and magazines gave extensive coverage to the social scene at the fashionable seaside resorts. Everyone with sufficient discretionary income headed for the coast in July and August, while the affluent urban neighborhoods resembled ghost towns. Wives,

With its relaxed manners and easy access to physical exercise, the beach was one of the earliest sites to offer equal opportunity for pleasure to both sexes. (Otto Bacher, *A Group of Sea Nymphs*, 1889, Bettmann Archive)

children, nannies, and servants of the well-to-do were packed off to elegant hotels and summer houses at the beach. Only husbands remained behind, to pursue business during summer weekdays. Availing themselves of the "summer arrangements" railway companies offered, men made frequent sorties to the beach, arriving at dinnertime and departing a day or two later in the early morning.

CONSPICUOUS CONGREGATION

Going to the seashore provided much more than a health cure for nineteenth-century Americans. It also gave them an excuse to congregate and, in the case of the upwardly mobile, a way to acquire and display good taste and status. At the seaside—among other places—a nation of shopkeepers, artisans, and professionals gradually metamorphosed into a new middle class, converted from an ethic of hard work and abhorrence for ostentation to an ethos of consumption, indulgence, and emotional fulfillment in purchases and play. The beach resort created a world where experiences were for sale: for the poetically inclined there was communion with nature; for the socially mobile, entree to a select circle; for the pious, community and religion; and for the restless, gambling, carnival, and the sporting life. Although they would hardly admit it, sober, hardworking artisans, tradesmen, farmers, and teachers were acquiring a taste for the fun of spending money.

By the mid-nineteenth century, coastal resorts crystallized along the spreading railroad lines, which were the critical link between city and sea, between oppressive heat and refreshment. More and more Americans came to value vacation travel and diligently set about putting aside a part of their income for what they increasingly viewed as a new necessity of life. After all, medical authorities were telling them sea air, sand, and water were wonderful cures for various ailments: for nervous disorders ranging from St. Vitus' dance to hysteria; diseases of the abdominal, excretory, and reproductive organs—exempting pregnancy and menstruation; and "hay" asthma as well as respiratory disorders. Depending on their symptoms, actual invalids and hypochondriacs were steered to the full regimen of bathing options—sun, cold salt water, hot salt water, sand—practiced in the health spas of Europe. "Change of scene" or sea air was prescribed for patients such as the novelist Edward Bellamy, who left an account of his treatment for nervous breakdown and exhaustion on Nantucket in the thinly disguised autobiographical novel *Six to One: A Nantucket Idyll.*

Following the British lead, American cities built swimming baths in the latter half of the nineteenth century and provided instructors paid for by local boards of education to teach the rudiments of swimming to all who applied. (Culver Pictures)

In fact, city living itself was increasingly considered detrimental to physical and mental health. The intense heat of the American summer, especially in the cities of the Northeast and the Midwest, provided an irresistible incentive for fleeing to the seashore. There was some speculation, too, that the American character was especially drawn to the sea by a sort of elemental affinity. "There is nothing so restful to the restless American," wrote Francis H. Hardy in *The Cornhill Magazine,* "as the sight and sound of the unresting sea."

There was even speculation that the beach might become a unique staging ground for "educating the country into accepting a consistent set of social standards and customs," as journalist J. Howe Adams hoped it would.

It appeared to Adams that the American beach could potentially be an even more democratic setting than the baseball stadium. In 1889, foreign observers writing in *The Cosmopolitan* viewed the American love for the beach as a glue that would help cement a heterogeneous society. It was a place where the country's "liability to fall apart from its own weight, as an unwieldy, helpless mass, as had occurred at the outbreak of the Civil War, might be counteracted."

Such, at least, was the theory. Practice was another matter. People from all walks of life and backgrounds were thrown together on large stretches of sand within easy reach of cities. Generally, however, the nineteenth-century beach was bound to disappoint social utopians. Seaside resorts seemed to evolve along existing social lines: people of the same circles and professions tended to go to the same resorts. In fact, exclusivity was one of their chief attractions. The earliest resorts on the New Jersey shore and in New England developed by carving out their own social niches, in which they surrounded the vacationer with agreeable company and created a bubble of psychological comfort. Class and income determined congeniality, and developers explicitly pitched their product to these social markers. If they wanted to attract the wealthy, they used the epithet "exclusive" in their promotional material. This code word meant the patrons would not have to worry about rubbing shoulders with middle-class or lower-class visitors. They also promised to exclude "excursionists," which meant the working-class day trippers.

When a group of prominent Boston investors opened an "exclusive" resort in Cape Arundel, Maine, they publicized the fact that "Every precaution has been taken to guard against an invasion of excursionists." By and large, resorts tended to be self-regulating, and status gradations were explicitly drawn. One stretch of the Maine coast, for example, accommodated three adjacent resorts, each catering to a distinct demographic niche, with almost no socializing across property boundaries. Opulent professionals and intellectuals came to York Harbor, where they commissioned grandiose, architect-built cottages in the vicinity of a small private beach and a refined hotel. Next door at York Beach, congregated people several rungs lower on the social scale, who stayed in rows of humble cottages. Even farther down the beach, at Long Sands, were the excursionists, who came for the day by trolley. It was to these intermediate zones—the day beaches and middle-class resorts—that most nineteenth-century vacationers gravitated.

For the most part, a seaside holiday—a fortnight or a month at the beach—came to be seen as an earmark of middle-class status, much like owning a piano or a Tiffany lamp. Because going to the "wrong" beach could compromise status, the middle-class vacationer took great pains to find the right "fit" between aspirations, self-assessment, and resort. A businessman could put himself and his family out of their depth in the flamboyant affluence of Newport, whereas an upwardly mobile young couple might feel "cheapened" at Nantasket Beach. In the novel *The Rise of Silas Lapham,* William Dean Howells, novelist and editor of *The Atlantic Monthly,* chronicled the social ordeals of a wealthy parvenu who, ignorant of Boston social standards, blundered into renting a cottage in plebeian Nantasket.

Parents of marriageable daughters carefully weighed the social advantages of Nahant, where the snobs of Beacon Hill spent their summers, against the easy sociability of Mount Desert Island, where the sporting set congregated and where bachelors with freer morals flocked. Young women and spinsters considered to be "hopeless" came here husband hunting. In fact, long before Club Med, the matrimonial function of these beach resorts was well known. Authorities on etiquette prescribed correct courtship decorum. "An attractive young girl sometimes suffers, at a watering place, from the reprehensible habit society men have of amusing themselves by selecting one young lady and monopolizing her society for the Summer," wrote Mrs. Robert A. Pryor in "The Social Code" for *The Delineator* of June 1895. For their part, caricaturists satirized the blatant intentions of "predatory" females and the vanity of "unmanly" suitors. For a girl without connections or sober advice, navigating the treacherous terrain of the "marriage mill" was quite an accomplishment, and depended on what beach she and her guardians had chosen for their summer vacation.

Americans flocked to the beach not only to ogle, recreate, and strut but to revel in an unprecedented liberalization of morals. Observers throughout the century were fascinated to discover that the aphrodisiacal potency of water was shared by watchers and bathers alike. There was something magical about the beach that dissolved constraint and melted reserve, and not a small share of the credit went to the bathing costume. "The haughty dowager, the exquisite maid, the formal-minded matron, the pompous buck, the pretty dandy," wrote J. Howe Adams during the 1890s, "donned with their unconstricting garb of bath-flannels, a devil-may-care disregard for the modes and conventions of fashion that reminds one strongly of [Herodotus'] comment on the close relation between womanly pudicity and its outer garb."

BEACH COTTAGES AND BOARDING HOUSES

As the herring population dwindled, and the economy up and down the coast of New England slumped, the fashion for seaside holidays brought a new measure of prosperity to the Atlantic coast. Affluent summer people traveled to dilapidated old coastal towns and villages like York, Maine, and fell in love with the deteriorating colonial architecture. Anxious to own a piece of the past, they bought up the ancestral homes of old sea captains and fishermen, restored them, added a wing here and a veranda there, and settled in for summers of sailing, swimming, and croquet on the lawn.

These outposts expanded with the construction of grand hotels and somewhat less grand rooming houses. Tourists from cities in the South, the Midwest, and even the West sought out the New Jersey shore, with its gentle sandy beach, for ocean bathing. Farther north, as the coast became rockier and the temperature of the water dropped, resort life focused on boating, sailing, horseback riding, and inland sports. As in British resorts, guests distracted themselves with sketching, science walks, and social events. In isolated coves or on remote sandy beaches of New England and Long Island, there were also hunting retreats, the "red-shirt" lodges named for the color worn by hunters. In these exclusively male retreats, the guests devoted themselves to hunting, shooting, heavy drinking, and swimming in the nude. Presumably, while taking their ease at these lodges, some of the men sent their wives to the handful of medicinal spas on the East Coast, such as the renowned Old Point Comfort, at the mouth of Chesapeake Bay. Though modeled on those at Brighton or Dieppe, these never achieved the popularity or cachet of their European counterparts.

A vigorous flowering of American beach culture occurred in the 1860s and 1870s. Seasonal resorts began to mushroom farther down the Atlantic coast, spurred by the growth in extensive and inexpensive rail service, an urban middle class, and growing familiarity with medical precepts that promoted the healthfulness of the seashore. Resort developers saw great potential in a new class of accommodations that would target a less affluent public than had frequented the grand hotels. Until then, the hotels had been the only option for visitors from the city without the means to construct their own palatial homes or without entree to high society.

The first private cottage was built in 1850 in Long Branch, New Jersey, by Commodore Stockton, who had earlier constructed a shooting-and-fishing lodge at Squan Beach. Soon modest-sized cottages began to sprout all along the seashore from Cape May to Bar Harbor, forming, as an 1886 article in *Harper's* described it, "an almost continual chain of hotels and summer cottages." One of the earliest such communities developed as Cottage City on the Island of Martha's Vineyard. A prototypical planned resort community, Cottage City was designed to attract a clearly defined public of solidly middle-class families. Though it did not exclude day trippers and fashionable sightseers, it was predominantly the summer home, as William Dean Howells remarked, of "inland people of little social importance."

In 1886, Charles Dudley Warner described Cottage City in a story for *Harper's*. Crossing on the New Bedford boat, he studied the vacationers bound for the resort and noticed at once that they little resembled the party he had recently left behind at Newport. "Most of the faces," he observed, "are of a grave, severe type, plain and good, of the sort of people ready to die for a notion." These were people, noted Warner, "who abandon themselves soberly to the pleasures of the sea and of this packed, gregarious life, and get solid enjoyment out of their recreation."

The appeal and popularity of cottage resorts challenged builders and engineers with an entirely new set of problems. Most construction prior to that time had been set far back from the beach, and the large hotels dealt with their seasonal water-and-sewage requirements in conventional ways that were adequate to the population they serviced. But building cottages close to, and in some cases directly on, the sand challenged old conventions. Extensive supplies of fresh water had to be identified, tapped, and channeled to the building sites, not always an easy matter. Much of the fresh water along the seacoast had a brackish or unpleasant smell, but by drilling deep underground, it was possible to tap into good reserve; frequently one had to go to the expense of running water pipes from artesian wells dug well inland. The earliest cottages were often built with cesspools and drinking wells placed close to each other and to the house, a situation that led to outbreaks of intestinal disorders and malodorous emanations. The newer fashion of so-called trapped water-closets, set at some distance from the freshwater supply, helped immeasurably, except when unusually high tides drove sewage back through the horizontally laid pipes.

Yet solutions were gradually found, and a formula was elaborated for the standard beach cottage. It was generally a two-story structure, set a foot or two from the ground on brick piles or wooden pillars. A fireplace in the main room provided warmth on cool days and took the edge off the damp air. Bathhouses or dressing rooms became standard; so did "piazzas," or porches, which surrounded the house on three sides to afford shelter from the sun and were large enough to accommodate a family and all its visitors. From the poles supporting the piazza's roof the renters generally suspended a hammock, which, with its appropriately marine connotations, provided many agreeable hours of rest and relaxation. The hammock was an extremely popular accessory around the turn of the century, when it became available in a wide array of styles: fringed or plain, covered or bare, cushioned or not.

Paradise by the sea had become a reality for the middle masses. In the rooming house or private cottage, the seasonal guest would find long- and short-term housing at an affordable price. In Atlantic City, for example, nearly fifty thousand visitors stayed in boarding houses and private cottages in 1890—the same number as were housed in the luxurious hotels. The impact of the building boom on summer resorts was quite dramatic. The arrival of these low-cost options allowed men of middling means to send their wives and children away for the entire summer, and not deprive themselves of the benefits of the seashore.

Cottage life, however, was not without its disadvantages. The trials and tribulations of renting and inhabiting these accommodations spawned an entire genre of anecdotes. Tiresome negotiations with landladies, unanticipated fees, the restrictions and controls of landlords, foul-smelling cesspools, the cumbersome crowded trip to the shore, the annoyance of unsavory neighbors, the dreadful discovery of insect infestations—these were the commonplaces of beach humor. Still, anyone who could, headed for the seashore as soon as the first heat wave touched down in the cities. Even people from smaller towns and villages packed up their belongings and joined the general exodus. A summer on the beach had become the general marker of middle-class affluence. It was, quite simply, the thing to do.

HEAVEN ON THE BEACH

Biblical teachings had often maligned the sea. But once tamed, sweetened, and lightened—and freed of terrifying associations—the beach was simply a force too powerful to be ignored by those who aimed at transporting the soul to an elevated, and drier, place. The road to higher ground was littered with formidable barriers. The heat waves that sent urban Americans to the healing and cooling sea also stoked the fires of lust and a host of sinful inclinations, among them gambling, drinking, sloth, and a general disregard for the Sabbath. So what were morally upright Americans to do if they were loath to forgo the innocent pleasures of the beach? The eventual result was seaside resorts founded along sectarian lines and strategically barricaded against the incursion of sin.

Clergymen actually began recommending seashore holidays. Some of them declared from the pulpit that, contrary to the adage that empty hands are the devil's workshop, leisure did not necessarily lead to vice, but could actually be good for the soul. With the proper guidance and in the right surroundings, a distinct religious advantage could be derived from a sea holiday. In Brooklyn Heights, New York, for example, the Reverend Henry Ward Beecher counseled his congregation of socially ambitious professionals to take a week or two, or even four, by the sea. It would do them good to "forget the city and lay aside its excitements" and to take the time for "the most earnest reflection, and for the most solemn resolutions for the future." Indeed, in his series of sermons, Beecher wrote of vacations as another form of religious obligation. "God says some things to the soul . . . along the sea-shore, or in the twilight forests, which he never speaks through books or men."

One of the earliest establishments dedicated entirely to Christian leisure by the sea was Wesleyan Grove on Martha's Vineyard, a triangle of land twenty miles long, nine miles wide, and about a hundred square miles in area, off the tip of Cape Cod. It began with the wave of Methodist revivalism in 1835, when thousands of people flocked to camp meetings in town "commons" and county fairgrounds up and down the Northeast. On Martha's Vineyard, a small number of local Methodists decided to hold their revival in a lovely but rather inaccessible spot—that was one reason they had chosen it—in a great grove of oak trees. On August 24, 1835, they gathered in the arbor to preach sermons, pray, confess their sins, and proclaim their faith. All through the following week, they renewed their faith and accepted new converts beneath the canopy of leaves, breaking long enough to picnic on cold chicken, potato salad, and pickled beef. By night they piled up beds of straw, and those who had thought of bringing tents cozied up inside them. The revival was, by all accounts, a stirring experience. When the believers dispersed, they promised to return the following year.

Until then, Martha's Vineyard had been a sleepy, sparsely inhabited outpost of some three thousand souls—five or six hundred of them whalers and fishermen. But now that would change. The following year, worshippers came to Wesleyan Grove—so the camp came to be called, after the founder of Methodism—from Nantucket and New Bedford. As its fame spread, celebrants began coming from all over New England, and eventually from all over the East Coast. Over the next two decades, the camp meetings at Wesleyan Grove enjoyed tremendous success. The number of tents multiplied, and oak trees were chopped down to make room for them. Large communal "society tents" were set up by home churches to house and board entire congregations, and a vast tented tabernacle, with benches for four thousand people, was built in the center of the site. There, protected from the hot August sun, the faithful worshipped in peace, until the day when a violent storm ripped apart the canvas and brought the entire structure tumbling down. Eventually, a handsome cast-iron-and-wood pavilion rose in its place.

At the culmination of the week-long meeting, the camp staged a special event, Big Sunday, which brought thousands of excursionists from the mainland by steamers and boats. In 1859, twelve thousand people joined the inhabitants of the four hundred tents to hear the Big Sunday preaching. But rather than welcoming this development as a sign of their success, the camp leadership were alarmed. A secular spirit of merriment and play had begun to accompany the day trippers: some did not listen as attentively to the pious words as they might have, and others joined in the singing with a gusto inspired less by the Holy Spirit than by alcohol.

For some years, gradual changes had begun to appear in Wesleyan Grove. At first a few, then more and more families began to set up their own tents instead of living in the communal quarters. By 1855, there were 150 private tents. Then, in 1859, a Providence regular named William Lawton decided to have a little cottage built in Rhode Island, shipped in sections—fancy scrollwork and all—to Martha's Vineyard, and erected in the Grove. Soon everybody wanted one. For the next ten years, Vineyard carpenters were busy sawing, planing, and hammering more than two hundred cottages in a distinctive "gingerbread" style bristling with geegaws, curlicues, gimcracks, balconies, fancy railings, and ornate balconies.

Apparently, the sybaritic spell of the shore was simply too compelling and eventually began to erode the religious orientation of those who had been coming to Wesleyan Grove. Once the worshippers had become houseowners, their expectations and attitudes toward the revival meetings changed. Why not come to the meetings a few days or even weeks early and enjoy the sun, the sailing, fishing, swimming, the lovely sights, the peace? By the mid-1860s, the retreats at Wesleyan Grove had taken on a recreational tone. Though the national Methodist weekly, the *Christian Advocate*, still found "the singing superb, the preaching superior, the congregations immense," it bewailed the fact that the number of converts had plummeted to *one*. At the same time, the number of converts to swimming, boating, and cricket had grown exponentially. Though banned from campgrounds for the duration of the meeting, the game was played enthusiastically in the weeks and months before and afterward.

Finally, in 1869, demoralized by the evidence of so much secularism in their midst, the Methodist camp leaders decided to enclose the grounds with a seven-foot-high picket fence. That might have kept irreverent excursionists from the Grove, but it did nothing to keep them from coming to the Vineyard. A building boom ensued, the profane took up residence on the island, but within the campground, life continued in its stately course.

Meanwhile, farther to the south, a shrewd, far-seeing Methodist minister by the name of Stokes advised a number of his sea-loving but sin-hating congregation members to invest in three hundred acres on the Jersey shore. In the 1880s, this tract of land, which boasted about a mile of sea frontage, was so far removed from any other settlements, or even possibilities of settlement, that the state of New Jersey granted the Ocean Grove Association, as it styled itself, a charter to dispose of the management and arrangement of the land as it saw fit. As part of this liberal dispensation, the state also guaranteed that by law no alcoholic beverages could be sold within a mile of Ocean Grove.

The settlement began modestly enough, in rough canvas tents used for a camp meeting lasting ten days. Within twenty-five years, a colony of fifteen hundred permanent structures had been established, and a spacious tract of tents was retained for indigent members of the community. For three months of the summer, Ocean Grove hummed with a resident population of twenty-five thousand, and when revival meetings were on the agenda, their number topped 150,000. The magnificent "tabernacle," eventually brilliantly illumined by electrical lights, had acoustic properties envied by every theater manager south of Manhattan. It was reported that the voice of a speaker using a normal tone could be heard in every part of the cavernous space and even reached the horizon of the sea.

Every transgression that made life outside Ocean Grove such a pleasure was banned within its limits. No liquor or tobacco could be sold *at any time.* No card playing or dancing was tolerated. On Sundays, the gates were locked and no vehicles were allowed within the precincts. No shops were open, so someone who happened to need a quart of milk had to trudge across to Asbury Park. Six to ten religious services were held, double the number available the other six days of the week. It was rumored that fully 99 percent of the residents attended at least two religious services daily, and even managed to squeeze in tours of a large model of the city of Jerusalem. True, many appeared at devotions still clad in their bathing costumes, dripping from the surf. For all their love of piety, their devotion to bathing kept pace with that of their sinful brethren across the way.

SIN AND SEA

Up the coast, at the northern end of New Jersey, the storms of life were brewing in the resort town of Long Branch, which acquired a reputation as the summer capital of the United States when General Ulysses S. Grant summered there during all eight years of his presidency. Boasting a splendid five-mile seafront boulevard, Long Branch had a seamy underside that many years later would resurface in Atlantic City.

Most of the respectable families vacationing here had no idea that Long Branch was distinguished as the gambling capital of the Jersey shore. But for the cognoscenti, Long Branch was Mecca. In some twenty-six gambling houses, open six months of the year, they tried their fortune with Lady Luck. A typical gambling house looked, from the outside, like nothing so much as the cottage of an affluent gentleman. Two stories high and surrounded by wide verandas, it gave little clue as to what went on beneath the glass-and-slate rotunda protruding from the top at a height of some sixty feet or behind the lush screen of potted plants that ornamented the verandas.

Gambling was, of course, against the law in New Jersey. But the operators circumvented legalities by not hiring or admitting any locals. At the entrance, they posted a townie to screen visitors: no permanent residents of Long Branch were allowed in. Everyone else was more than welcome, though no one was pressured to gamble.

Inside, the premises were dripping with the kind of luxury to which international travelers had become accustomed in the casinos of the grand hotels in Europe. Throughout, deep, soft Turkish rugs, in a yellow, gold, and blue pattern, dampened the sound of footfalls. Crystal chandeliers blazed with light night and day, reported *The Cosmopolitan,* because "it is always night in American gambling-houses." Pink-bottomed cupids frolicked on the blue-and-gold walls. Proceeding deeper into the emporium, the visitor entered the great gambling room, situated directly below the dome. The floor here was covered in even thicker yellow rugs, the walls painted a virginal white and studded with lights, crystal sconces, and chandeliers. The salon, although filled with three hundred men in evening dress intent on play at faro, roulette, baccarat, was as hushed as a cathedral. No one spoke above a whisper. The only noise was the percussive clacking of ivory chips stacked, scattered, collected. Waiters in livery hovered discreetly in the background, ready to escort

In the 1920s, the stately band music of the previous century's resorts was replaced by the syncopated rhythms of jazz. (Bettmann Archive)

players or observers to the magnificent banquet room, which served meals free of charge around the clock. Tremendous amounts of money thus passed through the establishments and percolated like rainwater into the local community, whose grocers and tradesmen were scrupulously patronized and made an integral part of the food chain of vice and pleasure.

SUTRO BATHS

Far from the mild Jersey shore, on the chill coast of northern California, San Franciscans engaged in their own fantasies of the Riviera. Here the sea bathing and revelry for which nature had so poorly equipped their coast were supplied by artificial means through the magic of engineering. An engineer who had grown wealthy by devising a tunnel for draining the flooded shafts of Nevada silver mines gave San Francisco the equivalent of Mediterranean bathing in oceanside swimming pools. In 1896, he opened Sutro Baths, a remarkable complex of health and pleasure situated high above the Pacific. Two railway lines ran directly to the entrance of what was then the largest glass-roofed building in the world. Visitors stepped into a balmy hothouse of palm trees reaching to the ceiling and stuffed jungle creatures lurking in the lush foliage. In the main amphitheater, seven swimming pools, holding two million gallons of seawater and ranging in temperature from icy to warm, overlooked the ocean. At any one time, ten thousand bathers swam, swung from the rings and trapezes, and dived from the springboards and platforms. Tiring of the water, they could watch swimming and diving competitions, or lounge on a tropical beach, or dine in one of the restaurants.

Across San Francisco Bay was the Fleishhacker, another gargantuan swimming facility. Its Italian Renaissance changing rooms were the height of elegance, and the open-air pool, touted to be the largest in the world, could accommodate hundreds of swimmers at one time. The size was something of a liability, however: the temperature of the water was always on the cold side, and a constant fog hovered over the swimmers.

CONEY ISLAND

The gambling establishments of Long Branch were exclusively for the amusement of "high rollers." The day tripper, however, was not left out of the pleasure loop for long. If, for the middle and upper classes, going to the beach was supposed to Do You Good—physically, spiritually, and intellectually—the working class, with typical bluntness, wanted one thing only: to Have Fun. No need to disguise the fact with edifying walks along the beach or with religious-revival meetings on the sand at sunset. Given long days at the factory or the piecework shop, and with no one at home to help with the washing, cooking, cleaning, or childrearing, time was a precious commodity. Almost as precious as money. And what everyone wanted was a place to go, a short, cheap ride from the city, a place that rolled all pleasures—licit and illicit—into a one-stop "orgiastic escape from respectability" from, as Richard Le Gallienne wrote in 1905, "the world of What-we-have-to-do into the world of What-we-would-like-to-do, from the world of duty that endureth forever into the world of joy that is permitted for a moment."

The place in question was Coney Island, a narrow sandbar five miles long lying nine miles out of Manhattan, at the foot of Brooklyn. Until 1829, only the wind and the seagulls disturbed its shifting sands. Then a road of broken seashells brought it within commuting distance of Long Island. Now and then, when cholera made its periodic visitations, wealthy Brooklynites took refuge with their families in the only available hotel, the Coney Island House. When the Civil War broke out, a handful of hotels, some bathhouses, and a few chowder huts persuaded local entrepreneurs that the place had potential. They even had visions of rivaling Newport, until they troubled to visit the beach. Evidently, the clientele here had a considerably lower threshold for modesty and hygiene than the public at the Rhode Island resort. As late as 1870, signs still had to be posted warning "Bathers Without Full Suits Positively Prohibited by Law," so Coney Island presumably saw its fair share of skinny-dippers. As for cleanliness, the bathers were not squeamish. What difference did an occasional rotting horse carcass make? The water was fine, and that was all that mattered.

In the 1870s, railroad lines were providing regular and frequent service to the Island. True, the trip out was a depressing excursion through the purgatory of urban industrialization, coal yards, soap factories, ash pits, threadbare fields with occasional signs rising up to promise suburban villas of the future. But what a sight greeted them at the other end: miles of fine sand, of waves tamely washing the shore, and a veritable paradise of bathing pavilions, piers, beer gardens, restaurants, hotels, and towers. Many of these structures were designed in the most fantastic of architectural styles, and there were mechanical rides and gigantic banners gaudily advertising everything from freaks to frankfurters. Playground to the urban masses, and safety valve of New York City, this carnival-in-residence received some ten million visitors annually, a good number of them coming to swim. West Brighton Beach, according to Baedeker's 1893 *United States,* "beggared description" on a fine Sunday in summer, when it "swarmed with all the peripatetic shows of a popular seaside resort." Strolling puppeteers, vendors and musicians, gamblers and prostitutes peddling their wares presented a riveting garnish to permanent attractions such as the colossal Elephant, with restaurant and dancing rooms in its interior, capable of feeding as many as four thousand in one seating; and such as the sideshows and the thrilling rides. Three enormous new hostelries beckoned—the Manhattan Beach, the Oriental, and the Brighton Beach.

A postcard from the period shows the Manhattan Beach Hotel, a long wooden affair with turrets, canopied windows, and endless verandas. Built in 1877, it was for a long time the classiest of the new grand hotels. Guests staying in the 258 rooms were fed by a kitchen equipped to turn out twenty thousand meals a day. Acres of impeccably groomed lawns and gardens flanked the expansive boardwalk. Every night, guests were treated to open-air concerts. A circular pavilion catered to the whims of diners seeking a less formal atmosphere than the dining rooms. According to a guidebook published in 1879, "One part of the pavilion is devoted to fish dinners, which are prepared by a special cook, and another part is reserved for the gratuitous use of the excursionists." Everybody who was anybody in New York signed up for rooms. "The most exclusive and prominent clubs in New York," the same guidebook announced, "the Union and the Union League, have selected it for a sea-beach branch, and have rented suites of the largest rooms permanently." To ensure that nothing would disturb this select clientele, the hotel management hired private detectives to patrol the grounds.

In 1878, the Hotel Brighton Beach opened its doors. A vast Stick-style extravaganza, the Brighton Beach matched the Manhattan Beach in all its amenities, and even topped it by offering champagne on draft at ten cents a glass. Unfortunately, however, it was situated just a hair too close to the amusement district cropping up in West Brighton. The truly respectable visitor cringed at such proximity. Just ten years later, on April 3, 1888, the Brighton Beach itself moved, all six thousand tons of it hoisted onto 120 railroad cars and inched inland over newly laid track. It seems the ocean was eating away at the beach in front of the hotel at an alarming rate. If nothing was done, guests would soon be swimming up to the bar. It was easier in those days to move the hotel than to extend the beach and numerous grand establishments had to be relocated because the sea had engulfed their foundations. By the end of June, the Brighton Beach was open for business in its new location.

In 1880, Manhattanites were given the welcome option of traveling to Coney Island by steamer. That year, the Iron Steamboat Company put a squadron of handsome little boats to work ferrying passengers. With their classical names—*Cepheus, Cetus, Cygnus, Pegasus,* and *Sirius*—the boats catered to the middle-class yen for travel to exotic locales. Though virtually at Manhattan's back door, Coney Island easily qualified, and the approach from the sea heightened the impression. "Coney Island," wrote the *Scientific American,* "that marvelous city of lath and burlap, should always be approached by the sea, as then, and then only, can the beauty of this ephemeral Venice be appreciated." As the giant paddle wheel churned the waves and a string of smoke trailed from the tall black stack, the passengers settled on one of the three decks to enjoy the procession of tugboats, yachts, ocean liners, and assorted aquatic vessels plying the waves. "Then," wrote Albert Bigelow Paine, "the Island rose up out of the sea—a horizon of towers, domes, spidery elevations, and huge revolving wheels." This glimpse of the Island evidently made a tremendous impression: here was America's first great tribute to the technology of pleasure. Industrial forms—grids, mechanical contrivances, welded towers, elevated rails, industrial-scale sheds, and gargantuan warehouses—were spot-welded to the beach with a single objective: to replicate and even outdo the thrills and spills and adrenaline rushes of a dip in the wild, cold surf.

Sin, like virtue, does not just happen. It takes planning, shrewd calculation, discipline, and a genius for knowing what customers want even before they do. In the case of Coney Island, the genius was John Y. McKane. "Houses of prostitution are a necessity on Coney Island," the hard-boiled onetime carpenter and eventual "ruler" of the resort ordained. In the 1870s and 1880s, he occupied virtually every post of importance, from chief of police to superintendent of Sunday schools, and controlled every concession and license on the Island. Things got so bad under his rule that sin-debauched and crime-soaked Coney Island aroused the ire of neighboring townships and finally attracted the attention of the reform movement of the 1890s. In 1894, McKane was at last dispatched to Sing Sing.

At that point, Coney Island passed under the rule of George C. Tilyou. By dint of hard work and vision, this local boy who made good transformed Sodom-on-the Sea into the premier carnival beach in the world. A shrewd, untiring developer with a long, aristocratic face, Tilyou brought the first painted scenery to the island. At the age of twenty, he was already running his own theater, Tilyou's Surf Theater. But, after he testified against McKane in legal proceedings, he lost his real-estate holdings. However, like one of those pop-up carnival dolls that just won't stay down no matter how hard you push them, Tilyou refused to admit defeat. As soon as McKane was packed off to prison, Tilyou set to work making his fantasy real.

In 1893, he had gone to the World's Columbian Exposition in Chicago and seen the great Ferris Wheel. This, he thought to himself, would be just the thing. He was not the first to see a useful lesson in the architecture of world's fairs. Before him, the Centennial Exhibition of Philadelphia had inspired the fantasy structures of Coney Island of the early 1880s, based on Brazilian and Japanese motifs. Set back from the beach, the three-hundred-foot Observation Tower, a spidery iron structure reminiscent of the Eiffel Tower, had come from the 1876 fair.

Tilyou tried to buy it, but St. Louis, looking ahead to the 1904 fair, beat

During the "Roaring Twenties," bathing beauties and beauty pageants became a fixed element of beach life. (authors' collection)

him to it. Unfazed, he returned to Coney Island and commissioned a Ferris wheel half as big. Truth be damned, he promptly let it be known: "On this site will be built the largest Ferris Wheel in the world." The hype worked: investors snapped up the concession space in the vicinity of the future attraction, the money went to Tilyou, and by the time the Ferris wheel was delivered by the Pennsylvania Steel Company, he was flush. Ten thousand people rode on it every day. By night, it was illuminated by 460 incandescent lights and "could be seen 38 miles at sea," as Tilyou liked to boast. It was said that immigrants coming from Europe saw Coney Island's Ferris wheel long before they caught sight of the Statue of Liberty. And they lost no time making their way out to this Mecca of delights.

Tilyou, in the meantime, was looking around for his next inspiration. Coney Island's racecourses—all three of them—gave him an idea. Why not give the crowds a chance to take part in a simulated horse-race? The British had come up with a ride that did just that. In 1897, Tilyou imported the novelty, which he called Steeplechase Park, and set it up along the perimeter of his fourteen-acre amusement park. From the top of the cavernous entrance to the Steeplechase ride, the trademark "Steeplechase Man" beamed his hideous grin to the multitudes, who made this ride "one of the biggest winners ever known, both in profit and in popularity." Consisting of a wooden course gently falling and rising for a half-mile, the circuit included eight elevated tracks, on each of which a wooden simulacrum of a racehorse was installed. Riders mounted the dummies, then were towed to the top of the track, to the starting gate, and released to compete. They could actually control the speed of the mount by the way they maneuvered around turns and down descending grades. The slope was much too gentle to provide hair-raising thrills, but riders mobbed the concession for the erotic kick of straddling the horse while clutching a paramour. Richard Snow, in *Coney Island: A Postcard Journey to the City of Fire*, remarked, "Nothing on Coney Island gave quite the same sense of jaunty intimacy as sitting astride that horse, the man behind the woman, arms around her waist holding the reins, and gusting along through the summer evening." From the Steeplechase, couples headed for the Barrel of Love, where they tumbled around in each other's arms.

When the entire complex perished in flames in 1901, Tilyou built a tremendous factorylike structure in its place. This glass-and-cast-iron shed became Tilyou's Pavilion of Fun, where a quarter purchased admission to twenty-five big attractions and where, according to Tilyou's publicity, "25,000 people laugh at one time." Distributed along more than five acres of hardwood floor, Tilyou's rides and novelties provided every experience of which the body was capable—movement, nausea, shock, terror—all of which, in Tilyou's words, "caused laughter enough to cure all the dyspepsia in the world." He installed heaving patches of floor, hidden air jets which sent skirts and petticoats ballooning over the knees, chairs dispensing electric shocks, stairways that flattened into slides, elevators that crashed, oiled and slippery floors—perilous but apparently beloved amusements no longer possible in our own litigious age.

In the meantime, another entrepreneur, Captain Paul Boyton, had been successfully developing the neighboring Sea Lion Park. Boyton had held the world spellbound some years earlier when he swam across the English Channel in an inflated rubber suit. Now he gave visitors the thrill of a lifetime in a ride called Shoot the Chutes, where they scudded down a huge water slide in flat-bottomed boats that debouched into an artificial lagoon. According to Robert Hughes, "One felt the rapture of a seagull swooping to the waves—the long, swift glide down the wet incline, and the glorious splash into the flying spray!" Boyton also ran one of the three roller coasters of Coney—the Flip-Flap, a centrifugal pleasure railway that gave passengers serious cases of whiplash as it jerked and lurched them through a terrifying series of loops and dips.

The sun, surf, and sand lured crowds of Manhattanites to Coney Island, but it was the glitz, the entertainment, and the hair-rising rides that kept them coming back for more. (Culver Pictures)

But Tilyou was not to be outdone, and again an international exposition gave him a splendid idea. At the 1901 Pan-American Exposition in Buffalo, he came across a trip-to-the-moon attraction operated by a pair of entrepreneurs named Fred Thompson and Elmer Dundy. They installed the lunar voyage as well as the Giant See-Saw for Tilyou and did so well that by next season they were able to purchase Boyton's Sea Lion Park, rebuild it, and open it on the evening of May 16, 1903, as Luna Park.

"By day a paradise . . . At night, Arcadia," "Electric Eden . . . Night as Noon-Tide," and "Harnessed Lightning in Flashing Fountains," proclaimed advertisements written by Thompson and Dundy. The twenty-two-acre extravaganza was a triumph of kitsch architecture and the masses' thirst for spectacle. Filled with towers, minarets, spires, trellises, lagoons, gilded domes, flags, pennants, and arches, Luna Park looked like a story-

Dressed in the unisex style of the 1920s, couples dance on the beach at Coney Island. (authors' collection)

book Baghdad. At night, it flamed with 1.2 million lightbulbs. Here revelers tumbled every which way in the Tickler, a kind of twisting and turning slide filled with tubs on wheels; or in the Helter Skelter, a precipitous slide on a doormat; or in the Trip to Mars by Aeroplane. They took camel- and elephant-back rides, inspected the Bauer Sisters' Candy Delicatessen, where every imaginable cut and preparation of meat was offered up in Pure Candy, and gawked at the people strolling for pleasure.

At the very heart of Coney Island's thrills were the spectacular reproductions of natural catastrophes which were constructed immediately on the heels of the actual events. It seems fitting that one of the most popular of these was devoted to the flood which had swept across Galveston, Texas, in 1900, leveling the city and killing over seven thousand people. Shortly thereafter, New Yorkers could witness Galveston before and after the flood, watching water—both real and fake—rushing in from a painted gulf, and hundreds of model buildings collapsing on themselves.

If Tilyou's Pavilion of Fun and Thomson and Dundy's Luna Park catered to workers and the day trippers, Dreamland aimed squarely at the pocketbooks of the well-heeled middle-class. Opened in 1904, it was designed by the New York architectural firm of Kirby, Petit, and Green, and enjoyed the unique distinction of being subjected to a serious and lengthy review by the critic Barr Feree in the *Architects' and Builders' Magazine*. Water, light, and gentility were the governing themes. Replicas of shrines sacred to Western culture abounded: there was a copy of the Doge's Palace in Venice, a series of Venetian-canal scenes, a Pompeii Building with a gigantic fresco of the Bay of Naples, finely detailed miniatures of steam engines, and a scaled-down model of Old Nuremberg peopled with three hundred midgets recruited from all parts of the world. There were lions and lion tamers, leopards, tigers, pumas, and hyenas that had been tortured into talent. There was Wormwood's Monkey Theater, where anteaters, chickens, monkeys, and lemurs performed a three-act drama entitled *The Pardon Came Too Late.* At the end of the iron pier, the giant Dreamland Ballroom reverberated to the sounds of big bands into the early hours of the morning.

Six years after it opened, Dreamland vanished in a puff of smoke. A great fire swept through the wooden-and-canvas structures, and all that remained of the architectural confectionery was the haunting waltz "Meet Me Tonight in Dreamland." World War I came soon after, and then the subway from Manhattan. For a nickel, anyone could ride out to Coney Island, and in a single season, the number of visitors more than doubled. Nathan Handwerker opened his Coney Island hot-dog stand on the corner of Surf Avenue and launched a beach tradition. But, gradually, the sensationalistic rides and displays no longer gave the same adrenaline rush as they had before the war. By the 1940s, Luna Park, too, had perished in flames. Steeplechase finally closed in 1965. By the 1970s, the fantastic carnival had shrunk, into a few blocks of Surf Avenue. The bathing pavilions vanished; the rides were dismantled, hauled away, or simply left to decay. All that remained was, once again, sand.

CHAPTER

8

SWIMMINGLY AT THE BEACH

Ipswich, Massachusetts, August 1918. The bay is sapphire with flashes of gold and silver reflecting the sun. A woman stands at the edge of the dock that juts from the expanse of tightly clipped lawn flowing from the sprawling, shingled house with forest-green shutters. Big white homes, each with its complement of tennis court, studio, guest cottage, and boathouse, line this stretch of beach like a necklace of pearls. From the porch, her husband, strong-jawed and burned mahogany-brown from days sailing in the bay, watches her silhouetted against the shimmering whitecaps, the sea spray, the raggedy rainbows. He sips sun-ripened tea. His dark hair blusters about in the hot breeze. The cedar planks on which the young swimmer stands burn her feet, giving the rest of her body its cue for excitement. In just a few seconds, the chilly sea will be a welcome, refreshing haven.

She wears a tight-fitting one-piece swimsuit of black wool—short-sleeved and brief-skirted. Conditioning and trainers have invested her body with a curvaceous splendor of line and muscle. The women of Ipswich have been buzzing about this human fish since she arrived from Boston's Beacon Hill on the Fourth of July. Day after day, they have studied her in the crosshairs of their binoculars and opera glasses. They have felt the challenge of her sweet and fit body, and of her femininity bursting upon them, with every morning plunge she takes into the Atlantic. At dinner last night, the Harvard professor who summers in the neighboring cottage called her a titan of estrogenic prowess.

Unconscious of her spectators, she walks to the edge of the dock and takes a deep breath. With arms outstretched and hands locked, she pushes off and performs a swan dive into the sea. For a brief moment she soars—like a cormorant with waxed wings—and then sends a small spray of jewels skyward as she pierces the shimmering surface. To dive from the dock, to fly into the air, turn in mid-flight so the heels are pointing skyward and the head is down, so as to enter the water headfirst, is a subtle and daring trick, not learned in a day, and not finessed without an occasional bump to the bottom or a close shave with a fractured skull. Two weeks earlier, diving from the pier two houses to the north, a Yale athlete broke his neck; he was buried at sea a week later.

Feeling the sour tickle of salt against her tongue and the bracing cold against her skin, she swims the Australian crawl from her dock to another, two hundred or so yards down the beach. Facedown, her full body length outstretched on the water's surface, her feet sculling like propellers, arm after arm in overhead strokes—like two hoes sowing a field—she swims back and forth, gliding through the sea, knowing only the potency and poetry of motion.

■ ■ ■ ■ ■ ■

Those who happened to live by the seashore historically tried to copy the graceful moves of marine creatures accessible to their scrutiny: dolphins, seals, sea lions. If, on the other hand, potential swimmers were landlocked, the amphibian frog or the hydrophilic canine offered handy flotational models. From all available evidence, it appears that, wherever indigenous people habitually swam in buoyant salt water, they favored some version of the crawl, a stroke using alternating overarm motions and a sort of flutter kick. The buoyancy of the sea helped to stabilize the body sufficiently to allow the arms to be raised with ease. South Sea Islanders, North and South American coastal Indians, and the peoples of the Mediterranean have always swum with overarm strokes. Manilius, a first-century Roman poet, left an evocative description of this technique.

> For just as the dolphin glides through the water on swift fins,
> now rising above the surface and now sinking to the depths,
> and piles up waves and sends them off in circles, just so will
> each person born under the sign of the Dolphin fly through
> the waves, raising one arm and then the other in slow arcs.

Oddly enough, this dolphinlike stroke seems to have vanished from Europe—along with magnificent public baths, aqueducts, seaside villas, and the voluptuous enjoyment of water—after the fall of Rome, to be rediscovered only on the eve of the twentieth century.

In the long interim, swimming itself fell into disrepute. Coastal peoples turned their backs to the sea, which clerics and preachers had filled with diabolical monsters. Swimming, it was suggested in allegories and fables, went against a divine order that had fixed each creature its proper place. And prevailing medical opinion reinforced this moral injunction by claiming that water debilitated the body.

De Arte Natandi, published in the sixteenth century, championed the breaststroke. (Title page, in Everard Digby, *De Arte Natandi*, London, 1587, Bettmann Archive)

By the sixteenth century, however, a new respect for swimming emerged in the earliest extant writings devoted to the sport. Sir Thomas Elyot in the *Boke Named the Governour,* published in London in 1531, alluded to swimming as an important part of the education of a gentleman. Published seven years later, Nicolaus Wynman's *Colymbetes: Sive de Arte Natandi Dialogus et Festivus et Lucundus Lectu,* identified the breaststroke as "the scientific stroke" which had to be mastered by all sea enthusiasts. This sentiment was amplified by Sir Everard Digby in his *De Arte Natandi (The Art of Swimming),* published in England in 1587. Although the author was executed in 1606 for his part in the Gunpowder Plot to blow up King James I and the Parliament, *De Arte Natandi* continued to be one of the most influential texts in promoting the breaststroke over all other forms of swimming. For nearly four hundred years, the breaststroke would be the master stroke of Western Europe. It provided good stability, especially in fresh water, and the head-held-high position seemed well suited for keeping the breathing apparatus clear in the turbulent sea or river waters of the north.

In *The Virtuoso* of 1676, the English dramatist Thomas Shadwell satirized the efforts of Sir Nicholas Gimcrack to master the "scientific" breaststroke. "Milord prostrates himself upon a table," Shadwell wrote, "as he holds between his teeth a thread attached to the belly of a frog paddling in a bowl of water." Lady Gimcrack elaborated on her spouse's training ritual, explaining that, when "the frog strikes, he strikes, and his swimming master stands by, to tell him when he does ill or well." Though taking such pains with his lessons, Sir Nicholas had little interest in putting his skill to the test. Instead, he explained, "I content myself with the Speculative part of swimming, I care not for the Practick." Apparently, this "dry-dock" approach to learning the stroke was commonplace to the end of the nineteenth century; as late as the 1920s, sports magazines and fashion journals ran learn-to-swim articles that showed pupils balancing facedown on stools, their faces occasionally submerged in a basin of water to get a "feel" for the sport. Until the crawl advanced to the position of "master" stroke in an age obsessed with speed, the breaststroke dominated, and was revered by beachgoers and swimming enthusiasts as the "poetry of motion."

SWIMMING TOWARD THE BEACH

The year 1785 is memorable in the annals of swimming, for it was then that the first school of swimming was established, on the River Seine in Paris. Floating baths—cramped, rickety affairs crudely installed next to boats— had already been available on the Thames and the Seine several years earlier. An awning completely covered the boat, and another was built out over the bathing area, a circular enclosure marked off by planks attached to stakes driven into the riverbed. The pale, naked bathers—there being few genuine swimmers to speak of—clung to the sides of the boat like so many eels.

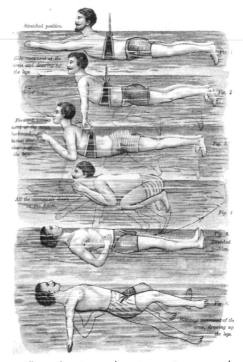

The French had attempted to open a swimming school in 1777, five years after the third reprinting of Melchissédec Thévenot's *L'Art de nager,* which had originally seen the light of day in 1696. A highly respected Oriental scholar, founder of the French Academy of Sciences, and royal librarian, Thévenot embarked on his treatise in order to remedy what he considered an oversight in the repertoire of available athletic pursuits. Swimming, he pointed out, was "an old sport which hitherto had not received the investigation necessary to improve in efficiency." His comprehensive treatment established the breaststroke as the "scientifically" correct mode of aquatic propulsion, and it was this stroke that he urged upon the youth of Paris. In

Well into the nineteenth century, swimmers modeled the breaststroke on the circular leg movements of the frog. The head was held high and completely out of the water. (Bettmann Archive)

1777, the Abbé Arnaud, a convert to Thévenot's ideas, applied for patronage to various academies and the royal entourage. He sought to attach a bath to the pilings of a bridge on the Seine, but was denied permission from authorities unpersuaded of the plan's usefulness. Eight years sufficed, however, to change the official climate. In 1785, the very same officials who had disdained Abbé Arnaud's proposal gave their support to swimming promoter J.-P. Turquin and even helped him obtain the endorsement of the very same French Academy of Sciences which Thévenot had established.

Turquin was a shrewd tactician. He understood the importance of stressing the therapeutic angle over the hygienic. His school would teach swimming in order to amplify the beneficial effects of cold water, to add to the armamentarium of cold-water therapies. This was completely in tune with the most progressive treatises. Diderot's *Encyclopédie* of 1765 maintained:

> Swimming has an advantage over a simple bath, because the vigorous, repeated movements made to overcome the resistance of the water are more conducive to making it penetrate the interior and give suppleness to the muscular activity of all parts of the body, to promoting the easiest and most favorable secretions and excretions, in a word, to setting the seal of health on the finest constitutions.

Turquin's school was dedicated to the civic ideal of moral, mental, and physical fitness, and swimming was the crown jewel of cold-water therapy. This instruction was to be carried out in an enclosed rectangle bounded by four boats firmly anchored in the Seine with cabins for changing and resting. The pupils were all from the highest circles of society—no one else could afford the lessons. At a time when only those with incomes exceeding four hundred livres a year—the very richest citizens—were obliged to pay taxes, subscriptions to Turquin's school cost ninety-six livres for the first class and forty-eight livres for the second.

BRITISH IN THE SWIM

At least as far as swimming was concerned, the nineteenth century belonged to the British. Surrounded on all sides by water, their island crisscrossed by rivers large and small, dotted with lakes and ponds—and their capital, London, boasting six permanent pools and floating baths moored at the Waterloo and Westminster bridges—the English were ideally situated to promote swimming. Add to their geographical predisposition a keenness for classical culture with its idealization of aquatic diversions, and a seemingly whimsical pleasure took on the shape of a national destiny. British Romantic poets and artists discovered sea swimming as an ideal vehicle for expressing their rebellious and individualistic moods. The beach was both a

Unsurpassed in long-distance swimming, the British considered their aquatic prowess a matter of national pride. The exploits of such swimmers as Captain Matthew Webb, who swam the English Channel in 1875, kept the general public spellbound. (Bettmann Archive)

zone for introspection—for confronting the self—and a springboard for adventures in the waves that tested the limits of their physical and moral fiber. From this double agenda, and with Britain as its champion, the fashion for swimming gripped the imagination of Europeans and Americans.

British travelers ranged far and wide across the Continent and to the Americas, and everywhere took with them the distinctly British rituals of sea bathing. At Dieppe, on the French Atlantic coast, British bathers astonished natives at the end of the eighteenth century by their habit of bathing during the coldest days of the year. Aristocratic Britons systematically swam their way across the bays, gulfs, and lagoons of the Mediterranean, recording their progress in private diaries and marking the sites of their various swims on maps. The sight of their pink-skinned and freckled bodies splashing in the waves continually amazed continentals. And their experiments with long-distance swimming—especially those of Lord Byron—were greeted with open-mouthed wonder. In their view, English lunacy—and obsessive swimming was taken as one of its manifestations—knew no bounds.

By dint of their charismatic personalities, their art, and the exposure they obtained through far-ranging travels, these pioneers of natation succeeded in seducing all of Europe into the waves. In Germany, for instance, swimming was almost unknown in the eighteenth century. But the popularity of Rousseau's philosophy of a "return to nature" and his view of self-betterment as expounded in *Émile* made the public receptive to the idea of swimming. After another German, Goethe, an ardent enthusiast, began to proselytize the sport, it was swiftly adopted as an "educational" form of exercise.

Goethe, in particular, was impressed with the vigor and style of British artists and thinkers with whom he had come into contact when they came

to pay their respects to him in Weimar. He knew that virtually all of them were excellent swimmers, and he could not help attributing their dash and the beauty of their women to this physical activity. In his novel *Wilhelm Meister*, he makes frequent reference to the benefits of swimming, particularly in cold water, which "transformed bourgeois sensual exhaustion into a fresh and vigorous existence." Goethe was convinced that by emulating the British in this respect, the Germans could reclaim some of the original-

When swimming rose to the status of a spectator sport, underwater dance and acrobatic performances were staged in large water tanks and swimming pools. ("Dick" Whittington)

ity, naturalness, health, and sensual enjoyment that their "unnatural" and unbalanced educational system had nearly succeeded in eliminating.

So intense was the general public's fascination with swimming that exhibitions were frequently held far from the seashore: in auditoria and music halls where special glass viewing tanks, or "crystal aquaria," were constructed, and in natatoria set against backdrops depicting beach scenes. Part sideshows and part sporting events, aquatic ballets and swimming demonstrations were often held in large pools before vast crowds, with celebrities carving out their own specialized niches. Among the more idiosyncratic performers was Charley Moore, a speed champion and one-legged "ornamental" swimmer, who wound his one leg in a half-pretzel configuration around his head as he floated in the pool. Another was Elise Wallenda, a diminutive athlete, who undressed, wrote a postcard, sewed a button, and then had a snack—all underwater. By comparison, James Finney, who held his breath for more than four minutes, was tame. Among the most popular performances were long-distance endurance races, in which swimmers competed for days on end, and underwater breath-holding competitions, which often culminated with one or more contestants being hauled out of the pool unconscious.

SCHOOLS OF SWIMMERS

Learning to swim in a lake or an artificial pool was one thing, but it did little to prepare people for the unique challenges of the ocean, where they might be immobilized by cramps, swamped by waves, caught in currents, dashed against rocks, or assaulted by marine creatures. Accordingly, as more and more beachgoers began to swim, resorts and eventually coastal municipalities began to introduce lifesaving stratagems to bail out poor or incapacitated swimmers. Lifeguard observation towers, cork-filled life belts, and the surf reel—a giant spool of strong rope—became standard pieces of surfside equipment. Color-coded pennants were run up on beaches to alert swimmers to daily water conditions. In Australia, large bells were sounded whenever sharks were sighted, so that surfers could flee to shore. Volunteer and community-subsidized lifesaving clubs experimented with resuscitation techniques to cope with the growing numbers of emergencies. The Australians, who took the initiative in developing the surf-lifesaving movement, organized numerous local clubs that trained men and women in lifesaving techniques and outfitted its members in distinctive uniforms.

There was no shortage of antidrowning devices or swimming prostheses. Strips of cork had been buoying up poor swimmers since Roman times. Air

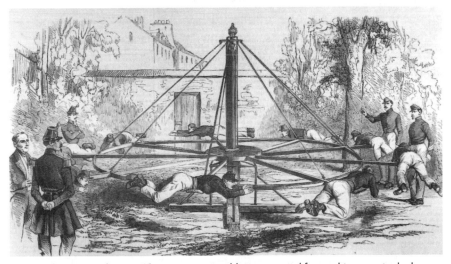

The French army used a special apparatus resembling a carousel for teaching recruits the breaststroke on dry land. By contrast, the German army made use of water tanks in which recruits were suspended from ropes attached to a metal framework. (Bettmann Archive)

belts, cork jackets, and inflated bladders of questionable utility found their way into seagoers' duffel bags—which, as it often turned out, was where they belonged. There were also various swimming contraptions designed to provide support: everything from pole-and-sling machines to the "chump's raft," a mobile aquatic playpen consisting of a wooden frame about six or seven feet square in which the swimmer was suspended.

Popular magazines of the 1880s offered instructions for using simple swimming devices, such as this sling, which holds the bather suspended just beneath the surface of the water. (authors' collection)

Numerous patents were issued on inventions to make swimming more efficient. One such apparatus consisted of flat plates made of wood, tin, leather, or waterproof fabric that were worn on the arms and legs. Correctly manipulated, the plates were supposed to propel the swimmer through water at amazing speeds. The Swimming Stocking—a collapsible, umbrella-like contraption worn on the ankles—used resistance to augment the force of the kick.

Other machines provided ingenious ways of maneuvering the body through water. The simplest was the water "skee," described in the patent application as providing the "wonderful sensation of shooting through the air and skimming the surface of the water." Consisting of a nine-foot board with an upturned prow, the skee was equipped with a copper air tank at each end for buoyancy. Swimmers straddled the board and used their legs to operate bicycle-type pedals positioned above a propeller. Mounted on this device, "skee-ers" pedaled out beyond the breakers and rode the waves back into shore as on a surfboard.

In many respects, the skee was the direct predecessor of the jet ski, which would make its debut in California in 1970. That was when an American named Clay Jacobson had the idea of combining the motorcycle with the water ski in a single, turbo-propelled machine that would provide safe and speedy mobility on water. He sold his design to Kawasaki, the Japanese motorcycle manufacturer, and in 1973 the mass-produced jet ski was launched. The silence of the sea was shattered at resorts on both coasts of the United States, as hundreds of thousands of these brilliantly colored hydro-jets plowed through the waves, spewing nauseating fumes and running over unsuspecting swimmers.

DIFFERENT STROKES

When competitive swimming was established on an organized basis, in 1869, the pressure to develop faster navigation techniques accelerated dramatically. On January 7 of that year, a group of representatives from several London swimming clubs met at the German Gymnasium to introduce order into competitive swimming. For years, amateurs and professionals had been racing together in canal locks, rivers, ponds, beaches, and swimming "baths" of various sizes, competing for money purses that had been collected by the spectators. There was no standard measure, no standard stroke, no standard distance, and no record keeping. That night, however, the Metropolitan Swimming Club Association was born, and within less than a month, reproducible standards were drawn up for swimming races.

Another milestone in the evolution of the crawl was the invention of the stopwatch, by E. D. Johnson, in 1855. A version of the chronograph, the stopwatch was first used for timing swim meets in 1869. From that moment on, swimming came under the sway of science. Speed, strokes, and efficiency were submitted to scientific quantification and scrutiny. And, in an effort to standardize racing conditions, competitive swimming was yanked out of the infinite variability of natural bodies of water, and moved to pools constructed in standard dimensions.

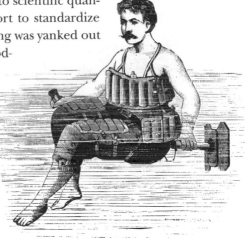

The introduction of competitive swimming in England was a powerful stimulus to experiment with natatory techniques. Until 1906, swimming competitions were stylistic free-for-alls. What mattered was speed, pure and simple. Swimmers who came up with a trick for beating the competition often won the purse, a place in history, and a spate of emulators. The underarm sidestroke, a precursor of the crawl, was improved by a

Cork and canvas were the principal ingredients of this bizarre 1880s lifesaving jacket. (Bettmann Archive)

slight modification to the position of the arms. By raising the arm above water in the recovery rather than drawing it back underwater, swimmers found they could shave precious minutes from their time. Thus was born the classic English overarm sidestroke, which remained a staple of racing for more than two decades.

Over time, various refinements were added, most of them by a succession of British swimmers whose names they still bear. The "Jarvis kick" was the brainchild of J. A. Jarvis, a champion by virtue of the twist he added to the leg kick, and, in his words, "giving a continuous grip of the water and making the stroke a continuation of screw and wedge." In 1872, John Trudgen, a native of the West Indies, stunned competitors by winning the English 160-yard handicap with a peculiarly jerky technique that had disqualified an earlier swimmer, W. Payton, from a breaststroke race in 1859. Trudgen swam in the breaststroke position, head held high above the water, legs delivering powerful frog kicks, while—here was the innovation—*each* arm was alternately swung forward over the water. It had been speculated, on the

Worthy of Jules Verne, T. Beck's Life Preserving Apparatus was designed as a complete flotation-cum-shelter system that would keep the swimmer dry and afloat by means of the buoylike floating upper chamber. (Bettmann Archive)

slimmest evidence, that something resembling the trudgen had been used over two thousand years ago by the Assyrians, but when the ungainly stroke broke an impressive succession of records, it was perceived as the very essence of modernity.

The trudgen's popularity, however, was short-lived. The propulsive bursts and disconnected movements required to execute the stroke were extremely strenuous, and required the kind of lung capacity and muscular coordination that few could muster. Swimmers looked for more efficient, less taxing ways of attaining speed: streamlining the body by narrowing the sweep of the legs, experimenting with breathing techniques, replacing the breaststroke kick of the trudgen with a side scissors kick.

Eventually surfaced the crawl, which James H. Sterrett, one of the great American amateur-swimming coaches,

hailed in 1917 as "undoubtedly the greatest stroke that has ever been invented or discovered in connection with swimming." The crawl would finally allow swimmers to enter previously uncharted aquatic-speed zones. Although the precise origin of the crawl is still uncertain, if you dig back far enough in the nineteenth century for its beginnings, you will find a native Samoan woman of competitive spirit, and three Australian brothers, named Syd, Tums, and Dick. On a visit to Samoa, Syd, the oldest, was showing off his good form at the beach when a young woman stepped out of the crowd of onlookers and challenged him to a race. Syd liked to think of himself as a strong, fast swimmer. After all, his father, the Englishman Fred Cavill, had started a swimming bath at Lavender Bay in Sydney Harbor soon after immigrating in 1879. He figured he had nothing to fear from this native girl. But the young woman beat him, in the hardest race of his life. To make matters worse, she did it using only her arms: her legs appeared not to be kicking at all.

Syd was understandably deflated, but he had enough heart to learn from his failure. He followed her example, tied his legs together, and found that he could swim almost as fast as the Samoan girl. Now he understood that the side scissors kick he had been taught was totally counterproductive. Excited by this discovery, Syd wrote his brother Tums, who wasted no time testing the legless stroke against another champion swimmer, Sydney Davis. Tums came in first. Then, he untied his legs and raced again. He lost. The lesson was not lost on Dick, the third Cavill brother. The scissors kick had to go. But what could replace it?

Then Dick remembered having once seen a fast young sprint swimmer doing a peculiar straight-legged kick that he claimed to have learned from natives in Colombo, Ceylon. Dick Cavill tried it, liked it, and, several days later, used the technique in a hundred-yard championship swim. Though he had not quite gotten the hang of it, he held the lead for the first fifty yards. Then his energy ran out, and he fell behind. The prize for that race may have gone to the sidestroke, but in the grander scheme of things, the winner was clearly the "Australian crawl." Coaches watching the competition from the sidelines knew speed when they saw it. They returned to their home clubs anxious to teach the new stroke to their swimmers; within months, news of the "crawl" and the "crawlers" had spread to all corners of the world. Europeans were "crawling" by the turn of the century, and by 1904, Americans had embraced the new wonder-stroke.

Much experimenting went on for the next half-century to produce the swift, streamlined techniques that now win Olympic medals. The whole business of moving through the water took on an increasingly scientific character. If, in the nineteenth century, the breaststroke had captivated the imagination of poets, writers, and artists, the crawl would attract scientists and engineers in the twentieth century, all working to apply principles from their disciplines to refining and accelerating human aquatic mobility. In fact, swimming became an object of scientific research, as investigators attempted to learn more about the physical characteristics of successful swimmers, measuring height, weight, shape, and body composition to determine what type of build was best suited to the sport. Coaches joined with scientists to analyze the physiological and psychological effects of training methods and nutrition. Engineers and architects contributed deeper pools, wave-reducing lane dividers, and sloping starting blocks. Mathematical formulas describing the relationship among stroke, resistance, and velocity were derived to predict the upper limits of swimming performance. Racing swimmers were not convinced that they had reached the limit of their speed. In the 1960s, swimsuit manufacturers were recruited to experiment with tailoring and textiles that would minimize "drag" and actually direct the movement of water around the body. The Speedo company of Australia designed a revolutionary form-fitting racing suit that reduced drag around the swimmer's body by using textiles that mimicked the slick skins of marine mammals. Streamlined, airtight goggles enabled swimmers to spend long periods of time in chlorine pools, increasing their training sessions without risking eye irritation and infections. As a result of so much systematic research, the world fifteen-hundred-meter record in the crawl improved by 31 percent between 1932 and 1988, from 21:35.3 to 14:58.27.

As the requirements for competitive swimming shifted from endurance in the nineteenth century to speed in the twentieth, the ideal body type of the swimmer gradually altered. In the nineteenth and early twentieth century, the prevailing shape of competitive swimmers—and of those aspiring to look like them on the beach—tended to be squat and bulky, with short and heavy muscles. As the twentieth century advanced, however, the emphasis on speed favored a tall, lithe, lean physique, long-limbed and finely muscled. A streamlined, gradually tapering body was found to be the most important single factor in reducing resistance and allowing the water to flow past more easily. Thus, by dint of persistent inventiveness and diligent study, we acquired increasing skill in moving through water and adapted our awkward terrestrial bodies to aquatic propulsion by studying the natural shapes of fishes, birds, and even insects.

SWIMMER'S MYSTIQUE

In Europe, the new century had rolled in with a healthy respect for the rights of the human body. Emboldened by the sexual theories of Sigmund Freud, progressives in *fin-de-siècle* Germany placed a new emphasis on body culture, or *Leibeskultur,* a celebration of the human body stripped of all social taboos and restrictions. As early as the 1890s, the free body-culture movement, or *Freikörperkultur,* promoted macrobiotic diets, homegrown vegetables, nature "cures," and, most radically of all, nudism. Young people wanted to liberate the body from belts, corsets, brassieres, and to give it free rein in the pursuit of self-expression. Swimming—and free sexual mores—were two of the most important ways of manifesting this spirit of physical liberation. Reveling in a "return to nature," the young flocked to beaches in the French Riviera, the Adriatic, and the Aegean, seeking out a more

primitive milieu where they could both enjoy the pleasures of the uncon-
strained body and play out their rebellion against an older generation
thought to be caught up in hypocrisy and repression.

The artistic avant-garde fanned the flames of revolution in physical sensuality that saw the beach as its most logical proving ground. Just before the
outbreak of World War I, the artist Emil Nolde, for instance, traveled to the
South Seas, where he was entranced by the contrast between what he perceived to be the vital "natural" life of beach-loving natives and the artificial,
diseased existence of civilization. In his view, "primitive men" who lived by
the sea were at one with nature, and a part of the whole. "I sometimes have
the feeling that they are the only real human beings left," he wrote, "and
that we, on the other hand, are malformed puppets, artificial and full of
conceit."

These sentiments ran like a powerful current throughout the turn-of-
the-century generation, and surfaced in all pockets of avant-garde European culture. In the period between the world wars, body consciousness
shaped the Nazi adulation of the athletic youth. Hitler was drawn to the ancient barbarian and antique Greek traditions of corporeal elegance. Ad-
miring a photograph of a beautiful female German swimmer, he once
commented, "What splendid
bodies you can see today. It is
only in our century that young
people have once again approached Hellenistic ideals
through sports."

In fact, the swimmer had
been taking shape in German
culture as a symbol of national
virility and might for some
years. In the fiction of Thomas
Mann—including *Tonio Kröger,
The Magic Mountain,* and *Death
in Venice*—the swimmer, more
than any other athlete, personi-
fied the health and vitality denied to the intellectual and the
artist. In *Death in Venice,* when
the desiccated and dying poet
Aschenbach reclined on his
chaise longue on the miasmic
Venetian Lido, he watched
avidly as the young boy Tadzio

The German-designed "Water-Walker" of the 1870s consisted of a wooden-hulled kayak for each foot and a balancing pole to keep the walker upright. (Culver Pictures)

splashed in the waves, recalling Narcissus and Phaedrus. The figure of the boy "conjured up mythologies, it was like a primeval legend, handed down from the beginning of time, of the birth of form, of the origin of the Gods."

On the other side of the Atlantic, American poets and artists were exhibiting similar symptoms of beach fever. Thomas Eakins, in his haunting painting *The Swimming Hole* and in a series of Arcadian waterscapes, celebrated the beauty of the nude swimmer. Walt Whitman, like Eakins a passionate swimmer, fervently believed that the sport was the font of spiritual and physical restoration. In his "I Sing the Body Electric" he lauds the sensation of swimming naked through the "transparent green-slime," or lying supine and rolling "silently to and fro in the heave of the water." Once, swimming at Étretat, he had let himself be carried out by the tide and, as he described it, felt "like some expert swimmer, who has tired himself, and to rest his limbs, allows them to float drowsily and unresistingly on the bosom of the sunny river. Real things lost their reality. A dusky mist spread itself before my eyes." The surrender to the seawater became a passage into another, more real state of being where things revealed themselves with a new luminosity and meaning, and the trivial, quotidian concerns of a mercantile life dropped away into oblivion.

Even in revolutionary Russia, beach mania became one of the symptoms of the utopian fervor of the 1920s. The film maker Dziga Vertov, originator of the documentary film, included exhilarating footage of swimmers and bathers on the Black Sea in his *Man with a Camera*. Some bathers recline in awkward, angular poses on the shingly beach, others slather themselves with thick black mud. Young Pioneers splash in the waves, as recently demobilized Red Guards demonstrate the finer points of aquatic propulsion.

The poetic symbolism of the swimmer spilled over to the figure of the diver as well. The Romantics had wreathed the diver in the mystique of the transgressor into taboo regions, depicting him as the ill-fated cousin of Icarus, who was punished by the gods for his proud ambition. During the period between the two world wars, the image of the swan dive was burned into the subconscious on both sides of the Atlantic as the quintessential representation of grace, beauty, and freedom. American divers of the 1920s dominated both the 1924 and the 1928 Olympics. In 1924, Caroline Smith won her medal with an exquisite swan dive. Hollywood extravaganzas teemed with girls looping and arching from the tops of waterfalls, Jane sailing into the arms of Tarzan, and Annette Kellerman effortlessly gliding from a prison tower one hundred feet above the sea in the 1914 film *A Daughter of the Gods*.

The image of the diving girl became one of the most enduring logos of the period. In 1920, an obscure American knitting mill located in the far-flung Pacific Northwest began decorating its stark black wool swimsuits with a bright-red image of what eventually became known as the Jantzen diving girl. Depicted in profile executing an impeccable swan dive, she became the consummate embodiment of intangible American ideals: youth, grace, sex appeal, and athletic prowess. A cultural icon was born, and soon it flashed from the haunches of swimmers and bathers all over the country, from gigantic posters in the heart of Paris, and even from decals glued to the windshields of Henry Ford's iron horses.

BUSINESS AND THE BEACH

Corporate hegemony over the swimsuit-and-beach culture was just beginning. Between 1900 and 1920, the public undressing of America would be orchestrated less by governmental bodies and more by market-driven entrepreneurs seeking to capitalize on—and satisfy—vast hordes of American beachgoers. Sleek, snappy, and streamlined, the tubular swimming suit had that irresistible aura of utopian dreams bred by the great machines of mechanical reproduction. But, as might be expected, the overall look of the finest one- and two-piece suits of the era borrowed much of its inspiration for the ideal female form from Art Deco's iconographic bestiary: deer, gazelles, antelopes, greyhounds, thrusting dancers, and lissome, pharaonic nudes. French swimsuits in scaled-down "salesmen's" models demonstrated how the sophisticated design sensibilities of Art Deco could transform a garment that was, in essence, an oversized body-sock into a revered work of haute couture. Appliquéed with the vivid patterns of Aztec-Deco, or with a bijouterie of diamonds, dots, and zigzags, the tubular suit came to represent the dizzying horizons of European fashion and propelled its wearers into the cutting edge of the future.

If Parisian ateliers whetted the popular appetite for this glamour rag, American knitting mills on the West Coast would eventually deliver the promise to millions of bathers from sea to shining sea. The bathing suits of Europe were exotic, interesting, and alarming, but they were rarely practical, and few specimens were within buying range of the great majority. America changed all that. Within the span of a mere decade, the design and fabrication of the bathing garment was delivered into the knitting, cutting, and sewing departments of mass-production factories.

The corporate age of the swimsuit had dawned. Almost simultaneously, three apparel manufacturers from Oregon and California embarked on a series of profitable adventures in the skin trade. Oddly enough, before launching their swimwear lines, each of these companies—the Portland Knitting Company of Portland, Oregon, and the Los Angeles–based Bentz Knitting Mills and West Coast Knitting Mills—had specialized in knitted underwear and sweaters. By the end of the decade, Jantzen, Catalina, and

Cole—as they would eventually be known—would develop into the Ford, Chrysler, and General Motors of the swimwear trade. From their headquarters on the West Coast, this mighty triumvirate oversaw the production of swimsuits for the masses. By drastically cutting prices, they succeeded in democratizing fashion for the beach and, coincidentally, in dictating the standards for taste and decency in dermal exposure.

The commodification of swim fashions began in earnest in 1909, when Carl Jantzen of Portland, Oregon, got the itch. An avid sportsman and accomplished knitter, Jantzen knew there had to be something more comfortable than the scratchy, body-clinging wool bathing suits he made for his

The faster motorboats of the 1920s and 1930s took waterskiing to new heights of acrobatic virtuosity. (authors' collection)

rowing mates so they could brave the nasty, rain-sodden winds hissing along Portland's Willamette River. So Jantzen, a quiet but persevering man, went after that "itch." He teamed up with John and Roy Zehntbauer, country boys from Missouri with roots going back to a two-room log cabin. In January 1910, the three men founded the Portland Knitting Company. By 1918, the company had decided to advertise—its annual advertising budget for that year was a mere six hundred dollars—and change its name to Jantzen Knitting Mills. With the kind of spunk, hard work, and boundless optimism that makes for the best rags-to-riches stories, Jantzen and the Zehntbauer brothers revolutionized the knitting industry, generating patent upon patent in sportswear. Over the next two decades, under their direction, skin and entrepreneurship would meet to spark a multi-million-dollar bathing-suit empire based upon flesh and its allure.

It was Jantzen who realized early on that if he was to sell swimsuits—and continue to sell them—the American public would have to do more than go to the beach to stroll, frolic, embrace, or escape the stresses of modern life. First and foremost, they would have to learn to embrace swimming as a mainstream leisure activity. In 1926, Jantzen Knitting Mills inaugurated a coast-to-coast "Learn to Swim Week" campaign. Complete with "graduation" certificates, competitions, and department-store tie-ins, a high-powered advertising program expanded the market for Jantzen's beach products. Newspaper ads, posters, and store displays announced the dates of local "Learn to Swim" programs. Swimming clubs were set up in public and private pools and on beaches throughout the country, and plugs for the sport were offered by spokesmen drawn from the ranks of champion swimmers such as Duke Kahanamoku, Norman Ross, Lewis "Happy" Kuehn, and William "Buddy" Wallen. Plaques were issued to member swimming pools, which presented certificates from the local Board of Health showing bacteria count and other tests to prove water purity. Jantzen wanted to make sure its product's image would be untainted by association with drowning accidents, infections, or other unsavory footnotes to the sport of swimming. Most important, the company's designers worked at making bathing costumes that would be aquadynamic, modest, and attractive.

Once consummated, the marriage of health, beach, and swimwear man ufacturer seemed made in heaven. Making swimsuits for the mass market became a growing business, with firms such as Jantzen—as well as Cole and Catalina in California—competing for an ever larger share of the market. More than any other item of apparel, the evolving swimsuit was profoundly influenced by cutting-edge technology: innovations in textiles, plastics, and even engineering sooner or later found their way into the square yard of fabric that regulated the public undressing of America. Jantzen, perhaps more than any of his contemporaries, understood that creating more comfortable, attractive, athletic, and utilitarian swimsuits would help establish the beach as a premier leisure destination—and, in the process, would keep his mills humming.

VENUS COMES TO THE BEACH

The nineteenth century had encouraged swimming among boys and men but it did not fully extend the privilege to women. According to Victorian notions, athletic exertion could seriously impair a woman's ability to conceive and carry a baby to term. Maternity and swimming simply did not mix, nor did practicality and respectability. To swim, one had to move. To move, one had to have unimpeded limbs. But the female bathing costume of the age forbade mobility. Anything less than the obligatory regalia of stockings, bloomers, blouse, gloves, hat, and slippers was downright immodest—a provocation to public morality.

When women took to the beach, they were subjected to incessant scrutiny by the male sex. In the eighteenth century, male bathers had armed themselves with spyglasses at the seashore, the better to observe the then unclad female of the species immersing herself in the waves. In a satirical account of early-nineteenth-century beach culture, the British Mr. Jolly has a disagreeable encounter with the French police when he strays into the women's sector of the beach at Calais, where he is accused of insulting

Esther Williams's glamorous aquacades—films featuring elaborate water-ballet routines and slim plots—created a public demand for opulently ornamented swimsuits in the 1940s. (authors' collection)

the honor of Gallic womanhood by his overlong scrutiny of the bathers. Since the beach was institutionalized in bourgeois rituals of leisure, it served as a haven for voluptuaries of all ages. Their eyes screened by tinted glasses or shaded by oversized hats, voyeurs could freely indulge their fancy for the female form, although there were many among them who specialized in young boys.

Once outside this suffocating environment, however, women satisfied their craving for physical freedom at the beach as unabashedly as men. Mary Wollstonecraft, author of *A Vindication of the Rights of Women* and mother of Mary Shelley, author of *Frankenstein,* swam alone in the waters off Scandinavia. Rose Macaulay bathed in the night sea off Spain and Portugal. The adventurous breed of Victorian woman travelers left various rapturous accounts of solitary swims in out-of-the-way pools and bays. Mary Kingsley swam naked—at night—in a lake in West Africa. Constance Gordon Cumming swam in the South Pacific, and Marianne North in the Atlantic north of Boston.

But it was an Australian girl who had struggled with polio in her childhood who became the Joan of Arc of female swimming. After taking up the sport to strengthen her legs, Annette Kellerman became a world-renowned champion. She devoted her life to the sport, because, as she wrote in *How to Swim,* "swimming is a pleasure and a benefit, a clean, cool, beautiful cheap thing we all from cats to kings can enjoy." Even more, it was an exercise in egalitarianism, linked to utopian notions of the sinless, beautiful human body and of a pluralistic, forgiving society. "There is nothing more democratic than swimming," she wrote. "Bathing is a society event but swimming out beyond the surf line is just plain social. Every one is happy and young and funny. No one argues. No one scolds. There is no time and no place where one may so companionably play the fool and not be called one."

Famed for her spectacular form—both in and out of the water—and as a star of swimming meets, vaudeville, and motion pictures, Kellerman was the first to prove that, when it came to practicality, less was decidedly more. In 1907, this striking brunette offered the first practical alternative to aquatic nudity in the form of an improvised, tight-fitting black wool one-piece which nearly overnight made her name a household word.

"I want to swim," Kellerman announced to a disbelieving public. "And I can't swim wearing more stuff than you hang on a clothesline." The original Kellerman suit did away with skirts and sleeves but kept the trousers, though cut off two inches above the knees. By the simple expedient of donning this abbreviated outfit, she turned the beach into the world's first public—and free-of-charge—open-air peepshow. When she appeared on Boston's Revere Beach dressed only in this clinging suit, Kellerman was arrested for indecent exposure and denounced as a wanton. Dark prophecies were made as to the future of America. However, only two years later, when Adeline Trapp, the first woman to swim across the East River, emerged from the waves in similar attire, she was unmolested by the law. The world of the bathing suit had finally begun to mimic the complexities of modern life: when it came to recreating in the water, one could, at last, choose between fashion and function.

DRAWING LINES IN THE SAND

The swimsuit on the beach tells the square-inch-by-square-inch history of how skin went public in modern times. In the swimsuit, flesh and fabric combined to serve sport, sex, culture, and continually shifting zones of eroticism. In a very real sense, the beach became a geological setting for the *pas de deux* between flesh and fabric, choreographed by the forces of concealment and disclosure, and played against the shifting sands of civilization and its discontents.

When a practical swimming garment finally became available, the history of the bathing costume took two divergent tracks. On one side stood the ornate bathing dress, and on the other, the wool knit swimsuit. One—decorous, ornamented, and impractical—was squarely within the camp of fashion, keeping pace with developments in outerwear and reflecting changing notions of the ideal female form. The other—immodest, stripped down, and practical—stood cleanly outside the territory of style. It was a piece of athletic equipment and, therefore, uniquely chaste. As long as the wearer exercised discretion and remembered that each suit had its place, there were no problems. Suits that were clearly meant for sports were one thing. They might have demystified the contours of the female anatomy, but naughty they were not.

It so happened that fashion in the Western world took a turn toward re-duction at just about the time that Annette Kellerman introduced her suit. A minor revolution also was in progress in perceptions of the ideal female form. Throughout the first decade of the twentieth century, the full-blown sinuousities of Art Nouveau still inspired the exemplary female form. Gus-tav Klimt's curvaceous Salomes haunted the fashionable imagination. As fashion historians pointed out, sometime around 1912 a tremendous change occurred. As if by magic, corsets and stays disappeared, to be re-placed by the human body as the sole basis and shaper of form.

The bathing costume instantly followed suit. Suddenly fashion maga-zines were filled with drawings of lithe, columnar *élégantes* in dresses that bared graceful arms and exposed delicately stockinged legs at the knee. The tunic and peg-top line current in other modes made their appearance on the shore, though in greatly shortened form. Arms were thrust into view through high-cut armholes, and sleeves in the shape of caps, petals, and cross-lacing were purely ornamental. The leg, from ankle to calf, was bared under a thin covering of silk stockings and, along with the armpit, emerged as a new erotic zone.

Introduction of the new bathing dress provoked a great deal of discom-fort and uncertainty among both bathers and guardians of moral authority, turning the beach into a no-tactics-barred arrest zone. In an era character-ized by more formal and rigid standards for daily costume, the question of how much—or how little—to wear could take on critical importance. At least during the first two decades of the century, wearing less than the norm was a cause for criminal arrest. The trouble was that what constituted the norm was usually left undefined.

The last summer before World War I was memorialized in the American press by a spate of stories documenting skirmishes on the beach between proponents of diminished swimwear, and die-hard traditionalists who in-sisted on the Victorian skirt-and-trouser models. In Atlantic City, a woman was assaulted by a mob for wearing a suit that revealed a short span of thigh. In Chicago, young women were escorted from the beach by police because they had bared their arms and legs. On Coney Island, bathers in the new, clinging wool "tube" suits were hauled out of the surf by police

The advent of the hydrodynamic swimsuit on the eve of World War I transformed the beach into a school for scandal, provocation, and civil disobedience. (authors' collection)

matrons. Private resorts and clubs took the matter into their own hands and quickly issued detailed regulations specifying appropriate beach apparel, though the penalty for underdressing was only a discreet reprimand; here, at least, the pressure to conform kept people in line.

But in the crowded, anonymous conditions of municipal beaches, an anarchic spirit began to manifest itself among young bathers. The example of celebrity swimmers such as Annette Kellerman, Adeline Trapp, and Gertrude Ederle inspired thousands of budding suffragettes to take up swimming in practical, form-fitting jersey maillots. Civic leaders and moral arbitrators responded by drawing up sumptuary guidelines and a protocol for dealing with violations. The "Bathing Suit Regulations," issued in May 1917 by the American Association of Park Superintendents, set the standard that was adopted by most public beaches throughout the nation. White and skin-colored suits were discouraged, as were male and female décolletages exceeding an imaginary line drawn between the armpits. It was stipulated that:

> Blouse and bloomer suits may be worn with or without stockings, provided the blouse has quarter-arm sleeves or close-fitting arm-holes, and provided bloomers are full and not shorter than four inches above the knee. Jersey knit suits may be worn with or without stockings, provided the suit has a skirt or skirt effect, with quarter-arm sleeves or close-fitting

arm holes and trunks not shorter than four inches above the
knee, and the bottom of the skirt must not be shorter than
two inches above the bottom of trunks.

Those fateful two inches landed many a young woman in jail. Self-
appointed modesty brigades patrolled public beaches, tape measure and
regulations in hand, a scourge to fun-loving youth well into the 1920s.

Men did not fare much better. It took an astonishingly long time for the
public to become desensitized to the sight of the bared male chest at the
beach. Since bathing attire had first become mandatory in the early nineteenth century, public nudity was considered scandalous. Every square
inch of epidermis became hotly contested ground, with each advance toward nakedness decried as a plunge into social anarchy and moral turpitude. This climate virtually guaranteed that every effort to tamper with
coverage would yield a tangle with the law. One upstanding citizen who re-
sented having to choose between practicality and decorum whipped off an
indignant letter to the editor of *The New York Times*. "I am a middle aged
man," he wrote in 1914, "and would not go to dinner clad in pajamas; but
when I go for a swim and put on a bathing suit which is correct for that purpose, I would like to be free from the thought that some officious police-
man out for a record might cause me the discomfort that many suffered
recently." What he and his male friends had suffered were legal repercus-
sions for wearing a tubular, one-piece suit that, in fact, did showcase the
taboo terrain of the male torso. To restore decency, American men stuck to
a two-piece costume consisting of mid-thigh trunks worn under a long,
sleeveless jersey that covered the groin.

The campaign for modesty in swimwear was answered by an equally stri-
dent position calling for the liberalization of beach attire. In 1918, before
the National Association of Drugless Physicians, Colonel Shingshah Ghadiall, founder of New York City's Aerial Police Squadron, voiced a strong
protest against Atlantic City's beach law mandating all women in bathing
raiment to wear stockings. "Why should beautiful women . . . be compelled
by an unmoral, un-American and inhuman law to cover their limbs?" the
colonel declared in the midst of a discussion about "unexplained anatomy
and the centers of psychic force in man." According to *The New York Times'*
piece covering Ghadiall's diatribe, the colonel then added, with prophetic
insight: "What is the difference I ask you between a woman's foot and a
man's foot? If Atlantic City would be truly moral it would tell women to dis-
card their clothing or don trousers. I hold she has that right no less than a
man."

A full-page spread in the *Ladies' Home Journal* brought the full horror of
the new licentiousness of the beach before its readers in August 1913.

"How Much of This Do You Want *Your* Daughter to Share?" shrieked the headline, which was surrounded by a collage of photographs meant to chill the blood of every self-respecting mother. "The pictures on this page are from photographs taken at the 'bathing hour,' on various public beaches that dot the Atlantic Coast from Cape May to Cape Ann," explained the editorial. "They accurately indicate the free-and-easy familiarity that is continuous on these great midsummer playgrounds from the opening of the season to its close."

Chaos was clearly threatening to erupt on the home front. While Europe was going up in flames and mustard gas, America was rushing toward wrack and ruin on the backs of scantily clad bathers. Fashion was ripping apart the fabric of society. Something had to be done.

CHAPTER

9

SUN ON THE BEACH

Tarawa, Gilbert Islands, November 1943. The rising sun spreads a deathly pallor across the flotilla of landing craft crawling toward the smear of beach beyond the breakers. The metallic sea heaves beneath a leaden sky. A boyish Marine from South Carolina draws camouflage netting over his steel helmet and braces against the awkward cant of the boat. He feels for the reassuring lump of a Penguin paperback, H. G. Wells' *A Short History of the World,* in his trouser pocket. The first wave of landing-craft vehicles (LCVs) lurch across the coral reef into the quiet water, trembling as their treads grip the shallow bottom of the lagoon.

Staring hard at the beachhead, he takes in the chaos of Sherman tanks, flamethrowers, and downed planes tumbled over and piled one on top of another on an inferno of sand impaled with the charred trunks of bare palms. Geysers of sand and fire spurt from the ground. Bursts of light explode from concrete bunkers that appear and disappear through the thick pall of smoke. After a night of bombing, the coconut-covered island has been battered into a mass of craters and fire-swept undergrowth.

Holding high his semi-automatic, the Marine leaps from the swaying boat. Water seeps into his boots. Encumbered by his sodden uniform and canvas haversack, he slogs through chest-high waves. Salt burns his eyes. The breaking surf percolates in the space between his head and helmet. Through the earsplitting roar of gunfire, he hears the high-pitched scream of another Marine, driven mad by the flotsam of severed heads and limbs drifting out to sea. In the crush of LCVs, one of the vehicles slews around and capsizes, spilling men and weapons into the churning water.

The soldier stops long enough to haul a casualty from the aft compartment of the craft, then presses ahead, squeezing through a gap in the barbed-wire fence that sways just beneath the surface of the water. He studies the beach. The dry expanse of sand seems to lie far away, across an immensity of water so blue and clear that, for a moment, he longs to tear off his clothes and luxuriate in its liquid warmth. But a hail of bullets churns up the placid surface, and he is back in the Gilbert Islands, in one of World War II's bloodiest battles, and he knows he has no choice but to sprint to land and throw himself into the nearest mortar-fire crater.

Which he does, only to find himself surrounded by blood-soaked fragments of human flesh and bone: headless bodies, legs, arms, shoes with feet still in them. Crawling on his belly, he sees two members of his squad hosed down by machine-gun fire. There is a blinding flash a few yards in front of

Corpses and disabled landing craft littered the beach at Tarawa in 1943. (National Archive/Corbis)

him. Time stops. The stench of death rises from the ground, and, pressing his back into the crater's soft curve, he realizes he has been flung into the depths of hell itself.

■ ■ ■ ■ ■

Long before the beach became hell for the soldiers who fought in the grisly aquatic theaters of World War II, it was nothing less than a paradise in the minds and dreams of soldiers who fought the inland battles of World War I. Paul Fussell, the eminent literary scholar, documents how the craving for warmth, light, and dryness—in short, for the constituents of the beach—had been incubating in the cold, muddy trenches during the nasty winter of 1917. One of the most popular cards soldiers sent home from the front, Fussell tells us, depicted palm trees on a beach framing a giant sun. As soldiers from both sides huddled in their dripping, reeking quarters, shivering uncontrollably—more from cold than from fear—rushing to down a few drops of tea before it froze over, they dreamed of a compensatory landscape drenched with sunshine, and bubbling with life and freedom. For some this "other" place was home; but for most it was a fantasized site somewhere far away, imaged in the mind's eye as a dimly remembered seashore seen once on a travel poster or in an illustrated family Bible.

British novelist Alec Waugh recalled how cold it was in the trenches during the winter of 1917, as he plotted his escape to tropical beaches he would visit thirteen years later. Another writer, H. M. Tomlinson, remembered that winter "on the hills of Ancre before the village of Miraumont, when the earth was marble, and every shell scattered frozen marl which flew like splinters of masonry." Their days and nights, like those of thousands of soldiers on both sides of the conflict, alternated between frenzied exchange of gunfire and mad scrambling to safe position, on the one hand, and, on the other, interminable hours of shivering boredom relieved by a furtive cigarette, muted conversation, and reading. The trenches were labyrinthine libraries; books circulated as a fragile antidote to the barbaric destruction and butchering.

Among the most cherished reading material were accounts of travels to tropical lands, such as Norman Douglas' *South Wind,* which evoked the broiling sun of a Capri-like island where "paganism and nudity and laughter" flourished. The beach was very much on the minds of soldiers engaged in the Great War. In his poem "When It's Over," Max Plowman imagines a soldier planning what he will do when released from service: "I shall lie on the beach / Of a shore where the rippling waves just sigh / And listen and dream and sleep and lie."

For most intellectuals of the period, the hundreds of thousands of mangled, dismembered, and charred corpses represented an obscene defilement of humanism and the ultimate desecration of the human body. To escape this debasement, Plowman's soldier longs for the beach as a public place where people can gather without fear, for nothing more than the simple pleasure of a nap in the sun. The beach is a place where the body—so badly abused by the war—could be displayed as a beautiful, precious object, lovingly bared to the elements, and proclaimed to be, once again, a thing of value freed from the threat of hostile forces.

Hawaii's reputation as an Eden of swaying palm trees, soft sands, warm waters, and luscious haole women was disseminated in films such as *Song of the Islands,* starring Betty Grable, Victor Mature, and Hilo Hattie. (authors' collection)

Civilians immobilized *behind* trench lines also nurtured vivid dreams of sunshine and flight to beaches. And so, in the period following the end of the war, they were eager to resume the good life, and nowhere with more vigor than on the sunny beaches of America and the Mediterranean. There was now, however, a new, vaguely desperate inflection to pleasure. With the carnage and destruction behind them, most survivors shrank from the unanswerable questions the con-

Crowding every spare inch of urban beaches, Americans during the Depression reveled in the messy vitality of Sundays by the sea. (Paul Cadmus, *Coney Island*, Los Angeles County Museum of Art)

flict had posed. Everyone knew that the war was over, but no one could tell what it had meant and what it boded for the old values of freedom, dignity, and justice. The contrast between the rhetoric of industrial progress and the reality of the trenches, between the benevolent image of human nature and the brutal demonstration of its bestiality on the battlefield, was too stark and too painful for most to face.

"The storm has died away," French poet Paul Valéry remarked in a 1922 lecture, "and still we are restless, uneasy, as if the storm were about to break. Almost all the affairs of man remain in terrible uncertainty." International relations, economic life, culture had been injured. "But among all these injured things," Valéry continued, "is the mind. The mind has indeed been cruelly wounded. It doubts itself profoundly."

One popular response to this self-doubt was a collective flight from reality that manifested itself in the funfest of the Roaring Twenties, with its frenzy of gin-swilling flappers, spirited dance steps, jazz rhythms, outrageous Dadaist antics, and a mass stampede to the beach as an outpost of "anything-goes" merriment, madcap revels, and delirious fun. Who cared about deciphering the fundamental meaning of life? Aside from a few pockets of intellectuals and deep thinkers, postwar Americans and Europeans, flush with their *carpe-diem* attitudes, proclaimed that the meaning of life lay in life itself, in the act of living. Best of all, in living for the day, and from day to day. The mere fact of survival, they believed, had entitled them to put suffering, pain, and introspection behind them.

Getting everything out of life meant getting it fast. People clipped their words, invented cocktails with an instant punch, wore clothes that slipped on and off at the flip of a wrist. "Sweet young things" in Europe and America embraced the cult of nudity and the beautiful body. Fashion designers slashed yards off the new "glad rags," exposed bare arms, legs, and bosoms, and wrapped the body in clinging, transparent fabrics. Hair stylists "bobbed" and "shingled" women's hair. More than ever before, young people sought distraction in movement: automobiles, dancing, and sports, for which—with the advent of the nine-hour workday—they had more time. For a few brief, dizzying years, America was on the move, as were war-weary Europeans who threw themselves into travel, migrating to uncharted beaches in the Adriatic, the Aegean, the Caribbean, South America, and even as far away as the South Pacific. Lured by the lush imagery of travel posters, they boarded express trains and luxurious ocean liners bound for exotic seaside destinations.

HERE COMES THE SUN

The most exciting new thing to appear at the beach was the sun. Like everything that had seemed so immutable and divinely ordained in the nineteenth century, attitudes toward the sun were given a thorough revision during the catastrophic years of the Great War. Put simply, the eighteenth and most of the nineteenth centuries were heliophobic. Ozone and water were the main attractions, and beachgoers ventured to the oceanside only during the early hours of the morning or late afternoon and early evening, when the force of the sun's rays was considerably blunted. For at least a century, medical science held that heat and sunshine dried up the body's necessary fluids and left it debilitated, softened, and prone to physical ailments and moral corruption. Not by chance, observers concluded, were the great collapsed civilizations of antiquity located in subtropical climes aflame with torrid sunshine.

Class prejudice was an even more potent sunblock. As long as the majority of the population in Europe and America was agrarian and plebeian, only the elite could boast of perfectly pallid complexions and flash them as an instant badge of superiority. In paintings of beach scenes from the period, swimmers and bathers, both male and female, were invariably depicted with white skin. This pallor was deemed not only to be more aesthetically pleasing than dark skin—in that it made the body more closely resemble sculpture—but it was also thought to signal racial purity and class privilege.

Consequently, nineteenth-century beachgoers had taken elaborate steps to guard against skin darkening, devising everything from bathing costumes to architecture to block the sun's rays. For the incautious—or excessively susceptible—there was an entire armamentarium of preparations, from homemade concoctions of lemon juice and witch hazel used to bleach freckles, to commercially available nostrums of mysterious composition, guaranteed to "remove sunspots and excessively high color." Ladies donned hats with enormous brims, carried parasols, hid under scarves, capes, veils, and even masks to protect any bit of skin that costume might have left exposed. On beaches—where the danger of sunburn was greatest—covered walkways, pavilions, gazebos, verandas, and tents were erected for the duration of the bathing season. There were beach chairs with awnings, and hammocks with attached sunshades. At high noon, a nineteenth-century beach had the uninhabited look of a desert.

By the early 1920s, the situation had completely changed. Not only were beaches most populated during the peak sun hours, but precisely those locations and seasons that the nineteenth century had avoided now became most desirable. People "in the know" streamed south—to the Riviera, Mallorca, Ibiza, Portofino, Venice, Abbazzia, Sicily, and, in the United States, to North Carolina, Florida, and the Gulf Coast—and, what's more, they did so *in the summer.* This mass impulse to expose the body to the sun was to a great degree the result of global trauma inflicted by the Great War.

The sun was a pervasive image in Art Deco design of the 1920s, and interest intensified in the sun worshippers of ancient Egypt and the sun cults of the Incas and Mayas. Writer D. H. Lawrence maintained that he, like the ancient Greeks, found a "white unsunned body . . . fishy and unhealthy." By immersing themselves in the sea, people could wash away the memories, the guilt, and the pain; by basking in the sun, bake themselves back to health and vitality.

The fad for heliotherapy drove the radical redesigning of the swimsuit. Large sections of the back were slashed, sleeves eliminated, and trunks abbreviated for maximal skin exposure. (Jantzen Archive)

Young Germans in the Weimar Republic revived the Nietzschean belief in nature as the source of human energy. The sun became a mobilizing social force that brought thousands outdoors to seashores, lakes, rivers, and open-air swimming pools. When Stephen Spender visited Germany after the war, he was converted to the idea of the sun as the "symbol of the great wealth of nature within the poverty of man." As he watched tanned young men on the shores of rivers and lakes, he realized that sunbathing for them was not only therapeutic but a rite of purification and spiritual healing. "The sun healed their bodies of the years of war," he observed, "and made them conscious of the quivering, fluttering life of blood and muscles, covering their exhausted spirits like the pelt of an animal."

ESCAPE TO PARADISE

Resort destinations such as Cap d'Antibes or Cannes, which had previously shut down during the summer, now began to see a trickle of eccentric visitors swell into a flood. A cadre of artists, bons vivants, film stars, deposed aristocrats, and bohemians did for the Riviera what, in the eighteenth and nineteenth centuries, the British royal house did for Brighton, Weymouth, and the Isle of Wight. "There was no one at Antibes this summer," wrote F. Scott Fitzgerald, "except me, Zelda, the Valentinos, the Murphys, Mistinguett, Rex Ingram, Dos Passos, Alice Terry, the MacLeishes, Charles Brackett, Maude Kahn, Esther Murphy, Marguerite Namara, E. Phillips Oppenheim, Mannes the violinist, Floyd Dell, May and Chrystal Eastman, ex-Premier Orlando, Etienne de Beaumont." He might have added Cole Porter, Pablo Picasso, Man Ray, and the painter Fernand Léger. In short, everybody who was anybody came to summer on the Riviera.

They came by steamer, motorcar, and train, glad to be going to beaches where they could count on a steady supply of hot sun. The new coastal road, the *moyenne corniche*, gave them quick access to the scattered outposts of other sun worshippers. In customized Bugattis and Rolls-Royces, they sped from one end of the coast to the other, for a beach party at Noailles, a luncheon at Cap Martin, then a visit to the artists who settled in Cagnes and St.-Tropez. Until the 1920s, trains making the north–south run were so crowded that reservations had to be made at least two weeks in advance, and even then the best a passenger could hope for was a hard seat in a second-class compartment. The legendary Train Bleu changed all that. When it made its first run, on December 8, 1922, it inaugurated a new age of luxury travel. With its interconnecting compartments and refined blue-and-gold exterior, the Calais–Méditerranée Express, as it was officially called, came to be known as the "Train of Paradise."

No one, of course, can take the blame for having invented sunbathing. Countless anonymous Scandinavians, Germans, and elderly arthritics had been soaking up the rays of the afternoon sun to chase the chill of winter from their bones. But when it comes to making sunbathing at the beach fashionable, then the name of Coco Chanel inevitably arises. In 1923, the young designer appeared on the Riviera as brown as a sailor. A year later, Prince Jean-Louis de Faucigny-Lucinge stunned friends by taking his bride to the Riviera in the summertime. The prince and his new wife spent their honeymoon pursuing the Chanel tan. "It was delicious," they recalled in later years. "We immediately started sunbathing, exaggerated sunbathing. It was a study, it took time, hours and hours of sunbathing."

By 1929, when it began daily runs to the Riviera, the Blue Train was conveying passengers to a spate of new Edens on the beach. These resorts were distinctly different from the prewar establishments that had provided swimming in small, rocky coves, from pebbly shores, or on man-made breakwaters. The new resorts were built around the paradisiacal ideal of the tropical beach. Converts to suntanning looked for sandy beaches to go with the tropical vegetation that an earlier generation had imported

After World War I, sun worshippers inaugurated the summer—which had been the nineteenth century's dead season—on the French and Italian Rivieras. (authors' collection)

and that now flourished in wild profusion. They gravitated to Juan-les-Pins, considered the prettiest resort on the Riviera.

As these beaches grew more and more crowded, efforts were launched to clean up other naturally sandy stretches on the Riviera and, wherever possible, to expand them by importing sand. Decades of fly-infested seaweed were peeled away to expose small patches of creamy beach. So desperate were hoteliers to accommodate their guests that they even considered constructing artificial beaches. In the case of Monaco, the venture was ill-fated.

The city hired Elsa Maxwell, who had revitalized the Lido in Venice, to modernize its facilities. Maxwell's solution—covering a giant rubber mat with sand—ended in failure, for the rubber disintegrated and the sand washed away.

What the Riviera lacked in inexhaustible sandy seashore, the islands of the Caribbean provided with unstinting generosity. The earliest tourists to this region were attracted by its bracing climate and balmy air. As early as 1905, visitors seeking to take advantage of Jamaica's great natural beauty, sun, and warm, healthy climate were regularly ferried from England. Travelers from other countries favored other islands. The choice of destination was completely determined by the reach of the European colonial empires. Thus, for example, the British frequented Barbados and Jamaica, the French vacationed in Martinique, the Dutch in Curaçao, and the Americans in Cuba and the Bahamas. The "season," as in Europe, was limited to the winter months, and, because of the difficulty and expense of travel, was confined largely to the wealthy few. For many North Americans after World War I, Jamaica, Cuba, and the Bahamas became what the Riviera was to cosmopolitan Europe. Moneyed visitors purchased houses or rented old plantation mansions, where they presided over elaborate seaside rituals. Hollywood film stars of the 1930s, writers, and playwrights sailed down to the islands in their large yachts, and spent their summers re-creating the good life of the colonial plantocracy. In Cuba, Ernest Hemingway set the tone for macho carousing and gambling.

THE AMERICAN RIVIERA

Stateside, however, Americans with a yen to find the elegance of the Côte d'Azur closer to home had to go no farther than Palm Beach, Florida, on an island separating Lake Worth from the Atlantic. Verdant, balmy, and relentlessly exclusive, this enclave of the rich and famous got its start in 1878, when the Spanish brigantine *Providencia* ran aground, spilling her cargo of twenty thousand coconuts along the blistering shore. The settlers stuck them in the sandy soil, and soon the windswept, barren strip was alive with susurrant groves. Twenty years later, Henry Morrison Flagler, a founder of Standard Oil and a real-estate developer with a knack for making thriving resorts out of sleepy seaside hamlets, paid a visit. He had already brought the railroad to St. Augustine, where he built the resplendent Ponce de Leon Hotel to provide a destination for his rail passengers. Now he would repeat the formula by extending the rail line east, right up to the Lake Worth Cottage Colony. This sleepy hamlet of ramshackle cottages—home to no more than nineteen families—had little to recommend it to the fashionable clientele Flagler wanted to attract, but the palm trees were delectable. Following his unerring instinct for identifying spectacular locations, Flagler commissioned a magnificent, sprawling hotel, the Royal Poinciana.

From its inception, Palm Beach was an exquisitely curated resort of grand hotels, opulent villas, and gambling casinos catering to an elegant "fast" crowd. Architecturally, Flagler wanted his new hotel to recall the rambling wooden "cottages" of Bar Harbor, Newport, and Southampton, which he considered the signature style of the American shoreline. Besides, building in wood was faster and cheaper than building in stone; Flagler was in a rush. Within a year of his first visit, a vast canary-yellow six-story structure in the so-called Shingle style was ready to receive the stylish guests arriving by Flagler's Florida East Coast Railroad, for which he had also provided a private railway car for their annual migration.

At the turn of the century, the newly formed Palm Beach Improvement Company undertook a series of massive projects to resculpt the island's natural topography. The marshy grasslands and lagoons were filled in; a seawall was constructed. Roads were laid. Even though access to the island resort was problematic, and would continue to be so until the early 1950s, visitors kept pouring in through a combination of ferries and precarious bridges.

The more socialites the beach resort drew, the sharper became the lines of demarcation between the disadvantaged and the privileged. This was a pattern with which Europeans had become familiar as they had watched the gradual social polarization of their resort towns: from ostensibly classless Edens to which the elite came to indulge in salubrious "simplification," to exclusive enclaves to which the have-nots were admitted only as the invisible hands of the mythical Psyche's paradise. Ministering to the needs of their employers, workers were expected to vanish in their off hours, lest they ruin the carefully cultivated aesthetic effect of seaside architecture, costume, and customs. In Palm Beach, the original inhabitants were housed in a neighborhood called "The Sticks" on account of its flimsy construction. The story was told that, when Henry Flagler unveiled his Royal Poinciana Hotel in 1894, he invited the Sticks residents to a great circus in West Palm Beach. As they were engrossed in the performances of freaks and high-wire artists, a fire mysteriously swept through their part of town, burning it to the ground. Even though fires were a seasonal occurrence, arson was suspected; Flagler was rumored to have instigated the fire, hoping to rid the new resort of its undesirable elements.

If Flagler got the ball rolling, two bons vivants—Paris Singer, heir to the sewing-machine fortune, and architect Addison Mizner—were responsible for making Palm Beach into a Mediterranean-style venue for pleasure. Together, they infused a cosmopolitan *joie de vivre* into the beach routine, and plotted to provide a truly theatrical backdrop for pleasure.

Their first collaboration had entirely philanthropic motives. Sympathetic to the psychological trauma of soldiers who had fought in World War I, Singer engaged Mizner to design a convalescents' hospital. The sun, the silence, and the sea, Singer thought, would do miracles for the shattered nerves of veterans. The construction, however, proceeded at too desultory a pace to be of any practical use to traumatized troops. By the time the Moorish-style structure was completed, its purpose had passed: the war was over and the soldiers were demobilized. Singer decided to turn his hospital into a private club; it became the hub of the good life in Palm Beach.

In New York, Mizner had built many vacation homes on Long Island, only a few in his beloved Mediterranean style. But in Palm Beach, he had virtual carte blanche to dictate the residential idiom. Backed by Singer's inexhaustible funds and licensed by his clients' aesthetic docility, Mizner went about redesigning paradise. The two friends gave Palm Beach a fairytale beauty concocted of Mediterranean-style shops, clubs, and mansions with fabled names, such as El Mirasol, Amado, Casa Nana. Among the clients were many Midwesterners: George S. Rasmussen (founder of a grocery-store chain), the Pillsburys, the McCormicks, and many other scions of industry.

The baronial dwellings—"castles by the sea," as they were known—followed an established formula: stucco walls, spiral staircases, soaring beamed ceilings, cypress paneling, loggias, balconies, cloistered walkways, and lushly landscaped gardens that spilled out onto the powder-fine sands rimming the island. The resplendent domiciles were completed at a frenzied pace, within just six months, yet nothing about them betrayed the haste of their construction. The wood used inside and out was specially aged in Mizner's workrooms, where it was flogged with chains, scraped with broken bottles, painted, stripped, and blasted with buckshot for that prized worm-eaten effect. Entire rooms were purchased abroad, from villas and monasteries, and reassembled in their new settings. Mizner left nothing to chance: he even had the green oranges on his clients' trees painted to look ripe.

Singer's and Mizner's brand of unabashed make-believe set the tone for subsequent development on Palm Beach. Allusions to bohemian revels and to the Mediterranean cropped up everywhere: in place names, gardening styles, and methods of construction. However magical these projects may have been, they were nothing compared with the palatial Mar-a-Lago ("Sea-to-Lake"), which Marjorie Merriweather Post, doyenne of the highest reaches of society, built between 1923 and 1927. Part Alhambra, part château, Mar-a-Lago had 115 rooms based on every stylistic idiom, from Rome's Chigi Palace and Venice's Accademia to Hollywood stage sets. As flamboyant as its various tenants, the estate would eventually pass into the hands of Donald Trump, another real-estate developer in the intrepid mold of Palm Beach's Flagler.

Beachside frolics continued unabated throughout the decade, as long as the weather and the market cooperated. Palm Beach socialite Charles Munn, Jr., of the mechanical mail-sorting-machine-and-racetrack-machinery fortune, entertained the likes of the Duke and Duchess of Windsor, and defined the inner circle of Palm Beach society by the odd stratagem of including the names and telephone numbers of his friends in his Christmas cards. Beach clubs with euphemistically worded exclusionary clauses sprang up at the least hint of undesirable parvenus seeking admission. The beach, in fact, bred myriad arcane rituals of inclusion and exclusion by which a self-defined elite maintained its supremacy and set, for the rest of the nation, the norms of leisure conspicuously indulged.

DECO HEAVEN

What Palm Beach was to the rich and famous, Miami Beach—its glitzy cousin sixty-two miles to the south—was to the solidly middle-class. The 1930s brought large numbers of visitors from large East Coast cities—New York, Boston, Philadelphia, and Baltimore—where they were accustomed to life in apartment houses or small homes. Their needs, trimmed even more by the austerity of the Depression, were modest. Moreover, many were one or, at most, two generations removed from immigrant origins, and brought lower expectations of comfort.

Moderately priced hotels in the pastel colors and exotic geometries of the Tropical Art Deco style spread along Miami Beach's south side. (authors' collection)

It was for these visitors that a vigorous construction campaign got under way between 1934 and 1940. Hundreds of hotels and apartment houses were built, although no longer in the historicist styles of the original resorts, but in a new, stripped-down idiom. Now appeared the modernist aesthetic that came to be known, generically, as Art Deco: a collection of styles that included ZigZag, Moderne, Streamline, Depression Moderne, Mechano Deco, and Cinema Style. Located in the area roughly bounded by 5th Street to the south, 23rd Street to the north, Ocean Drive to the east, and Lenox Court on the west, these new structures followed, according to Polly Redford, author of *Billion-Dollar Sandbar,* "the then 'modern' architecture of the day, a style whose angular lines, flat sundecks, and staring windows suggested a series of stranded ferry boats parsimoniously cut up and converted into hotels."

Emblazoned with names such as Neron, Cavalier, Cardozo, Carlyle, Delano, Haddon Hall, Claremont, Mayfair, Majestic, and Richmond, the new hotels rose from Collins Avenue and Ocean Drive like overscaled, marzipan-covered pastries. Tinted sunshine-yellow, seafoam-green, flamingo-pink, and turquoise-blue, they broadcast a vision of life as carnival. The fashion for Art Deco—launched in Paris in 1925—had legitimized an arsenal of decorative motifs and architectural devices that had never before appeared on structures devoted to pleasure: glass block, tubular railings, brash cylindrical volumes, ornament based on images of machine gears, rocket fins, and pharaonic regalia, as well as medallions, "bosses," moldings, parapets, and finials in clean geometric patterns. Facing into the tropical breeze, the hotels and apartments sat squarely in the sandy soil, each with its central tower hovering like a fantastic sculpture above the stepped-back flat roofs.

Unlike the earlier generation of resort hotels, which were deliberately uniform in style—the same historicist architecture cropped up in Newport, Rhode Island, and in Newport Beach, California—the Tropical Deco structures of Miami Beach studiously related to their setting. With their porthole windows, balconies reminiscent of the generous decks of ocean liners, flagstaff finials, and wave-shaped friezes, they invoked the colors, shapes, and motifs of their marine environment. The novelty and sparkle of these structures connoted a newfound optimism, and a determination to found a brave new world here, on the shores of a mild and caressing sea, in a climate predictably sunny, warm, and healing.

Every winter, as the Northeast sank beneath a chill blanket of snow, asthmatics, consumptives, arthritics, and pensioners boarded the *Champion* at Manhattan's Pennsylvania Station, bound for Miami Beach sunshine.

Like birds migrating south for the winter, tourists from the Midwest motored to Florida, taking the Dixie Highway from Chicago to Miami. (Marion Post Wolcott, *Picnic on the Beach, Sarasota, Florida,* 1941, authors' collection)

While the train sped southward, they snacked on picnic fare brought along in hampers; at night, they waited for the porter to bring around pillows and blankets and help them tilt their seats way back. When the lights were dimmed, they slept fitfully, awakened in the middle of the night, when the train stopped at a designated location south of the Mason-Dixon Line and all the black passengers were forced to relocate to cars at the rear of the train.

A little more than twenty-four hours after leaving Manhattan, the train pulled into the grimy old railroad station in Miami. By cab or trolley, tourists rode to their rented apartments, some of which went for as little as three dollars a week, located in the candy-colored buildings of the southern reaches of the resort. Only the inexperienced settled for first-floor flats, where the Florida dampness made furniture tacky to the touch and gave rugs a musty, mildewy smell. The tiny kitchens were clean, but always host to the beetles and bugs, mice and salamanders that stubbornly refused to be exterminated.

Many of the "winter people" nailed mezuzahs to the side of their apartment doors. They came for protracted stays of three, four, even five months, bringing along children and small pets. During the week, the children went to schools where they studied with classmates from all over the country. In the late afternoon and on weekends, families walked the few blocks from their rented quarters to the ocean, wooden beach shoes clattering on the warm pavement.

The coarse dark-green grass that grew close to the sand scratched the bottoms of bare feet. There was no boardwalk here, as on the Jersey shore, no undertow, and no rope to hold on to. The bathhouses were just as dark and cramped as those at home, but the exteriors were made of yellow or lavender stucco and the roofs were red tile. The water was warm and clear and blue-green, and at low tide one could walk way, way out and still only get wet up to the knees.

In the evening, after the supper dishes were put away, it was time to go to movies in one of the swank Deco theaters. The curtains would rise on *Moon over Miami,* or the latest aquacade starring Esther Williams, queen of bathing beauties, who swam underwater, always smiling with beautiful, straight white teeth and shiny red lipstick, and dived without a splash, to the wordless admiration of the handsome young men in the background. The longer you sat in the dark, the more aware you were of the taut sunburned skin on your back, until all you could think about was a long, soothing vinegar bath. The Deco phase of Miami Beach was its moment of populist glory. By the end of the 1930s, the number of hotels had swelled to three hundred, so that at any one time the city housed as many as eighty-five thousand visitors.

SUITED FOR THE SUN

In the 1920s, swimming had played the decisive role in transforming the bathing dress into a functional, hydrodynamic garment suitable for the aquatic athlete; in the 1930s, the principal design-generator for the swimsuit came from the new "sport" of sunbathing. Tanned skin was all the rage during the Depression decade. Dr. Shirley W. Wynne, commissioner of health for the City of New York, promoted tanning as a cure for everything from tuberculosis to surgical conditions. "The sun-tan fad is the best thing that has ever happened to the people of America," the health commissioner decreed. "The sun is the greatest bottle of medicine in the universe."

Even better, this perpetual blaze of melanin-inducing photons from that fireball in the sky was free. Absolutely free. But since only those with ample leisure could acquire a seamless gloss of brown, tanned skin was an immediate marker of class, physical fitness, and glamour. Suddenly everyone was a heliophiliac in quest of a tan—and of a suit that afforded maximum exposure.

In 1931, the swimwear industry was revolutionized by the introduction of Lastex, a rubber yarn manufactured and patented by the Adamson Brothers Company, a subsidiary of the U.S. Rubber Company. Before 1930, elastic yarn used in apparel was cut from sheets of rubber. Finally, a technique was developed for extruding liquid latex into a fine, round rubber thread. When covered with two tightly wound layers of yarn, the thread could be used in a wide variety of swimsuit fabrics. Cotton, rayon, silk, wool, and acetate were the most common materials used to sheathe the latex-rubber threads. This new yarn also had several limitations. For one, the rubber thread

To protect fragile skins from sunburn, there were gasoline-pump-shaped tanning-oil dispensers at which women queued up to be sprayed, and the "Tan-O-Meter," a color-graded chart that prescribed optimal exposure times. (UPI/Bettmann)

at the core of the thread did not take dyes readily and showed, or "grinned through," when the yarn was stretched. It also tended to loose its elasticity, primarily because the rubber was susceptible to deterioration from contact with natural body oils, cosmetics, and suntan lotions.

Publicists for every major firm claimed the distinction of being first to introduce the "miracle fiber" in their own suits. The shaping power of Lastex fueled a whole new way of thinking about swimwear and the ways in which the human body could be exhibited in public. Since every curve and dimple was faithfully reproduced in the fabric, it became desirable, once again, to find ways of suppressing anatomical "defects," smoothing over taboo zones, and enhancing strengths. For the woman who was concerned that the swimsuit was the only thing between her ungovernable flesh and the unforgiving world, Lastex was the perfect solution. "What's he got that I haven't got?" queried a chubby male specimen staring dumbfounded at "Mr. Muscles," preening for a cluster of bosomy beauties in a Catalina ad for Lastex trunks. "LASTEX APPEAL—that's what he's got!" was the snappy reply.

By the mid-1930s, Lastex had become a household word. Not surprisingly, most swimwear manufacturers tried to distinguish their Lastex suits with enticing names. The B.V.D. Company collaborated closely with Adamson Brothers to develop woven Lastex fabrics for their swimsuits, registering the results with unique product names such as Sea Satin, a Lastex-and-rayon-acetate woven satin fabric. With its slightly crinkled appearance, this blend was similar to Schiaparelli fabrics produced in France in 1933. In 1937, B.V.D. introduced a printed "mesh sea-satin" called Aqualastic in styles designed by tennis player Helen Wills. Apparently, so amenable to the vagaries of the human form was Lastex that A. J. Spaulding introduced a one-size-fits-all suit that would "dry in a twinkle."

SKIN AND SEA

In 1930, psychologist John Carl Flügel published an influential study, *Psychology of Clothes,* in which he voiced an opinion that was to become typical of the entire decade: "Dress is after all destined to be but an episode in the history of humanity, and man (and perhaps before him woman) will one day go about his business secure in the control of his body and of his wider physical environment, disdaining the sartorial crutches on which he perilously supported himself during the earlier tottering stages of his march towards a higher culture." This was a curiously utopian sentiment, one of the escapist fairy tales into which the culture retreated during the gloom of hard times. Ironically, nudity in those days did not suggest poverty. Rather, it had the mystique of innocence, evolutionary advances, and boundless opportunity for motion and, by implication, for promotion. To the futurologists of the thirties, the brave new world could only be nude.

The beach was the perfect arena for exploring these novel attitudes. Here one could revel in the embrace of the elements: the caress of the wind, the tug of the wave, the warm breath of the sun. Time seemed to stand still. The body, freed from constraining coverings, could rediscover its pagan beauty. Small wonder, then, that with the weight of so many social and cultural changes, even bathers on American beaches were beginning to rebel against the most tangible symbol of a discredited past: the restrictive, concealing bathing costume.

The cult of the athletic, tanned body spread from Weimar, Germany, to America. (authors' collection)

The *Miami Herald* noted that ordinances regulating bathing attire no longer held the force of law. "To expose a leg on the beach several years ago brought condemnation of a member of the fair sex in the minds of her associates. Then, by degrees, the many yards of bathing paraphernalia have been discarded for a few ounces of wool, cotton, or silk. The legs were allowed a chance to feel the sun rays. The back was given free rein as the bottom of the bathing suits became higher and the tops became lower." What's more, the beach patrol turned a blind eye to sunbathers who let their tops down, provided they were discreet about it. "There are many inconspicuous places along the beach which afford bathers a modest environment where suits can be dropped to the waist permitting the sun to penetrate the body."

At least partly in response to this sun-worshipping craze, radical reductions were introduced into the basic maillot design. Armholes were enlarged, and the décolletage was cut much deeper. Finally, the back of the suit was stripped away nearly to the waist. Styles with names like the Sungoddess, the Sunaire, and the Shouldaire offered what were then unprecedented expanses of uncovered skin, most of them in the back. "What is Jantzen's answer to nude bathing?" read an ad in 1933. And the response: "Jantzen's Molded-Fit swimming suits, super-light, super-soft that flex with every body movement like one's own skin!"

A spirit of playfulness and play-acting invaded the beach, transforming it into an open-air theater. A fashion story in the *Ladies' Home Journal* of June 1931 made this suggestion: "A brigand. A pirate bold. A wily Mexican. A heathen Chinee. A dashing Spaniard. The grocer's boy. A Basque fisher-man. A bronzed skipper. A desert sheik. A lovely lady in a Lysistrata robe . . . You'll play most of them yourself *on the beach* this summer. And the girl next door will do the parts you don't."

Male styles kept pace with the shrinking trend in women's suits. But the battle to expose the male chest was long, arduous, and far from decisive. The new "thrill" in 1933 was the "Men's Topper," admirably modeled by Warner star Dick Powell, who, as it turned out, had the hair airbrushed off his chest for the promotional photograph. "Zip!" announced the Jantzen swimwear catalogue copy, "In six seconds the change is made from a com-plete swimming suit to a smart high-waisted sun shorts. . . . The patented fastener makes the change effortless without fumbling with buttons and belts arrangement."

Wading through miles of red tape, men finally won the right in 1937 to hang their swimsuit tops on a hanger and go down to the sea in trunks. In the summer of 1936, the no-shirt movement was a hot issue—hotter, in fact, than the perennial fuss about female undress. The United Press reported that topless men were banned from the beaches of Atlantic City because the city fathers wanted "no gorillas on our beaches." Cleveland held out for men's trunks covering the navel. Galveston insisted on tops for men's suits, "but no special regulations concerning color or style of garment worn by women." The situation was so unstable that beach travelers found it pru-dent to consult updates on swimwear regulations across the country. In New York City, the rule was "anything goes"—but "within reason." Men could appear in abbreviated one-piece suits or simple trunks, but they were not allowed to roll down their one-piece suits to the waistline. That would have smacked too loudly of undressing in public—and might have thrown open the possibility of even further disrobing.

TAN PLANNING

As swimsuits shrank to permit greater exposure to the sun, medical science slowly mobilized its authority to promote the sun.

President Franklin Delano Roosevelt's sojourn on the coast of South Car-olina in the spring of 1943 focused attention on the therapeutic value of seaside sun. Admiral McIntire, the president's medical adviser, was widely quoted as saying, "All traces of winter ailments vanished under the magic of salt air, lots of sleep and rest and long hours of sunbathing." The following year, *The Journal of the American Medical Association* endorsed thalassother-apy—the sea-sun-and-air cure—for conditions ranging from the common cold to tuberculosis. A stay of six to eight weeks was considered optimal for patients suffering from chronic bronchitis, nervous exhaustion, or arthritis. According to E. K. Gubin, a writer for the medical journal *Hygeia*, scientists had determined that not all sunshine was created equal. Because the air of the beach is exceptionally pure, "more of the sun's rays strike the earth." And because of the reflective properties of water and sand, the radiation at the beach is amplified. Ultraviolet rays, which are responsible for tanning and for producing vitamin D in the tissues of the epidermis, were thought to be especially concentrated by the seashore.

But there was "dark side" to the sun craze, which, unfortunately, medical practitioners of the period failed to appreciate. Though few sun worshippers of this period died from acute solar overexposure, it is likely that thousands eventually suffered from skin damage and cancers caused by unprotected exposure. In fact, the pain associated with sunburn was probably the most enduring deterrent to sunbathing, even after social taboos relaxed sufficiently to include a tan among markers of class, privilege, and wealth. People did not yet worry about skin or collagen damage, even though the prematurely wrinkled faces of fishermen and fishwives gave them clear warning about the long-term effects of sun damage. They worried only about short-term effects: blistering, peeling, and freckling.

The Sun Ray Health Resort in Miami, Florida, provided a nude sunbath facility supervised by a uniformed nurse to ensure a medically correct exposure. (UPI/Bettmann)

In retrospect, the idea that something as insubstantial and invisible as a light film of liquid could promote the "seared-bronze" shade of skin to which sunbathers of the 1920s aspired and, more important, could even guard against burning, was patently implausible. After all, the earliest "sunblocks" had always been architectural: awnings, followed by hats, umbrellas, capes, and shelters. But by the late 1920s, chemists had begun experimenting with preparations could block the harmful action of the sun's rays. Microscopic particles of zinc oxide and titanium dioxide, when mixed into a thick paste, promised to provide an effective physical barrier. But its brilliant white color was unattractive on bare skin—the areas on which it was spread remained completely white—and so it was used only by lifeguards and skin-cancer patients.

The original formulations of zinc oxide made tanning an all-or-nothing proposition. Eventually, physical sunscreens would be developed that were transparent. These space-age preparations, referred to as "microfine powders," were manufactured so that the particles of zinc and titanium dioxide were so small they became invisible.

When all was said and done, the most dependable sun protection still came in the form of self-control. Through trial and error, sunbathers had learned that, by gradually increasing the length of time they spent in the sun and building up a "foundation," they could avoid the acute symptoms of sunburn and at the same time maintain their tan for some time after exposure. Careful timing and synchronizing progressively longer tanning sessions with specific times of the day allowed sun worshippers to fine-tune the precise shade of tan they desired. Some American beaches and European resorts even posted billboards that provided color-coded charts with recommended exposure times.

The first chemical breakthrough came in 1943, when chemists succeeded in synthesizing a complex string of molecules called para-aminobenzoic acid (PABA), an organic sunscreen. Although by varying the

concentration of PABA in the sunscreen solution, chemists could offer a range of tanning options, they were not able to eliminate allergic reactions. During World War II, other organic sunscreens were developed for use in the military, with or without additives such as insect repellents and water-proofing silicones. In the late 1940s, when demobilized soldiers and their families again flocked to beaches, cosmetic manufacturers and pharma-

In 1932, cellophane paper sun blankets were the latest word in tanning protection. (UPI/Bettmann)

ceutical companies stepped up production of these products. Some beach resorts in Europe and America even set up sunscreen-spraying stations. Modeled on gasoline pumps, these were brightly colored, coin-activated dispensers, usually operated by an attendant wielding a trigger-action nozzle.

ABANDON ON THE BEACH

In the United States, the Depression years segued into a time of dreams and fantasies of a tomorrow that would grant everyone everything the pres-

ent had denied. Footloose and fancy-free, designers—along with artists, ac-
tors, and filmmakers—kept pumping the adrenaline of optimism into
America's veins. At the end of the 1930s, the era's most innovative designers seized their greatest challenge when they were recruited to design the
1939 New York World's Fair. The theme of the fair, "Building the World of
Tomorrow," was the perfect culmination for an era of deprivation, and the
ideal vehicle for the talents of the brave new designers. Together they summoned up a vision of a future America where science, technology, and design molded a healthy, just, and happy society.

At about the same time, an "Aquacity of Tomorrow," an amusement park
conceived on the theme of water and its joyous benefits to humanity, rose
on the bank of the Columbia River in Portland, Orgean. Jantzen Beach, as
the park was called, was a clean, wholesome outdoor playground that
sprang from and catered to the messy vitality of the popular imagination.
In 1926, Paul H. Huedepohl, an outdoor-amusement expert, had joined
Jantzen Knitting Mills' promotional arm. A visionary authority on water
sports, he dreamed of building the perfect swimming pool, modeled on
the modern beach resort. Within a decade, his idea grew into a plan for a
lively amusement park that would become Portland's answer to New York
City's Coney Island.

A local architect, Richard Sundeleaf, was engaged to design a place
where, the architect explained, "thousands came to ride the Big Dipper,
swim in the pools, have a family picnic under the trees and then dance the
night away, to the big band sound in the Golden Canopy Ballroom." Flashing as many faces as a Halloween crowd, the Golden Canopy Ballroom was
part palace, part warehouse. The future-oriented design melded Beaux-
Arts gentility with industrial pragmatism. To keep in shape for those long
nights of "Dancin' at Jantzen," Portland's fox-trotters spent their daytime
hours pursuing the "secret of health and beauty" in the crystal waters of the
park's four swimming pools. "Health builds a likable personality," ran the
company's come-on, "and swimming in the great outdoors in clean safe-
guarded pools is the ideal place to find it." The Natatorium, as the bathhouse was called, and a spectacular poolside fountain gave this healthful
pursuit an aesthetic dimension. A cascade of graduated streamlined plates,
"over which a million gallons of pure crystal-like water flowed each day,"
was placed in the mammoth bathing pool. The perimeter of the pool was
buried beneath several tons of Columbia River sand, justifying the park's
appellation of "beach." This was the first time someone had tried to replicate the seashore far from the coast, an experiment that would be repeated
on a massive scale in the 1996 Phoenix project in Japan. This particular experiment, however, was short-lived: the sand was constantly clogging the
pool's filtration system and was soon eliminated. Some twenty-five hundred

bathers passed through this aquatic Eden every day, and a good number of them flexed their muscles and tucked in their tummies in zippy Jantzen suits.

By night, this "Aquacity of Tomorrow" was ablaze with thousands of flickering electric lamps as the soft river air vibrated with music. In its heyday in the 1930s and 1940s, as many as 4,000 dancers crowded nightly in the Jantzen Beach Golden Canopy Ballroom to hear the swing kings of the time. They danced to Tommy Dorsey, Stan Kenton, Benny Goodman, Dick Jurgens, and Woody Herman, gaining musical—and aquatic—respite from the cares of the Depression and war years.

BELLICOSITY AND THE BEACH

Then came World War II, and the beach took an ugly fall from paradise. Beginning in November 1939, when a British private patrolling the mudflats on the Channel coast recovered a German magnetic mine, the beaches of the Atlantic, the Mediterranean, and, within two years, the Pacific turned into death traps, where thousands of men were mowed down, ripped apart, and incinerated by the most modern tools of destruction. The names of some of the most beautiful beaches of the world—Dieppe, Anzio, Normandy, Salerno, the Solomons, Leyte Gulf, Two Jima—could never again be uttered without resonating with gunfire and the moans of the dying. In their devastation and menace, the violence staged by war would indeed re-create the horrifying visions of beach-as-hell whose full measure had already been taken in the Bible.

Even far from the front, however, the war effort indelibly altered the look and feel of the recreational beach. Japan's occupation of Southeast Asia meant no more rubber. And that, in turn, meant no more elasticized swimsuits, beach balls, rubber bathing caps, beach shoes, flotation rings, or floats. It also brought to a halt weekend and day trips to the beach: automobile tires were no longer available to civilians, and gasoline was strictly rationed. Beginning in December 1941, when tankers bound for the East Coast of the United States were sunk by German U-boats, the ordinary consumer was entitled to a mere four gallons—soon to be reduced to three—of gasoline a week, enough for sixty miles of strictly "nonpleasure" driving. To make those gallons and tires go farther, a national "Victory Speed" limit of thirty-five miles an hour was imposed. Cars themselves, and soon bicycles—along with anything else made of metal—became scarce. Automobiles languished under dust covers, bicycles rusted in cellars, and the casual beach outings of the 1930s became just another memory.

Weeds sprang up in the seams of deserted highways, and seaside resorts turned into ghost towns. Here and there, a grand hotel was requisitioned for military use. In Miami Beach, for example, posh hostelries were turned into dormitories, barracks, and hospitals for thousands of soldiers. When American involvement in the war was announced, beach hoteliers and resort entrepreneurs feared for the future of their investments. Wild rumors circulated that the playland would shut down overnight. This was not to be. Instead, the resort became a staging area for military maneuvers, romper room for off-duty troops, and schoolhouse for officers-in-training. In 1942, the Army Air Corps stationed four thousand men in six hotels, converted the municipal golf course into a drill field, and cordoned off adjoining neighborhoods.

War had come to paradise. On February 19, 1942, Floridians could look up from their morning papers to see thick clouds of smoke rising over the marine horizon. German U-boats were scoring hits against Allied tankers and supply boats. Some months later, a Mexican tanker was hit just south of Miami Beach and burned for hours within sight of the grand estates. The city was plunged into total blackouts and adopted defensive precautions. Every morning, the soldiers were roused before sunrise for reveille, or "roll out," which, as Private R. C. Bolton noted in the army publication *Yank,* was literally that: "Practically all of these hotels have front steps. These are very attractive in the daylight and make excellent places for the boys to sit during their off moments, if any. However, at 5:30 a.m., you can't see these steps even while you are falling down them, which is what usually happens."

The hub of off-duty activity was the magnificent Miami Beach Municipal Pier, an amusement structure built at the southeastern tip of Miami Beach and equipped with a theater, a gambling casino, restaurants, and bathing facilities. Renamed the Servicemen's Pier in early 1942, it leased swimsuits to an international cast of soldiers who were now stationed on the bases. Toward the end of the war, Russians came to sunbathe on the pier. There were even some German prisoners of war among the foreign visitors: stationed across Biscayne Bay and put to work in Miami Beach cleaning and repairing streets.

Before it was all over, the tropical city would become one of the great army command posts, where a quarter of all the officers and a fifth of all the enlisted men of the Army Air Forces of World War II were trained. By the late summer of 1943, 188 hotels, 109 apartment houses, and eighteen private homes had been turned over to the military. This, it turned out, was Miami Beach's salvation. Had the armed forces never come, it is doubtful that the resort could have survived the drastic drop in tourism that resulted from severe wartime travel restrictions.

Elsewhere, however, a bleak, pinched mood of deprivation settled into every nook and cranny of life, and there were few opportunities to escape to the beach. Civilians shivered in lines, waiting to buy minuscule portions of coffee; they shivered watching *The Maltese Falcon* in glacial movie theaters; they shivered in bed at night, praying for GIs slogging through blood-stained breakers on hostile beaches.

"To evoke a French beach at that time," wrote British novelist Cyril Connolly, "was to be reminded that beaches did not exist for mines and pill-boxes and barbed wire, but for us to bathe in." But the seaside resorts of England were far from inviting. In April 1942, the Germans launched the so-called Baedeker Blitz, named for the popular guidebook which had steered tourists to memorable sites throughout Europe for over a century. Seaside resorts, particularly those along the North Sea and the English Channel, were prime targets of these hit-and-run bombing raids, both because they formed the nearest land border to occupied Europe, and because Britain's defenses were concentrated there. When France fell in 1940, the British began moving guns and troops into holiday beach cottages around Dover and the Channel resorts. The grand hotels and dance halls of beach resorts were converted into army headquarters and officers' convalescent homes. Scaffold poles festooned with rolls of barbed wire stretched as far as the eye could see. Mines were hidden in the sand that was covered by water at high tide, making bathing lethal. Ugly concrete blockhouses and bunkers squatted along the cliff tops. The pillboxes installed on the sand were disguised as ice-cream stalls or bathing cabañas. Pleasure beaches were ringed with antitank blocks and deep ditches called tank traps, which filled with water and were designed to deter violation of land by heavy artillery. Tourists were promptly dispatched inland, and the year-round citizenry in seaside towns was encouraged to follow.

In a curiously satisfying twist of history, the invasion of Normandy on D-Day, June 6, 1944—an event that in the popular mind signifies the turning point of World War II—could not have come about without the help of the seaside holiday. Believing that occupied France could best be reclaimed by way of the sea, the Allies spent years preparing the assault on the eight-and-a-half kilometer stretch of the Cherbourg Peninsula. With no access to the occupied territory, the Allied planners pored over "oblique" reconnaissance aerial shots and old surveying maps and mariners' charts, but they lacked details of topographical features, such as the gradient of the beach or the location of dunes, which could be critical to the success of the attack. What information the military lacked about topography and ground cover, the civilian sector provided in the form of old tourist postcards of the beach and holiday snapshots by the sea commemorating the leisure "thalassophilic" invasion of the previous one hundred years. Droves of vacationers seeking the cure had been coming to the chilly, therapeutic waters of the Channel to combat the double foes of ill health and boredom. Now, in an odd Eros-in-the-service-of-Thanatos twist of fate, the intimate me-

mentos of their revelry and rest—hand-tinted images and linen postcards as detailed as espionage photos—became invaluable for delivering a crippling blow to the German army. Discreetly solicited over the BBC, images of vacationers on the Normandy beaches poured into Allied headquarters, providing crucial information about water depth, topographical landmarks, tidal patterns, and sand formations.

Combatants on both sides had used the beaches of the world as great "walls" of defense and subjected them to a brute geometry of grids, sectors, embankments, and crudely rectilinear bunkers. Nowhere was this more apparent than in a series of drawings of the beach made by General Rommel, which show it imprisoned in a network of crosses, rectangles, and polyhedra as an extreme materialization of that human drive for power over ungovernable nature. The rigid geometries of war—the standing at attention, the grid of formations, the deadly straight line of the bullet—had incubated a deep yearning for the irregular topography of the beach, with its impertinent and ever-shifting curves, and the joyous surprises of changing dunes and tide pools.

When peace finally came, so did a curiosity to visit the sites of war along the beaches of Hitler's so-called Atlantic Wall. A number of seaside resorts in Britain and France that had thrived as tourist destinations before the war were eager to put up monuments and open museums. In short, the "holiday-to-hell" vacation was inaugurated. Visitors made pilgrimages to the five beaches—Sword, Juno, Gold, Omaha, Utah—of Operation Overlord, with their commemorative monuments, cemeteries, beached Sherman tanks, sunken landing craft, and remnants of artificial harbors. In the Musée du Débarquement at Omaha Beach, tourists inspected displays of memorabilia, painstakingly rendered scale models, and grainy documentary films showing but a fraction of the 6,939 vessels, eleven thousand airplanes, and quarter-million troops landing during that first week of the invasion. In place of the hellish din and chaos of machines, bodies, and explosives, visitors now found, among the labeled remnants of war, a serene landscape of umbrellas, bathers, cabañas, and mobile homes generously distributed among carefully parceled strips of terrain.

BIKINI BEACH

By far the most explosive sartorial event of the forties was the introduction, in 1946, of the "bikini," or, as it was originally christened, the "Atome." The appearance of this infinitesimal garment sent shock waves around the world and brought joy to war-weary males in every port. After all, scarcely a year earlier, *Life* magazine had sounded the apocalyptic refrain on the theme of shrinking swimwear: "There is—or seems to be—nothing more to cut off." But if the evolutionary path of the bathing suit had steadily marched toward diminution, nothing in the recent past had prepared the beach for this. Never before had the female anatomy so teasingly called attention to the sum total of its erogenous zones. Conceptually, if not literally, the bikini's components resembled the black censoring stripes that appeared on pornographic pictures. In both cases, the function was the same: to permit the scantily clad female body legal circulation in a public arena.

The bikini actually claimed a nearly mythical origin in its antiquity, having been fully conceptualized on Minoan wall paintings dating from 1600 B.C. and in Roman mosaics from the fourth century A.D. In fact, six years after the bikini's "invention," its prototype was discovered by an Italian archeologist excavating a luxurious Roman villa on the island of Sicily. In the villa's capacious family gymnasium, Gino V. Gentili was confronted with a mosaic depicting eight female gymnasts sporting a diaperlike panty and a strapless bandeau.

Jacques Heim and Louis Réard, the two Frenchmen who nearly simultaneously launched the modern bikini, had no clue, however, that they were reinventing the wheel. Heim, a couturier, designed the suit to be sold in his beach shop in Cannes. He called the suit the Atome in honor of its size. The sky was the limit as far as its advertising went. One sun-baked morning early in the summer of 1946, beachgoers at Cannes raised their tanned faces to the heavens to find an apocalyptic message scrawled by skywriting planes against the Mediterranean sky: "Atome—the world's smallest bathing suit."

On July 1, 1946, the first postwar atom-bomb test blasted Bikini Atoll out of the South Pacific. Less than three weeks later, sun worshippers on the French Riviera were roused from their torpor by another message delivered from the heavens. This time the smoke loops spelled out "Bikini— smaller than the smallest bathing suit in the world." The man behind the aerial graffiti was Réard, a mechanical engineer who had brought the Atome a step closer to the subatomic. Applying all the years of his professional training to the challenge of providing minimal strategic coverage to the female body, Réard shaped 129 square inches of cotton into a smaller version of Heim's Atome. No one knows why Réard decided to call his suit after the radioactive atoll in the Pacific, but the name stuck.

The bikini could titillate with impunity, its three triangles performing an infinite *pas de trois* along the body's erogenous zones. In the years to come, the garment that, according to fashion guru Diana Vreeland, "revealed everything about a girl except her mother's maiden name," would inspire countless variations on the theme of three patches, some serious and some blatantly comical. The bikini was worn for the first time by French model

Micheline Bernardini at a poolside fashion show at the Piscine Molitor in Paris on July 5, 1946. A number of American foreign correspondents covered the event for the *Herald Tribune,* whose July 6, 1946, Paris edition ran nine bylined stories.

Two events shook the summer of 1946: the atomic test on Bikini Atoll and the unveiling of the world's skimpiest two-piece bathing suit. (National Archive/Corbis)

The quintessential tease, this sketchy garment was a provocation to fashion as much as to convention. It was, after all, the purest expression of the minimal formula of dress required by both. On the one hand, the bikini compressed the latest "look" into less than a square foot of fabric. In this respect, it was a kind of bonsai of apparel that displayed the salient features of style in miniature. All the subtle inflections of fashion could be expressed in the details of textile, fastenings, ornament, and the shaping of the bosom. As subsequent history would show, the bikini was more than a skimpy garment—it was a state of mind.

10

ENGINEERING PARADISE

Levittown, Christmas vacation, 1957. Snow swirls against the wood siding of the split-level ranch house. In the living room, a man spreads a Rand McNally roadmap on the sectional sofa and traces his finger along a network of blue and red lines running north to south. Two children sprawl in front of the Motorola television set, munching egg-salad sandwiches and absorbed in the madcap antics of Lucille Ball. A toddler sways in a swing seat near the picture window. In the kitchen, the refrigerator door slams shut. A woman in a powder-blue shirtwaist dress enters carrying a large wicker basket and sets it down by the front hall, next to a heap of suitcases, pillows, swim rings, golf clubs, beach mattresses, canvas folding chairs, and a mysterious lumpy object which, it turns out, is a collapsible beach cabaña built by the man of the house in his garage workshop.

At dawn the next day, Mom helps Dad pack the gear and the kids into the Pontiac Star Chief. Snow is still coming down as they pull into the Texaco station to tank up for the six day drive south. The black asphalt of U.S. 1 runs some twelve hundred miles down to Miami Beach. By late afternoon of each day, Mom anxiously scans the procession of flashy, neon-lit motel signs—Sea Breeze Court, Wind'n'Surf, Komfy Kabins—looking for one that might actually deliver what it promises. One night it's a rat trap for sixteen dollars—ten for the adults and two per child. The nearest place to eat is three miles down the road. The children are cranky, the parents irritated, and everybody is too tired to eat. The last night out, they find a Holiday Inn, where for six dollars they get a double room with a free television set, a restaurant, and a gift shop. The kids love the big bouncy beds, the paper covers on the drinking glasses, the miniature bars of soap. Dad loves the fact that there's no extra charge for the children.

Near Augusta, the southbound traffic thickens into a caravan of Buicks and "Woodies" piled high with suitcases and stuffed with pale children. The air grows warm. At roadside diners, the kids head straight for the section marked "Whites Only." Forty miles out of Miami Beach, they start seeing billboards advertising Arthur Godfrey at the Kenilworth, Pickin' Chicken, Joe's Stone Crab House, and miniature golf. There are palm trees everywhere.

They cross the causeway into Miami Beach and find their way to 1330 Pennsylvania Avenue, a pink stucco U-shaped building with a goldfish pool in front. The apartment they rented is ugly and smells of mildew and stale cigarettes. Mom opens the windows while the children go looking for the bedrooms. All they find is a tiny kitchen, a breakfast nook, a bathroom with a big water bug in the tub, a cramped bedroom, and an alcove with a door in the wall. Dad opens the door and pulls down the "Murphy bed," where the big kids will sleep. It's not paradise, but it will do.

The next morning, Mom packs a lunch in the wicker basket and Dad shoulders a folding chair and the portable dressing room. The family drives to the 13th Street beach on Ocean Drive. The kids carry Dad's old army blanket, the bag with towels, suntan lotion, and dry suits. There is no boardwalk, but the sand is soft and yellow, and it goes on for miles. They find a quiet spot in front of the twelve-story Tides Hotel, a glamorous Deco beacon amid smaller hotels in a pastel palette—the Marlin, Kent, and Leslie—on Ocean Drive. There is no end to the variety, and Dad, an engineer, studies the Mayan vegetative friezes and plaques, the Moorish twisted columns, the cut-glass sconces, the fluted pillars, and the use of the most advanced technological materials, including glass block, chrome, Vitrolite, and raked concrete, all of which capture the excitement of skyscrapers by the sea.

The waves here are shallow and long and gentle, and the water is a deep emerald color. Dad takes the kids to the water's edge, where he points out bluish bubbles floating on the surface of the waves—dangerous, stinging jellyfish called men-of-war. There will be no swimming today, but there is still a lot to do. The kids amuse themselves with the "Goofy Ball," a beach ball with an unexpected cockeyed bounce that sends them scurrying in pursuit.

At night, they celebrate with dinner in the La Ronde Room of the fabulous Fontainebleau Hotel. Dad invites Mom to dance to the music of Vaughn Monroe and his orchestra. The kids sneak out to run up and down the grand spiral staircase in the white marble lobby. Tomorrow, and for seven more days, they will swim and play in the surf and lie in the sun, as a united family.

⸎ ⸎ ⸎ ⸎ ⸎ ⸎

If separation had been the theme of the war years, togetherness was the rallying cry of the 1950s. Never before had the nuclear family been pumped

An aerial view of a summer Sunday in the late 1940s at Jones Beach, New York, attests to the tremendous draw of the seashore. (Culver Pictures)

with so much mystique. Celebrated in everything from women's magazines to television situation comedies, the family was the darling of popular culture and of an economy retreading for peacetime production.

After nearly fifteen years of austerity, American consumers were hot to shop. They wanted cheap modern homes, filled with labor-saving devices. They craved the fast, flashy, and increasingly affordable automobiles that rolled off the assembly lines of General Motors, Ford, and Chrysler. They longed for powerboats, water skis, and motorized beach toys. Gas was cheap and, thanks to the vast networks of pipelines and refineries built during the war, plentiful.

Even as automobiles, highways, and far-flung housing developments ruptured close-knit families, and television and a fledgling youth culture eroded generational bonds, sitcoms such as *I Love Lucy, The Adventures of Ozzie and Harriet, Leave It to Beaver,* and *Father Knows Best* served up rosy icons of family unity. The sullen alienation expressed by such apostles of rebellion as Marlon Brando, James Dean, and Elvis Presley did not take teenagers much beyond the local drive-in. For the time being, Americans were convinced that they had never had it so good, and nowhere was the cult of the joyous American nuclear family expressed with more verve than on the nation's beaches.

PACKAGED PLEASURES

Thanks to the automobile, the airplane, and affluence, the seashore was accessible to the broadest public in history and available for development as

After World War II, Americans embraced vacations with the fervor of converts to a new religion. Summer holidays and winter getaways to the beach were cherished, planned long in advance, and venerated as a respite from work and school. (authors' collection)

never before. Until the 1950s, beach options had largely fallen into two categories: the select resorts located at considerable distances from urban centers, which catered to the affluent; and the popular and congested bathing sites within easy reach of large cities, which drew short-term visitors of the day-tripping variety. The middle-class beachgoers had been largely dependent on railways and steamboats to take them to sites that toed the precarious line between respectability and affordability. Their beach excursions took them to rooming houses and modest hotels at the periphery of exclusive enclaves, or to seasonal cottages within easy reach of home.

The transportation revolution changed all that. Travel by car, airplane, bus, and recreational vehicle had never been cheaper. Bitten by the bug of mobility during their far-flung military travels, enlisted men and women were anxious for geographical novelty. This meant a craving for new, unfamiliar locations, for holidays in out-of-the-way places where in the interwar years only people of means could afford to vacation: Cuba, the Caribbean, Europe.

With the introduction of the commercially successful Boeing 707 in 1958, the age of air travel for the masses arrived. British vacationers by the thousands signed up for inexpensive holidays on Spain's Costa Brava and the Balearic Islands of Mallorca and Ibiza, as well as in Italy, Greece, and the French Riviera. Other Northern Europeans quickly followed suit, packaging their own sea-and-sun tours to the Mediterranean. With air travel shrinking the Atlantic Ocean into a lake and, more important, contracting the distance from the mainland to Hawaii, more and more Americans jumped on the beach-hopping bandwagon. Cruise-line companies, hit hard by aircraft competition, scrambled for a piece of the burgeoning beach-holiday market and came up with the fly-cruise concept. Chartered airplanes flew passengers directly to ports in the Caribbean or the Mediterranean, where they embarked on luxury liners for picture-postcard-perfect beaches and duty-free shopping opportunities.

BRINGING HOME TO THE BEACH

An ad for the Trotwood, "The Trailer of Complete Relaxation," proclaimed that it "makes your dreams of carefree Traveling and Living come gloriously true. Plenty of room for four persons, and you can cook, eat and sleep as easily as at home." Traveling to the beach by camper promised independence, flexibility, and spontaneity, without the tedium and expense of motels, or the constraint of a long-term rental. Suburban homes on wheels, campers were equipped with "every comfort and convenience: everything you need to make you happy and contented, no matter where you choose to be." In the galley, housewives concocted quick meals in energy-and-time-saving pressure cookers which made up in speed for whatever they lost in taste and texture. Since many GI wives had begun their married lives in makeshift trailer housing, they were experienced in the art of improvising nourishing "dinner-in-a-dish" recipes, such as tuna-fish casserole, hearty trailer toss, or "boo-yaw."

By the early 1950s, so many Americans took campers to the beach that trailer parks by the seashore and along the Great Lakes resembled seasonal suburban sprawls. In 1940, there had been thirty-five hundred trailer camps throughout the United States. A decade later, that number had more than doubled. Unfortunately, the unsavory element frequenting trailers was also increasing, particularly during the weekdays, when the "respectable" weekend traffic slacked off and various criminal elements took over. According to FBI Director J. Edgar Hoover, the conditions in trailer parks along the nation's highways was "pestilential." He explained that, "with prostitution growing more nomadic and gravitating toward tourist camps, 'drunk rolling,' pocket-picking, and

Wartime technology was retooled to produce the commodities of beachfront leisure, including mobile homes, barbecue grills, portable radios, and beach toys. (Bettmann Archive)

the use of knockout drops for robbery . . . have now appeared in seaside re-treats." Divorce detectives—"that lowest of parasite upon law enforce-ment"—and marijuana sellers rounded out the cast of miscreants allegedly endemic to these transient communities.

In an effort to make camper parks at the beach safer for families and "de-cent people," the American Automobile Association made an inventory of the nation's facilities, and issued a regularly upgraded directory of safe and unsafe parks. The trailer industry responded by encouraging the develop-ment of parks limited exclusively to trailers and run in conjunction with au-tomobile dealerships. The result was an efflorescence of trailer parks along the warm beaches of the southern United States, on the Gulf Coast, and in southern California.

Run as mom-and-pop operations or as national franchises, these instant villages-by-the-sea offered water-and-sewage hookup, a hot shower, and a laundry. A Chicago firm by the name of K-A-R-A-V-A-N Industries sold, ac-cording to its brochure, "buildings, service, and equipment, individually owned but exactly alike." The illustration accompanying the ad shows the trailers standing in a beautifully landscaped park enclosed by a picket fence. In reality, however, the picturesque factor rarely extended beyond the names, such as Paradise Trailer Court or Briny Breezes Park. Typically, the ground was scraped flat and cleared of all vegetation. Gravel paths ran from each plot to the dirt road. When empty, the camp had the dreary, pinched look of a construction site. In the summertime, however, when every spot was taken and the spaces between trailers were filled with color-ful awnings and beach umbrellas, the park seemed festive, like a seaside carnival.

FINE-TUNING THE CLIMATE

More than any other technological breakthrough, air conditioning was responsible for transforming the beach holiday from a seasonal to a year-round option, and for spurring growth, especially in Florida. Without it, southern beaches were habitable only eight or nine months of the year, the optimal season extending from December through April. Visitors stayed away from June through August, and those locals who could afford to trav-eled inland or farther north.

Although available commercially since the 1930s, air conditioning was not used extensively in Miami Beach until 1946. By 1955, every major hotel and apartment house had been equipped with it, which meant that even on sweltering days guests could retreat from the sun to cool restaurants, lounges, movie theaters, and hotel rooms. Now hotels and rooming houses were kept busy year-round, and the resort became more attractive for the waiters, hotel housekeepers, hair stylists, gardeners, and other service personnel who were taking up permanent residence.

Something similar was taking place in beach resorts throughout the South and on the West Coast. Controlling the environment inside beach facilities expanded their appeal and allure. Guests could move from the searing heat of the sand into the temperate microclimate of their lodgings. Technology brought them one step closer to controlling the variables of nature and attuning the natural world to the body, rather than, as had overwhelmingly been the case before, the other way around. Artificial cooling breezes took one of the last liabilities out of the hostile element of the beach. In the 1970s and 1980s, chemicals would take care of the sunburn problem, and by the end of the millennium, artificial beaches enclosed beneath domes—complete with sand, regulatable waves, palm trees, and sunlight—would truly take the beach into the realm of utopia.

BEACH OR BUST

By affording a protracted public display of the female torso, and of the breast in particular, beach life in postwar America did more to focus attention on—and develop fashion modifications for—this erogenous zone than any human activity that had preceded it. In addition, demographic changes profoundly affected how people wanted to present themselves on the beach, and these changes were reflected in swimsuit construction. The broad public was still hypnotized by the mannered, padded, and contoured silhouettes of the 1940s, and by swimsuits that, as much as anything, addressed the "pin-up" sensibilities nurtured by a decade of conflict, anxiety, and familial dislocation. With their bold protuberances, architectonic styling, and glittering fabrics, swimsuits were uniquely tailored for an era locked in a consuming romance with the automobile and all its stylistic mannerisms, from chrome-plated hubcaps to flamboyant excrescences affixed to the rear ends of De Sotos and Fleetwoods.

In fact, like automobiles of the era, the signature 1950s swimsuit silhouette counterposed jutting angles against bulbous shapes and amoeboid curves. Pointed breasts—or "high beams," as they were jocularly known in the vernacular—surmounted wafer-thin torsos which flared gracefully from wasp waists to slim hips—all, thanks to the zealotry of foundation experts, within easy reach of most women. The "Merry Widow" corset and radical developments in foundation garments had a powerful impact on the look of women on the beach. Engineered with rubber elastic fibers and fortified with boning, underwiring and doubled panels, these sartorial infrastructures represented what fashion historian Ellen Melinkoff called the "Sherman tank line of corsetry." Girdles were manufactured in a range of controlling styles, from the strangulating "all-in-one" extending from bosom to mid-thigh, to the long-line panty and sheath models.

Promotions for swimwear promised to turn the ugliest duckling into a siren. Consumers were coached on improving their beach presence with "Color Charts" in which accessories, belts, caps, shoes, and swimsuits could be matched to hair color. Five-foot-high Animated Color Wheels by Hazel Adler guided shoppers in "scientifically" selecting the ensemble most flattering to their complexions. The Jantzen Size-O-Weight, a denial device for the cellulite set, registered *size* on the scale, rather than pounds. "Hundreds of alert merchants have installed the Jantzen Size-O-Weight over the past year," read an ad to retailers. "They have found it *makes* sales. Because the dial registers size not pounds, it overcomes the *reluctance* of some customers to give their weight and obviates the *unconscious* mistakes of others."

Purveyors of American beachwear found themselves feeding an appetite for hourglass curves, luxurious fabrics, and unambiguous sexual symbolism. "During a war, a man hates nothing more than to see a girl in pants," explained Fred Cole, who by the mid-1950s had manufactured some thirteen million swimsuits. "Today, we are in a disturbed period, and again femininity is very important." When it came to the swimsuit, femininity expressed itself primarily through the choice and treatment of fabrics. "Women are going to look more like women on the beaches this summer," *Harper's Bazaar* announced in 1951, and offered up a sampling of "feminizing" looks which ran the gamut from the black lace of the boudoir to the crinoline petticoat of the sock hop, embracing as well the bloomer of the toddler's romper suit, the sophisticate's sheath, and the debutante's flounces. Beachwear also provided the American woman with an unprecedented range of "looks"—from homey to sophisticated, from ingenue to demimondaine.

Jayne Mansfield, the decade's archetypical va-va-voom girl, explained in 1952 that a woman who looked right in a swimsuit must have "a flat tummy, a firm bosom and a nice derriere. Then you're in business." Because so many women lacked these requisites—or thought they did—the sportswear industry invented a milestone in the history of swimwear design known as the "constructed suit." Never before in the history of American fashion had so much engineering gone into constructing a garment. In its most sophisticated variation, the swimsuit developed an awesome capacity to control, dissimulate, and glorify the female body. Constructed as cunningly as corsets, many suits were boned at the sides to produce a smooth, long torso. Bras were wired, lined with a layer of foam rubber or molded with pellon, a fabric used to stiffen petticoats, to shape the fashionably high, pointed bosom.

As quickly as the petrochemical industry produced new types of plastics, foams, and rubber compounds, these found their way into the support structures of bathing-suit brassieres. In the days before cosmetic surgery had perfected breast-augmentation procedures, padding was the only solution for small-busted women. In the late 1940s and early 1950s, constructed swimwear began to feature sewn cups which were shaped entirely by complicated cutting and stitching. The shapes that could be achieved by this method, however, did not correspond to the geometrically pure ideal of the fifties. The new bustline looked considerably more mannered, more artificial, than the pneumatic but rounded bust of the pin-up decade. Moreover, the sewn bra cup was made with seams, which had a tendency to show through the stretch fabrics.

The new fashion dictated a substantial, pointed bosom cantilevered over a pinched waist in a manner reminiscent of the canted roof of a Googie coffee shop or drive-in restaurant. The foundation industry rose to the challenge with devices that sculpted the bosom while augmenting it. Brassieres came equipped with everything from ventilated foam-rubber pads to nippled rubber cones—or "falsies"—and inflatable prosthetics that could be blown up to the wearer's specifications. Always in the business of providing secular role models, Hollywood churned out a torrid array of ideal body types. The hyperbolic dimensions of beach-cum-sex goddesses Marilyn Monroe, Jayne Mansfield, and Jane Russell invaded living rooms, colonizing the American subconscious with anatomic archetypes. Such films as *The Petty Girl* proposed that, with proper handling, even a prim schoolteacher could be a curvaceous glamour girl. Every woman wanted movie-star curves, and nowhere more so than on the beach.

Postwar jubilation introduced a new playfulness to swimsuit fashion. Reflecting their contact with military theaters abroad, American designers scoured the globe for grace notes and exotic touches to enhance beach fashions. Gathering impressions from distant ports-of-call, they brought back with them a taste for bright and bold

Manufacturers turned out fantasy swimwear for the mass market that covered the entire gamut of looks. (University of Southern California Archives of the Performing Arts)

prints—Mexican, West African, West Indian, and especially Hawaiian—that spoke of balmy winds beneath an azure sky. Depending upon her most recent itinerary, globe-trotting Carolyn Schnurer, the grande dame of adaptive design, took her inspiration directly from the native costumes of Africa's Gold Coast and from wrought-iron grillwork she spotted in Istanbul. Suits with names like "The Persian Gulf," "Scottish Moor," "Zanzibar,"

In 1949, Charles L. Langs, a chrome-plater of Cadillac grilles from Detroit, designed the first adhesive brassiere. Good for only a single dip, the strapless, wireless, and backless garment was sold with glue for "rejuvenating" the adhesive. (Time Life Pictures Archive)

or even "Traveler's Check" displayed their provenance in instantly recognizable cuts and textiles.

Any soft material could be pressed into service as padding under street clothing, but swimsuits were appreciably less forgiving. A bosom enhanced by Kleenex tissues or nylons could not stand up to the buffeting of waves, much less to the intense scrutiny of beach bums. Bust pads fashioned from nylon horsehair, a coarse nylon mesh material that became available at the turn of the decade, were somewhat more reliable. They bestowed the requisite conical shape to the breast, but unfortunately had no "memory," and the stress of powerful swimwear fabrics tended to crush them. Moreover, if the discrepancy between the pads and the wearer's endowments was too great, these cups collapsed under the least pressure. For manufacturers and bathers, the future of the "new look" in the swimsuit depended on finding a better bust pad that could withstand the aquatic stress test.

In 1951, Herbert Nigetson, founder of Metric Products, Inc., solved this problem with a seamless molded cup which combined a plastic copolymer shell, fused onto polyurethane foam, with a soft stretch nylon fabric. The "Curvelle," as this bra cup would eventually be known, was ideal for swimwear. It was fast-drying, impervious to swimming-pool chemicals, and comfortable to wear. Metric's contour-formed rubber cups could be molded into any shape and had the outstanding ability to "remember" their contours. The manufacturer guaranteed that the wearer "could lie on her stomach or embrace her lifeguard without worrying about losing her figure."

SEX ON THE BEACH

While some manufacturers were promoting a more conservative approach to swimwear—and claimed the beach as a site for wholesome recreation—others were capitalizing on the beach as an evolving locus for erotic pursuits. Jantzen, for one, commissioned *Esquire* illustrator Alberto Varga (the company dropped the "s" because it was too "gassy") to create a new image for the Jantzen girl. That new image was closer to pound cake than the cheesecake Varga eventually produced for *Playboy*. Things got spicy, however, in an *Esquire* calendar that Jantzen mailed to 3,123 "preferred swimsuit accounts."

"She's young . . . she's thrilling . . . and ideal to every American man. You'll be seeing her this summer . . . in Jantzen's stunning swimsuit." The quips put the final icing on the cheesecake. Miss January's annotation read, "I've been in more triangles than the one I'm wearing." Others, like "I can't stay late, my wife isn't as dumb as your husband," or "May, so delightful, and what a month for men, Daddies who have lost their *spring* discover it again," were sending shock (and shlock) waves through the minds of Jantzen's preferred customers.

These successful campaigns encouraged Jantzen to continue its search for marketable flesh of the living-and-breathing variety. With the rise of the movie industry in the 1920s, America's most salable skin was, as it still is today, on the beaches of southern California. In the late 1940s, Jantzen searched throngs of virile adolescents in sunny southern California, and found James Garner. America's favorite TV detective was barely eighteen years old when Jantzen discovered him at, of all places, Hollywood High School. They offered him fifteen dollars an hour, and he just couldn't turn them down. This solid hunk of testosterone made such waves modeling their line of "savage swim trunks" that in 1947 he was chosen "Mr. Jantzen."

That season, Jantzen's style books for wholesalers and retailers featured not only Garner but a fair-skinned, fair-haired young beauty named Norma Jean Baker modeling the risqué "Double Dare" bathing suit (so-called because it afforded a glimpse of the upper thigh through two circular portholes). Baker (later known as Marilyn Monroe) seemed radiant as she stuck a two-pronged skewer through the six-inch wiener balanced between her thumb and four fingers. Another photograph revealed a somewhat less provocative, but equally metaphorical, Monroe. Wearing the "Temptation," a no-frills solid-body two-piece, she had the look of a playful predator as she admired the desiccated remains of a fish still affixed to a hook.

Only a **Jantzen** *fits so perfectly*

The early-1940s marketing campaigns of Jantzen, one of America's premier swimwear manufacturers, represented the beach as the site for wholesome family recreation. (authors' collection)

Although it is not known who took the photographs of Monroe and Garner—they remained sequestered in Jantzen's archives for years—the services of both were commissioned in 1947 through a modeling agency, long before either was a nationally recognized star. Unlike the modeling photographs of Douglas Fairbanks, Jr., Dick Powell, Loretta Young, and others obtained through the Warner Brothers/First National trade arrangement with Jantzen in the mid-thirties, the pictures of Monroe and Garner were independent of film-industry linkups. Tapped by manufacturers since the early thirties, Hollywood stars became a standard fixture for beach-side promotions. Established screen celebrities such as Rita Hayworth posed for swimwear spreads in family magazines, and matinee idols lent their names to popular models—as Frank Sinatra did to the "Swoonsuit" of the forties.

ENGINEERING PARADISE BY THE SEA

Miami Beach was to the seashore what the constructed swimsuit of the 1950s was to bathing attire: a highly engineered setting, mechanically contrived to serve the single objective of delivering the perfect experience of sun, sand, and surf. This apotheosis of beach-as-everyday-life had taken root less than a century earlier in the swamps and bogs of Miami's eastern barrier island, which in the ensuing decades would be razed, filled, dredged, and landscaped into the perfect projection of God's City on the Sea. The story of South Florida's evolution from a crocodile-and-mosquito-infested swamp to a sybarite's Shangri-la by the 1950s is the story of ambition, hype, and technological wizardry pressed into service for the pleasure principle—the saga of creating paradise from silt and scratch.

Long before Deco jewels lined Collins Avenue and Ocean Drive, much of the area was a mere bar with a cluster of mangrove trees to the south trapping the sand that grew into a beach on the east. At low tide, when the brownish water shrank from the dark, slimy roots, crabs scuttled across the ooze. At dusk, clouds of mosquitoes rose whining from the thick foliage and prowled the jungle in search of human blood. Wild oranges, lemons, limes, and guava grew in profusion, and coco plums, which made a tasty sauce when cooked, were plentiful. In the spring and early summer, the air was perfumed with wild acacia, verbena, and lantana. In winter, all that could be heard was the cry of cranes and the scuttle of raccoons across rotting logs.

What would one day be Miami Beach began as an agricultural dream. In 1513, Ponce de León rounded the tip of Key Biscayne, and other explorers followed, along with their priests, merchants, and traders. No gold or silver was found, nor were many souls converted either to Christianity or to Western dress. The natives saw no reason to trade their Spanish-moss loincloths for the cumbersome pantaloons and tight weskits of the colonialists, just as, four centuries later, tourists from Chicago, Indianapolis, New York, and New Jersey would find no reason to wear anything but the modern equivalent of the natives' costume.

As unstable as its geography, the name of this playground by the sea changed with each successive tenant. Early maps showed it as the Tongue of the Mainland, and then, successively, Boca Ratonnes, the Peninsula, Ocean Beach, Alton Beach, and, finally, Miami Beach. The indigenous nomads lost this territory to the Spanish; then the Spanish, in 1763, lost it to the British, who twenty years later gave it back as a bad bet. The settlers who withstood the hurricanes, pestilential heat, and brackish drinking water made a wretched living stripping wrecked ships—and, if need be, engineering shipwrecks by removing markers and extinguishing signals so they would have ships to strip.

The United States gained control of the property in 1821. Some years later, two powerful hurricanes roared across northern Biscayne Bay and gouged out two sections of the peninsula, stranding the southern tip as an island. Until 1876, there were few humans inhabiting the coastal areas, other than the occasional shipwrecked sailor, for whose benefit signs had been posted in English, French, and Spanish to indicate the location of freshwater wells. This early trilingual courtesy would lay the foundation for the exuberant cultural mix that would make Miami Beach the melting fleshpot of cultures at the end of the twentieth century.

In the 1870s, the United States government erected one of its lifesaving stations—a manned outpost with provisions for stranded sailors and survivors of shipwrecks—the Biscayne House of Refuge, on the site of today's Miami Beach. At about the same time, an adventure capitalist named Henry B. Lum paid a visit to the remote sandbar. He was the secret link between the California Gold Rush and what would soon become the rush to Florida's Gold Coast. An enterprising New Jerseyite, Lum had headed west as the first rumors of California gold began circulating on the East Coast. He had no luck with prospecting, but by selling bread to miners at the inflated rate of a dollar a slice, he soon saved up enough to buy a neat parcel of land back in New Jersey. His plan was to open a nursery and supply plants to the great estates along the Hudson River Valley.

As his business thrived, his slumbering wanderlust awakened, along with a thirst for new challenges. Lum traveled to Miami and one afternoon found himself tramping across the sands of the godforsaken barrier strip, tripping over roots, and wiping the sweat from his eyes. At the very end of the beach, he saw something that sent shivers of excitement running down his spine. Jutting out of the sand were three palm trees. Only a visionary horticulturist could look at those three sorry specimens on the southernmost tip of the peninsula and see a fortune in them. But even as he was being stung by sand flies rising in clouds from the stinking seaweed, Lum resolved to abandon New Jersey forever. He would return to this tropical land and set himself up in the coconut-growing business. Here, he thought to himself, a new Arcadia will blossom.

With two other entrepreneurs from Middletown, New Jersey, Lum bought up virtually all of what would one day become Miami Beach. The long, slow process of the "New Jersey–fication" of the South Florida shore was under way. Additional investors from New Jersey bought into that stretch of coast. On the striated foundations of indigenous populations— Spanish, British, and Yankee—the future Miami Beach was consecrated into the polyglot cosmopolitanism which by the end of the twentieth century would be its greatest glory.

First, however, came a detour into commerce that would forever mark the character of Miami Beach as a mercenary retreat hell-bent on profiting from the human weakness for self-indulgent fantasy. Lum and his two original investors went about turning the beach into a coconut plantation. They hired twenty-five hands from New Jersey lifesaving stations; purchased several condemned government lifeboats, some cheap, sound mules, tents, tools, provisions, and a small prefabricated house; and shipped the whole lot down to the festering peninsula. While waiting for a chartered schooner to deliver the first of four shipments of coconuts from Trinidad, the men cleared trails about thirty feet apart, from the beach back to the mangrove swamp, in which to plant the coconuts. When the schooner arrived, they unloaded the shipments one at a time into the old lifeboats, and then again onshore. On that first shipment, thirty-eight thousand coconuts were unloaded and planted. More would follow.

The task of creating a plantation was daunting. The vegetation was so thickly intergrown that the surveyors were unable to lay guidelines on the ground. The best they could do was to have some men climb the highest trees and call out the landmarks to the workers below, who then hacked their way through the underbrush and vines, balancing long bamboo stakes to plant at twenty-foot intervals. The men had to be on constant lookout for coral snakes, rattlers, leeches, and crocodiles. There was nothing paradisaical about the preparation of paradise.

As soon as the first sprouts appeared, the rats and rabbits that infested the peninsula abandoned their customary diet of salt sea oats for the novelty of coconut shoots. The planters were reduced to desperate measures. They spread out corn and apples dosed with strychnine, but the rodents, unfamiliar with these Northern delicacies, ignored them. Chicken wire and palmetto leaves were erected around the base of young coconut trees, and some of the seedlings were saved. At first, however, the battle with nature went against the humans, so much so that in 1890, Lum admitted defeat and returned to New Jersey.

PUTTING TOGETHER THE PIECES

Only a physician could conceive that what South Florida needed to spur its growth was a new circulation system. In 1884, Dr. John Wescott of St. Augustine dreamed of converting southeastern Florida into a commercial shipping center, and came up with a scheme for an inland waterway that would link up with the natural bodies of water just west of the Atlantic Ocean. He established the Florida Coast Line Canal and Transportation Company to raise funds, buy land, and dig waterways to connect the St. Johns River, near Jacksonville, to Biscayne Bay, 340 miles away. Sooner rather than later, he, too, ran out of money. The digging was both onerous and chaotic, and the resulting link, when finally completed in 1912—long after Wescott was out of the picture—was useless for commercial shipping. Only five feet deep and fifty feet wide, it was too shallow and narrow for cargo ships.

It was, however, just the right size for pleasure boats, and when eventually developed into the Intracoastal Waterway, it would be a great drawing point for amateur mariners. These were making their way south along the network of railways Henry Flagler was threading all through South Florida. By 1896, Flagler's railroad had reached Miami—just in time for developer John Collins to begin purchasing large tracts of real estate with the object of improving them for resale. He reportedly plotted his campaign in a room in Flagler's Royal Palm Hotel, located in what would become downtown Miami, reputed to be the largest wooden structure in the world. Hype had arrived along with architectural hyperbole. Incorporated in 1896, fledgling Miami was drawing speculators and entrepreneurs the way saltwater taffy draws flies. No one, however, paid much attention to the barrier strip immediately east of the city, except on Sunday afternoons when the heat became genuinely insufferable. Then bathing parties were organized to what the local press described as "a very nice beach and good surf just north of Norris' Cut," on the peninsula.

The author of an article that appeared in the *Miami Metropolis* one week after the city's incorporation in 1896 suggested: "If a pavilion and a few bath houses were erected on the beach so that people could find a shady spot to shelter them from the sun when they wished to sit down to luncheon or where they could take refuge in case of a rain squall, we believe a hundred people would go over to Norris' Cut every Sunday. There are a thousand people at Miami who have nothing to do and nowhere to go every Sunday, and there must be at least one in ten who enjoy looking at the 'sad sea waves' and taking a dip in the old ocean."

This advice did not pass unheeded. A two-story dance hall was erected on the beach in 1904. It wasn't much of a place—"mostly roof, very high and shaped like the famous pyramids of Egypt," according to the subsequent developer, Avery Smith, who took over the lease for the building and some adjoining land. The terrain was still so untouched that Smith reported feeling "like Robinson Crusoe on his South Sea Isle. We saw the land, the sea and all that nature had put there but that was about all there was at that time. I was greatly impressed with what I thought was an opportunity to establish a pleasure resort, and transportation proposition in connection with it." Five years later, his vision became a reality. Smith's Biscayne Navigation Company constructed wharves at Miami and on the peninsula and began to run ferryboats twice a day.

Smith's resort, built on the bones of the old, was christened Fairy Land and, according to a prospectus, offered an "average temperature of sea water 76 degrees, winter season. All modern improvements. Large recreation pavilion for picnics." Most important, it afforded year-round bathing. This last feature would clinch the site's success.

Progress, in the form of channel dredging, steadily gnawed away at the peninsula. In 1905, after months of around-the-clock digging, the sandy finger of land was severed from the mainland by a passageway called Government Cut. The waters of Biscayne Bay were now joined with those of the ocean to yield a brand-new island, roughly seven and a half square miles in area, with a beach eight miles long, that would soon bear the name "Miami Beach." The entire population of Miami, then thirty-five hundred, turned out for the final dip of the dredge that would complete the cut. At the last moment, something went wrong with the dredging machinery, so that what was to have been a biblical surge turned out to be a mere trickle. A group of dignitaries seized shovels and manually attacked the intervening strip of sand to excavate a tiny stream between the two bodies of water.

The new island, complete with bathhouse and ferry service, was in the hands of John Collins. All this time, he had been struggling to establish an avocado plantation on the site of the former coconut groves carved out by Lum. But he, too, had bad luck: the winds dried up his crops. Finally, he appealed to his children in New Jersey for money. They agreed to help him out on condition that he build a bridge across Biscayne Bay. They reasoned that if people could actually drive their cars there instead of waiting for the ferry, perhaps the island could be made into a resort, even something along the lines of New Jersey's Atlantic City. Where their father had seen only mangoes, tomatoes, and potatoes, they saw the promised land of leisure, Florida-style.

When word of the projected bridge got out, Miami's Realtors whipped up a feeding frenzy, offering an initial 415 lots, 50 by 130 feet in size, priced from four hundred to twelve hundred dollars, and urging "procrastinators to BUY, and BUY NOW!" One company enticed prospective owners to "think of buying a lot in such a desirable location for such a price. The improvements now in progress indicate its desirability—Boardwalk, Casino, Sewers, Rock Roads, Electric lights, Telephones and Street Cars will follow as a matter of course."

All the perks of modern life—efficiency, affordability, accessibility, sociability, utility, hygiene, and diversion were packed into a tidy parcel. The beachside home promoted family unity and cemented social bonds, and even, it was implied, advanced the cause of democracy by bringing together a geographically scattered citizenry in a common appreciation for natural beauty, without sacrificing any of the advances of modern technology. As in that far-off biblical time, the "Ocean Beach" experience would know no boredom, no sense of a breach between work and play, effort and relaxation, no social or functional cleavage between servants and masters. Each individual would be perfectly integrated and harmonious, and each family would preside over its own flawless, seasonless corner of heaven. Give us this day our daily beach.

COMMUTING TO PARADISE

The Collins Bridge was completed and officially unveiled on May 22, 1913, formally opening Miami Beach to the automobile. A photograph taken at the bridge's inauguration shows an unbroken string of square-topped automobiles, bumper to bumper on the low structure, which hovers above the choppy waters of the bay like a thin strand of spiderweb. There is a decidedly precarious look about the whole arrangement, but the dignitaries gathered at the base appear jubilant. Ladies in white lawn dresses and straw hats festooned with feathers and flowers peer joyously over the shoulders of their white-shirted men. A few bicyclists are on hand, waiting their turn to cross. On the other side, automobiles queued up for a spot on the turntable used to point them back toward Miami.

Over the next year, eight miles of beach were carved up into lots, and an infrastructure of roads began to appear. For several weeks at a stretch, residents of Miami, across the bay, would wake up in the morning to the sight of thick clouds of smoke rising from the burning palmetto and mangrove and roiling above the sandy spit. What could not be burned was chopped up and used to reinforce landfill. As the jungle was cleared to accommodate human habitation, the natural fauna was forced out into the open. Rattlesnakes, raccoons by the hundreds, and rats by the thousands, not to mention swarms of mosquitoes, poured out of the shrinking jungle. The workmen wrapped their feet and ankles in layers of newspaper to keep from being bitten, and all donned wide-brimmed hats with heavy nets to protect the face and neck. Not until many of the mangrove swamps had been drained and the mosquito population brought under some semblance of control would it actually be possible to strip down without worrying about the possibility of major blood loss.

In the span of less than eight months, 350 acres of the peninsula were transformed from a wilderness to a park. Dredging crews deepened the bay and then filled in a bulkhead constructed on the west side of the land. Carl Fisher, the land developer who was the prime mover in Miami Beach's phenomenal growth, had learned from the east–west Lincoln Highway the advantages of involving local industrialists and financiers in bankrolling a project. Now he applied the same strategy to creating a highway from Chicago to Miami; it would eventually reach as far north as the Straits of Mackinac in Michigan's Upper Peninsula. Despite frenzied enthusiasm, Dixie Highway generated considerable local squabbling: everyone wanted a piece of the action. Finally, two routes were laid. The eastern began at Sault Ste. Marie and continued through Toledo, Dayton, Cincinnati, Asheville, Augusta, Savannah, and into Florida through Jacksonville; the western route ran from Chicago through Indianapolis, Louisville, Nashville, Atlanta, and Tallahassee. Both roads led to Miami. The entire "pipeline-for-tourism" was now finally in place. Vacationers from the Midwest took to the Lincoln and Dixie highways in staggering numbers, lured by the novelty of automobile travel along what Carl Fisher's promotional literature booster described as the "wonder trail . . . running like a gleaming thread of gold from sea to sea, girding the continent with startlingly new and romantic values."

The only thing this new beach lacked was a name, and that was formally bestowed in 1915 when the three developers Collins, Fisher, and J. N. Lummus met to incorporate their holdings as "Miami Beach." In the next fifteen years, until the stock-market crash of 1929 put a damper—never a brake—on development, the geographical reshaping of paradise went on unabated. Driven by greed and fantasy, developers deepened the bay, constructed bridges, extended and reshaped the contours of the land. In short, they played God with nature. New, perfectly geometrical landfill islands appeared in the bay: Flag, Star, Palm, Hibiscus, and Venetian islands materialized in the 1910s. In 1921, four more—Rivo Alto, DiLido, San Marino, and San Marco—were dredged out of the bay bottom, and three years later the grounds of the new Nautilus Hotel were augmented by the addition of Collins and Johns islands.

To complement those already running east and west, more islands were planned to run north and south. Even though they lay seven feet beneath the water, they appeared on maps, each with its charming Italian name. The new causeway, islands, and islets forever altered the flow of water in the bay. The causeway acted as a dam along the upper bay and blocked the tidal flushing that had naturally kept the waters clean. Soon fish were dying, mosquitoes were once again proliferating, and a foul smell rose from the still waters. More cuts had to be made to drain the bay.

Rivaling the Egyptian pyramids in scope, engineering, and the sheer number of its builders, Miami Beach was a living monument to modern America's passion for instant gratification. Even though periodically shaken by man-made and natural disasters—boom-and-bust real-estate cycles, hurricanes, shifting de-

Emulating seaside restaurants on the Riviera, where patrons were served luncheon in the surf, residents of Miami Beach structured their lives around the water. (UPI/Bettmann)

mographics and fashion—Miami Beach had one thing going that was always in demand: the perfect combination of sand, sun, and ocean.

MOVING INTO GOD'S WAITING ROOM

World War II gave Miami Beach a genuinely international inflection. On its beaches and along its palm-shaded avenues formed an unholy alliance of sun worshippers: gangsters and racketeers in the late 1940s, Cubans fleeing Fidel Castro in the 1950s; Colombian drug lords in the 1960s and 1970s; and, eventually, American, Italian, French, and German designers, financiers, models, and celebrities in the 1980s and 1990s.

The population density of the resort city soared. Mass tourism had arrived, along with the "total-resort" experience that began with hotelier Morris Lansburg's "American Plan": for a single price, guests received accommodations, breakfast, dinner, and admission to a nightclub show. The more the city expanded its tourist facilities, the more customers it had to attract. Entrepreneurs courted every zoological fraternity, political party, and professional organization. Facilities were built to house professional basketball teams, championship boxing matches, and beauty pageants. Nightclubs gave top billing to stars such as flamenco dancer José Greco, singer Georgia Gibbs, Johnny Mathis, the zany Ritz Brothers, Connie Francis, Tony Bennett, Martha Raye, comic Don Rickles, Milton Berle, Arthur Godfrey, and many others. With so many options in the menu of diversions and so little time allotted to them, the seaside holiday was transformed into a tightly scheduled prix-fixe menu of entertainment. Stimulation and frenzied consumption of leisure activities exterminated relaxation.

Meanwhile, the area south of Lincoln Road presented a less glittery face. By the 1950s, neighborhoods with Art Deco hotels and apartment houses had grown shabby. The brilliant colors of the stucco had faded and chipped. The intricate scrollwork and cast-iron railings were flaking and pocked with rust, and the bodies that occupied the webbed beach chairs that lined the entryways were frail and old. The southern part of Miami Beach had aged. The population of mainly Jewish New Yorkers, New Jerseyites, and European refugees who had started coming when the Deco palaces were young had returned permanently. Dressed in the fashions of their youth, fragile old ladies and gentlemen took the sun on hotel porches that local wags called "God's Waiting Room." They looked out across the palm trees lining Ocean Drive at a jumble of bulwarks, groins, and jetties, and, beyond them, at an angry sea chewing at the last few feet of beach that had survived the ceaseless engineering of the tropical paradise.

OUTCASTS FROM PARADISE

Miami Beach of the 1920s and 1930s was a place that stubbornly insisted on seeing itself as a racially homogeneous utopia and was zealous in engineering not only its natural but also its social landscape. Until World War II, the fantasy resort was quite solidly White, Anglo-Saxon, and Protestant: no Jews or African Americans in this paradise. Even as racial hatreds began to erupt to the surface and self-defense organizations such as the National Association for the Advancement of Colored People and the Anti-Defamation League of B'nai B'rith came into being, the realty offices typically issued deeds restricting ownership to Caucasians. All others were thereby implicitly excluded.

Signs were posted on apartments and hotels that identified them as "Restricted" or "For Gentiles Only." In the 1921–22 winter season, the proprietor of the socially ambitious Helene Apartment House sent out a prospectus that included a rate sheet and a "No Hebrew" card. The prestigious Flamingo Hotel and the Lincoln Inn were a little less crude, though they, too, admitted only those Jewish guests who had secured high social standing. Even these reluctant courtesies were abruptly and temporarily terminated in the spring of 1925, when young, mainly Jewish speculators from the North swept into town, bought up options on property before it went on public sale, then, in turn, sold and resold their options at higher prices, driving up the original price of the property as much as four or five times. For six frenetic months, these wheeler-dealers holed up in cheap

hotels, three or four to a single room. Realtors quickly learned to recognize them from afar by their inevitable golf knickers, which the "Binder Boys"—so called after the name of their financial maneuver—favored for their imperviousness to wrinkles and dirt.

In the late 1930s, when the resort city moved into a new middle-class phase, the most southern sections became hospitable to Jews, most of them from New York and New Jersey. Kosher meat markets, groceries, and delis appeared. As soon as Jews began to frequent the public beaches and the Roman Pools opposite the Roney Plaza

Weight lifters worked out on the beach along Ocean Drive. (authors' collection)

Hotel, a backlash developed among the self-appointed, anti-Semitic elite. They withdrew into restricted private clubs, such as the Bath Clubs, the Indian Creek Country Club, the Surf Club, and the vigilantly exclusive Miami Beach Rod and Reel Club. Here, members sipped on Prohibition bourbon through the afternoon as they lounged in their tented beachside cabañas. Women in floppy pajamas and in bias-cut silk sarongs with Paris labels shuttled between the sea and the dance floor beneath the palms, where they were dipped and pivoted by tipsy companions to the wail of Argentine tangos. As the sun flamed in the west, the action shifted to the indoor bars and restaurants, and, later still, to the gambling casinos that thrived in open violation of the law. Miami Beach, ever permissive and obliging, looked the other way.

AFRICAN-AMERICAN SANDS

Not until civil-rights legislation was enacted in the 1960s would African-Americans enjoy unrestricted access to the sands and waters of Miami Beach. Until then, African-American chauffeurs, day workers from Miami, live-in domestics, and hotel help gathered on the beach along Ocean Drive. Their presence, though scant, was from the beginning vexatious to the developers. "We have a problem on our hands," wrote an associate of Carl Fisher in a memo concerning their using the ocean for bathing and swimming, "that is going to be a little difficult, I am afraid, to handle and the longer it goes the more difficult it is going to be."

In 1918, a wealthy African-American Miami developer by the name of D. A. Dorsey came up with a proposal that might have worked. Principal owner of what is now Fisher Island, Dorsey wanted to build a resort for African-Americans there, but ran into insurmountable obstacles. Others applied themselves to the task, spurred by Fisher's advice: "The Negroes should have a place of their own to bathe, where they can get suits and bathe in the Ocean the same as white people, and if I knew where we could build such a place for them at not too prohibitive a cost, it would be to our advantage to build it." Yet nothing ever went beyond talk, and for the next four decades they had to go to the mainland if they wished to bathe in the sea.

As all along the southern Atlantic coast, segregation kept the beach sharply divided between the white haves and the African-American have-nots. But a phenomenon that would ultimately bring them together was brewing in the African-American dance pavilions of Myrtle Beach. Since the late 1930s and early 1940s, African-American couples had been dancing something called the "shag," an exuberant melding of the jitterbug, the lindy, and the swing, to the music of Lucky Millinder, the Tympany Five, and a host of touring orchestras. Gradually, a distinctive sound emerged, concocted of equal parts horn, saxophone, and rhythm, with roots in gospel and swing. Bands with big horn sections added rhythm for a kick and saxophone for "guts." The result was irresistible, not only for the African-American musicians and beachgoers whose synergy kept the Myrtle

Beach pavilions hopping, but also for white kids in the know. But the juke-boxes and the radio stations were not carrying the then forbidden fruit of this music. For one thing, its lyrical content—unabashedly sexual and bawdy—kept the songs off the radio stations altogether. The only way people living inland could catch the "underground sounds" of the era was by making the trip to the dance pavilions of Myrtle Beach. Hence the name "beach music."

It was not until the early 1950s that "beach music" really exploded into a full-blown force. African-American GIs who had returned from the war with broadened perspectives and ambitions began to take over the beach in earnest. For the first time, they had the leisure, the money, and the inclination to come to the beach, not just for the day—as they had done in the past—but for weeks and even months at a time. Colonizing separate stretches of coastline in the Carolinas, they brought with them not only their own language and dress but also a perspective and experience that found expression in the racy, earthy lyrics of songs with titles like "Annie Had a Baby," "60 Minute Man," "It Ain't the Meat It's the Motion," "Rockin' & Rollin', Ballin' & Squallin'," and "Meet Me with Your Black Drawers On." From its epicenter in Fat Hal's Beach Club on Ocean Drive in North Myrtle Beach, beach music sent shock waves up and down the African-American clubs along the ocean strip.

This music went straight for the id like a roaring freight train and, unlike the sixties West Coast phenomenon of white "surfer" music, was not generational in its appeal. Bands such as the Catalinas, the Embers, the Drifters, the Lonely Teardrops, and the Ravens cut across generational lines. As beach-music historian Dale Van Horn described it, beach music "is an idiom, a sound, a lifestyle. It's the magic of the summer sun playing tricks on the waves. It's the glow in the eyes of two young people from two different places who meet and find something special. It's a pale yellow moon, ocean spray, sand and seagulls—a part of life that shouldn't be missed and can never be forgotten."

CHAPTER 11

CASTAWAYS

Hanalei, Kauai, 1968. The island is an exhilarating labyrinth of rocks, sub-terranean rivers, ocean pools, and rain forest. The beaches are full of swag-gering pelvises and salt-dried pompadours. The bearded, long-haired man in a tie-dyed T-shirt and cutoff jeans drives his VW Luv Bug on a precipitous oceanside road that, by way of single-lane wooden bridges, passes over rivulets tinted red with the earth's mud and iron. The island of Kauai is as far as he can get from the Statue of Liberty, the Smithsonian, and the Pen-tagon. His friends tell him Hawaii is where civilization can blow off a little steam now and then. He speaks almost exclusively in metaphors, so it is hard to know exactly what he means. Back home, the Vietnam War is taking its toll, turning college campuses into powder kegs. He has come to this beach because, to use the words of Jack Kerouac, there is more ecstasy to be had here, more life, more kicks, more darkness, more music, more night.

And more water. Today, flash-flood warnings have gone up for the Hanalei-Haena area, on the northwestern part of the island, where the film *South Pacific* was made. During the night, monsoons of warm, liquid air blow steady gusts that seem propelled to shore by giant silk-bladed fans out at sea. Just before dawn, ominous thunderheads coalesce in the sky. Sur-reptitiously they glide into the moist Hanalei Valley, dropping cataracts and splaying open a few landslides. At times like these, lightning illumines the coast like a strobe flash, freeze-framing the frenzied palms flailing against the metal roofs of wooden houses. Climatically, culturally, and emotionally, the place is about turbulence and surrender.

He ignores the weather warnings, and pulls the car over onto a strip of gravel alongside the beach. He watches the sun rise above the rim of the Pacific, lighting up a mushrooming black cumulus cloud with an edge of brilliant cerise—nature's eye candy for this hippie's overactive retina. Grad-ually, the sky pales, and the frosting of night stars melts away.

He makes his way into the Shell Side Restaurant, an establishment that takes its name from the one-pump gas station that shares common walls with a small general store and a post office the size of a closet. This is the westernmost restaurant in the United States. The very last stop. A sign on the wall boasts that the world's best papaya cheesecake is made here, and that the coffee-liqueur drinks are topped with cream as fluffy as surf foam. In the dim light, he spots a local grower from whom he scores an ounce of the world's best pot. The natives call it "Kauaian Electric," and one puff packs enough "voltage" to get him "electrocuted." He knows that, what Kingston is to Blue Mountain coffee, what Lima is to cocaine, what Havana is to the tobacco leaf, Hanalei is to the world pot trade.

He has listened to Peter, Paul, and Mary's song "Puff, the Magic Dragon," whose hero "frolicked in the autumn mist in a land called Hannah Lee"—a song about this very place, where people puff the magic and drag in by the sea of paradisaical surrender. This is why he came here, to the cutting edge of the continent, having traveled three thousand miles from his home in Sacramento to this idyllic volcanic remnant on the trailing edge of America's Manifest Destiny, on the rim of a tectonic plate, on an island where exotic cultures have clashed and then converged. And he's digging it to the max, in the parlance of the moment.

Stifled by the cities and the culture he has inherited from his parents, this man is convinced that on the distant island of Hawaii he will find the perfect wave, the perfect beach, the perfect drug-and-sun-induced "high" that will last an eternity. The days are simple. He writes in his journal, reads Kerouac and Castaneda, smokes marijuana, surfs, swims, makes love, and meditates. His mission is to evolve into a neurosis-free, wild and crazy hipster, adopt a life of simplicity, or turn into a deeply and perpetually tanned, guilt-free polygamist. To the max!

He picks up a surfboard and heads into the waves, paddling with long, confident strokes. Far out, at the point where the big swells break, he turns his board and faces into the sea and waits, patiently, for a wave to summon him. At last, he sees it coming: a rounding of the water, ripening

The monokini and the thong constituted the unisex nude look on the French Riviera of the 1960s and 1970s. (UPI/Bettmann)

into a hump, and then the wall of water rises up, solid and dark at the base, thinning on top, its transparency shot through with gold and green and the palest of pale blues. Gracefully, he rises to his feet, pivots his board so it hovers along the side of the wave, and expertly threads a needle through the roaring, racing tube of water. One wrong move and he will be hurled by that giant force and pulped against the coral bottom before being sucked out to sea in the fierce undertow. But the young man, hair streaming, muscled arms outflung, gives a quick flip of his hips, and soars like an angel.

■■■■■■

The year 1964 was the dividing line between the era of the nuclear-family vacation to Miami Beach, on the one hand, and the commune on the beaches of Hawaii or Mazatlán, on the other—or, on a larger scale, between the epochs of the status quo and the counterculture. The free-speech movement rocked Berkeley, and from this epicenter, rebellion spread like a seismic wave across the land. The civil-rights movement gained momentum in the South. President Johnson launched his domestic "War on Poverty" even as, in Vietnam, the Tonkin Gulf incident embroiled the U.S. in a tragic and divisive war. "Baby boomers" reached adulthood to the driving rhythms of the Beatles and the Rolling Stones, the psychedelic riffs of Jimi Hendrix and the Doors, and the desperately cynical idealism of Bob Dylan. LSD, "flower power," and the first blasts of the Green Movement were in the air, with the modernist gospel of "less is more" applied to everything from money and energy-inefficient technology to clothing and self-restraint. Primitivism was the new good, and they pursued it by not cutting their hair, shaving their beards, or supporting their breasts. "Letting it all hang out" meant discarding etiquette and embracing nudity and free love, especially on the beach.

In fact, the difference between the "before" of the Eisenhower years and what came after, blossomed to a startling head on the beaches of the world—in marijuana-peppered seaside colonies of Mexico, Greece, Jamaica, Costa Rica, Ibiza, and Hawaii. During the years of the Vietnam War and the 1970s, the beach was "primitivized"—returned to an imagined state of nature where mostly single young adults came for spiritual invigoration, and to escape the discordant realities and false needs of a world whose center would no longer hold.

Throughout the 1950s, American beaches had been turned into extensions of the backyard patio. There were young children to think about, and young children meant beaches with small waves, restrooms, food concessions, lifeguards, showers, and plenty of parking. Beachgoers had an unprecedented array of gadgets and toys to pick from. There were light-

weight rubber rafts, foam
sailboats, plastic aquatic
games—everything from volleyball and bounceball to
basketball, horseshoes, and
water polo—waterborne re-
cliners, even shoes for walking on water at a brisk three
miles per hour. The four-
hundred-million-dollar-
per-year plastics industry
churned out an entire bestiary of floating devices: sea
horses, panda bears, alli-
gators, snakes, and seals.
There were dumbbells and
inflatable paddleboats, surfboards and piper-boards—
twenty-eight-inch-wide
wooden disks coated with a
smooth layer of plastic to
make them skim on sand—

During spring break, college students flocked to beaches
from Fort Lauderdale, Florida, to San Pedro Island, Texas.
(UPI/Bettmann)

beach buggies and sand sailboats. Swimwear manufacturers offered beach
hats with built-in wigs and swimsuits with built-in bosoms. And, to record it
all for posterity, Kodak marketed a Brownie eight-millimeter "idiot-proof"
movie camera for less than twenty-seven dollars.

By the mid-1960s, however, the now grown boomer babies wanted nothing to do with the beach as dream backyard—white, predictable, nestlike,
and serene. Even *Life* magazine was telling its readers, in 1961, that "This
summer it isn't enough just to go down to the water, jump in and swim." Instead, on exotic beaches far from home the young set up communities
where they could shed materialism, hypocrisy, and clothing. The same
ethos that had bred their "back-to-nature" movement gradually permeated
mainstream culture. In Florida and especially in southern California during the 1960s and 1970s, the distinction between holiday and everyday became blurred, as did the boundary between aquatic and terrestrial
activities. The beaches of southern California would leave their influence
on everything from concepts of style and modes of behavior to notions of
beauty and health. The sun-streaked hair, tanned glowing skin, tight mus-
culature, and springy step of the vacationer would become the common at-
tribute of the southern Californian and, eventually, disseminated by
Hollywood, set a new standard for American pulchritude. *Life* called the

"undeniably healthy look" of its beachgoers "California's most remarkable natural resource."

UTOPIA ON THE BEACH

If the grand resorts of the nineteenth and early twentieth centuries had been carbon copies of the social life of the cities, these low-tech, low-maintenance settlements of the 1960s and early 1970s were unprecedented improvisations on the theme of Eden. Whether in Bora Bora or the Seychelles, in Tahiti or in Tasmania, the alienated children of affluence learned to create their own primitive gardens of Eden in the primal conditions of the beach.

No place attracted them so much as the beaches of the tropical belt, where they could live on next to nothing, sleep under the stars, wash in the warm sea, and eat off the bounty of the land. "We go to live at the beach," members of a hippie commune announced in a *Life* magazine interview in 1969, "with no need for the previously expensive media of electric technology. The energy we perceive within ourselves is beyond electric; it is atomic, it is cosmic, it is bliss." Like their earlier Romantic counterparts, they gravitated toward beaches that had not yet been spoiled by tourism, where an "authentic, meaningful, traditional way of life" could still be found, and where they would be immune to the harassing of local police protecting the interests of large hotels.

Seeking alternate values and a simple lifestyle, young Americans share the beach with a cow in Goa, India. (Martin Parr, *Tourists on the Beach with a Cow, Goa, India,* 1995, Magnum Photos)

A tight domestic economy discouraged many students from entering the job market, rerouting them in a titanic out-migration to seek adventure and Nirvana abroad on unpopulated beaches. Transcontinental travel was cheap. Airline price wars, prompted by the explosion of empty seats in newly introduced 747 jumbo jets, whacked the price of a flight to Europe to its lowest point in history. For $167.80, one could fly one-way from New York to Luxembourg. Frommer's *Europe on 5 Dollars a Day* steered the young to hostels, tent cities, camps, and cafeterias with soup-kitchen prices. Sooner or later, the ragged Grand Tourists of the Woodstock Generation found themselves on pristine beaches where conditions were right for regressing to their preindustrial ideal of life. On the beaches of places with such musical names as Hvar, Santorini, and Mykonos, living was easy, and no one bothered the international barefoot brigade if they slept all day by the sea and drank cheap wine deep into the night.

In Europe, the narcissists of the "Me Generation" gravitated to spots off the beaten track in the Mediterranean, the Adriatic, the Aegean, and to the shores of the Black Sea. On Ibiza, off the coast of Spain, they congregated on the northern side, packed into modest hotels on a tiny slice of beach caught between rocky promentories; many camped out on the sand. On Hvar and Korčula, islands off the Dalmatian coast, they scouted out flat rocks under the pitch pines along the shore and draped sheets across the lowest branches for shade. They learned to eat the sweet flesh of sea urchins scraped from the shallows and spent their days sunning like lizards on the rocks or floating in the tideless sea. On the island of Crete, they made their way to the tiny coastal village of Màtala, whose caves, famous since Ulysses sheltered in them, offered free accommodation. They cared little that the ancients had buried their dead in these hillside caves, or that lepers had dwelt in them for centuries. For the young Americans, what mattered was that they were on the beach and that America was very far away.

Hippies set up communes on public beaches. (Hiroji Kubota, *Hippie Wedding on Laguna Beach*, 1996, Magnum Photos)

Closer to home, there was Baja California. Every day, psychedelically painted VW vans crossed the border into Mexico, bumping and lurching down the washboard road that ran from San Diego to Cabo San Lucas. Along the coast, stretches of sand alternated with fantastically sculpted outcroppings. The Pacific rolled landward in heaps upon heaps of dark-blue water; to the east, in the Sea of Cortés, lay some of the world's richest fishing waters, teeming with marlin, tuna, dorado, hammerhead shark. College-age gringos wandered from beach to beach, camping out each night at a new cove. The sea was the temperature of their blood, and they dived into it with the abandon of the sea lions who barked at them from the cliffs. At Bahía de Concepción or Bahía de Los Frailes, there were no sounds of outboard motors or plane hums to signal the proximity of civilization. When they got hungry, they dived for abalone or rooster fish or bartered with local fishermen for a piece of marlin.

Meanwhile, on the Yucatán Peninsula, other children of the Age of Aquarius followed faint roads through the jungles to the beaches at Tabasco, Carmen, Campeche, Cancún, Acumal, Tulum, Chetumal, and Belize. Sometimes the road swerved inland and tunneled through thick, claustrophobic jungle. Then, suddenly, through a break in the wall of green, a white beach appeared and, beyond it, the dancing sea. Hammocks were slung between palm trees, and in short order another utopia took shape. Bronzed and naked, festooned with bracelets and earrings of Mexican silver, the young men and women lazed in the shade or splashed in the water. They looked like modern-day versions of Rousseau's noble savages.

CALIFORNIA DREAMIN'

"I'd be safe and warm," the Mamas and the Papas sang in their 1966 hit, "California Dreamin'," "if I was in L.A." The quintessential California-dreamin' beach is found on the seventy miles of almost continuous white sand that runs between Malibu and Balboa. This has been a historically democratic strip, much of it open to public access, with no restrictive covenants limiting usage to everything below the high-tide line, as on the Eastern Seaboard. Only the cheek-by-jowl clustering of houses along some of the sections keep the public from the sand. This strip is embedded in the longer stretch of coastline that runs from Santa Barbara to San Diego. Dedicated to the proposition that only life in the sun and surf is worth living, this stretch of shore is a mosaic of disparate communities, each with its distinctive character and inflection of pleasure.

Santa Barbara, at the northern gateway to the "strip," started out as a mission pueblo and, through time, tenaciously held on to its respectability. From the early 1920s, monied Republicans gathered at the beachside Biltmore, where they weathered the earthquake of 1925, the Great Depression, Prohibition, and World War II, while sipping martinis on the veranda and lounging by the Coral Casino Pool, with its seven lanes and high-diving tower. Tourists of modest means came to Ventura and Oxnard, fishing towns where people worked for a living and holidays were for outsiders. They stayed at Chautauqua Grounds, a city of white tents arranged in tidy rows around a red wooden clubhouse, everything functional but purely utilitarian, in keeping with the work ethos of the beach below. The sand here smelled of fish, sugar beets, and hot tar. In the evenings, mothers sat children down on the beach and scrubbed the tar balls off their feet with huge handfuls of sand. There was oil everywhere, and the spidery tracery of oil wells took the place of lifeguard towers.

A twenty-mile stretch of unspoiled wilderness led to Malibu, the territory of Hollywood stars, a dreamy strip of sand that repelled outsiders, not so much through restrictive legislation as because the houses were built so close to each other as to form a virtually unbroken wall. On the other side of this rampart-of-dreams, the beach was the private preserve of celebrities. From the cantilevered decks of their spacious retreats, stars tanned in the nude, indifferent to paparazzi and fans.

If Malibu was the backlot of Hollywood stars, the mouth of Santa Monica Canyon was the sandbox of Los Angeles. Beginning in the 1870s, families traveled here for weekend picnics, bringing or renting white canvas tents which they pitched all along the base of the canyon, out of reach of high tide and its biting winds. They usually stayed a while to justify the dusty two-day trip from downtown L.A. Once the stagecoach began a regular run, and more and more people congregated on the shore, the beach itself no longer sufficed as entertainment. People wanted to have the best of the beach and the best of the city, all wrapped up in one big package. A local entrepreneur gave it to them in a big semipermanent tent where, in the fantastic light of swaying Chinese lanterns, they could dance to honky-tonk tunes banged out on an upright piano. It was good, clean, cheap fun, even on Saturday nights, when the stevedores, oil drillers, and sailors wandered in from Santa Monica and, once the railway link was made, from Los Angeles.

In the twentieth century, Santa Monica became the Coney Island of the West. Vacationers poured in on the Red Cars of the railway at twenty-minute intervals. They arrived on the crowded beach and headed to the arcades, carousels, and Whirlwind Dipper on the Concrete and Pleasure Piers. They strolled along the paths of Bernheimer's Chinese Gardens and queued up for admission to a concession called the Camera Obscura that showed the world turned upside down. By the end of the day, a massive change of shifts took place on the piers and the beach. One group of sunburned day trippers boarded the Red Car for the ride home, while another, decked out in festive clothes, rushed to replace them at the amusements.

The California beach experience has always been about make-believe. Surfing, weightlifting, Rollerblading, beach volleyball, slalom skateboarding, and bicycling—all these physical diversions were, in one way or another, vehicles for a single vast collective daydream of paradise regained in the form of perfectly tuned bodies, endless leisure, and enduring harmony with nature. The brainchild of Abbot Kinney, a developer obsessed with spot-welding the Pearl of the Adriatic on the shores of the Pacific, Venice Beach

In southern California, youth culture of the 1960s took shape around the
primal celebratory rites of adolescence. (authors' collection)

was the very crystallization of the fantasy. In 1905, he commissioned a maze
of canals to be dug through the quaggy sands and brackish inland marshes of
his site. Ornate Venetian bridges were flung across the canals, and genuine
Venetian gondoliers were imported to pole the gondolas. Windward Avenue
was lined with Corinthian columns and arched loggias that were intended to
suggest Piazza San Marco, and a miniature railway ran along the perimeter.

If Kinney's intent had been to impart the elegance and grandeur of the
original Venice to a déclassé California shore, history had a different
agenda. In 1927, oil was struck, and Kinney's fantasy-by-the-sea had to make
way for reality. Oil drills sprouted on the lawns, residents moved away, and
the stylish city fell into disrepair. By the late 1960s, when architectural historian Reyner Banham first saw it, Venice presented a spectacle of urban
desolation. Bridges wrapped in barbed wire spanned a slimy canal flanked
by rusting oil machinery and nodding pumps. Only a two- or three-block
stretch of the original arcaded shopping street still survived on Windward
Avenue, and a narrow strip of houses ran down to the beach, where muscle
builders flexed biceps, gay couples snuggled, and hippies strummed gui-
tars beneath the ironic gaze of Jewish pensioners.

BEACH-BALL BINGO

Just down the coast lie Playa del Rey, El Segundo, Manhattan Beach, Her-
mosa Beach, Redondo Beach, and Huntington Beach. Between the rusting

railway tracks of the old interurban electric railway and glorious expanses of sand crowd four or five streets of stucco boxes and wood cottages. Concrete "boardwalks," closed to automobiles, rim the residential sections at a slight elevation above the sand. In the 1960s, these were beaches where people in their twenties came to hang out and scowl at the small, rubber-tired trams that ferried the old, the overburdened, and the lazy across short distances. The beach was the center of their lives.

Although some members of a growing beach cult here came to do nothing, most were drawn to two quintessentially Californian sports: beach volleyball and surfing. Half-naked demiurges and nymphs served, spiked, and dunked the ball, pivoting on the sand with the grace of ballet dancers. They were dead serious about their game, in the humorless fashion that marks the southern California attitude toward recreation. Sport is a religion here, and athletes are its high priests.

On Pacific Palisades State Beach, beach volleyball had been played for more than fifty years. Old-timers reminisced about the early, innocent days, when players were unconcerned about winning but reveled in the sheer pleasure of hurling their bodies through space. In the 1960s, a virus of commercialism began to invade the competition. Winning began to mean more than impressing women on the beach. Corporations nosed out the potential profit spike in the sport's irresistible combination of flesh and flash. Backers and sponsors appeared, at first offering humble rewards—a free pair of shorts, a gift certificate, a round of beer—but in the late 1970s, things changed. Marketers for Jose

Elevated above the crowd, 1930s lifeguards survey the beach with Olympian detachment. (Bettmann Archive)

Cuervo tequila and the Miller Brewing Company started giving out ten-thousand-dollar tournament prizes in exchange for conspicuous display of their logos at tournaments. By the 1980s, the sport was professionalized, and teams outfitted in logo-loaded shorts and baseball caps traveled from city to city in flashy semi-trucks. Spreading beyond southern California, the sport appeared in shopping malls thousands of miles from the Pacific. In cities such as Phoenix, Philadelphia, and Atlanta, promoters trucked tons of sand into makeshift arenas to create instant artificial beaches.

HAWAII SURF-O

No one knows exactly when native islanders first began to clutch wooden planks to their bellies and hold them before a breaking wave to hitch a ride to the shore. Surfing historians speculate that the sport goes back three or four thousand years, and trace it to the ancestors of the present South Sea Islanders, who migrated from the shores of South Asia and dispersed among the islands and archipelagos of Oceania. In New Guinea, Melanesia, Micronesia, and the western half of Polynesia, surfing was the province of children and youths, who threw themselves on short boards and paddled out beyond the surf line to catch a curling crest to shore. But among the main islands of East Polynesia—New Zealand, Tahiti, the Marquesas Islands, and Hawaii—longer boards were developed, and the sport became more than a casual pastime for adolescents. Men and women of all ages surfed with passion and impeccable skill in a sport that, in fact, assumed a crucial significance in their culture. When the sea offered a sudden run of good waves, the thatch houses of a whole village stood empty, and the entire community—men, women and children—enjoyed themselves in the rising surf and rushing white water.

Though such early European explorers as Captain James Cook and Captain William Bligh, who first witnessed surfing in Tahiti in 1778 and 1789, respectively, were enthralled by the skill and beauty of the sport, neither they nor later colonizers had much sympathy for the natives' evidently ungovernable passion for the surf. But as California surfers were well aware, surfing had profound religious significance for Hawaiians. The making of surfboards was carefully circumscribed by protocol. Before shaping the boards from the sacred koa or wiliwili trees, the skilled craftsmen offered prayers and sacrifices to the deities of their animist beliefs. It was because surfing was integrally woven into the fabric of Hawaiian culture that the Calvinist missionaries, who began arriving there in 1820, took a dim view of the practice. "The appearance of destitution, degradation, and barbarism, among the chattering, and almost naked savages, whose heads and feet, and much of their sunburnt skins were bare, was appalling," wrote Hiram Bingham, who led the first party of missionaries. "Some of our number, with gushing tears, turned away from the spectacle." On his visit twenty-seven years later, Bingham observed a marked decline in the use of the surfboard.

If religious colonialism had brought surfing to near extinction, economic imperialism brought it back. In 1898, the Republic of Hawaii, then little more than a governorship controlled by the powerful sugarcane planter Sanford Dole, was annexed to the United States as the Territory of Hawaii. The annexation brought political and economic stability, and a new breed of haoles, as the Hawaiians called the occidental settlers. The nineteenth-century Europeans and North Americans had as little use for surfing, which they considered the devil's pastime, as they did for swimming. The intrepid Mark Twain, however, came to Hawaii in 1860 with something more than moralizing in mind. His funny bone always ready for action, he gave surfing a try. "None but natives," he proclaimed after his unceremonious failure, "ever master the art of surf-bathing thoroughly." He, like most visitors, was firmly convinced that the ability to balance on a board was racially determined.

Hawaii's twentieth-century settlers—or, more precisely, their young sons—thought otherwise. Having overcome the fear of the sea, the young haoles knew how to swim practically from the day they could walk. Every afternoon and weekend, sunburned schoolboys came to watch the natives surf on the beach at Waikiki. Watching, however, was not nearly so thrilling as trying out the big boards for themselves, and under the patient tutelage of master surfers, they began to learn. Surfing was being revived, and the master movers in this event were kids from the mainland. In 1908, a group of American businessmen looked at the Waikiki riders and saw dollar signs. Under the leadership of Alexander Ford, and with the publicity generated by

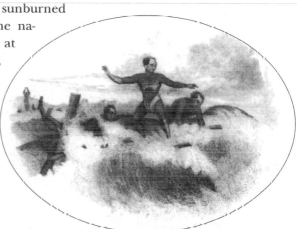

By the end of the nineteenth century, the fabric of the indigenous Hawaiian culture was in tatters, and surfing had all but disappeared. The surfing temples were in ruins, and the great sports festivals and other religious aspects of the sport had been largely forgotten. (Bettmann Archive)

Jack London's story on the "royal sport" of surfing, the group founded the Hawaiian Outrigger Canoe Club for the unique purpose of "preserving surfing on boards and in Hawaiian outrigger canoes." By 1911, a handful of wave riders had grown to hundreds; by 1920, to thousands. Native Hawaiians—swimming champion Duke Kahanamoku and George Freeth—traveled to California as unofficial ambassadors of surfing, gradually gathering converts to their beach sport.

The solid redwood board on which the Irish-Hawaiian George Freeth rode the waves at Redondo Beach in 1907 was eight feet long and weighed two hundred pounds. During the next forty years, some of the bulk was stripped away, but boards were still unwieldy, between ninety and 120 pounds. To steer, the surfer had to drag one foot down the face of a wave while balancing on the other. It was a hard stunt to pull off. Thanks to the military-industrial complex, all that would change. After World War II, fiberglass, originally developed for wartime use in aircraft and ships, was put to work sheathing the new plastic-foam core of the prototypical modern surfboard. Easier to handle, and cheaper because it was mass-produced, the streamlined new board featured a single fin. By the beginning of the 1960s, a portable, maneuverable, and totally "bitchin' " board had evolved. Gracefully tapering and leaning against the boardwalk, the surfboard became a iconographic billboard on the beaches of southern California.

By that time, Californians turned the sport into a self-contained package of mythology, music, and icons. Between 1964 and 1975, surfboarding was primarily the domain of young men on their way to becoming men. Shaking off the constraints of family, trying to find their own way in the world, young surfers formed a testosteronal fraternity, complete with its own dialect. They talked about "loopers" and "loomers," "malihinis" and "Kamaaianas," "elephant guns," "quasimodos," "el spontanios," and "mysteriosos." They "grabbed the rail," "hanged five," and "walked the noose." Surfers

Surfers often opt for areas that include obstacles—such as the pier at Huntington Beach—that test their prowess with often deadly precision. (Hiroji Kubota, *Surfers under the Pier at Huntington Beach, California*, 1971, Magnum Photos)

congregated on the cutting edges of vast continents or islands—if nothing else, to free themselves from that interference, that static of the nonbeach world, that corrupts the harmony of those who do not live entirely in the imagination. As Tom Adler, author of *Surfing from San Onofre to Point Dume*, explains, it was on the surfing beaches of California "where manifest destiny encountered the indomitable sea . . . where the urban power brokers and chosen few came to recreate and carve up the big civic pie from their wooden Adirondack beachside chairs." Surfing, in fact, attracted an eccentric following, including Gary Cooper, movie producer David O. Selznick, and astrophysicist George Ellery Hale, who would spend afternoons at the tony Bel Air Bay Club trying to master the Zen of body surfing.

In an exquisite reconstructed beachside memoir Adler paints an intimate portrait of "penniless surfing 'professionals' who chose to live in the obscurity of lifeguard headquarters" so they could remain close to the sport they so loved. Photographs chronicle the evolution of the world's first municipal lifeguard organization, inaugurated in Santa Monica. Seasonal volunteers with little money, some lifeguard surfers lived in lifeguard stations during the winter, without heat, indoor toilets, and electricity. "Golden boys seldom went hungry in the land of illusion," stressed Adler, "where looking good is a form of currency in itself."

Addicted to the adrenaline gush and endorphin highs produced by the glide of fiberglass across water, these surfers were, in every sense of the word, New Age explorers of the sea, crossing aquatic boundaries and tangling with a tumultuous realm that man had never before dared to enter. Unlike fifteenth- and sixteenth-century explorers, who traveled thousands of miles to uncharted, far-off beaches, modern surfers ventured only a few hundred yards from shore. But in this circumscribed parcel of sea, the technology of modern surfboards made it possible for surf enthusiasts to engage with nature in an entirely new way: to play "chicken" with the power of the seas. They dreamed up death-defying stunts, such as riding the waves between the pilings of the Huntington Beach Pier, or the intricacies of tandem surfing, in which surfer-and-acrobat duos balanced on a single board, performing ballet moves while skimming the waves. At night, they would gather at clubs which specialized in Hawaiian food and music, like the Hula Hut, The Club Zamboanga, Sweeny's Tropicana, and Holo Holo.

Design advances in the ultra-light, ultra-sleek short board made it possible for humans to explore uncharted—indeed, life- and limb-compromising—aquatic territory at the margins between ocean and land. Here, for hours, days, and months at a stretch, over and over each day, exhausted but determined, they surged toward the ocean's wellspring of energy. They flocked to the waves of California, Hawaii, and Australia to harness the power imparted to the breaking surf by wind, sun, planets, and currents for a blistering journey to shore. It was exploration in every sense of the word, creating an intimacy with the sea that would have dazzled the Romantics of the mid-nineteenth century. For the first time in the history of beach athletics, it was possible to blaze through a pipeline of water so dense and powerful that only the most courageous would even contemplate the journey. They navigated treacherous, Brobdingnagian waves with more speed and alacrity than had ever been possible.

An entire genre of music—West Coast surfer rock—mythologized and eulogized the magic of surfing. In no uncertain terms, this was "white boys'" music: nervy, upbeat, and almost seraphic in its note of triumphant rebellion. Jan and Dean swept the charts with "Surf City," "Ride the Wild Surf," "Honolulu Lulu," and "Tell 'Em I'm Surfing," until the Beach Boys eclipsed them with their squeaky-clean ballads. Sun-bleached, healthy-looking boys with irresistible sex appeal, the Beach Boys were surfers raised to iconographic status. The stuff of their songs was typical adolescent-male-rite-of-passage material transposed to the dangerous surf zone.

One sure sign that surfing had entered the mainstream was the commodification of surf wear. Morbidly vain, surfers affected total nonchalance with respect to costume. If, instead of Hawaiian surfer shorts, they opted for cutoffs, their jeans had to be baggy Levi's "ruined to perfection," in the oxymoronic phrase of surfer-author Mark Christensen. Their uniform invariably included, as described by Christensen, an "extra-large short sleeve madras shirt bled blobby, worn over extra-large Penny towncraft 'polo neck' T-shirts, and hair in an over-the-ears winged bouffant favored by the cartoon gremmies in *Surfer* magazine." Soon teenagers in malls three thousand miles inland shuffled around in knee-length baggy Hawaiian prints and combed peroxide through their hair for that fresh-off-the-curl look. By 1997, surfing would be a $1.4-billion industry that produced about 375,000 surfboards and 545,000 wetsuits for sale in more than three thousand specialty stores. And, like swimming in the 1920s, the sport of surfing was being groomed for a slot in the 2000 Olympic Games in Australia.

HOLLYWOOD ON THE BEACH

Between 1917 and 1925, when the movie industry on the East Coast ran into hard times, producers with high hopes came to Los Angeles. They had heard that the mild climate made shooting films out of doors both easier and cheaper. The sun was always shining, so there would be fewer problems lighting the sets. Land, moreover, was to be had for next to nothing, especially in Hollywood, a twenty-minute ride out of town on the Red Car. Mack Sennett launched what would become the cinema's passionate love affair with the beach, by filming his bathing girls cavorting through improbable plots on the seashore. His beach scenes capitalized on the erotic thrills and spills that the waves could provide, and were just a hop, skip, and jump away from the antics that filled the stages of burlesque theaters of the day.

The marriage of beach and celluloid was consummated over the decades in films that depicted the sands as the site of transgressive love, as in *From Here to Eternity*, or as a locus for good clean fun. Throughout the 1940s, the "aquacade," a film genre totally inspired by swimming, became a Hollywood staple. The live water-show had been popularized in the 1930s by such swimmers such as Annette Kellerman, mermaid extraordinaire, who stunned the world with her swimming records and beach exploits. The genre really took off when Billy Rose, an entrepreneur and popular lyricist, installed Eleanor Holm as an aquacade headliner who, in her day, was celebrated as the most beautiful athlete in the world. The spectacle made its debut in landlocked Cleveland, Ohio, and established the formula that would be repeated for the next three years, as the show moved to New York and eventually to San Francisco. Eleanor Holm would strut onto the dramatically illumined stage in silver high heels and cape. While the orchestra played "Blue Danube," she dramatically removed her cape, revealing an impeccable figure sheathed in a silver leotard, and then dived flawlessly into the black water of a giant pool onstage. There, she would be joined by Johnny Weissmuller, Olympic medalist and screen Tarzan, and together they would perform an involved aquatic ballet.

The speed-swimming champion Esther Williams replaced Holm in the San Francisco series and performed it so successfully that she was tapped to star in a series of Hollywood aquacade films, beginning with *Neptune's Daughter*. Her generous curves, which fit perfectly the erotic specifications that appealed to GIs tutored by the pin-up art of the war years, were set off

Hollywood's contribution to the erotic spell of the beach can be seen in *From Here to Eternity* (1953). (authors' collection)

to perfection in a feverish rash of "apple-pie-on-water" escapist films made by MGM. Decked out in gorgeous swimsuits, the statuesque swimmer was at her best in pools decorated in Hollywood baroque, where she performed aquatic ballets to Busby Berkeley routines.

It was, however, with the genre of the "beach movie" of the 1960s that southern California beach culture finally found its perfect medium. Beginning in 1960, when MGM released *Where the Boys Are,* Hollywood introduced a series of innocuous fantasy films about college students on the beaches of California, Florida, and Hawaii. Hardly a critical success, *Where the Boys Are* was a smash hit with the nation's teenagers, and a new subgenre of Hollywood films was born. Described as "sunny, sexy, and totally amusing," the beach-party movie developed around an elementary formula of young love, raucous rock and roll, and squadrons of bikini-clad starlets dancing with wild abandon at the drop of a strap. Released in 1963, *Beach Party* introduced Annette Funicello (Dee-Dee) and Frankie Avalon (Frankie), the Fred Astaire and Ginger Rogers of libidinal youth. Between 1962 and 1966—the golden years of the genre—Annette and Frankie snuggled and volleyballed their way through such mawkish comedies as

The more than one hundred beach movies produced during the 1960s tapped into the cultural myth of the beach as a Garden of Eden. (authors' collection)

Bikini Beach and *How to Stuff a Wild Bikini.* Thronged by dozens of wriggly, top-heavy beach bunnies, Elvis Presley crooned his way from *Blue Hawaii* and *Paradise Hawaiian Style* to *Girl Happy* and *Fun in Acapulco,* which featured the compelling topography of Ursula Andress.

Who could forget Frankie Avalon and Annette Funicello fighting off the likes of Eric Von Zipper, big surf, and bad music? In 1964, Frankie and Annette starred in *Muscle Beach Party,* which also introduced Little Stevie Wonder to the world, and bragged in its advertising posters: "When 10,000 biceps go around 5,000 bikinis you *KNOW* what's gonna happen!" Actually, it was only 4,999 bikinis, because Funicello's contract with Walt Disney Studios would not allow the consummate beach-blanket bunny of the 1960s to bare her belly button. The former Disney Mouseketeer appeared only in one-piece and conservative two-piece suits through all the beach-party movies. The rest of America's nubile population was bound by no such clauses.

With their teen-o-centric thematics and adult-o-phobic polarization of characters, Hollywood's rocking beach reels helped establish the world of youth as a separate culture of innocent hedonism, a paradise of noble savages whose naïveté and ingenuousness were a shield against the cynicism, complacency, and materialism of their elders. With their sanitized romance, mild personal eccentricities, and never-never land of bourgeois youth, these films were precursors to such 1990s TV dramas as *Baywatch,* and tingled the nerves of pubescent viewers who saw the beach as a safe haven where mundane social intercourse was set in comic opposition to muffled erotic impulses. By showcasing the glorious fun provided by being not far from in a state of nature, these films contributed to the "less-is-more" ethos of the 1960s counterculture.

NAKED ON THE BEACH

By the mid-1960s, nudity was no longer the exclusive province of eccentric heliophiles sequestered in private clubs or restricted preserves, where they could indulge in sybaritic extravaganzas unencumbered by clothes. Bare skin had acquired a symbolic cachet for the culture at large, and the beach was one of its principal proving grounds. The political left measured its radicalism by the number of square inches of skin it exposed for public consumption. Thousands of young, college-educated radicals and free spirits flaunted miles of skin as a way of taunting adult authority figures and traditional values. Nude was natural, and natural was good.

The first bracing ripples of what would soon be dubbed the "Nude Wave" crept onto American shores. Over the course of the decade, the bare midriff would emerge from under wraps that retreated lower and lower beneath the navel. The bosom burst out of diminished tops, peeked from plunging décolletages, swelled from the sides of shrunken "bib" tops, and, for one delirious season, would explode in all its unadorned glory for the topless look. Backs came and went, sometimes as far as dorsal cleavage. From Los Angeles to Long Island, women began to peel down in suits whose chief feature was brevity. And, not surprisingly, it was the raging hormonal imperative of the baby-boomer psyche that was considered the perpetrator of this great undress. "American fashion is now dominated by teen-agers," explained one Westhampton, Long Island, matron to a *Time* magazine reporter in 1965. "They have the figures and the courage to wear these suits, and adults—happily or not—are following their lead." But, as *Sports Illustrated* writer Liz Smith noted, "In the beatitudes of bareness there is no substitute for youth." The excess poundage of the ripe sex goddess melted away into the skin-and-bones angularity of such models as Twiggy, Verushka, Peggy Moffitt, and Suzy Parker.

What is fascinating is that, although the bikini was officially launched in 1946, it wasn't until the political and cultural climate in America became sufficiently permissive, in the 1960s, that it entered the mainstream. A creeping relaxation in sexual mores—and a new candor about everything from the dimples and curves of one's anatomy, to snagging the attention of the opposite sex—encouraged the acceptability of the bikini. Asked by an inquisitive photographer for the *New York Post* why she wore a bikini, a bather at New York's Fire Island bluntly replied, "Husbands are scarce. You know any better way for me to beat the competition?" During the early 1960s, a casual stroller along the country's beaches was sure to spot bevies of bikini-clad teenagers trailing swains like seaweed. Pink or blue gingham, slathered with eyelet ruffles, was wildly popular with adolescents. The suit's mounting popularity proved, once and for all, that the art of forecasting styles for the beach was as treacherous as predicting the weather. Between 1960 and 1964, at least one fashion prophet was sure to announce each season, "Bikinis are finally out," only to have the nation's beaches prove the enormity of his mistake. And if important designers perennially decreed the bikini "unimportant fashionwise," the public—and mass manufacturers—thought otherwise.

One fashion expert claimed that only "a man hunter, sun worshiper, or someone very young (at least in heart) will dare to wear a bikini." Sales clerks reported a heavy influx of young married women with good figures who brought their husbands along for approval. An exclusive sportswear shop in Beverly Hills, California, noticed that bikinis were far more acceptable to boyfriends than to husbands, and adopted an ad urging men: "Buy your girl a bikini—it's the least you can do for her." By 1967, 65 percent of women under twenty-five had already switched to the bikini, and mature women were rapidly following suit. It captured the Hollywood imagination in a way that no other item of attire before or since could rival, inspiring Brian Hyland, subsequently immortalized as the troubadour of this mythical garment, to compose his chart buster, "Itsy Bitsy Teenie Weenie Yellow Polkadot Bikini."

The year 1964 marked the transition between the eras of dress and undress on the beach. That year, set against the backdrop of an increasingly polarized society, stripping down at the beach went to unprecedented extremes. To the wildly discordant reviews of fashion critics, statesmen, and church dignitaries, the Viennese-born designer Rudi Gernreich unveiled his "topless" suit for women. The one-piece garment was an austere black knit extending from mid-midriff to the upper thigh, bare above the waist except for a pair of skinny suspenders that met above the navel and climbed up the chest, just grazing the inner curve of the breasts. The provocative garment, however, completely missed the point of what the age

The "Scandal Suit" from Cole of California epitomized the "less-is-more" ethos of the mid 1960s. (Jane MacGowan, *Scandal Suit*, 1964, Cole of California Archive)

considered erotic. Specifically, in a decade when the navel was considered sexy, the "topless" suit tried to capitalize on the breasts. The suit covered up those anatomic regions—the navel, the hips, and the tummy—which the bikini rendered sexy, while it uncovered those areas—the breasts and the upper midriff—whose concealment was essential to the erotic bite of the bikini. Paradoxically, unlike the miniskirts and see-through blouses of the 1960s, it exposed too much, too suddenly.

Sparking endless gag lines, Bob Hope predicted, "Instead of *Playboy*, the guys will be buying *Ladies' Home Journal*." Art Buchwald spoke of 1964 as "the year the bottom fell out of the top," and the *New York Daily News* reported the arrest of a California barmaid serving drinks in a topless suit under the headline "Martini with a Peel."

Some of the harshest criticism came from the world of fashion itself. Norman Norell, the high priest of American couture, had nothing kind to say of the experiment. "There is no news in the no-top bathing suit," he remarked astringently to *Women's Wear Daily*. The French were deeply affronted by the implication that they had been superseded at their own game and protested with banner headlines asserting, "The Americans Have Invented Nothing. . . . The bare-breasted look already here 32 years ago." The Kremlin blasted the suit as an emblem of "capitalist decay," and the Vatican fulminated and anathematized the garment for "negating moral sense." In an editorial in *L'Osservatore Romano*, Raimondo Manzini gave the official position of Roman Catholicism: "One ought to be ashamed of giving space and attention to degrading chronicles of the industrial-erotic adventure of the 'monopiece' that, adding an unsated avidity for money to subfeminine shamelessness, has given rise to so much clamor." And Gina Lollobrigida, the very incarnation of mammarian amplitude, reviled the topless suit as an attack on femininity. One Los Angeles department store staged a humorous display inspired by the topless suit. In the shopwindow one hanger, labeled "Yesterday," held an old-fashioned Annette Kellerman suit; another hanger, labeled "Today," supported the Gernreich topless; and a third, captioned "Tomorrow," supported nothing at all.

12

PARADISE FOUND (AND LOST)

Aitutaki Atoll, Cook Islands, 1997. He does not think that there is anywhere, in any language, a word billowing enough for the pleasure he feels as the South Pacific reaches out to warm him. Stroke by stroke, his body remembers an ancient self with fins and gills that opened like flowers, feeling with every snapping frog-kick of the breaststroke that his legs will lock and become one so that he might shimmy like a dolphin and swim all day and far into the night.

During years in sodden, chill Seattle, hunched over a keyboard and diode screen, he had dreamed of becoming again a body of blind feeling sprawled in the maternal lap of aquamarine. Retired, at the age of thirty-four, the silicon tycoon searched long and hard for this perfect getaway.

After surfing the Net, interviewing friends, and reading travel magazines, he came to realize how hard it was to find—and how expensive to rent—a remote, unspoiled corner of paradise.

At last, far from the cacophony of telephones, fax lines, and e-mail, with only a sliver of plastic umbilicating him to his millions, he is here. He feels ambition draining from every pore as he dives, again and again, into the luminosity of the sea, into the glittering pandemo-

With the availability of the perfected Aqua-Lung and efficient snorkling gear, visitors to tropical beaches gained access to one of the last frontiers: the world beneath the sea. (Paul Fusco, *Snorkeler on the Beach*, 1984, Magnum Photos)

nium of pink and lavender and blood-red sea grasses, undulating fans, yellow damselfish, and crimson clownfish.

Later, in the morning sun. The "Chippy" millionaire stretches out in a hammock in the shrinking shadow of a palm tree. He swings gently, back and forth, rocked by the faint breeze, his mind blank, inhaling, exhaling the sweet air. A striking brunette in a monokini runs into the waves. Three young natives paddle past, peering curiously at him and at the scattering of huts set into the manicured jungle of coconut palm, banana, breadfruit, bougainvillea, hibiscus, and fragrant white *tiarea*. The smell of fish barbecuing and baguettes baking perfumes the air. The sun climbs higher, and his skin begins to tighten under the onslaught of tropical rays. He smears

The new fad for eco-tourism takes visitors to remote beach outposts equipped with traditional, environmentally sensitive accommodations. (authors' collection)

more sunblock on his shoulders. The waiter comes to summon him to lunch. The paper millionaire follows the winding path past the *fare*—the traditional thatched-roof hut for which he is paying seven hundred dollars a night, without meals or electricity—to the open-air bungalow where the three other hotel guests are already digging into their meal. The couple at the far end has the abstracted look of honeymooners. The brunette is sitting alone. Tonight he will invite her for a drink.

After a fine meal of Polynesian delicacies, he meets his native guide for a tour of the reef at the far end of the lagoon. This is the first of his scheduled excursions. Later in the week, he will go bird-watching in the rain forest with an ornithologist, fish for bonefish with an aborigine, and join a marine biologist for a shark-watching expedition. The light canoe glides silently across the turquoise waters, then cuts across the choppy stretch to the outer reef. When they reach it, the native secures the boat, and then the tourist slips into scuba gear and drops deep into the gentle current.

Scattered across the sea floor are clusters of pinnacles thirty to forty feet high. Their crests reach nearly to the surface of the water and seem oddly barren. Despite himself, the diver feels a shiver of terror and awe run up his spine. He wonders whether there really is no danger of sharks. But then the tide turns and begins to flow, and suddenly the pinnacles explode into a spectacular tapestry of plumed, soft coral as they inflate their delicate branched bodies with water and spread their arms across the flow. Multitudes of small fish feed on the plankton. There are lionfish and Moorish idols, angelfish and nudibranchs, and a strange transparent formation—not quite jellyfish—that ripples and swells a dozen feet above him. Intrigued, he swims for a closer look. It is a large plastic bag, snagged in the crotch of a coral formation.

Disgusted, he surfaces and hauls himself on board the canoe. The guide begins to paddle back to shore. As they round the spit into the lagoon, they see the pristine stretch of sand, the thicket of jungle with its chaste sprinking of thatched roofs, and, beyond them, boldly silhouetted against the golden sunset, the black tracery of a giant crane. He feels cheated. He had come a long way to get here, and he would have to go even farther to get nowhere.

∎∎∎∎∎∎

Like the melancholic of the eighteenth century, we are lured by the hydrotherapeutic promise of the sea. We come for the air, as did the urban bourgeoisie and consumptives of the nineteenth century; for the athletic prowess of the 1910s, and the sun of the 1920s. We come to congregate and to be alone, to submit our dulled senses to the therapeutic sublime, and to restoke the libido. Like the Romantics, we come to be spiritualized, to recover from broken hearts and broken lives, and to decipher the tangled ways of our souls in the chaos

On the beaches of the Black Sea, Romanian bathers improvise mud baths. (Abbas/Magnum)

of the turbulent sea. We come, as in the 1950s, to reaffirm our domesticity, and, like the hippies of the 1960s, to discover our ideal selves. We experience the beach as a place of bourgeois delights and comforts; as an escape from the edginess of urban areas, as did the English of the Industrial Age.

Sunbathers in St.-Tropez monopolize the beach. (Elliott Erwitt, *Sunbathing, St.-Tropez, France,* Magnum Photos)

In short, the same laws of diversification rule the social, therapeutic, and hedonistic practices at the beach that operate in the culture at large. Now, when we go to the beach, we deconstruct our experience of it according to precisely those milestone events that civilization claimed were important reasons to experience the beach.

During the last twenty years, the beach has given exhibitionism a new inflection. The desire to see and be seen has always brought people to the beach, but never before have bathers so systematically and deliberately sculpted their bodies for public scrutiny. If, in the past two hundred years, fabric did the work of providing form, now skin and muscle must provide the perfect scaffold to the swimsuit, despite phenomenal advances in elastic textiles. Witness the fact that the bathing garment is now styled to showcase buttocks, upper thigh, and hip, parts of the body most susceptible to sag, flab, and cellulite. The ideal body now boasts bulges and declivities in places and shapes rarely given by nature. Only the machine, in conjunction with rigorous training regimens and near-starvation diets, can produce the lean slabs of muscle that have come to constitute beauty.

The beach is no longer the site of the natural, but of the artificially shaped and surgically carved body. The back-to-nature movement of the 1960s led squarely into the self-indulgence of the "Me" decade with its designer jeans, status labels, and trendy quests for the right image to go along with a meticulously groomed "lifestyle." A new physical ideal began to emerge from exercise studios, aerobic classes, bodybuilding salons, and surgical clinics. The new anatomic archetype was the machine-tuned superbody, one that was architectonically shaped—muscle group by muscle group—to conform to a Platonic vision of beauty.

The sixties catechism that had preached the equality of natural forms grew less convincing as time weighed heavily on once firm bosoms and thighs. "Discipline" and "artistry" were suddenly no longer bad words when it came to putting the body on show. What nature could not deliver, the high-tech culture of Universal exercise machines could. Bolstered by the new feminism, unprecedented professional opportunities, and a fresh generation of positive-thinking magazines, American women ran to gyms and health clubs, striving to seize control of their bodies, convinced that by doing so they would in some way be seizing control of destiny, grunting and groaning their way into muscle definition, transforming their bodies into manifestos of self-determination and self-reliance. People now come to the beach to show off how well they have aged, how beautifully they have maintained their bodies. On a very basic level, working out became the political gesture of the times, just as going bare had been during the earlier decade. Self-affirmation by self-exposure became the newest motive for coming to the beach. Millions of beachgoers added conspicuous posing, running, and stretching to the repertoire of motives drawing them to the beach.

PARADISE IN DECLINE

For over two hundred years, the forces of urbanization and industrialization had been chauffeuring people to the seashore. When the British first transported their health spas from inland sites to the margin of the sea, they domesticated an alien environment to make it hospitable to human practices and the frail human constitution. Spot-welding their protocols for civilized behavior to these remote outposts, they began exerting some mea-

Clad in monumental concrete, the beach at Blackpool, England, bears witness to the triumph of civilization over nature. (Ian Berry, *Blackpool, England*, Magnum Photos)

Monte Carlo compensates for its meager shore-front by constructing a brutalist, artificial beach. (Leonard Freed, *Monte Carlo, Monaco,* Magnum Photos)

sure of control over the hostile forces of the beach. With breakwaters, groins, and moles they altered the lay of the land and arrested the seasonal waxing and waning of the strand. Through architectural forms and urbanistic templates, they constructed beach communities, provided beach services, and improvised facilities for recreation.

In the nineteenth century, the Riviera was a winter haven for consumptives, misanthropes, and sinners. By the end of this century, the Côte d'Azur had become a holding pen, where—in the month of August—the great cities of the north dumped their populations. The same can be said of the beaches along the Adriatic, the Aegean, and the southern Mediterranean. Summer on the beaches of these seashores is the season of crowds, congestion, and pollution. Along much of the coast, the terrain is either too steep to offer new building sites or already filled to capacity with high-rise hotels, exclusive resorts, and luxurious villas. Existing sewage systems are overtaxed, so that untreated effluent washes up on the beaches and clouds the ordinarily limpid waters.

Automobiles choke the narrow roads, filling the air with exhaust and noise. There is nowhere to park. In 1975, the British writer Alec Waugh described his trip from Nice to Antibes as a "trip through the wilderness of cranes, bulldozers, excavations and churned up soil that separated the airport, the race course, a vast new supermarket and an immense two-flanked block of flats." He laments, "In the old days your eyes were constantly delighted. Now they are very often not. Beauty is not spread prodigally at your feet. You have to search it out. Charming places are not obvious."

All along seashores in the Northern Hemisphere—in the British Isles, the Atlantic beaches of Europe and the United States, the American West Coast—as well as "Down Under," in Australia, the desire to escape crowded urban areas for seashore vacations has resulted in sprawling colonization. As long as tourists traveled by rail or boat, and then dispersed by foot or carriage to centrally located hotels, they had little impact on the countryside. Resort communities tended to develop in a rough T-shape, with a railway station located at the intersection of the T; a pier, pavilion, hotels, restaurants, and shops thrusting in the direction of the sea; resorts and housing radiating along the beach on either side. But once automobiles and private ownership of second homes entered the equation, the liberating, solitary, spiritually uplifting beaches of the nineteenth century became a thing of the past, and seashore development took on a new shape. With the growing suburbanization of the seashore, the beach has lost its character as a pristine natural environment.

Instead, vast stretches of coastline are parceled out into tiny plots colonized by second homes of dubious architectural distinction, and shabby trailer parks, alternating with strips of shopping malls, and recreational facilities, here and there punctuated by the odd wildlife refuge or state park. These are glutted on hot summer weekends with visitors who depart on Sunday afternoon, leaving behind cigarette butts, plastic containers, and the charred remains of bonfires. Summer visitors and owners of weekend homes often end up retiring by the seashore. Local and national planning commissions are hard put to mediate between the needs of tourists, second-homers, and local residents, all of whom want a piece of the beach pie.

After the late 1960s, new high-rise condominiums and apartments began to take the place of small hotels and rooming houses. Year round residents chafed under high tax burdens to finance public facilities—sewage treatment, water supply, solid-waste disposal—needed to accommodate the in flux of visitors. At first, it appeared as if the new constructions might contribute to the local economy. Soon, however, it became evident that the opposite was the case. In resort after resort—from Westerland, on Germany's North Sea, to Atami, Japan—the high-rise condominiums and apartments slowly drained the life out of the communities. By replacing many old hotels, these new housing developments also displaced the large staffs that had been employed in them. Instead of eating in local restaurants, tourists brought their food with them or cooked in their own kitchens. Many of the condominiums remained vacant during the week, and even

Dune buggies tear up the natural sand formations of the seashore. (Dennis Stock, *Dune Buggy on Beach, California,* Magnum Photos)

then were used only seasonally, so that patronage of the local shops declined.

Even as the central core of the old resort communities withered, the beaches swarmed with unprecedented numbers of tourists. Wishing to avoid the congestion, visitors rented automobiles and went in search of more distant, less crowded beaches. In the process, they faced long commutes on roads not equipped to handle the peak loads. The quality of air, water, and sand suffered under the onslaught. Vacated at day's end, a popular beach had the look of a gargantuan trash bin, covered with cigarette butts, swizzle sticks, bottles, cans, plastic containers, newspapers, and every imaginable kind of refuse.

The resort beaches of the Caribbean are testimonials to the dynamic whereby development ends by replicating the pathology of the very places people try to escape. Once it became possible, with the flick of a computer screen and a telephone call to a travel agent, to transplant oneself to an exotic paradise, and once it became possible to supply these outposts with the absolutely uniform comforts, services, and architecture of the urban center, the beach lost its allure as a place where the natural and the civilized were faced off in a productive tension that made man alternate between the primitive and modern. Entirely divorced from nature, packed into cubicles ten feet square, shepherded through long corridors of high-rise hotels, ferried beachside in bone-chilling elevators, the holidaymakers of numerical tours experience only the discrepancy between cultures: the indigenous and the tourist.

PRIMITIVE BEACH

Once beaches as destination points were absorbed into urban culture, select hotels and travel agencies began to offer beach experiences that afforded the opportunity to return to the wilderness. Owners of exclusive, expensive resorts in Ibiza, Mallorca, or Portofino, on handkerchief-size islands in the South Pacific, the Sea of Cortés, and the Caribbean realized that their guests pined for more than a perfectly controlled, civilized environment. As an increasingly important amenity, they began to show guests how to go back to discovering their beaches the way the original explorers, or Indians, or fishermen did 150 years ago. Organized eco-tours into national preserves were journeys back in time. In this way, the experience of untouched nature could only happen through a laborious and highly contrived ritual.

Small, ecologically "correct" boutique resorts were developed on sands impeccably groomed, on grounds planted with an ecologically correct mix of flora, and in bungalows painstakingly "contextualized" to the indige-

To safeguard bathers from the perennial threat of shark attacks, developers at Bondi Beach, Australia, constructed swimming pools at the ocean's edge. (David Hurn, *Bondi Beach, Sydney*, Magnum Photos)

nous—and mostly erased—culture. Exotic, indigenous beaches were painstakingly and self-consciously redecorated to appear "authentic," as though they had not in fact been expressly constructed, in the manner of stage props, for an ethnographically accurate experience of the beach.

In Bahía de Los Frailes, on the Sea of Cortés, a retired investment banker from San Francisco sets up an exquisite string of hand-crafted cabañas, furnished with a well-chosen collection of antiques and crafts. Expensive, and in the best of taste, the small hotel caters to tourists from Italy, France, and the West Coast of the United States. It offers eco-tourists everything they crave: unspoiled nature, gourmet meals, running water, and privacy. There are no telephones, no fax machines, no television sets to intrude into the restorative retreat. The terraces look out over one of the most fertile bays in the world. Each night, the chef grills the fish the tourists caught, and if they had no luck, a native fisherman is quickly dispatched. The visible hired help are local; those in "administration" are invisible and foreign. Ironically, to obtain the simulacrum of the primitive, unspoiled beach experience, the traveler has to pay astronomical sums of money to be deprived of service and comfort.

THE VANISHING BEACH

The beach itself has eroded over time, literally washing away. Here as well, too much of the civilizing and domesticating impulse eventually turned against us. Once the beach became the infrastructure, it was subject to the same erosive forces as everything else.

The Ritz Carlton Hotel in Naples, Florida, sits on a picture-perfect stretch of beach fringed with palmetto, mangrove, cabbage palm, and seagrape. It seemed odd, for this reason, that in January 1996, at the height of the tourist season, the beach was empty and that the neat blue cabañas laid out with mathematical precision were uninhabited. On either side of Ritz Carlton's beach, vacationers were lounging on blankets, playing bad-minton, promenading. Only here there was no one. One step onto the sand, and the reason was clear. Instead of sinking into soft powder, the foot scraped against a rough conglomerate of gravel, shell, and coral. What had at a distance appeared to be calcareous sand turned out, on closer inspec-tion, to be a dusty, unyielding layer of construction-grade cement-in-the-making. Large chunks of rock poked out here and there. If ever a beach looked dead, this one was clearly suffering from rigor mortis.

Why this particular segment of beach? After all, the sand to the left and right was the typical mix of ground-up seashells, coral, and quartz that one finds along the gulf-side Florida beaches. What had happened to the beach here? As it turned out, just two months earlier, the Ritz Carlton—along with other luxury hotels, condominiums, and time-shares along a two-mile stretch—had had no beach to speak of. At high tide, during storms, or dur-ing "syzygy"—the infrequent alignment of earth, moon, and sun that boosts tides by as much as three feet or so—the waves of the gulf were breaking at the very roots of the mangroves that now stood seventy-five feet from the low tide. Through a combination of natural transport by currents and storms, and erosion triggered by the erection of inflexible structures such as seawalls, jetties, and groins, the generous beachfront of Naples, Florida, had shrunk over the years until there was literally nowhere to set down a chaise longue. Developers who had invested millions on the false premise that the shoreline was as stable as dry land were in a panic. The very economy of Naples, built on the formula of winter sun, sand, and sea, hung in the balance. With the beach gone, the tourist-and-retirement trade would soon be a thing of the past.

What Naples was experiencing in 1995 was old hat to resort communities up and down the Atlantic Seaboard, along the Gulf Coast, on the Pacific, as well as in such countries as Britain, Germany, and the Netherlands, where oceanfront property has been heavily developed. Sea level has been rising. In New Jersey, for example, it is seventeen inches higher today than it was in 1900, and the pace is accelerating. Meanwhile, no new sand is being added to the beaches naturally. Elsewhere in the United States, entire coastal areas are disappearing into the sea. Coastal engineers and geolo-gists estimate that about 86 percent of California's eleven hundred miles of exposed Pacific shoreline is receding at the average rate of six inches to two feet a year. South of San Francisco, Monterey Bay is losing five to fifteen feet annually. Cape Shoalwater, in Washington, has been shrinking at the rate of one hundred feet a year since the turn of the century, which amounts to more than two miles since 1910. In 1987, parts of Chambers County, Texas, lost nine feet of the coast to Galveston Bay. Since 1970, Louisiana has shrunk by three hundred square miles. At Boca Grande Pass, an inlet on the Gulf Coast of Florida, the sea carried away some two hundred million cubic yards of sand.

The evidence has been steadily mounting that the sea is staging a new offensive against the land. Around the world, more shores are retreating than advancing. Though fluctuating sea levels are part of a natural cycle, scientists suspect that the current increase is different, augmented by what they believe to be fundamental changes in the climate due to the "green-

Hurricanes such as this one in 1991 wipe out beach communities on Fire Island, New York. (UPI/Corbis-Bettmann)

house effect." Since the Industrial Revolution, we have been burning vast quantities of fossil fuels, such as coal, oil, and gas, whose by-product—carbon dioxide—has been increasingly blocking the escape of excess heat into space. In the gradually warming atmosphere—one-half degree Celsius to date, with an anticipated increase of one and a half to four and a half degrees Celsius in the next century—the polar ice caps have been melting, so that sea levels are now expected to rise at least a foot in just another half-century.

Industrial development and demographic pressures have also had a hand in the inverse process of subsidence, particularly along the Gulf Coast. Extraction of groundwater and petroleum from subterranean layers of sand and clay has forced the land, already virtually at sea level, to drop another three feet a century. Scientists predict that in some parts of coastal Florida, where the land is flat to begin with, the sea may advance by as much as five hundred feet in the next fifty years. On the West Coast, beach-front developers have to worry about an additional complication. At irregular intervals that range from two to seven years, a warm-water current in the Pacific shifts eastward in a pattern called El Niño, or the "Christ Child"—named thus because it appears off South America around Christ-

mastime. El Niños swell sea levels, producing unusually high tides and severe winter storms. The great one of 1982–83 elevated the sea ten to fourteen inches, with catastrophic results which can only increase in severity
with progressive global warming.

Official watchdogs such as the Environmental Protection Agency take a
dim view of our ability to hold back the rising waters. Its wholesale advice to
homeowners and beachfront developers is the disquieting "abandonment
of low-lying areas in an orderly fashion." But for two hundred years, resort
municipalities, hoteliers, and private developers have been imposing patterns of control on nature's inexorable patterns of change, redecorating
the shoreline according to their own notions of comfort, beauty, convenience, and safety. When people who build along the shore notice the sea
coming closer to their front doors, they work hard to hold it back.

Historically, the Dutch have been leaders in engineering high-tech solutions, building involved defensive structures. Their most recent project,
completed in 1986, was a $2.4-billion concrete-and-steel "mega-dike" one
and a half miles long across the eastern Scheldt River estuary, consisting of
sixty-two five-hundred-ton gates that are left open to the tides but can be
shut when a storm threatens. Across the English Channel, the British installed an equally expensive series of superdikes, the Thames Barrier, to
protect Londoners against inundation from waters that have swelled some
twenty-three inches over the last century. In the Adriatic, Italians will have
spent over two billion dollars on rescuing Venice and the Lido through a
combination of dikes, floodgates, and "mud jacking," or injecting material
to raise the surface of the islands.

Beaches, dunes, and barrier islands must move or they die. We humans
think we must stop beaches from moving or we will die. Or, at the very least,
lose our possessions and imperil our fortunes. And so we have been erect-
ing breakwaters to create safe harbors. We have been removing sand from
harbors, bays, and estuaries with dredges and jetties, and moving it to
beaches, where it "belongs" and where we "secure" it by groins. We hold
back migratory barrier islands by channelizing and dredging their inlets
and flattening their dunes. We secure crumbling cliffs by spraying them
with cement. We pile up junked cars on the shore—as desperate ranchers
did on Galveston Bay—in the hope that they will keep the waters from
washing out roads and pastures. On clay banks we plant dense patches of
cord grass, and we jury-rig protective barriers of old air-force parachutes in
the water to absorb the force of waves. From Texas to Long Island, we improvise barricades of wire mesh, old tires, and driftwood; in California, we
plant plastic kelp and lay sausagelike tubing along the beach to trap sand
normally washed away at high tide. But, as beach conservationists Wallace
Kaufman and Orrin Pilkey tell us, by immobilizing our beaches, we only

hasten and, in many cases, even cause their destruction. Beaches must move—or die.

Since the mid-nineteenth century, the New Jersey shore has had the dubious distinction of leading the field in beach erosion. In fact, Kaufman and Pilkey call the phenomenon of beach destruction through immobilization the "New Jersey–fication" of the shore. First wooden breakwaters were installed, followed up with stone groins to control, direct, and modify the force of waves and currents. More development engendered more coastal engineering, which in turn made the shore more vulnerable to ravaging storms. The beaches hemorrhaged sand out to sea, and coastal engineers applied themselves to creating more and more ambitious cement, stone, and rebar tourniquets. The results are disappointing, if not alarming: a saw-toothed shorefront with steep, narrow beaches, token slivers of sand piled high with rocks. When hurricanes and winter storms assault the coast, the protective barrier of sand that mitigated their force is not there. The violent forces of wind and sea gnaw away with unmitigated fury at the weekend cottages, expensive year-round homes, and vacation resorts.

The very beach homes in which we seek isolated retreats from the havoc of modern life in turn wreak havoc on the beach. All along the West Coast, houses perched atop cliffs overlooking the ocean create new runoff patterns for rainfall and irrigation that weaken the land, and contribute to its erosion. On the East and Gulf coasts, resort development on many of the 295 barrier islands has dramatically contributed to beach erosion. The dunes, the beach's most important line of defense, are usually the first target of the developer's bulldozer. Atlantic City in New Jersey, Virginia Beach in Virginia, and Hilton Head in South Carolina were all built on leveled dunes. In the 1970s, aspiring to re-create Miami Beach's phenomenal oceanfront values, developers in Ocean City, Maryland, began building high-rises on the dune line and bulldozed away the dunes so that hotel guests on the lower floors would have an open view of the ocean. Within ten years, the ocean was lapping at the foundation pilings. Just south of Myrtle Beach, at Garden City, South Carolina, the dunes were cleared to accommodate large-scale condominium developments. Now storm waves grind away at the protective seawalls and carry off chunks of swimming pools.

As they face sea-level rise and the inevitable erosion of the beaches, coastal communities have few options. The lure of building on the rapidly disappearing flat sandy beaches continues unabated. But as it becomes increasingly clear that attempts to stabilize the shoreline are futile, coastal communities have begun to look at other strategies. One possibility was explored in 1985 by a group of geologists meeting at the Skidaway Institute of Oceanography in Savannah, Georgia, to chart a new national strategy for beach preservations that called for a retreat from the coastline. States soon began to pass regulations to achieve that goal. North Carolina required all new construction to be situated behind the thirty-year flood line. New York State considered limiting beachfront construction to movable buildings, and set about implementing its 1981 Coastal Erosion Management Act to ban rebuilding of storm-damaged buildings within a specified distance from the shore. Florida prohibited new construction on land that is likely to erode within thirty years under "natural conditions" or that cannot withstand hurricane winds up to 140 miles an hour. California and Maine have also placed limits on new and rebuilt coastal construction. Another possibility involved implementing fiscal disincentives by rethinking federal flood insurance. Traditionally, federal flood insurance reimbursed owners for rebuilding, rather than for relocating houses to safer ground. Environmentalists, such as Pilkey, believe that such insurance programs actually encourage building in dangerous places, and penalize owners who might wish to move their homes. Such a fiscal solution would involve elaborating formulas that insure homes without guaranteeing a post-storm location for them.

So far, the most promising solution for preserving the imperiled beaches does not involve fortifying the coastline with seawalls costing from fifteen hundred to five thousand dollars per foot, or retreating from the water's edge, but, rather, rebuilding the beaches. Known as "beach renourishment," this relatively low-tech antierosion scheme involves replacing sand that has been washed away with sand mined in another location. Think of it as the sand equivalent of hair transplants. At a cost of twelve hundred dollars per foot, renourishment has turned out to be competitive with seawalls, and, at least according to environmentalists, far less disruptive of the natural ecology.

Renourishing has the advantage of restoring the beach to its original appearance, and, it is argued, its original function of deflecting the force of the waves. Since 1971, the United States Army Corps of Engineers has embraced "non-structural" solutions—renourishment foremost among them—to beach erosion. The agency's Shore Protection Manual, a guide to coastal works in the world, recommended "artificial fill with periodic nourishment to restore and preserve a beach is the preferred method [to handle erosion]. It is the natural method, is aesthetically pleasing, and permits a variety of recreational uses." Many beaches in South Carolina, New Jersey, Florida, and California have been renourished over the past two decades. Los Angelenos have renourishment to thank for their entire twenty-five-mile crescent of Santa Monica Bay.

Feeding a beach, however, is neither a cheap nor a permanent solution. From 1950 through 1993, the Corps of Engineers, which oversees renourishment financed by the federal government, participated in fifty-six major projects at a total cost of almost nine hundred million dollars. Critics—and there are many of them—complain that these projects are, at best, a subsidy for coastal property owners and, at worst, a complete waste of money, the equivalent of using taxpayers' funds to build sand castles that wash away in the first big storm. There is also some concern that the added sand might have adverse effects on reefs and other offshore ecosystems. But the most powerful argument is that renourishment is temporary. Residents of Monmouth Beach, New Jersey, were dismayed when much of the sand that had been pumped at great expense quickly disappeared. Coastal engineers point out that, unless the erosive forces that destroyed the beach in the first place have been diagnosed and addressed, erosion will continue, and the new sand will go the way of the old. As a rule, engineers expect a large amount of new sand to disappear from artificial beaches in the initial stages of the reconstruction, as waves, currents, and storms reshape the new beach and give it a natural profile.

The Naples Beach renourishment project was an entire decade in the planning before it moved to implementation in the fall and winter of 1995–96. Complicated financing had to be arranged, with the federal government, the county, and the municipal tourist department sharing in the cost. A coastal-engineering firm undertook a comprehensive longitudinal study of the target area going back to the 1890s to determine a hypothetically "original" profile of the beach. Next, a "borrow" area that closely matched the original sand of the beach was located about a mile offshore, under twenty-five feet of water. For thirty-six days, a hydraulic pump anchored offshore dredged sand from a hole that eventually became one thousand feet long, one thousand feet wide, and ten feet deep, and pumped it to a barge moored close to shore. There the material was mixed with water and, before being pumped to the beach in the form of "slurry," redistributed so that the hard surface matter, which was last, would be deposited first in the new site. This "dual layering approach" would place the finest sand at the top of the renourished beach.

Day by day, the new beach grew in one-thousand-foot increments, with 80 percent of the "fill" ending up underwater, and another 5 percent expected to erode within a year. Like a skin graft, the new sand had to "grow" into its new environment. Initially, it was a sticky, sodden, lumpy mass that needed to be raked and tilled repeatedly until it reached its natural weight and consistency. This it did—everywhere but in front of the Ritz Carlton Hotel, where the sand had been deposited directly as it had come from the borrow site: the fine material first, and the hard, grainy matter last. Fortunately, the mistake was easily remedied. Within a few weeks, the Ritz Carlton Hotel could once again boast of a picture-perfect beach, at least for another ten years, after which it would need another "treatment."

THE BEACH IN A MUSEUM

If there is one thing bioengineering has proved, it is that the natural can be perfected and refined. The ultimate step in the domestication of the beach is to "breed" the perfect seaside environment, and then to put it into a museum. During the last three centuries, we have applied all the resources of civilization to adapt the body, customs, and technology to the untenable strip of land washed by the sea. But always, as savage storms erased our beachfront communities and resorts, as the sun's rays disrupted the functioning of our bodies' cells, and as the ocean's currents thwarted our strength, we have had to admit defeat. Recently, however, the tide has turned in our favor: the natural beach has been cloned in a perfect artificial version. It is called, in honor of the mythical bird that, though consumed by fire, eternally rises up out of its own ashes, the Phoenix Resort.

Located in Japan, the artificial beach has finally been re-created as a sterilized, safe, enclosed environment, a distillate of all the elements we find at the seashore, with the danger, the discomfort, and the dread taken out. "Welcome to the great indoors," writes Howard G. Chua-Eoan, correspondent of *Time* magazine, reporting on the newest resort concept: the perfect outdoor vacation packaged in the vast sanitized pleasure dome of the Phoenix Resort Seagaia.

In 1988, Japan passed a Resort Promotion Act in an attempt to alleviate the frightful stress levels of its workers and to introduce them to the novel Western notion of leisure. That year, a consortium of local governmental bodies and eleven private firms created the concept for a state-of-the-art, technological paradise to be located in Miyazaki, on the Japanese island of Kyushu, once the nation's honeymoon capital. Completed in 1993, the Phoenix Resort Seagaia contained a 462-foot-wide ocean with a 280-foot shoreline under a 660-foot retractable roof. Complete with crushed-marble "sand" beaches and waves big enough for surfing, the indoor water theme park has accommodated ten thousand visitors a day since it opened. Artificial breezes play on artificial rocks and palm trees. A concealed sound system carries a mellifluous cocktail of water and bird sounds. In the Bali Hai zone, an artificial volcano erupts every fifteen minutes. A virtual-reality theater offers alternative sensory experiences. Caribbean dancers perform at regular intervals, and each night, when the "stars" begin to glimmer as a thousand points of artificial light in the dome, a laser light show plays on a water-spray screen. Golfers tee off on perfectly groomed Astroturf. Water rides, slides, tanning beds, restaurants, and boutiques serve up a predictable, orderly, controllable version of nature, where the sun is guaranteed to shine 365 days a year. Over 120 temperature and humidity sensors are programmed to take periodic readings, feed them back to a central computer, and make adjustments to provide a perfectly calibrated environment for leisure.

The Phoenix Resort, true to its mythological moniker, proved its indestructibility and indeed superiority to its natural prototype almost immediately. Within weeks of the opening, a savage typhoon ravaged the Miyazaki area. Vacationers fled from the seaside resorts and took shelter under the Phoenix dome. The raging winds of the typhoon beat impotently against the glass-and-steel walls of the structure. Inside, the artificial sun shone on, the wind never rose above a breeze, the birds kept on singing, and the waves tumbled with gentle regularity. Eden was finally under man's control.

DEATH ON THE BEACH

In the late 1960s and early 1970s, the beaches of the Mediterranean, the Atlantic, and the Caribbean began to effloresce with bacteria, particularly in the late summer months, when the hot cities disgorged their multitudes to the seashore. By 1975, so many of the coastal and inland waters of the United States were on the verge of putrefaction that Congress passed the Clean Water Act with the objective of "zero discharge." But, ten years later, sewage pollution still tainted municipal beaches and some of the most convenient and lovely shores had become health hazards. New York City was dumping raw sewage—some seven million metric tons annually—until 1987, when it began hauling it 106 miles out to sea. And yet, carried by tides and shifting currents, the pollution found its way into the shallows of New York Bight. Vacationers on the Jersey shore found themselves swimming in sludge slicks peppered with condoms and human feces. To protect bathers, resorts on the French and Italian Rivieras began hoisting flags when the bacteria count was too high for swimming. In the lukewarm Adriatic, infectious diseases spread through the tepid waves. Some summers, parents packed their offspring off to the mountains rather than run the risk of exposing them to polio or encephalitis or skin diseases at the beach. The healthful waters had lost their healing touch.

Even remote beaches in the South Pacific were not immune from civilization's infestation. On the remotest of atolls, travel writers were aghast to stumble across plastic soda bottles, those ubiquitous, virtually indestructible emblems of civilization, and white pellets of Styrofoam packing material flecking the shore. In expensive resorts in the Caribbean, early risers out for a dawn jog would invariably see beach boys from Haiti silently grooming the sand, raking up the night's harvest of plastic cups, disposable lighters, cans, bottles, tampon inserters, and diapers. Trash and solid wastes from naval vessels and merchant ships washed up on the margins of the seas long after plans were drawn up to draft an international treaty banning all ocean dumping of trash in the 1970s. Surfers in Santa Monica and in Melbourne, Australia, began to discover that sharks and Portuguese men-of-war were not the only dangerous organisms in the ocean. Far more frequent were the invisible *E. coli* and staph bacteria that ravaged their digestive tracts and ear canals after a day in the surf. Poisons leeching into the sands from insecticides and herbicides found their way into the fragile tidal organisms, which passed death up the food chain to fish and birds. Even inert plastics, aesthetically offensive—but otherwise innocuous—to humans, were agents of destruction. Plastic six-pack containers tightened like nooses around the beaks of sea birds. Discarded fishing nets became death traps for seals. Sea turtles, mistaking floating plastic bags for jelly-fish—their dietary staple—choke irremediably.

With every incoming tide, the waves trace the failures of our civilization in the ragged script of refuse left at the high-water line. We come to the beach still dreaming of Eden. We find in the shifting sands of the seashore a stern warning of the doom that hangs over us, and that this time is of our own doing.

AND YET, THE ALLURE ENDURES

Nature may have been conquered or dismantled, but one lure—deeply human—remains. Sex is part of the catechism of the beach. Beaches are advertised to the modern world as places to retreat for sexual adventures, with photographs depicting men and women locked in passionate embrace against Technicolor sunsets. Resorts entice visitors with images of anatomically perfect couples lolling on the sand by day and, by night, gazing into the velvety horizon, drinks in hand. Evenings, honeymooners smile blankly at the soft-porn suggestiveness of cabaret dancers decked out in skimpy versions of native costumes. The fantasy of sexual fulfillment is as much a part of the package of practices we expect to find at the beach as was, in the eighteenth century, the dream of perfect health.

Ecologically, demographically, and therapeutically, the beach may appear to have gone to hell. Yet, despite the stress of numerical tourism and the concomitantly diminished availability of pleasures we have learned to associate with this marginal zone, the beach continues to be a powerful and persistently democratic magnet. For the affluent who can afford to be choosy about how to escape the boardroom, the trading floor, the studio, and the surgery, Palm Beach, Malibu, Fisher Island, and the Hamptons are the twentieth century's fertile socioeconomic crescents, where the cream of society establishes communities dedicated to leisure. The expensive homes they commission are capriccios of often brilliant styles. Inserted into the last remaining expanses of undeveloped seashore, these homes stand

out like sculptures, sentinels to in-
dividualism and shrines to intellectual trends. Stark modernist cubes,
impressionistic assemblages of geometric volumes, pop-art saltboxes,
postmodernist palaces, and historicist cottages sit cheek by jowl
in some of the most prestigious
beachside communities—in the
Hamptons of Long Island, Malibu,
on the shores of Lake Geneva and
Lake Michigan.

As the beaches closest to the
large urban centers are increasingly swallowed by suburban
sprawl, the exclusive enclaves move
farther and farther afield. Commuting to them on weekends re-
quires courage and inventiveness.
Penny-pinching Manhattanites en
route to the Hamptons take the
cheap Hampton Jitney through
bumper-to-bumper traffic; others
pay upward of $250 to ride in full-
service beauty salons on wheels,

Many seashore communities sponsor sand castle-
building competitions. (Paul Richards, *Camelot '85.
World's Tallest Sand Castle*, UPI/Bettmann)

equipped with marble bathrooms, leather seats, and high-tech beauty im-
plementa. The superrich jet in on their private planes.

The material trappings of beach holidays may have changed dramatically
over the last hundred years, but the domestic rituals have largely remained
the same. Weekend "cuckold trains" have been augmented by planes and
trains to haul husbands to wives and children happily ensconced at the
summer beach. As, forty-some years ago, Marilyn Monroe and Tom Ewell
flirted with adultery in Billy Wilder's *Seven Year Itch*, spousal beach holidays
continue to offer pretexts for adulterous affairs—or at least fantasies. Men
continue to suffer in the city so the wife and kids can be in paradise, playing out scenarios of summertime separation celebrated and anatomized in
the fiction of Fitzgerald, Updike, and Cheever. During the sweltering week,
the urban males suffer what psychologists call "the dread that results from
aloneness" as they return at night to empty homes. As the weekend approaches, they make the tedious commute to the beach, where they either
enter into domestic Nirvana or are made to feel like the proverbial fifth
wheel, disrupting the holiday routine with their unfamiliar presence.

Either way, as Sunday evening rolls around and with it the prospect of returning to the city, the visiting paterfamilias suffers the characteristic symptoms of separation described by John Cheever in his story "The Summer
Farmer." "There is a moment early on Sunday," Cheever wrote, "when the
tide of the summer day turns inexorably toward the evening train. You can
swim, play tennis, or take a nap or a walk, but it doesn't make much difference. Immediately after lunch, Paul was faced with his unwillingness to
leave."

Even during those weekends at the beach, however, the silicon mi-
crochip has come home to roost in the sand. Of all recent inventions in
electronic gadgetry, none has done more to destroy the tranquillity of the
beach than this tiny mechanical brain cell. It has made possible the minia-
turization and, consequently, the transportability of the office. Now, thanks
to small, battery-powered laptops, cell-phones-cum-fax-machines, CD players, and television sets, the beach's sacrosanct status as escape from the
workday has come under assault. It is now entirely possible to bring the office to the beach. The people who most need to be isolated from their
workstations are now literally inseparable from their electronic prostheses.
The laptop-toting executive on the beach is redefining leisure: the term no
longer refers to time set aside from work, but to a place apart from the normal workplace. At the turn of the twenty-first century, a beach vacation for
the most affluent and successful segments of society denotes a change of
place, not of schedule.

The search for the perfect beach continues. For some, this might be a
parenthesis of peace within easy reach of crowded cities. Such are the "secret six" beaches of New York City discovered by writer Ivan Held in
Queens, Staten Island, and Brooklyn, where sun worshippers spread out
towels on sand that is still more silica than cigarette ashes, and bathers can
swim in water unencumbered with raw sewage and tar balls. Surfers overrun Rockaway's Beach 89 and Beach 38, which take their cybernames from
the numbers of the streets feeding into them. Nudists from New Jersey and
New York still find companionable privacy at the southern part of Gunni-
son Beach at Sandy Hook, one of the oldest nudist haunts on the East
Coast. Much farther south, college students perform their annual spring
migrations to the beaches of Fort Lauderdale and drive their cars along
Daytona Beach, bringing together the three linchpins of the perfect sand-
and-surf experience: automobiles, sun, and water.

Whatever the beach, it is still possible, in the presence of the timeless
wash of waves, the sibilance of sand, and the warm kiss of the sun, to forget
the nagging sense of fealty to cash, work, and responsibility. After all is said
and done, we still come to the beach to slip through a crack of time into
the paradise of self-forgetfulness.

Boys leaping (authors' collection)

What constitutes a magnificent, world-class beach destination is, to some degree, a matter of personal preference. Some "paradises by the sea" have a decidedly urban twist, and balance the serenity of an immaculate private beach with the cosmopolitan edge and artistic vitality of life just on the other side of the resort wall. Other beach outposts are truly of the sea, drawing upon the natural beauty of the site to provide a seamless transition between nature and excursion. Most beach aficionados, however, will agree that fine accommodations, spectacular views, sensitivity to the local culture, lush gardens, and proximity to unspoiled beaches should always be part of the equation. Based on our travels, and drawing upon testimonials from well-seasoned travelers—among them, avid surfers, divers, yachtsmen, and swimmers—who have made beach holidays a central part of their life, the following list of beach hotels and resorts constitutes our private shortlist of the world's eighty best beach destinations. To suit a wide range of tastes, we have included the full spectrum of options, from hand-thatched bungalows to grand resorts.

EUROPE

FRANCE

Château de la Chèvre d'Or
Eze-Village (Alpes-Maritimes)
Tel: (33) 04 92 10 66 66
Fax: (33) 04 93 41 06 72

Château Éza
Eze Village
Côte d'Azur
Tel: (33) 04 93 41 12 24
Fax: (33) 04 93 41 16 64

Château Hôtel de la Messardière*
Saint-Tropez (Var)
Tel: (33) 04 94 56 76 00
Fax: (33) 04 94 56 76 01

Château Saint-Martin*
Vence (Alpes-Maritimes)
Tel: (33) 04 93 58 02 02
Fax: (33) 04 93 24 08 91

Hôtel du Cap Eden-Roc*
Cap d'Antibes
Tel: (33) 04 93 61 39 01
Fax: (33) 04 93 67 76 04

Hôtel les Roches
Aiguebelle (Var)
Tel: (33) 04 94 71 05 07
Fax: (33) 04 94 71 08 40

La Réserve
Beaulieu-sur-Mer (Alpes-Maritimes)
Tel: (33) 04 93 01 00 01
Fax: (33) 04 93 01 28 99

Le Métropole
Beaulieu-sur-Mer (Alpes-Maritimes)
Tel: (33) 04 93 01 00 08
Fax: (33) 04 93 01 18 51

Résidence de la Pinède
Saint-Tropez (Var)
Tel: (33) 04 94 55 91 00
Fax: (33) 04 94 97 73 64

Villa Saint Elme
Les Issambres
Tel: (33) 04 94 49 52 32
Fax: (33) 04 94 49 63 18

GREECE

Casa Delfino*
Crete
Tel. (30) 821 87 400

Villa Vedema Hotel
Megalohori, Santorini
Tel: (30) 286 81 796
Fax: (30) 286 81 798

ITALY

Hôtel Des Bains
Venice Lido
Tel: (39) 41 526 5921
Fax: (39) 41 526 0113

Hotel Romazzino
Porto Cervo, Sardinia
Tel: (39) 789 977 111
Fax: (39) 789 96258

Hotel Splendido*
Portofino
Tel: (39) (0185) 26 95 51
Fax: (39) (0185) 26 96 14

Il Pellicano*
Porto Ercole (Grosseto)
Tel: (39) (0564) 83 38 01
Fax: (39) (0564) 83 34 18

La Posta Vecchia
Palo Laziale (Ladispoli)
Tel: (39) 069 949 501
Fax: (39) 069 949 507

Le Sireneuse*
Positano (Salerno)
Tel: (39) (08) 987 50 66
Fax: (39) (08) 981 17 98

Pitrizza
Porto Cervo (Sardinia)
Tel: (39) (78) 993 01 11
Fax: (39) (78) 993 06 11

PORTUGAL

Reid's Palace
Madeira, Portugal
Tel: 91 700 7171
Fax: 91 700 7177

SPAIN

Hotel Hacienda Na
Hamena*
San Miguel (Ibiza)
Tel: (34) (9) (71) 33 45 00
Fax: (34) (9) (71) 33 45 14

Hotel Puente Romano
Marbella (Málaga)
Tel: (34) (5) 282 09 00
Fax: (34) (5) 277 57 66

Hotel Santa Marta
Playa Santa Cristina
(Gerone)
Tel: (34) (9) (72) 36 49 04
Fax: (34) (9) (72) 36 92 80

La Residencia*
Deya (Majorca)
Tel: (34) (9) (71) 63 90 11
Fax: (34) (9) (71) 63 93 70

Marbella Club Hotel*
Marbella (Málaga)
Tel: (34) (5) 282 22 11
Fax: (34) (5) 282 98 84

AUSTRALIA, SOUTH PACIFIC AND PACIFIC RIM

AUSTRALIA

Bloomfield Wilderness
Lodge
Cairns, Australia
Tel: (61) (0) 70 35 91 66
Fax: (61) (0) 70 35 91 80

Cable Beach Club Resort
Broome, Australia
Tel: (61) (0) 91 92 04 00
Fax: (61) (0) 91 92 22 49

Green Island Resort
Cairns, Australia
Tel: (61) (0) 70 31 33 00
Fax: (61) (0) 70 52 15 11

Hayman Island*
Great Barrier Reef
Queensland, Australia
Tel: (61) (0) 79 40 12 34
Fax: (61) (0) 79 40 15 67

Kewarra Beach Resort
Smithfield
Cairns, Australia
Tel: (61) (0) 70 57 66 66
Fax: (61) (0) 70 57 75 25

Kim's Beachside Retreat
Toowoon Bay, Australia
Tel: (61) (0) 43 32 15 66
Fax: (61) (0) 43 33 15 44

BALI

Four Seasons Jim Baran
Bay*
Bali, Indonesia
Tel: (62) 361 70 1010
Fax: (62) 361 70 1020

Four Seasons Sayan
Bali, Indonesia
Tel: (62) 361 70 1010
Fax: (62) 361 70 1022

The Oberoi
Bali, Indonesia
Tel: (62) 361 73 0361
Fax: (62) 361 73 0791

FIJI

Toberua Island Resort
Suva, Fiji
Tel: (61) (6) 7930 2356
Fax: (61) (6) 7930 2215

Turtle Island Resort*
Yasawa Islands, Fiji
Tel: 61 (3) 629 4200
Fax: 61 (3) 629 8605

Vatulele Island Resort*
Fiji Islands
Tel: (61) (2) 326 1055
Fax: (61) (2) 327 2764

Wakaya Club
Fiji Islands
Tel: 800-828-3454

Yasawa Island Resort
Yasawa Island, Fiji
Tel: (61) (6) 966 3364
Fax: (61) (6) 966 5044

MALAYSIA

Pangkor Laut Resort*
Pangkor Laut Island
Malaysia
Tel: 605 699 1100
Fax: 605 699 1200

THAILAND

Banyan Tree Phuket*
Amphur Talang, Phuket
Thailand
Tel: (66) (75) 66 76 32

Dusit Rayadavee Resort
Hotel
Tambon Sai Thai, Amphor
Muang
Thailand
Tel: (66) (75) 62 07 40
Fax: (66) (75) 62 06 30

INDIAN OCEAN

Banyan Tree Maldives
Vabbinfaru Island
Maldives
Tel: 960 443 147
Fax: 960 443 843

Bird Island Lodge
Seychelles, Outer Islands
Tel: (248) 323 322

Le Galawa
Comoros
Tel: (44) 14 91 411 222

Royal Palm*
Grand Baie, Mauritius
Tel: (230) 263 8353
Fax: (230) 263 8455

Samana Villas
Aturuwella, Bentota
Sri Lanka
Tel: (94) 34 75 435
Fax: (94) 34 75 433

Silhouette Islands Lodge*
Seychelles, Outer Islands
Tel: (248) 344 154

Soneva Fushi
Kunfunadhoo Island
Baa Atoll, Maldives
Tel: (960) 230 304
Fax: (960) 230 374

SOUTH AFRICA

The Bay
Camps Bay, Capetown
Tel: (27) (21) 438 4444
Fax: (27) (21) 438 4455

UNITED STATES AND HAWAII

The Breakers*
Palm Beach, Florida
Tel: (407) 655 6611
Fax: (407) 659 8403

Delano*
South Beach, Miami
Florida
Tel: (305) 672 2000
Fax: (305) 532 0099

Four Seasons Resort Wailea
Maui, Hawaii
Tel: (808) 874 8000
Fax: (808) 874 6449

Halekulani*
Honolulu, Hawaii
Tel: (808) 923 2311
Fax: (808) 926 8004

Highlands Inn
Carmel, California
Tel: (408) 634 3801
Fax: (408) 626 1574

Hotel Hana Maui
Maui, Hawaii
Tel: (800) 325 3535

Little Palm Island
Little Torch Key, Florida
Tel: (305) 872 2524
Fax: (305) 872 4843

Manele Bay Hotel
Lana'i City, Hawaii
Tel: (808) 565 7700
Fax: (808) 565 2483

Post Ranch Inn
Big Sur, Monterey County
California
Tel: (408) 667 2200
Fax: (408) 667 2824

Ritz-Carlton
Laguna Nigel
California
Tel: (714) 240 2000
Fax: (714) 489 5810

Ritz-Carlton*
Naples, Florida
Tel: (941) 598 3300
Fax: (941) 598 6691

Ritz-Carlton
Manalapan
Palm Beach, Florida
Tel: (407) 533 6000
Fax: (407) 588 4555

Shutters On The Beach
Santa Monica, California
Tel: (310) 458 0030
Fax: (310) 458 4589

Tides Hotel*
South Beach, Miami
Florida
Tel: (305) 604 5000
Fax: (305) 604 5180

White Barn Inn
Kennebunkport, Maine
Tel: (207) 967 2321
Fax: (207) 967 1100

MEXICO, CARIBBEAN, SOUTH AMERICA, AND BERMUDA

Bahía des los Frailes*
Baja California Sur
Mexico
Tel: 415 956 3499

Hotel Twin Dolphins
Cabo San Lucas
Mexico
Tel: 52 (114) 3 25 90
Fax (U.S.): (213) 380 1302

Maroma*
Quintana Roo
Yucután, Mexico
Tel: 52 114 987 44 729
Fax: 52 114 98 84 21 15

Ritz-Carlton*
Cancún, Mexico
Tel: 52 98 85 08 08
Fax: 52 98 85 10 15

Villa Del Sol
Zihuatenejo, Mexico
Tel: 52 (755) 42239
Fax: 52 (755) 42758

CARIBBEAN

Ariel Sands Beach Club*
Bermuda
Tel: 441 236 1010
Fax: 441 236 0087

Cotton House
Mustique, Saint Vincent,
West Indies
The Grenadines
Tel: (809) 456 4777
Fax: (809) 456 5887

Four Seasons Resort Hotel
Nevis
Tel: (809) 469 1111
Fax: (809) 469 1040

Grace Bay Club
Turks & Caicos Island
British West Indies
Tel: (809) 946 5050
Fax: (809) 946 5758

La Samanna
Saint Martin
French West Indies
Tel: (590) 876 400
Fax: (590) 878 786

Little Dix Bay
Virgin Gorda
British Virgin Islands
Tel: (809) 495 5555
Fax: (809) 495 5661

Malliouhana
Anguilla
French West Indies
Tel: (800) 835 0796

Pink Sands*
Harbour Island
Bahamas
Tel: (800) 688 7678

SOUTH AMERICA

Copacabana Place*
Rio de Janeiro
Brazil
Tel: (021) 548 7070
Fax: (021) 235 7330

Hotel Villa Serena
Samana Peninsula
Dominican Republic
Tel: (809) 223 8703

*Authors' favorites.

"Accessories for the Shore: Games and Gadgets." *House and Garden* 79 (June 1941): 17–19.

Adams, J. Howe. "Bathing at the American Sea-Shore Resorts." *The Cosmopolitan* 19 (1895): 316–29.

———. "Bathing at the Continental Sea-Shore Resorts." *The Cosmopolitan* 19 (1895): 131–45.

———. "Bathing at the English Sea-Shore Resorts." *The Cosmopolitan* 19 (1895): 395–404.

Aeschylus. *Complete Plays*. Translated by Gilbert Murray. London: Allen & Unwin, 1952.

Aitchison, J. H. "Hot Baths of Rome." *American Architect and Architecture* 25 (1888–89): 118–19.

Allen, William H. "The Sea-Air Treatment for New York's Bedridden Children." *Review of Reviews* 32 (1905): 324–27.

Anstey, Christopher. *New Bath Guide*. 1766.

Apuleius. *The Golden Ass*. Translated by Jack Lindsay. Bloomington. Indiana University Press, 1962.

Aristophanes. *The Comedies of Aristophanes*. Translated by B. B. Rogers. London: Bell, 1902.

Ash, Jennifer, and Alex McLean. *Private Palm Beach: Tropical Style*. New York: Abbeville Press, 1992.

Asimov, Isaac, and Frank White. *The March of Millennia: A Key to Looking at History*. New York: Walker, 1991.

"At the Seaside." *The Cornhill Magazine* 4 (1861): 582–83.

"At the Seaside." *The Cornhill Magazine* 32 (1874): 414–26.

Austen, Jane. *Persuasion*. New York: E. P. Dutton, 1922.

Baedeker, Karl. *Belgium and Holland Including The Grand Duchy of Luxembourg: Handbook for Travellers*. Leipzig and London: K. Baedeker, 1901.

——— *The Riviera, South-Eastern France and Corsica, the Italian Lakes and Lake Geneva: Handbook for Travellers*. Leipzig and London: K. Baedeker, 1931.

——— *Southern France Including Corsica: Handbook for Travellers*. Leipzig and New York: K. Baedeker, 1907.

Banham, Reyner. *Los Angeles: The Architecture of Four Ecologies*. London: Penguin, 1976.

"Barrel-Hoop Bath House: Portable Dressing Room." *Popular Science Monthly* 144 (June 1944): 176.

Bascom, Willard. "Beaches." *Scientific American* 203 (August 1960): 81–92.

———. *Waves and Beaches*. New York: Anchor Press, 1980.

Basset, F. S. "Epithets and Conundrums of the Sea." *United Service Magazine* 4 (December 1890): 578–86.

"Bath House That Can Be Folded." *Popular Science Monthly* 143 (July 1943): 265.

"Bathing and Bodies." *Putnam's Monthly* 4 (November 1854): 532–36.

"Bathing and Swimming." *The Penny Magazine,* September 12, 1835.

"Bathing Pavilion." *Architectural Record* 78 (September 1935): 172–75.

"Bath in the Eighteenth Century." *Edinburgh Review* 202 (July 1905): 162–88.

"Baths, Public, and Wash-Houses." *The British Almanac for the Society of the Diffusion of Useful Knowledge for the Year.* pp. 40–54. London: Charles Knight, 1854.

"Baths and Bathing-Places, Ancient and Modern." *Eclectic Magazine* 7 (October 1870): 385–401.

"Baths for the Working Classes." *The British Almanac for the Society of the Diffusion of Useful Knowledge for the Year,* pp. 117–24. London: Charles Knight, 1848.

Baudelaire, Charles. *Fleurs du mal. The Flowers of Evil.* New York: New Directions, 1963.

Baxter, Sylvester. "City Ownership of Seaside Parks." *The Cosmopolitan* 33 (1901): 29–39.

"Beach Club to Sell a View." *Architectural Record* 104 (July 1948): 136–39.

Beard, J. Carter. "The Abysmal Depths of the Sea." *The Cosmopolitan* 14 (1894): 532–38.

Beecher, Henry Ward. *Plymouth Pulpit: Sermons Preached in Plymouth Church, Brooklyn.* Boston: Pilgrim Press, 1897.

Belloli, Andrea P. A., ed. *A Day in the Country: Impressionism and the French Landscape.* Los Angeles: Los Angeles County Museum of Art, 1984.

Benjamin, Lewis S. *The Life and Letters of Tobias Smollett.* Boston: Houghton Mifflin, 1927.

Bennett, Dery. "Paying for Sand." *Audubon* 95 (September–October 1993): 132.

Bennett, Tony. "A Thousand and One Troubles: Blackpool Pleasure Beach." *Formations of Pleasure.* London: Routledge & Kegan Paul, 1983, pp. 138–55.

Beowulf and Other Old English Poems. Translated by Constance B. Hieatt. New York: Odyssey Press, 1967.

Bigelow, Poultney. "Comfort on the High Seas." *Chamber's Journal* 80 (1903): 58–61.

Bloch, Marc. *Feudal Society.* Translated by L. A. Manyon. 2 vols. Vol. 1: *The Growth of Ties of Dependence.* Chicago: University of Chicago Press, 1961.

Blossom, Laurel. *Splash! Great Writing About Swimming.* Hopewell, N.J.: Ecco Press, 1996.

Blume, Mary. *Côte d'Azur: Inventing the French Riviera.* New York: Thames and Hudson, 1992.

Bosselman, Fred P. *In the Wake of the Tourist: Managing Special Places in Eight Countries.* Washington, D.C.: The Conservation Foundation, 1978.

Bougainville, Louis-Antoine de. *Circumnavigating the World on the Royal Frigate "La Boudeuse" and the Armed Transport "L'Etoile,"* 1771.

Breen, Ann, and Dick Rigby. *Waterfronts: Cities Reclaim Their Edge.* New York: McGraw-Hill, 1994.

Brent, John. "The World's Bathing Places." *Munsey's Magazine* 27 (1902): 549–57.

Brown, DeSoto. *Hawaii Recalls: Selling Romance to America.* Honolulu: Editions Limited, 1982.

Brown, Dona. *Inventing New England: Regional Tourism in the Nineteenth Century.* Washington and London: Smithsonian Institution Press, 1995.

Bruce, James. *Travels through Part of Africa, Syria, Egypt, and Arabia, into Abyssinia, To Discover the Source of the Nile.* Manchester, England: J. Gleave, 1823.

Brydone, Patrick. *A Tour through Sicily and Malta.* 2 vols. 1773.

Buck, Elizabeth. *Paradise Remade: The Politics of Culture and History in Hawai'i.* Philadelphia: Temple University Press, 1993.

Buckland, Gail. *The Golden Summer.* London: Pavilion Books, 1989.

Buffon, George Louis Leclerc. *Buffon's Natural History.* London: H. D. Symonds, 1797–1807.

Burke, Edmund. *A Philosophical Enquiry into the Origin of Our Ideas of the Sublime and the Beautiful.* Edited by James T. Boulton. London: 1958.

Burnet, Thomas. *The Sacred Theory of the Earth.* London: T. Kinnersrey, 1816.

Burney, Fanny (Frances). *The Diary and Letters of Madame d'Arblay.* 3 vols. London: Frederick Warne, 1892.

Burton, Robert. *The Anatomy of Melancholy.* Edited by Holbrook Jackson. New York: Vintage, 1977.

Byron, George Gordon, Lord. *The Complete Poetical Works.* Oxford and New York: Clarendon Press, 1980.

Calasso, Roberto. *The Marriage of Cadmus and Harmony.* Translated by Tim Parks. New York: Vintage International, 1994.

Cameron, Ian. *Lost Paradise: An Exploration of the Pacific.* Topsfield, Mass.: Salem House Publishers, 1987.

Cameron, Roderick. *The Golden Riviera.* London: Weidenfeld & Nicolson, 1975.

Carson, Rachel. *The Edge of the Sea.* Boston: Houghton Mifflin, 1955.

———. *The Sea Around Us.* New York: Oxford University Press, 1951.

Cartwright, Frederick F. *Disease and History.* New York: Dorset Press, 1991.

Chadwick, French E. "The Mastery of the Sea." *Munsey's Magazine* 34 (1905–6): 749–53.

Chopin, Kate. *The Awakening: An Authoritative Text.* Edited by Margaret Culley. New York: Norton, 1976.

Cicero, Marcus Tullius. *Correspondence.* Edited by R. Y. Tyrrell and L. C. Purser. Dublin: Longmans, 1890–1906.

"City Glorifies Its Old Swimming Hole." *Architectural Record* 104 (December 1948): 86–93.

Clark, T. J. *The Painting of Modern Life.* Princeton: Princeton University Press, 1984.

Coleridge, Samuel Taylor. *The Rime of the Ancient Mariner.* New York: Dover Publications, 1970.

Colwin, Cecil M. *Swimming into the 21st Century.* Champaign, Ill.: Human Kinetics Publishers, 1992.

Conrad, Joseph. "The Character of the Sea." *Appleton's Booklover's Magazine* 7 (1906): 28–32.

———. *Heart of Darkness: An Authoritative Text.* Edited by Robert Kimbrought. New York: Norton, 1963.

Cook, James. *A Voyage to the Pacific Ocean.* London: W. and A. Strahan, for G. Nicol and T. Cadell, 1784.

Cookridge, E. H. *Orient Express: The Life and Times of the World's Most Famous Train.* New York: Random House, 1978.

Cotterell, T. Sturge. "Bath Stone." *The Antiquary* 41 (1905): 87–92.

Coues, Elliott. "Sea-Side Homes and What Lived in Them." *The American Naturalist* 3 (September 1869): 337–49.

Cowell, F. R. *Everyday Life in Ancient Rome.* London: B. T. Batsford Limited, 1961.

Croutier, Alev Lytle. *Taking the Waters.* New York: Abbeville Press, 1992.

Cule, W. E. "By the Winter Sea." *Chamber's Journal* 80 (1903): 218–19.

"The Dangers of Washing." *The Spectator* 67 (July 1891): 124–25.

Dante Alighieri. *The Inferno of Dante: A New Verse Translation.* Translated by Robert Pinsky. New York: Farrar, Straus and Giroux, 1994.

Darwin, Charles. *The Collected Papers of Charles Darwin.* Edited by Paul H. Barrett. Chicago: University of Chicago Press, 1977.

Dean, Cornelia. "Is It Worth It to Rebuild a Beach? Panel's Answer Is a Tentative Yes." *The New York Times,* April 2, 1996, p. C4.

Debenham, Frank. *Discovery and Exploration.* New York: Doubleday, 1960.

"Decorative Effects in Country Bath-Dressing Rooms." *House and Garden* 60 (August 1931): 52–53.

Defoe, Daniel. *The Life and Adventures of Robinson Crusoe.* Edited by Angus Ross. Harmondsworth, England: Penguin, 1985.

Dening, Greg. *Mr Bligh's Bad Language: Passion, Power and Theatre on the Bounty.* Cambridge: Cambridge University Press, 1992.

Dickens, Charles. *David Copperfield.* New York: Dodd, Mead, 1943.

Diderot, Denis. *Selected Writings.* Selected and edited by Lester G. Crooker. New York: Macmillan, 1966.

Digby, Sir Everard. *De Arte Natandi.* England, 1587.

Diller, Elizabeth, and Ricardo Scofidio, eds. *Back to the Front: Tourisms of War.* New York: F.R.A.C. Basse-Normandie, 1994.

Douglas, Jack D., and Paul K. Rasmussen, with Carol Ann Flanagan. *The Nude Beach.* Beverly Hills: Sage Publications, 1977.

Douglas, Norman. *South Wind.* New York: Modern Library, 1925.

Dupont, Florence. *Daily Life in Ancient Rome.* Translated by Christopher Woodall. Oxford: Blackwell, 1993.

Durrell, Gerard. *My Family and Other Animals.* Harmondsworth, England: Penguin, 1959.

Ehrke, Ernest B. "Ten Bathing-Beach Commandments." *Good Housekeeping* 105 (July 1937): 34–35.

Eighteenth Century: Europe in the Age of Enlightenment. Edited by Alfred Cobban. London: Thames and Hudson, 1969.

Eksteins, Modris. *Rites of Spring: The Great War and the Birth of the Modern Age.* New York and London: Anchor Books, 1989.

Eldon, Abraham. *The Continental Oracle, or Maxims of Foreign Locomotion.*

Eliot, T. S. *Collected Poems: 1909–1935.* New York: Harcourt, Brace, 1936.

Elyot, Sir Thomas. *The Boke Named the Governour.* London, T. Berthelet, 1531. Menston, Yorkshire: Scolar Press, 1970.

Empson, William. *English Pastoral Poetry.* Freeport, N.Y.: Books for Libraries Press, 1972.

Escribe, Dominique. *La Côte d'Azur.* Nice: Éditions Serre, 1988.

E.S.D. "A Seaside Sanatorium." *London Society* (July 1870): 225–33.

Farber, Thomas. *On Water.* Hopewell, N.J.: Ecco Press, 1994.

"A Fashionable Bath in the Olden Time." *The Cornhill Magazine* 35 (1876): 195–207.

Ferri, Roger. "Beach Pavilion." *Kenchiku to Toshi—Architecture and Urbanism* (March 1992): 76–81.

Fielding, Henry. *Miscellanies.* Edited by Henry Knight Miller. Middletown, Conn.: Wesleyan University Press, 1972.

"Fifty Honeymoon Beaches: A Lover's Guide, a Room with a Beach." *Bride's and Your New Home* 61 (October 1994): 398–420.

Fish, Edmond S. "New Swimmin' Hole." *Saturday Evening Post,* July 5, 1941, pp. 14–15.

Fitzgerald, F. Scott. "Tender Is the Night." *The Portable F. Scott Fitzgerald.* Selected by Dorothy Parker. New York: Viking, 1949, pp. 169–545.

Flacelière, Robert. *Daily Life in Greece at the Time of Pericles.* Translated by Peter Green. New York: Macmillan, 1965.

Flaubert, Gustav. *Notes de voyages.* Paris: Louis Conard, 1910.

Floyer, Sir John. *On the Use and Abuse of Baths.*

Flügel, John Carl. *Psychology of Clothes.* New York: AMS Press, 1976.

Foote, Samuel. *The Works of Samuel Foote.* London: Sherwood, Gilbert & Piper, 1830.

"For Living Between Sea and Land." *Architectural Record* 104 (September 1948). 109–11.

Friedländer, Ludwig. *Roman Life and Manners Under the Early Empire.* Translated by Leonard A. Magnus. London: George Routledge and Sons, 1908.

"Fun on the Beach." *Life* 25 (July 1948): 64–71.

Fussell, Paul. *Abroad: British Literary Traveling Between the Wars.* Oxford: Oxford University Press, 1980.

———. *The Great War and Modern Memory.* Oxford: Oxford University Press, 1975.

Geithmann, Harriet. "Singing and Barking Sands." *The Mentor* 13 (September 1925): 53.

Goethe, Johann Wolfgang von. *Italian Journey.* Translated by Robert R. Heitner. Princeton: Princeton University Press, 1994.

———. *Wilhelm Meister's Apprenticeship and Travels.* Translated by Thomas Carlyle. New York: AMS Press, 1974.

Granville, A. B. *The Spas of England and Principal Sea-Bathing Places.* 3 vols. Vol. 1, *Northern Spas.* Vol. 2, *Midland Spas.* Vol. 3, *Southern Spas.* London: Henry Colburn, 1841.

———. "The Spas of England and Principal Sea-Bathing Places." *Fraser's Magazine for Town and Country* 25 (February 1842): 182–91.

Graves, Ralph. *Martha's Vineyard: An Affectionate Memoir.* New York: Abbeville Press, 1995.

Gubin, E. K. "The Seashore Can Make You Well." *Hygeia* 22 (September 1944): 668–69.

Guillaume de Lorris, and Jean de Meum. *The Romance of the Rose.* Translated by Harry W. Robbins. New York: E. P. Dutton, 1962.

Gutteridge, Noel M. "Australia, Land of Sun and Surf." *Hygeia* 18 (January 1940): 31.

Haas, Hans. *Challenging the Deep: Thirty Years of Undersea Adventure.* Translated by Ewald Osers. New York: William Morrow, 1973.

Hadas, Moses, trans. *Three Greek Romances.* New York: Bobbs-Merrill, 1964.

Halberstam, David. *The Fifties.* New York: Fawcett Columbine, 1993.

Hamilton, Edith. *Mythology.* Boston: Little, Brown, 1942.

Hamilton, John. *War at Sea: 1939–1945.* Poole, England: Blanford Press, 1986.

Hamilton-Paterson, James. *The Great Deep: The Sea and Its Thresholds.* New York: Henry Holt, 1992.

Hanna, Nick. *The BMW Tropical Beach Handbook.* London: Fourth Estate, 1989.

Hansard, William. "What Sent Me to the Sea." *Adelaide Nutting Historical Nursing Collection* 3 (1862): 263–71.

Hardy, Francis H. "Seaside Life in America." *The Cornhill Magazine* 74 (1896): 605–19.

"Hartwig's 'Sea and Its Wonders.' " *Nature* 9 (November 1873): 40–41.

Haung, C. James. *Leisure and Urbanism in Nineteenth-Century Nice.* Lawrence: Regents Press of Kansas, 1982.

Haviland, Alfred. "English Seaside Health-Resorts." *Knowledge* 3 (April 1883): 247–48.

Held, Ivan. "Secret Six for a Beach Fix." *New York Daily News* (August 1, 1997), p. 59.

Hemingway, Andrew. *Landscape Imagery and Urban Culture in Early Nineteenth-Century Britain.* Cambridge: Cambridge University Press, 1992.

Hemingway, Ernest. *The Old Man and the Sea.* New York: Scribner, 1952.

Herbert, Robert. *Monet on the Normandy Coast.* New Haven: Yale University Press, 1994.

Hern, Anthony. *The Seaside Holiday: The History of the English Seaside Resort.* London: Cresset Press, 1967.

Herodotus. *The History.* Translated by David Grene. Chicago: University of Chicago Press, 1987.

Herrick, Francis H. "Days and Nights by the Sea." *The American Naturalist* 22 (May 1889): 406–20.

————. "Nature at Sea." *Popular Science Monthly* 44 (1893–94): 69–80.

Hesiod. *Theogony.* Translated by Norman O. Brown. Indianapolis and New York: Bobbs-Merrill, 1953.

Hilber, Vinzenz. "The Struggle of Sea and Land." *Popular Science Monthly* 36 (1889–90): 222–26.

H.J. "Sea-Side Life." *Once a Week* (August 1862): 149–52.

Hoefer, Hans Johannes, and Merin Wexler, eds. *Great Britain.* Singapore: APA Productions, 1985.

Holloway, J. Christopher. *The Business of Tourism.* London: Pitman, 1986.

Holy Bible, The. Edited by C. I. Scofield. New York: Oxford University Press, 1917.

Homer. *The Odyssey of Homer.* Translated by S. H. Butcher and A. Lang. New York: Modern Library, 1950.

Hopkins, Gerard Manley. *The Hopkins Reader.* New York and London: Oxford University Press, 1953.

Horace. *The Works of Horace.* Translated by C. Smart. London: H. G. Bohn, 1850.

"Houses in Bath." *Saturday Review of Politics, Literature, Science and Art* 57 (1883–84): 824–25.

Howarth, Patrick. *When the Riviera Was Ours.* London: Routledge & Kegan Paul, 1977.

Howells, William Dean. *The Rise of Silas Lapham.* New York: Dodd, Mead, 1964.

Hutchinson, Woods. *The New Handbook of Health.* Boston and New York: Houghton Mifflin, 1934.

Huxley, Aldous. *Point Counter Point.* New York: Doubleday, 1928.

"Improved Sanitary Code for Public Pools and Beaches." *The American City* 62 (July 1947): 5–7.

Inkersley, Arthur. "Bathing in Ancient Rome, and Its Effects on Roman Character." *Education* 16 (November 1895): 134–40.

Ireland, Samuel. *Picturesque Views on the River Thames.* London: T. Egerton, 1801–2.

Ivy, Robert A., Jr. "Building by the Sea: The Southeast." *Architecture* (June 1985): 70–75.

James, Henry. *The American Scene.* Bloomington: Indiana University Press, 1968.

————. *The Art of Travel: Scenes and Journeys in America, England, France and Italy from the Travel Writings of Henry James.* Freeport, N.Y.: Books for Libraries Press, 1962.

Joyce, James. *Ulysses.* New York: Vintage, 1990.

Junk, Cletus. "A Municipal River Beach with a Seaside Personality." *American City* 53 (September 1938): 101.

Kant, Immanuel. "Analytic of the Sublime." *Kant's Critique of Aesthetic Judgment.* Translated by J. C. Meredith. Oxford, 1911.

Kaufman, Wallace, and Orrin H. Pilkey, Jr. *The Beaches Are Moving.* Durham, N.C.: Duke University Press, 1983.

Keats, John. *Complete Poetry and Selected Prose.* New York: Modern Library, 1991.

King, Austin J., and B. H. Watts. "Some Visitors to Bath During the Reign of James I." *The Antiquary* 14 (1886): 64.

Kirby, Donald Beach, and Wallace Wolcott. "West Coast Beach House." *American Home* 25 (February 1941): 13–15.

Klein, Roberta. "Exhibition Celebrates Miami Architecture." *Architecture* (February 1994): 30–33.

Kleinberg, Howard. *Miami Beach: A History.* Miami: Centennial Press, 1994.

Lang, A. "My Friend the Beachcomber." *Longman's Magazine* 6 (1885): 417–23.

La Pietra, Ugo. "Cultura balneare." *L'Architettura* 33 (August September 1987): 657–72.

Laqueur, Thomas. *Making Sex: Body and Gender from the Greeks to Freud.* Cambridge, Mass.: Harvard University Press, 1990.

Lawrence, D. H. *The Complete Short Stories.* 3 vols. New York, 1961.

————. *Sea and Sardinia.* Harmondsworth, England: Penguin, 1981.

Le Gallienne, Richard. *Vanishing Roads and Other Essays.* New York: G. P. Putnam's Sons, 1915.

Lenček, Lena, and Gideon Bosker. *Making Waves: Swimsuits and the Undressing of America.* San Francisco: Chronicle Books, 1989.

Lévi-Strauss, Claude. *The Savage Mind.* Chicago: University of Chicago Press, 1966.

"Life Goes on a Beach Vacation." *Life* 22 (April 1947): 136–38.

Lindbergh, Anne Morrow. *Gift from the Sea.* New York: Pantheon, 1977.

Lobban, J. H. "The Kingdom of Bath." *Blackwoood's Edinburgh Magazine* 177 (1904–5): 446–81.

Lucy, Henry W. "Seaport and Seaside." *Gentleman's Magazine* 13 (1874): 220–29.

Lundberg, Donald E., and Carolyn B. Lundberg. *International Travel and Tourism.* New York: John B. Wiley & Sons, 1985.

MacCannell, Dean. *Empty Meeting Grounds: The Tourist Papers.* London and New York: Routledge, 1992.

————. *The Tourist: A New Theory of the Leisure Class.* New York: Schocken, 1976.

McFall, Christie. *Wonders of Sand.* New York: Dodd, Mead, 1966.

McGee, W. H. "Encroachments of the Sea." *The Forum* 9 (1890): 437–49.

McKechnie, Samuel. *Popular Entertainments Through the Ages.* New York and London: Benjamin Blom, 1969.

Macleod, Fiona. "Sea-Magic and Running Water." *Contemporary Review* 82 (1902): 568–80.

Macpherson, James. *The Poems of Ossian.* Geddes, 1896.

Maillet, Benoît. *The Telliamed, or the Dialogue of an Indian Philosopher with a French Missionary.* Amsterdam, 1748.

Mann, Thomas. *Buddenbrooks: The Decline of a Family.* Translated by John E. Woods. New York: Knopf, 1993.

―――. *Death in Venice.* Translated by Kenneth Burke. New York: Knopf, 1965.

―――. *Stories of Three Decades.* Translated by H. T. Lowe-Porter. New York: Knopf, 1955.

Margan, Frank, and Ben R. Finney. *A Pictorial History of Surfing.* London: Paul Hamlyn, 1970.

Margotta, Roberto. *The Story of Medicine.* Edited by Paul Lewis. New York: Golden Press, 1968.

Marryat, Florence. "The Bath-Chair Man's Story." *Temple Bar* 22 (1867–68): 507–20.

Martin, Richard, and Harold Koda. *Splash! A History of Swimwear.* New York: Rizzoli, 1990.

Massingham, Hugh. *The Great Victorians.* Edited by J. Massingham and Hugh Massingham. London: I. Nicholson & Watson, 1932.

Maupassant, Guy de. *Pierre et Jean.* Paris: Garnier, 1959.

―――. *Sur l'eau: de Saint-Tropez à Monte-Carlo.* Paris: Encre, 1979.

Melinkoff, Ellen. *What We Wore: An Offbeat Social History of Women's Clothing, 1950 to 1980.* New York: Quill, 1984.

Melville, Herman. *Moby-Dick.* Toronto and New York: Bantam, 1967.

Merrill, Frederick J. H. "Barrier Beaches of the Atlantic Coast." *Popular Science Monthly* 37 (1890): 736–45.

Millot, J. A. *L'Art d'améliorer et de perfectionner les hommes,* 1801.

Monnier, Henri. *Physiologie du bourgeois* [N.p., 1841(?)].

Montaigne, Michel de. *Montaigne's Travel Journal.* Translated by Donald M. Frame. San Francisco: North Point Press, 1983.

Morse, Edward S. "A Stroll by the Sea-Side." *The American Naturalist* 2 (1868): 336–51.

Moseley, H. N. "The Fauna of the Sea-Shore." *Popular Science Monthly* 27 (1876–77): 623–25.

Nabokov, Vladimir. *The Gift.* New York: G. P. Putnam's Sons, 1963.

―――. *Speak Memory: An Autobiography Revisited.* London: Weidenfeld and Nicolson, 1967.

O'Neill, William L. *American High: The Years of Confidence, 1945–1960.* New York: Free Press, 1986.

"On the Sea and Sailors." *Academy and Literature* 65 (1903): 87–88.

Osborne, Duffield. "Surf Bathing." *Outing* 40 (August 1902): 517–26.

Ovid. *The Metamorphoses of Ovid.* Translated by Allen Mandelbaum. San Diego: Harvest, 1993.

Packard, John H. *Sea-Air and Sea-Bathing.* Philadelphia: P. Blakiston, 1880.

Park, Mungo. *The Life and Travels of Mungo Park: With a Supplementary Chapter Detailing the Results of Recent Discoveries in Africa.* Edinburgh: William P. Nimmo, 1875.

Patmore, J. Allan. *Land and Leisure in England and Wales.* London: David & Charles, 1970.

Pattullo, Polly. *Last Resorts: The Cost of Tourism in the Caribbean.* London: Cassell, 1996.

Payne, Blanche, Geitel Winakor, and Jane Farrell-Beck. *The History of the Costume: From Ancient Mesopotamia Through the Twentieth Century.* New York: Harper-Collins, 1992.

Pemble, John. *The Mediterranean Passion.* Oxford: Clarendon Press, 1987.

Pidgeon, D. "The Story of a Sea-Beach." *Gentleman's Magazine* 31 (1883): 277–81.

Poe, Edgar Allan. "A Descent into the Maelström." *Complete Tales and Poems of Edgar Allan Poe.* New York: Vintage, 1975.

"Portable Dressing Room for the Beach." *Popular Mechanics Magazine* 84 (August 1945): 103.

Powys, John Cowper. *Weymouth Sands: A Novel.* Simon & Schuster, 1934.

Pryor, Mrs. Roger A. "The Social Code." *The Delineator* (June 1895).

Quincy, Josiah. "Playgrounds, Baths, and Gymnasia." *Journal of Social Science* 36 (1898): 139–47.

Quinn, Edward. *A Côte d'Azur Album.* Zurich: Zurich Museum of Design, 1994.

Raban, Jonathan, ed. *The Oxford Book of the Sea.* Oxford: Oxford University Press, 1993.

———. Review of *Waterfronts,* by Ann Breen. *The New York Review of Books,* July 14, 1994, pp. 37–42.

Raymond, Karl B. "Bathing Beaches in Minneapolis." *The Playground* 18 (August 1924): 285–86.

Rearick, Charles. *Pleasures of the Belle Epoque: Entertainment and Festivity in Turn-of-the-Century France.* New Haven and London: Yale University Press, 1985.

Redford, Polly. *Billion-Dollar Sandbar: A Biography of Miami Beach.* New York: Dutton, 1970.

"Resort Hotel Makes Short Season Pay." *Architectural Record* 88 (July 1940): 95–97.

Reynolds-Ball, Eustace. "Sea-Sickness, and How to Avoid It." *Chamber's Journal* 81 (1904): 509–11.

Rice, Warner G., ed. *Literature as a Mode of Travel.* New York: New York Public Library, 1963.

Rilke, Rainer Maria. *Duino Elegies.* Translated by David Young. New York: Norton, 1978.

Roche, Daniel. *The Culture of Clothing: Dress and Fashion in the "Ancien Régime."* Translated by Jean Birrell. Cambridge and New York: Cambridge University Press, 1994.

Rollier, Auguste. *Heliotherapy,* 1923.

"Roman Baths at Bath." *The Antiquary* 15 (1886–87): 159–62.

Ross, Janet. "The Baths of Casciana in July." *Macmillan's Magazine* 52 (1885): 354–60.

Rousseau, Jean Jacques. *Émile, or, On Education.* Translated by Allan Bloom. New York: Basic Books, 1979.

———. *The Social Contract and Discourses.* London and New York: E. P. Dutton, 1913.

Russell, Beverly. "Fantasy on the Beach." *Interiors* 150 (October 1991): 56–59.

Russell, Percy. "Irish Seaside Resorts, from an Unconventional Point of View." *Knowledge* 7 (June 1885): 520–42.

Russell, W. Clark. "Sea Stories." *The Contemporary Review* 46 (1884): 343–63.

Sand, George. *Winter in Majorca.* Translated by Robert Graves. Chicago: Academy Chicago Publishers, 1992.

Saporta, Antoine M. de. "Properties and Constitution of Sea-Water." *Popular Science Monthly* 26 (1875–76): 529–41.

Schama, Simon. *Landscape and Memory.* New York: Knopf, 1995.

Schiller, Friedrich von. "On the Sublime." *Naive and Sentimental Poetry and On the Sublime: Two Essays.* Translated by Julius A. Elias. New York: Frederick Ungar, 1975.

"The Sea and Its Living Wonders." *Eclectic Magazine* 53 (July 1861): 289–98, 463–67.

"The Sea and the Sea-Side." *The Cornhill Magazine* 62 (1890): 191–200.

"Sea Bathing Places in England." *Fraser's Magazine for Town and Country* 25 (February 1842): 182–91.

"Sea-Coast Country." *The Spectator* 91 (July 1903): 87–88.

"Sea Coast Life in England." *Saturday Review of Politics, Literature, Science and Art* 57 (1883–84): 824–25.

"Sea—from Shore." *Putnam's Monthly* 4 (July 1854): 41–50.

"The Sea-Side Recreations of Mr. Jolly Green." *The Monthly Magazine and Humorist* 94 (1851–52): 63–79, 236–45, 334–48.

"Sea-Side Resorts for Londoners." *Chamber's Edinburgh Journal* 20 (November 1853): 305–9.

"A Sea-Side Story." *St. James Magazine* (October 1874): 36–52.

Seigel, Jerrold. *Bohemian Paris: Culture, Politics, and the Boundaries of Bourgeois Life, 1830–1930.* New York: Viking, 1986.

Seneca, Lucius Annaeus (the Younger). *On Benefits.* Translated by Aubrey Stewart. London: George Bell & Sons, 1887.

Sessa, Chiara. "Aggregazioni estive: Cultura balneare." *L'Architettura* 35 (July–August 1989): 584–85.

Seton, William. "The Sea and Its Inhabitants." *Catholic World* 79 (May 1904): 192–208.

Sévigné, Madame de Rabutin-Chantal. *Lettres Choisies de Mme de Sévigné.* Paris: Librarie Garnier Frères, 1923.

Shadwell, Thomas. *The Complete Works.* London: The Fortune Press, 1927.

Shakespeare, William. *Hamlet.* Cambridge and New York: Cambridge University Press, 1985.

———. *Pericles.* Cambridge, Mass.: Harvard University Press, 1963.

———. *Richard III.* Toronto and New York: Bantam Books, 1988.

———. *The Tempest.* Toronto and New York: Bantam Books, 1988.

Shelley, Percy Bysshe. *The Complete Works.* New York and London: Gordian Press, 1965.

Sheridan, Richard. *The Works of Richard Brinsley Sheridan.* New York: G. Routledge & Sons, 1874.

Siebert, Ted. *The Art of Sandcastling.* Seattle: Romar Books, 1990 (?).

Siever, Raymond. *Sand.* New York: Scientific American Library, 1988.

Smollett, Tobias. *The Expedition of Humphry Clinker.* New York: New American Library, 1960.

———. *Travels Through France and Italy.* London: Oxford University Press, 1907.

———. *The Works of Tobias Smollett.* New York: Bigelow, Smith, 1900.

Snead, Stella. *Beach Patterns: The World of Sea and Sand.* Barre, Mass.: Barre Publishing, 1975.

Snow, Richard. *Coney Island: A Postcard Journey to the City of Fire.* New York: Brightwaters Press, 1984.

"Solaria, Cafeteria, Beauty Shop Included in New Beach Club." *Architectural Record* 84 (August 1938): 35–39.

"Some Literary Ramblings About Bath." *The Cornhill Magazine* 27 (1872): 27–44, 543–61, 688–702.

Sophocles. *The Complete Plays.* Translated by Richard Claverhouse Jebb. Toronto and New York: Bantam Books, 1982.

Sprawson, Charles. *Haunts of the Black Masseur: The Swimmer as Hero.* New York: Penguin, 1992.

Stagl, Justin. *A History of Curiosity: The Theory of Travel 1550–1800.* Chur, Switzerland: Harwood Academic Publisher, 1995.

Stendhal. *Memoirs of an Egotist by Stendhal.* Translated with an Introduction and Notes by David Ellis. New York: Horizon Press, 1957.

"Street-Cleaning a Beach." *American City* 55 (July 1940): 45.

Stuller, Jay. "On the Beach." *Sea Frontiers* 40 (December 1994): 28–34.

Sundeleaf, Richard. Unpublished interview with Lena Lenček and Gideon Bosker. Portland, Or., June 1983.

Swain, Leonard. "God's Ownership of the Sea." *Bibliotheca Sacra* 18 (July 1861): 636–62.

Swinburne, Algernon Charles. *The Novels of A. C. Swinburne: Love's Cross-Currents, Lesbia Brandon.* New York: Noonday Press, 1963.

———. *Selected Poetry and Prose.* New York: Modern Library, 1968.

Swinglehurst, Edmund. *The Romantic Journey: The Story of Thomas Cook and Victorian Travel.* New York: Harper and Row, 1974.

Tanner, Tony, ed. *The Oxford Book of Sea Stories.* Oxford: Oxford University Press, 1994.

Thévenot, Melchissedec. *L'Art de nager.* 1696.

Thompson, Grahame. "Carnival and the Calculable: Consumption and Play at Blackpool." *Formations of Pleasure.* London: Routledge & Kegan Paul, 1983, pp. 124–37.

Tocqueville, Alexis de. *Journeys to England and Ireland.* Translated by George Lawrence. Edited by K. P. Mayer and J. P. Mayer. London: Faber and Faber, 1957.

Tomlinson, H. M. *All Our Yesterdays.* New York and London: Harper & Brothers, 1930.

Twain, Mark [Samuel Clemens]. *The Innocents Abroad: or, The New Pilgrim's Progress.* New York and London: Harper, 1903.

Valéry, Paul. *Collected Works.* New York: Pantheon, 1956.

Veblen, Thorstein. *The Theory of the Leisure Class.* New Brunswick, N.J.: Transaction Publishers, 1992.

Vigarello, Georges. *The Concept of Cleanliness.* Translated by Jean Birrell. Cambridge: Cambridge University Press, 1988.

Viola, Herman J., and Carolyn Margolis, eds. *Magnificent Voyagers.* Washington, D.C.: Smithsonian Institution Press, 1985.

Virgil. *The Aeneid of Virgil.* Translated by C. Day Lewis. New York: Oxford University Press, 1950.

"Visit to the North-West Coast of Tasmania." *St. James Magazine* (April 1874): 281–99.

"Voice from the Sea." *The American Whig Review* 14 (1851): 525–35.

Walker, Charles Clement. "Baths for the People." *American Architect and Architecture* 26 (1889): 207–8.

Walton, John K., and James Walvin, eds. *Leisure in Britain 1780–1939.* Manchester, England: Manchester University Press, 1983.

Waugh, Alec. *Hot Countries.* New York: Paragon House, 1989.

Waugh, Evelyn. "This Sun-Bathing Business." *Daily Mail* (July 5, 1930), p. 8.

"Weekend Resort at Ingierstrand, Oslo, Norway." *Architectural Record* 79 (March 1936): 207–10.

Wheeler, W. H. "Sea Coast Destruction and Littoral Drift." *Nature* 62 (August 1900): 400–402.

Whitman, Walt. *The Complete Poems.* Harmondsworth, England: Penguin, 1986.

Wilson, David. "A Sea in the Time of War." *Chamber's Journal* 80 (1903): 108–10.

"Winner of a Competition Held Under A.I.A." *Building News* 87 (March 1940): 49–52.

"Winter at the Sea-Side." *Temple Bar* 22 (1867–68): 342–48.

Withey, Lynne. *Grand Tours and Cook's Tours: A History of Leisure Travel, 1750–1915.* New York: Morrow, 1997.

Wollstonecraft, Mary. *A Vindication of the Rights of Women.* New York: Norton, 1967.

Woolf, Virginia. *The Voyage Out.* New York: Harvest, 1948.

———. *To the Lighthouse.* New York: Harcourt, Brace and World, 1927.

Wordsworth, William. *The Complete Poetical Works.* Boston: Houghton Mifflin, 1965.

Wright, Margaret B. "Seawomen." *Chautauquan* 14 (1891–92): 602–5.

Wynman, Nicolaus. *Colymbetes: Sive de Arte Natandi Dialogus et Festivus et Lucundus Lectu,* 1538.

Young, Sarah Gilman. "Baths and Boundaries." *American Art and Architecture* 13 (February 1883): 89–90.